The role and status of the Catholic Church in the church-state relationship within the Roman Empire from A.D. 306 to 814

Jean Carlos Zukowski

ADVENTIST THEOLOGICAL SOCIETY PUBLICATIONS

THE ROLE AND STATUS OF THE CATHOLIC CHURCH IN THE CHURCH-STATE RELATIONSHIP WITHIN THE ROMAN EMPIRE FROM A.D 306 TO 814

Project director: Iraceli Hubner Zukowski
Proofreading: Iraceli Hubner Zukowski
Book Design: Pedro Valença
Typesetting: Pedro Valença
Cover Design: Márcio Trindade

Zukowski, Jean Carlos
    The Role and Status of the Catholic Church
in the Church-State Relationship Within the
Roman Empire From A.D 306 to 814 / Jean Carlos
Zukowski. -- 1. ed. -- Berrien Springs, MI :
Adventist Theological Society Publications, 2013.

    Bibliography
    ISBN 978-0-9831147-1-0

    1. Church history -- Primitive and early church,
ca. 30-600   2. Church and state -- Rome -- History --
Primitive and early church, ca. 30-600   3. Clovis, King
of the Franks, ca. 466-511 -- Religion   4. Justinian I,
Emperor of the East, 483?-565   5. Vigilius, Pope, d.
555

1st edition - 2013
500 copies
Printed in U.S.A. by Lithotech

The the typesetting, cover and book design of this work were made by Unaspress, the publishing house of the Sao Paulo Adventist University (Unasp - São Paulo - Brazil).

UNASPRESS

This book is dedicated

to my wife Iraceli

and daughter Karoline

Contents

LIST OF ABBREVIATIONS... x

INTRODUCTION.. 1

BACKGROUND OF THE PROBLEM 1
STATEMENT OF THE PROBLEM 3
PURPOSE 4
JUSTIFICATION FOR THE RESEARCH.. 4
SCOPE/DELIMITATIONS 5
METHODOLOGY 6

ANALYSIS OF ANCIENT AND CONTEMPORARY
VIEWS ON CHURCH-STATE RELATIONSHIPS AT THE
TIME OF CONSTANTINE 11

INTRODUCTION 11
THE CHRISTIAN CHURCH AND THE STATE BEFORE CONSTANTINE ... 12
    CHURCH AND STATE IN THE NT 13
    OVERVIEW OF THE DEVELOPMENT OF CHURCH AND STATE UNDERSTAND-
    ING 16
    SUMMARY 21
ROMAN RELIGIOUS POLICY 22
SUMMARY 29
CONSTANTINE AND THE CHRISTIAN CHURCH 30
    THE EDICT OF MILAN (A.D. 313) 31
    THE DONATIST CRISIS.. 35
    THE COUNCIL OF NICAEA 41
    CONSTANTINE, THE BISHOPS, AND THE CHURCH 47
        CONSTANTINE'S CHOICE 48
        CONSTANTINE AND THE BISHOPS 51
        CONSTANTINE AND THE ARISTOCRACY 52
        CONSTANTINE AND THE CHURCH 52
    SUMMARY 59
    CONCLUSION 60

ANALYSIS OF ANCIENT AND CONTEMPORARY VIEWS ON CHURCH-STATE RELATIONSHIPS FROM CONSTANTINE´S SONS TO JUSTINIAN 63

INTRODUCTION 63
RELIGIOUS POLICIES FROM CONSTANTINE'S SONS TO JUSTINIAN 65
   RELIGIOUS POLICIES RELATED TO CHURCH AFFAIRS 65
      RELIGIOUS LEGISLATION RELATED TO CATHOLIC CHURCH AFFAIRS ... 67
      RELIGIOUS LEGISLATION REGARDING HERETICS AND SCHISMATICS ... 71
   RELIGIOUS POLICIES REGARDING NON-CHRISTIANS 72
      RELIGIOUS LEGISLATION AGAINST PAGANS 73
      RELIGIOUS LEGISLATION AGAINST JEWS 75
   SUMMARY 76
BISHOPS' RESPONSES TO IMPERIAL INTERVENTION IN CHURCH AFFAIRS 76
   THE DEVELOPMENT OF THE ECCLESIASTICAL SUPREMACY   OF
   THE BISHOP OF ROME 80
   SUMMARY 91
THE CHURCH IN THE WEST AND THE BARBARIAN INVASION 91
   THE POLITICAL SITUATION IN ITALY AFTER THE BARBARIAN INVASIONS 93
   SUMMARY 99
JUSTINIAN'S POLICIES ON CHURCH-STATE RELATIONSHIPS 100
   THEOLOGICAL CONTROVERSIES INHERITED BY JUSTINIAN -   CHAL-
   CEDON AND THE ACACIAN SCHISM 101
   JUSTINIAN'S ECCLESIASTICAL POLICIES 104
      JUSTINIAN AND THE BISHOPS OF ROME ON CHURCH-STATE RELATION-
      SHIPS 105
         JUSTINIAN AND POPES FELIX IV, BONIFACE II (530-532), JOHN II
         (533-535), AND AGAPETUS 106
         JUSTINIAN AND POPES SILVERIUS, VIGILIUS, AND PELAGIUS I 109
      THE POLITICAL IMPLICATIONS OF THE GOTHIC WAR FOR CHURCH-
      STATE RELATIONSHIPS IN ITALY 115
      THE CORPUS JURIS CIVILIS 116
         JUSTINIAN'S POLICIES REGARDING PAGANS, JEWS, SAMARITANS, AND
         HERETICS 123
   SUMMARY 125
CONCLUSION 127

ANALYSIS OF ANCIENT AND CONTEMPORARY

VIEWS ON CHURCH-STATE RELATIONSHIPS DURING CLOVIS´REIGN (A.D. 481-511) 131

INTRODUCTION 131
GAUL BEFORE CLOVIS.. 132
    DEMOGRAPHIC BACKGROUND 133
    POLITICAL BACKGROUND............................... 135
    RELIGIOUS BACKGROUND............................... 138
        THEOLOGICAL TRENDS............................... 138
        CHRISTIAN WRITERS AND MILITARY AFFAIRS.... 139
        THE CATHOLIC DIOCESAN SYSTEM............... 141
    HISTORICAL BACKGROUND 143
    SUMMARY 144
CLOVIS'S KINGDOM 145
    INTRODUCTION.. 145
    BEGINNING OF REIGN (481 OR 482)................ 146
    WAR AGAINST SYAGRIUS (486)....................... 147
    CLOVIS'S MARRIAGE (492-493) 148
    WAR AGAINST THE ALAMANNI (496 OR 506) AND CLOVIS'S BAPTISM (496 OR 508)... 148
    WAR AGAINST THE VISIGOTHS.......................... 155
    THE COUNCIL OF ORLÉANS.............................. 157
    THE SALIC LAW 159
    SUMMARY 161
FRANKISH EXPANSION AND THE CHURCH-STATE RELATIONSHIP DURING CLOVIS'S REIGN.. 161
    INTRODUCTION.. 161
    FRANKISH EXPANSION 162
        EXPANSION, NOT MIGRATION...................... 162
        ASSIMILATION OF LOCAL INSTITUTIONS AND RULERS.... 162
        GEOGRAPHICAL POSITION 163
        RELIGIOUS FACTORS................................. 164
    THE COUNCIL OF ORLÉANS.............................. 166
    SUMMARY 168
THE IMPACT OF CLOVIS'S CONVERSION DESCRIBED BY HISTORIANS AND THEOLOGIANS 168
    INTRODUCTION.. 168
    CLOVIS, THE CHAMPION OF CATHOLICISM 169
    MOVEMENT TOWARD INDEPENDENCE.................. 171

Historical Criticism 171

Conclusion 172

Analysis of ancient and contemporary and contemporary views on church-state relatioships from Pope Gregory the Great to Charlamagne 175

Introduction 175

The Merovingian Kingdom and Its Decline after Clovis 176

Carolingian Dynasty 180

    Charles Martel 180

    Pepin the Short 182

    Charlemagne 183

        Religious Reform 185

        The Temporal Authority of the Papacy up to Charlemagne ....
        187

        Church-State Relationships 196

Summary and Conclusion 203

Analysis and comparison of the models of church-state relationships during the rulerships of Constantine, Clovis, Justinian, and Charlemagne 207

Introduction 207

Similarities and Differences 208

    Emperors and Catholicism 208

    Emperor's Appointment 209

    Theology and Religious Tolerance 210

    Relationship with Bishops 211

    Legislation 213

Historical Development 214

    Constantine 214

    From Constantine's Sons to Justinian 215

    Church-state under barbarian government 216

    Justinian 219

Charlemagne 223
Summary and Conclusion 224

Conclusion
.... 229

Bibliography
.... 237

Primary Sources 237
Secondary Sources 245

Appendix
.... 279

Chronological list of bishps of rome, roman emperors, and
frankish kings from a.d. 280-816 279

LIST OF ABBREVIATIONS

ACO		*Acta Conciliorum Oecumenicorum*, Series I, ed. E. Schwartz and J. Straub (Berlin: Walter de Gruyter, 1914-1984)
ANF		A Select Library of Ante-Nicene Fathers of The Christian Church
CSEL		Corpus Scriptorum Ecclesiasticorum Latinorum (Vienna, 1866-)
CS		*Constitutiones Sirmondianae.* Clyde Pharr, *The Theodosian Code and Novels, and the Sirmondian Constitutions* (Princeton: Princeton University Press, 1952)
CJ		*Codex Justinianus*
CT		*Codex Theodosianus.* Clyde Pharr, *The Theodosian Code and Novels, and the Sirmondian Constitutions* (Princeton: Princeton University Press, 1952)
HE		Historia Ecclesiastica
MGH		Monumenta Germaniae Historica
	AA	Auctores Antiquissimi (Berlin, Hannover, 1877-1919)
	Cap	*Capitularia Regum Francorum* (Hannover, 1883)
	EKA	*Epistolae Karolini Aevi II* (Berlin, 1895)

Epp.	Epistolae (Berlin, 1887-)
Scr.	Scriptores
SRG	Scriptores Rerum Germanicrum in usum scholarum separatim editi (Hannover, Leipzig, 1885-1951)
SRL	*Scriptores Rerum Langobardorum* (Hannover, 1878)
NPNF2	A Select Library of Nicene and Post Nicene Fathers of The Christian Church, Series 2
LC	*Laus Constantine*
LLP	*Le Liber Pontificalis*, ed. L. Duchesne, 3 vols. (Paris: E. de Boccard, 1955)
LP	*Liber Pontificalis*
OC	*Oration of Constantine*
PG	*Patrologiae Cursus Completus, Series Graeca*, ed. Jacques Paul Migne, 161 vols. (Paris: 1857-1887)
PL	*Patrologiae Cursus Completus, Series Latina*, ed. Jacques Paul Migne, 221 vols. (Paris: 1844-1864)
VT	*Vita Constantini*

CHAPTER I

INTRODUCTION

BACKGROUND OF THE PROBLEM

From biblical and historical perspectives, there have always been complex interrelationships played out between the spiritual and the temporal powers on earth. The history of the church[1] reveals a fascinating interaction between church and state in which periods of collaboration and identification are contrasted with periods of antagonism, disjunction, and outright aggression. The Christian church has at times been totally independent of the state, and at other times there has been total control by the state over the affairs of the church. There have also been times when the church has exercised political authority over the state.

The first few centuries of the primitive church were characterized by a leadership that emphasized the spiritual rather than the political realm.[2] Up to the proclamation of the Edict of Milan in 313, which established a policy of religious freedom for all,[3] the

---

[1] The term church is used primarily to identify the Catholic orthodoxy led by the bishop of Rome in both the eastern and Western parts of the Roman Empire till the 11th century. Accepted practice by historians of the period is to include both eastern and western territories of the Roman Empire in defining the extent of the Catholic Church. Territories not included in this definition of Catholicism will be mentioned separately if necessary.

[2] David Hall says that "the earliest Christians formulated little in way of a systematic doctrine of church/state relationships. There was hardly enough leisure or protection for such. . . . The Christian was obligated to submit to the state, except in extremew circumstances that coerced denial of God. Further, the focus was placed on spiritual development rather than political organization." David W. Hall, "The Early Church and the State," Premise 3, no. 2 (1996): 8. See also F. X. von Funk, A Manual of Church History, 2 vols. (St. Louis: B. Herder, 1913), 1:17-77; Wilhelm Moeller, History of the Christian Church, 3 vols. (London: Sonnenschein, 1892), 1:159-183; Williston Walker and Robert T. Handy, A History of the Christian Church, 3d ed. (New York: Scribner, 1970), 45-80.

[3] After one year, the freedom of religion established by the Edict of Milan was restricted to the official Christian Church and some pagan religions. Non-Catholic Christians were not tolerated by the Roman Empire. One example of this is how Constantine dealt with the Donatist heresy. He used his troops to seize the Donatist churches and to exile their bishop. See Hubert Jedin and John Patrick Dolan, History of the Church, 10 vols. (London: Burns & Oates, 1980), 421

Roman Empire did not officially recognize the Christian church. In fact, there were periods of intense persecution of Christians prior to 313. The promotion of Christianity in the Roman Empire in the fourth century by the Emperor Constantine[4] the Great (313-317) considerably improved the status of the Catholic segment of Christianity. At the time of Theodosius I (379-395) all the citizens of the empire were required to join Catholic Christianity and, with one exception, all emperors after Constantine I professed to be Christian. Catholicism not only became one among several legal religions in the empire, but it eventually became the "official religion" of the empire.[5]

The gradual decay of the Roman Empire's power, the invasion of barbarian tribes, and the fall of Rome in A.D. 476 brought different nuances to the relationship between church and state. Because the capital of the empire had been moved from Rome to Constantinople about A.D. 330, the emperor had more influence on church affairs in the eastern part of the empire than the western part. Further, Roman Catholicism in the West was threatened by Arian barbarians. The conversion of Clovis to Catholicism and the expansion of his kingdom provided a new military power in defense and promotion of Roman Catholicism. East and West moved further and further apart until the West became completely independent, under the leadership of the papacy and the Germanic kings.

Church-state relationships during the centuries after Constantine oscillated between a strong influence of the state over the church and a jurisdictional supremacy of the church over the state. The leadership of the church expanded its presence and influence beyond the spiritual realm, to involvement in the political affairs of the state. The political role of the church in relation to the state became especially pronounced after the coronation of Charlemagne in 800 that initiated the formation of the so-called Holy Roman Empire. The "Investiture Controversy" which continued over the course of several centuries was a struggle between the pope and the emperor concerning which office was the ultimate authority under God to appoint and recognize civil and ecclesiastical leadership.[6] This controversy,

---

[4] Flavius Valerius Constantinus (272–337), commonly known as Constantine I or Constantine the Great, was the Roman emperor from 306 to his death. He was the first Roman emperor to approve Christianity as an official religion in 312 with the edict of Milan, and sponsored Christianity throughout his dominions. For more information on Constantine, see chapter 2.

[5] The Theodosian Code declared Christianity as the only official religion of the state. Clyde Pharr, The Theodosian Code and Novels, and the Sirmondian Constitutions (Princeton: Princeton University Press, 1952), 16.1.2; Henry Scowcroft Bettenson, Documents of the Christian Church (London: Oxford University Press, 1943), 31. From now on the abbreviation "CT" will be used to refer to the Theodosian Code, "CS" to refer to the Sirmondian Constitutions, and all quotations will be taken from Pharr's edition.

[6] For example, see Funk, 309-332; Walker and Handy, 179-300.

in which the papacy gradually emerged supreme,[7] epitomized the struggle for and attainment of political supremacy by the western church.

STATEMENT OF THE PROBLEM

The majority of historians, sociologists, and other authors, place the birth of the struggle for political supremacy between church and state with Charlemagne.[8] The main topics of this discussion are (1) the conflicting nature and role of church and state in relation to their duties in promoting justice and order in society; (2) the political and theological grounds for church and state jurisdiction over ecclesiastical and civil society; and (3) the different theories of church and state relationships in an ideal form of government.[9]

The analysis of all these variants is not an easy task. A description of the turning points in the history of church and state does not clearly reveal the shifts and trends that were in place before these turning points occurred. From Constantine to the establishment of the Holy Roman Empire, the balance of power shifted from a greater influence

---

[7] One example of this supremacy is the pontificate of Innocent III (1198-1216). The papacy reached its apex of power during his pontificate. Innocent became pope at a time when a power vacuum existed within the Roman Empire. He was the guardian of the young Frederick II. After Frederick had secured the imperial crown, a power struggle took place between the papacy and the empire. Innocent had a theocratic and hierocratic world-view. In his time all the temporal rulers of Europe appeared subservient to his domination. He intervened in the dispute between King John of England and King Phillip Augustus of France over the fief of Normandy; in the conflict between Philip of Swabia (brother of Henry IV) and Otto of Brunswick; in the Kingdom of France to persuade Philip II to restore his legitimate wife; in succession disputes in the Kingdoms of Norway, Sweden, and Bohemia. He also excommunicated King John of England and freed John's subjects from their oath of allegiance to their king. He had as vassals the Kings of Bulgaria, Aragon, Portugal, and Castille. In his time the papal curia became the busiest governmental center in the world. For additional information, see Leonard Elliott Elliott-Binns, Innocent III (London: Methuen, 1931); Raymonde Foreville, Le Pape Innocent III et la France, Päpste Und Papsttum; Bd. 26 (Stuttgart: A. Hiersemann, 1992); James M. Powell, Innocent III: Vicar of Christ or Lord of the World?, 2nd exp. ed. (Washington, DC: Catholic University of America Press, 1994); Charles Edward Smith, Innocent III, Church Defender (Baton Rouge: Louisiana State University Press, 1951); Walter Ullmann, A Short History of the Papacy in the Middle Ages (London: Methuen, 1972).

[8] See for example Sidney Z. Ehler and John B. Morrall, Church and State through the Centuries; a Collection of Historic Documents with Commentaries (London: Burns & Oates, 1954); Frank Stanton Burns Gavin, Seven Centuries of the Problem of Church and State (Princeton: Princeton University Press, 1938); Bennett D. Hill, Church and State in the Middle Ages (New York: Wiley, 1970); Jacob Marcellus Kik, Church and State; the Story of Two Kingdoms (New York: Nelson, 1963).

[9] See for example John Emerich Edward Dalberg Acton, Essays on Church and State (London: Hollis and Carter, 1952); Doug Bandow, Beyond Good Intentions: A Biblical View of Politics. Turning point Christian Worldview Series (Westchester, IL: Crossway Books, 1988); Albert Hyma, Christianity and Politics: A History of the Principles and Struggles of Church and State (Birmingham, MI: Brant Publishing Company, 1960).

of the state over the church to a greater influence of the church over the state. However, historical events that took place during this period, such as the barbarian invasions, the fall of the Western Roman Empire, and the conversion of Clovis to Catholicism, though might be interpreted as having caused a shift of power, also might be interpreted as resulting from a model of church and state relationships that was already in place and was itself the cause of the historical events that marked the shift of power.

An analysis of historical events from Constantine to the establishment of the Holy Roman Empire raises some questions regarding (1) the possible causes for the increase of authority of the Catholic Church over the state; (2) the influence of the Catholic Church in the political realm; and (3) the event(s) and/or trends which led to the shift of power in favor of the church. Was the claimed supremacy of the Catholic Church before the ninth century limited to only the spiritual realm? How much did the fall of Rome, the barbarian invasions, and/or the conversion of Clovis to Catholicism contribute to the shift of power in the relationship of church and state? Are there any indications of changes in the role and status of the church in the relationship between the Catholic Church and the state when it is compared to Constantine's, Clovis's, Justinian's, and Charlemagne's rulership? When did the church start to acquire political influence in the political affairs of the state?

PURPOSE

The purpose of this dissertation is to analyze and compare information from historical documents on the role and status of the church in the development of church-state relationships within the Roman Empire from A.D. 306 to 814 (from Constantine's ascendancy to the throne, to Charlemagne's death). The specific intent is to examine whether or not there is any evidence for a significant change or development in the church-state relationships from the time of Constantine to Charlemagne, considering the conversion of the Franks to Catholicism, the Religious reforms promoted by Justinian, and the decline of the Eastern Roman Empire's influence over the West.

JUSTIFICATION FOR THE RESEARCH

Four major reasons justify the present research. First, there is a lack of historical research on the development of the relationship between church and state from Constantine to Charlemagne. The church-state relationship from Charlemagne until the Reformation (800-1500) has been explored extensively by theologians and historians.[10] However, few scholarly works have explored how the church sought political supremacy and gained

---

[10] See, for example, Acton; Richard M. Golden, Church, State, and Society under the Bourbon Kings of France (Lawrence, KS: Coronado Press, 1982); Hill; Kik, Church and State; the Story of Two Kingdoms.

political power prior to Charlemagne.[11] Second, since there are divergent opinions on the historical development of the church's political supremacy prior to Charlemagne, this dissertation will examine whether any autocracy of the church in western Europe before the ninth century can be substantiated by the historical data. Third, even though many books have been written on Clovis and Frankish history, in most of these works the relationship between church and state is discussed in one chapter or less, or it is not present at all.[12] Fourth, even though scholars have explored the religious and political policies of Christian emperors from Constantine to Charlemagne, the similarities and differences between the religious policies of the Byzantine emperors Constantine and Justinian and those of the German kings Clovis and Charlemagne have not been examined.

SCOPE/DELIMITATIONS

This study is not intended to provide a historical account of the lives of Constantine, Justinian, Clovis, and Charlemagne. Due to the length of time covered in this research and the rich availability of primary and secondary sources on the reigns of Constantine, Justinian, and Charlemagne (including personal letters, financial transactions, historical accounts, judicial codes, theological treatises, panegyrics, church canons, sermons, etc.), and even though the primary literature about church-related historical events during Clovis's reign is not as extensive as that for other periods, an appraisal of the literature will be made in each chapter as needed.[13]

---

[11] See, for example, F. Heinrich Geffcken and Edward Fairfax Taylor, Church and State: Their Relations Historically Developed (London: Longmans Green, 1877); Jeffrey Richards, The Popes and the Papacy in the Early Middle Ages, 476-752 (Boston: Routledge & Kegan Paul, 1979); Thomas Robbins and Roland Robertson, Church-State Relations: Tensions and Transitions (New Brunswick, NJ: Transaction Books, 1987).

[12] Eyre Evans Crowe dedicates one page of his work to the subject: Eyre Evans Crowe, The History of France (New York: Harper & Brothers, 1869), 1:6; F. Dallais, Clovis, ou, le Combat de Gloire (La Roche Rigault: PSR âeditions, 1996). Even though Edward James discusses different aspects of Clovis's conversion to Christianity, he does not analyze church-state relationships in his book. Edward James, The Franks, The Peoples of Europe (Oxford, UK: Basil Blackwell, 1988), 121-161. Godefroid Kurth analyzes the church-state relationship during Clovis's reign and sees in Clovis's reign the beginning of a new era in Europe. Godefroid Kurth, Clovis, 2nd rev. corr. ed., vol. 1 (Paris: V. Retauz, 1901), 155-190. See also Ferdinand Lot, Naissance de la France (Paris: Fayard, 1970); John Moorhead, "Clovis' Motives for Becoming a Catholic Christian," Journal of Religious History 13, no. 1-4 (1984-1985): 329-339; Patrick Perin and Laure-Charlotte Feffer, Les Francs (Paris: A. Colin, 1987); Georges Tessier, Le Bapteme de Clovis: 25 Decembre 496 (?),Trente Journées Qui Ont Fait La France (Paris: Gallimard, 1996).

[13] For a list of the most important primary and secondary sources on the late Roman Empire—from Diocletian to the end of the fourth century—see Averil Cameron, The Later Roman Empire (Cambridge, MA: Harvard University Press, 1993), 13-29, 199-227. For the fifth and sixth centuries, see Paul Fouracre, The New Cambridge Medieval History 1: C. 500 - C. 700 (Cambridge: Cambridge University Press, 2006), 785-804, 805-910. For the period from the seventh century to the ninth century, see Rosamond McKitterick, The New Cambridge Medieval

Many events very well known today, such as Emperor Anastasius sending an insignia of consular dignity to Clovis, are presented only in secondary sources such as Gregory of Tours' *The History of the Franks*. Furthermore, the inclusion of much content of a miraculous nature in these secondary sources, written a half-century or more after the events, has led to much criticism and skepticism from the majority of modern historians concerning the historicity of the events these sources present.[14] This dissertation will not focus on a critical analysis of these secondary sources or appraisal of the chronological details of the relevant periods.[15] Most of the areas related to church-state relationships covered in this dissertation are not free of controversy. For each of these areas, an essay, a paper, or even a book could be written to explore all the opposing views. However, due to the space limitations of this research, opposing views will be discussed only if they are significant to elucidate the church-state relationships as presented in this dissertation.

The dates presented in this dissertation will follow those generally accepted by the majority of historians as the most reliable ones.[16]The main concern will be the importance of the events for the authors when they wrote about them. The specific focus will be on historical events related to the interplay between political and ecclesiastical powers.

METHODOLOGY

The history of the Christian church consists of a series of events that can be described in different ways according to the viewpoints of historians. Each historian portrays and interprets the most important facts in terms of his or her bias, interest, and focus. Histories may be written from political, theological, or economic

---

History 2: C. 700 - C. 900 (Cambridge: Cambridge University Press, 1995), 867-885, 886-1039.

[14] For the example cited above on Clovis's life, some of the critical works on these secondary sources are: Godefroid Kurth, Histoire Poétique Des Mérovingiens (Paris: A. Picard, 1893); idem, Clovis; idem, Études Franques, vol. 2 (Paris: H. Champion, 1919); Lot, Naissance De La France; Kathleen Mitchell, History and Christian Society in Sixth-Century Gaul: An Historiographical Analysis of Gregory of Tours' Decem Libri Historiarum (Ann Arbor, MI: UMI, 1983); Tessier; J. M. Wallace-Hadrill, The Long-Haired Kings, and Other Studies in Frankish History (London: Methuen, 1962).

[15] For further discussion on the chronological details of Clovis's reign, see Tessier, Le Bapteme, and Wallace-Hadrill, The Long-Haired Kings.

[16] For the later Roman Empire and late antiquity: Cameron, The Later Roman Empire; Fouracre, The New Cambridge Medieval History 1: C. 500 - C. 700; McKitterick, The New Cambridge Medieval History 2: C. 700 - C. 900. For the history of the Franks: James, The Franks; Kurth, Clovis: Le Fondateur; Perin and Feffer, Les Francs; Tessier; Wallace-Hadrill, The Long-Haired Kings; J. M. Wallace-Hadrill, The Barbarian West, 400-1000, rev. ed. (Malden, MA: Basil Blackwell, 1996); I. N. Wood, The Merovingian Kingdoms, 450-751 (London and New York: Longman, 1994).

perspectives, or again, for example, with the bias of a modem or postmodern mind-set. In each case, the resulting history presents a rather subjective insight into an illusory reality, which occurred sometime in the past.

Even though I recognize the influence of sociological, anthropological, cultural, and archeological factors on the interplay of secular and religious powers, the focus of this dissertation will be in the political, geographical, military, and economical aspects of the church-state relationships.

In this dissertation, the historical method[17] will be implemented. However, due to the extensive time frame involved in this research, the classification and nature of historical sources, and the appraising of the sources will be part of the body of the dissertation only when it will help to clarify questionable historical events and/or the historical reasoning of the primary and secondary sources. The main focus of this dissertation is to analyze the authors' reasoning in the choice or sequential description of historical facts rather than the reliability of the authors' description. The historical facts will be analyzed based on their importance to elucidate the development of the political and ecclesiastical power of the church.

My research consisted first of the analyses of the main general historical works, particular historical works on Constantine, Justinian, Clovis, the Goths, papal history, and specific literature on church-state relationships. The purpose of the first phase of my research was to broaden knowledge of the topic and the collection of primary sources cited in these works. In the second phase I analyzed all translated primary sources including those collected in phase one. In the third phase I analyzed and translated the significant sources—mainly in Greek or Latin—which have not been translated into English, French, or German, if they were to be quoted in the dissertation. In the fourth and last phase I analyzed the analytical citations and direct identification by Catholic, Protestant, and other historians of the church supremacy during the relevant period.

The chapters in this dissertation are arranged in the following way. The first chapter provides a general introduction to the research. The second chapter discusses conventional views on the Constantinian model of church and state relationships. The chapter describes the implications of Constantine's conversion to Christianity and his patronage of Catholic Christianity over other religions for the church and the state.

The third chapter investigates the relevant events in church-state relationships that occurred from Constantine's sons to Justinian. The chapter evaluates the interplay of

---

[17] There are three major operations in the historical method: (1) heuristic—the nature and classification of historical sources; (2) criticism—appraising of sources; and (3) synthesis and exposition—presentation of the results of the research. For further studies see: Gilbert J. Garraghan and Jean Delanglez, A Guide to Historical Method (New York: Fordham University Press, 1946).

church leadership and state leadership, the Byzantine political philosophy, as well as the development of the political supremacy of the church and the bishop of Rome.

The fourth chapter describes the relevant facts in church-state relationships that occurred from Clovis's ascendancy to the throne (481) and of his death (511) and his policies of church and state relationships. The chapter describes the political and ecclesiastical events that were significant in the interaction of the bishops of Gaul with kings and emperors. It analyzes how clerics and other Catholic writers have explained the role of the church in the first half of the sixth century, and how these writers explore and interpret the development of church-state relationships during this period.

The fifth chapter describes the Carolingian model of church and state relationships. The chapter focuses particularly on the roles of bishops, mainly the bishop of Rome and secular rulers in the interplay of church and state, which culminate later on with the formation of Holy Roman Empire.

The sixth chapter analyzes and compares the major church-state models mentioned in chapters 2, 3, 4, and 5. The chapter focuses particularly on the similarities and differences of these models, seeking to find turning points of the ecclesiastical and political supremacy of the church. Finally, a summary and conclusion is made.

CHAPTER II

ANALYSIS OF ANCIENT AND CONTEMPORARY VIEWS ON CHURCH-STATE RELATIONSHIPS AT THE TIME OF CONSTANTINE

INTRODUCTION

Constantine's policies of religious liberty and his support of Christianity as a legitimate religion led to a fundamental turning point in the relationship between the Christian church and the Roman Empire.[1] Constantine recognized Catholic orthodox Christianity as a *religio licita* and introduced the church leadership into the political life of the empire. His religious policy incorporated Christian values while retaining old elements of Roman religious traditions. From Constantine on, Catholic Christianity increased in political power and influenced the life of the state.

---

[1] Independently of the viewpoint of those who wrote about Constantine, it is almost unanimously accepted that Constantine's reign or events that took place in the empire under him led to a turning point in the history of the relationship between Christianity and the Roman Empire. Alistair Kee saw Constantine's reign, as a whole, being the turning point. Constantine Versus Christ: The Triumph of Ideology (London: SCM Press, 1982). Norman H. Baynes says that "Constantine marks in his own person a turning point in European history." Constantine the Great and the Christian Church (London: H. Milford, 1930), 3. Mark A. Noll, in his short presentation of Turning Points: Decisive Moments in the History of Christianity, presents the Council of Nicaea as the turning point; however, he stresses the significant role of Constantine in the Council. Turning Points: Decisive Moments in the History of Christianity (Grand Rapids, MI: Baker Books, 1997). G. P. Baker and others point out that the change in the nature of future European monarchies and the ascension of Christianity as a coercive power had their roots in Constantine's reign. Constantine the Great and the Christian Revolution (New York: Cooper Square Press, 2001). See also: Timothy David Barnes, Constantine and Eusebius (Cambridge, MA: Harvard University Press, 1981); Christopher Bush Coleman, Constantine the Great and Christianity (New York: Columbia University Press, 1914); H. A. Drake, Constantine and the Bishops: The Politics of Intolerance, Ancient Society and History (Baltimore, MD: Johns Hopkins University Press, 2002); Lloyd Burdwin Holsapple, Constantine the Great (New York: Sheed & Ward, 1942); John Holland Smith, Constantine the Great (New York: Scribner, 1971); Brooke Foss Westcott and Arthur Westcott, The Two Empires, the Church and the World (London: Macmillan, 1909); Daniel H. Williams, "Constantine, Nicaea and the 'Fall' of the Church," in Christian Origins: Theology, Rhetoric, and Community, ed. Lewis Ayres and Gareth Jones (London and New York: Routledge, 1998).

In this chapter, the analysis of Constantine's *renovatio*[2] will start with a discussion of Christian and Roman religion before Constantine. After that, the main historical events during Constantine's reign related to church and state relationships will be discussed. A final section will discuss the relationship between Constantine, the bishops, and the church. A summary will be given at the end of each section and for the whole chapter.

The christian church and the state before Constantine

The history of the development of the understanding of church-state relationships from the apostolic era until Constantine has been described by scholars from different perspectives. It has been examined using theological, political, historical, and sociological approaches, as well as combined approaches. In this section, some scholarly views on the subject will be presented, followed by background information on the New Testament (NT) concept of church and state relationships and the historical changes in the understanding of these relationships in the first three centuries of our era.

The most common way scholars approach the church-state relationship in early Christianity is looking at the attitude of the church toward the state both in the NT and in other writings. Thus, Gregory T. Armstrong[3] argues that there are at least three attitudes toward the state: (1) favorable, (2) positive but neutral, and (3) negative. The gospel of Luke is an example of a favorable attitude, Paul's letter to the Romans a positive or neutral one, and the book of Revelation a negative. He says also that although the church had a non-participative position "in regard to most civic duties," it "never advocated overthrow of the government" and "seemed content to live under the empire even with certain restrictions, provided it might worship unhindered and not be required to compromise its faith."[4]

Hugo Rahner says that the church had a positive and negative conception of the state, and this can be seen in the "yes" or "no" given by early Christians in their in-

---

[2] The term renovatio (rebirth) is used by historians to describe Roman emperors' policies in their attempt to promote the rebirth of the empire. Constantine's policies of religious freedom where Christianity had a pre-eminent role are considered as a renovatio by historians. See Michael Azkoul, "Sacerdotium et Imperium: The Constantinian Renovatio According to the Greek Fathers," Theological Studies 32 (1971): 431-464; Francis Dvornik, Early Christian and Byzantine Political Philosophy: Origins and Background, 2 vols. (Washington, DC: Dumbarton Oaks Center for Byzantine Studies Trustees, for Harvard University, 1966), 2:611-850.

[3] Gregory T. Armstrong at the time of this publication was Assistant Professor of Church History, Vanderbilt Divinity School.

[4] Gregory T. Armstrong, "Church and State Relations: The Changes Wrought by Constantine," The Journal of Bible and Religion 32, no. 1 (1964): 2. See also idem, "Politics and the Early Christian," Journal of Church and State 10 (1968): 448-450.

teraction with the state. He says that the church in this period "has never confronted the state with a no of inflexible refusal dictated by an otherworldly mysticism or with a yes of unqualified acceptance based on political indifference."[5]

Jacob Marcellus Kik says that according to Scripture, church and state work in two different realms; both are instituted by God, but they have different functions and purposes in society. According to him, "civil government operates in the realm of common grace and ecclesiastical government in the realm of special grace."[6] He concludes with the following:

> The State finds its origin in God, as moral Governor of the world; the Church, in the redemptive act of Christ the Mediator. . . . The State has jurisdiction over all its citizens, regardless of their beliefs; the Church has jurisdiction only over those who have professed faith in Christ. The State has the material welfare of its citizens as its aim; the Church, the spiritual welfare of her members. The State's enactments find their source in natural law; the Church's laws come from special revelation. The State may use coercion; the Church may only employ spiritual weapons.[7]

CHURCH AND STATE IN THE NT

Any attempt to understand the relationship between church and state in the history of the Christian church must have a section on the NT content concerning the topic.[8] As

---

[5] Hugo Rahner was a Jesuit and Professor of Church History and Patristics at Innsbruck in 1937, and from 1945 to 1962. His brother was the influential theologian Karl Rahner. Hugo Rahner, Church and State in Early Christianity (San Francisco: Ignatius Press, 1992), 3.

[6] Jacob Marcellus Kik, Church and State in the New Testament (Philadelphia: Presbyterian and Reformed Publishing Corporation, 1962), 18.

[7] Ibid., 27.

[8] Many books discuss the issue of church and state relationships by drawing conclusions from the NT. However, most of the present discussion is related to contemporary problems seeking to answer the question of whether or not the church should be involved in politics. See for example: Jean Héring, A Good and a Bad Government, According to the New Testament, American Lecture Series; Publication No. 221 (Springfield, IL: C.C. Thomas, 1954); Kik, Church and State: The Story of Two Kingdoms; Archie Penner, The Christian, the State, and the New Testament (Scottdale, PA: Herald Press, 1959); Walter E. Pilgrim, Uneasy Neighbors: Church and State in the New Testament, Overtures to Biblical Theology (Minneapolis, MN: Fortress Press, 1999); Mihail S. Popa, "New Testament Principles Governing the Relationship between the Christian and Civil Authorities and Their Elaboration in the Writings of Ellen G. White with Their Reflection in the Adventist Church in Romania" (Project report, Andrews, University, 1980); Géza Vermès, Scrolls, Scriptures, and Early Christianity, Library of Second Temple Studies, vol. 56 (London; New York: T & T Clark International, 2005); James Edward Wood, Church and State in Scripture, History, and Constitutional Law (Waco, TX: Baylor University Press, 1958); John Howard Yoder, Discipleship as Political Responsibility (Scottdale, PA: Herald Press, 2003). For the present section, the purpose is not to answer this question affirmatively or negatively. Rather, this section will present a background on church and state relationships in the NT and during the time of early Christianity.

Bennett D. Hill says, "the starting point for any study of the relations of Church and State, as well as for any other aspect of the history of Christianity or of the Christian Church, is the collection of texts which Christians have always accepted as the Word of God."[9]

John A. McGuckin says that the NT does not underline a Christian theology of politics, but it has an ambivalent concept of obedience and rejection of civil leaders.[10] Agnes Cunningham comments that this "apparent ambivalence on the part of Christians toward the state was due to at least two significant historical factors"—the common understanding of religious and civil functions as inseparable in the ancient Near East and Mediterranean world, and the Roman Empire's understanding of the supremacy of the state over the religious and secular spheres.[11] Even though the NT does not include a scriptural paradigm for a Christian political theology, it presents some guidelines—mainly in the Gospels, in some of Paul's letters, and in Peter's addresses to all Christians on how church-state relationships should be.[12]

The NT recognizes the existence of civil and spiritual leadership; however, there is no earthly theocratic concept of kingship. Jesus' statements that the kingdom of God is not related to worldly political supremacy[13] and the famous phrase pronounced in His discussion with the Herodians, "Render therefore to Caesar the things which are Caesar's; and unto God the things that are God's,"[14] present a notion of church and state relationships in which He would neither ally himself with those who were seeking a political messiah nor deny the authority of the Roman

---

[9] Bennett D. Hill (1934-2005), a former Chairman and Professor of History at the University of Illinois, received his Ph.D. from Princeton in 1963. He taught at the University of Maryland and was most recently a visiting professor at Georgetown University. He published two books and several journal articles. Hill, 1.

[10] John Anthony McGuckin is Professor of Byzantine Christian Studies, Columbia University. He is a priest of the Orthodox Church (Patriarchate of Romania) who came to New York from England in 1997 where he was formerly a Reader in Patristic and Byzantine Theology at the University of Leeds. John A. McGuckin, "The Legacy of the 13th Apostle: Origins of the East Christian Conceptions of Church and State Relation," St Vladimir's Theological Quarterly 47, no. 3-4 (2003): 253, 254.

[11] Sr. Agnes Cunningham, at the time of this publication, was a Catholic theologian, member of the Congregation of the Servants of the Holy Heart of Mary since 1943, and professor of patristic and historical theology at Mundelein Seminary, University of St. Mary of the Lake, from 1967-1992. She also served as a consultant to the Lumen Christi Institute at the University of Chicago. Agnes Cunningham, The Early Church and the State (Philadelphia: Fortress Press, 1982), 2.

[12] Cullmann says that the problem of church and state is an integral part of the NT, not something peripheral. Also, James E. Wood argues that those who deny the existence of a political philosophy in the NT do so because they are not willing to recognize the topic in the NT. Oscar Cullmann, "The State in the New Testament," in Church and State in the Middle Ages, ed. Bennett D. Hill (New York: Wiley, 1970), 6; Wood, Church and State in Scripture, 20.

[13] The books of Mark, Luke, and Matthew are full of parables and other passages where Jesus refers to the kingdom of God as spiritual and not worldly. In John 18:33-40, Jesus clearly says to Pilate that his "kingdom is not from this world."

[14] Matt 22:21.

government, carefully establishing the boundaries of things belonging to the state and to God.[15] Also, "in John 18 Jesus expressly denies any relationship with the secular government. . . . All four Gospels are rather insistent on the fact that Jesus was not executed for any political offense; this insistence certainly reflects the image which the apostolic Church wished to project."[16] The civil and spiritual leadership, the church and the state, work in different spheres of influence. As Cullmann argues, the state is nothing divine and the church is not a worldly political institution.[17]

In the NT there is a notion of messianic kingship[18] and a kingdom of God headed by Jesus Christ, first in heaven and finally being established on earth at His second coming. In His dialogue with Pilate, Jesus assumes His role as king, but says His kingdom is not of this world.[19] In many of His speeches, Jesus promised His disciples that He had to go to heaven but that He would return to Earth to establish His kingdom.[20]

Another two points addressed in the NT are the issues of power and citizenship. Civil authorities are established by God's allowance. According to Paul, all power comes from God.[21] The state is a temporal power with provisional settings until the final establishment of the kingdom of God. Christians are citizens of the world and should obey the authorities in everything that does not conflict with the law of God because, according to Paul, "to resist the authority [of the state] is to resist God."[22] On this issue of authority and power, John McKenzie argues that Paul's statement is not a new idea that contradicts Old Testament (OT) biblical thought:

> No nation and no person can have any power which is not committed to it by God; but the exercise of the power is not thereby authenticated. Assyria was the rod of God's anger for Israel (Is 10:5); Assyria was still Assyria, an object of judgment no less because it was an instrument of judgment. God brought down the kingdom of Judah and the city of Jerusalem through Nebuchadnezzar of Babylon; and Jeremiah preached submission to Nebuchadnezzar because God had given him the rule of the earth (Jer 25:8-11; 27:1-15) and counseled the Jews who had been transported

---

[15] Kik, Church and State: The Story of Two Kingdoms, 16.

[16] John L. McKenzie, "The Power and the Wisdom," in Church and State in the Middle Ages, ed. Bennett D. Hill (New York: Wiley, 1970), 9.

[17] Cullmann, 18.

[18] For more information on the notion of kingship, see: Ernest Barker, From Alexander to Constantine; Passages and Documents Illustrating the History of Social and Political Ideas, 336 B.C.-A.D. 337 (Oxford: Clarendon Press, 1956), 341-390; Lucien Cerfaux and Julien Tondriau, Le Culte des Souverains: Un Concurrent du Christianisme dans la Civilisation Gréco-Romaine (Tournai: Desclée, 1957).

[19] John 18:33-37. See Kik, Church and State in the New Testament, 28-37; McGuckin, 254.

[20] See for example Matt 24 and John 14:1-3.

[21] Rom 13:1-7.

[22] McKenzie, 11.

to Babylon to seek the welfare of the city (Jer 29:5-7). I think one recognizes in these passages the ideas in which Paul moves; and they permit one to say that Paul does not clearly give the Roman Empire any value which the Old Testament does not give to Assyria and Babylonia. If Rome has power, it must be because God has given it power. God gives it power as he gave power to the nations of the East, for the purpose of punishing evildoers; to resist this power is to resist God, and this is true both of Babylon and of Rome. No positive value is attributed to either state as such.[23]

Even though all power comes from God, in the NT the authority of the church is different from that of the state. Jesus' statements to the Herodians and to Pilate[24] point out that the jurisdiction of the church is in the spiritual realm, while that of the state is in the worldly realm. This does not mean that the church must be alienated from the world. The church must change the world, but not by the power of the sword; rather, by the life-changing power of the Spirit, the power of the truth.[25] Christians as citizens have to fulfill their civic responsibilities, which go beyond "obedience to lawful commands and payment of taxes," as revealed in 1 Tim 2:1-4.[26] Christians' prayers for the civic authorities demonstrate their concern for the welfare of the state, for the sake of those who live in it and the spreading of the gospel.[27]

OVERVIEW OF THE DEVELOPMENT OF CHURCH AND STATE UNDERSTANDING

In the three centuries preceding the recognition of Christianity as a *religio licita* by Constantine, the Christian church maintained an attitude of opposition to the state on spiritual matters (religious power in subjection to civil authorities), but at the same time, it was seeking state recognition on institutional and individual levels. Christians had times of relative peace as well as times of persecution. The Christian literature of these centuries portrays a continuing affirmation of God's supremacy over the empire, mainly in the stories of the martyrs; a continuing defense of Christians as good citizens, which made their persecution by the Romans unjust and senseless; and a recognition of the Roman Empire as a great tool in God's hands to maintain order and justice and also to benefit their own church.

The notion of church and state in the primitive church is grounded primarily in the NT. The apostolic church's allegiance was directed only to God, in opposition to any worldly institution, even though as citizens Christians were instructed to

---

[23] Ibid., 12.

[24] Matt 22:21, John 18:36.

[25] John 18:37.

[26] Kik, Church and State in the New Testament, 20.

[27] Ibid.

obey and pray for the constituted authorities. As Schmemann says, this "opposition between the Church and the world is undoubtedly the essential element in Early Christianity. And we must stress the fact that this opposition is not only of a moral or psychological nature, but is, above all, metaphysical. The Church is not of this world; between the Church and the world a great gulf is fixed, which it is impossible to bridge, a difference of nature and not merely of ideology or of belief."[28] Rahner argues also that "the Church continually opposes any state that wishes to build only in this world a kingdom of definitive happiness or in absolutist fashion seeks to force religion into a legal system that alone has full jurisdiction."[29]

In the first century, Christians were living as an independent community inside the empire, without the boundaries of nationality. As Francis Murphy says, "Christians tended to consort together in separate, independent groups based on a sacramentally conceived 'communion of belief.' Their community was governed directly by the law of God; and it was superior to the law of man as expressed in the state. Besides, the local Christian church belonged to a much wider community, that had God as its ruler."[30] Also, Christians had a cosmological understanding of the imminent end of the world and final establishment of the kingdom of God on earth—the second coming of Jesus—which led them to refrain from taking part in the political life of the empire. Their focus was not to change the world politically, but to bring the world to repentance in preparation to meet their savior.[31] Even though Christians gradually lessened their expectations of the imminent return of Christ to earth, they still maintained their independent way of living in the first three centuries, as witnessed by Origen when he said that Christians "do not belong to any nation. Christian believers are from one city or another, from one nation and another, without any group representing a whole people. Christians are not like the Jews or Egyptians who form a single nation or race. They come from, and are from everywhere."[32]

---

[28] Rev. Dr. Alexander Schmemann (1921-1983) was Dean of St. Vladimir's Orthodox Theological Seminary in Crestwood, New York, where he also occupied the chair of Liturgical and Pastoral Theology. Since 1958 he has been Adjunct Professor at the Graduate Faculty of Columbia University and was Lecturer in Eastern Orthodoxy at Union Theological Seminary. Alexander Schmemann, "Byzantine Theocracy and the Orthodox Church," St Vladimir's Seminary Quarterly 1, no. 2 (1953): 7.

[29] Rahner, 3-4.

[30] Francis Xavier Murphy (1915-2002) was a Catholic Priest who taught at the Vatican's Lateran University, Princeton University, and Johns Hopkins University. Francis Xavier Murphy, Politics and the Early Christian (New York: Desclée, 1967), 40.

[31] Ibid., 57.

[32] "Nos enim sumus non gens, qui pauci ex isu civitate credimus, et alli ex alia, et nusquain gens integra ab initio credulitatis videtur assumpta. Non enim sicut Judaeorum gens erat, vel Aegyptiorum gens, ita etiam Christianorum genus gens est una, sed integra, sed sparsim ex singulis gentibus congregantur." Origen, "Homily

The organization of early Christian communities followed the pattern of Jewish synagogues. Christians had, like Jews, an exclusivism of faith. The church was a divine institution independent of state control in religious matters, with "its own jurisdictional system to combat heterodoxy of belief, and to eliminate heretics from official positions as well as membership."[33] These similarities between Christians and Jews led the Roman Empire to initially identify the Christian church as a Jewish sect and extend to it the same religious tolerance granted to the Jewish nation. In this period, Roman authorities even protected Christians from Jewish persecution.[34] In the time of Nero, Christians began to be recognized as an independent religious group.[35] Even though the Roman Empire had a tolerant policy concerning religion, any institution that could be a threat to the stability of the state had to be eliminated.[36] Also, the incorporation of religion within the state was the policy of the Roman Empire, in which "no self-governing religious body was allowed to exist over against the State."[37] Christians' lack of national identity and natural opposition to any other religious allegiance contributed to the beginning of their persecution by the Romans. As Joseph Lecler[38] said, the Christians' dualistic views of religious society and civil society "represented in the ancient world a revolution without precedent."[39]

In the conflict between Rome and their faith, Christians were loyal to God. The answer of Polycarp before the proconsul in his trial reflects the attitude of Christians before the charge of recognizing Caesar as Lord. He said, "Fourscore and six years have I been His servant, and He hath done me no wrong. How then can I blaspheme my King who saved me?"[40] Cyprian, years later, manifested the same boldness and died refusing to recognize Caesar as Lord.[41]

---

1 in Psalm 36," in PG, ed. J. P. Migne (Paris: J.-P. Migne, 1857), Col. 1321.

[33] Murphy, 41.

[34] In the book of Acts, Roman officers saved Christians from Jewish persecution on different occasions. Paul used his status as a Roman citizen to his advantage. He even asked for Caesar's intervention in his case, since he realized that he would not have a fair trial in Judea. See Acts 16:36-40; 17:1-10; 18:12-18; 21:26 to 26:32.

[35] See: Jürgen Becker, Paul: Apostle to the Gentiles (Louisville, KY: Westminster; John Knox Press, 1993), 337; H. B. Mattingly, "The Origen of the Name 'Christians,'" Journal of Theological Studies 9 (1958): 26-37.

[36] Murphy says, "The nature of the Roman empire was such that any challenge to its total authority was looked upon as treason" (112). For more information on Roman religious policy, see the next section.

[37] Joseph Lecler, The Two Sovereignties: A Study of the Relationship between Church and State (London: Burns Oates and Washbourne, 1952), 8.

[38] Joseph Lecler was teacher at the Catholic University of Paris (L'institut Catholique de Paris).

[39] Ibid.

[40] Eusebius, The Church History of Eusebius, NPNF2, ed. Philip Schaff and Henry Wace (Grand Rapids, MI: Eerdmans, 1983), 1:15.16-27.

[41] Pontius, The Life and Passion of Cyprian, ANF, ed. Alexander Roberts, James Donaldson, and A. Cleve-

The political and social problems in Palestine around the first Jewish war also contributed to the intolerance against Christians, since Christianity was considered a Jewish sect by most of the Romans in the first century.[42] The hostility between Romans and Jews, and Jews and Christians, contributed to the desire of apologists and other Christian writers in the second and third centuries to seek recognition from the Roman Empire as good citizens and to clearly differentiate themselves from the Jews.[43]

Cunningham says that the Christian church had both internal and external responses to imperial persecution. Internally, Christians developed a theology of martyrdom and a renewed expectation of the coming kingdom of God with a revival of apocalyptic literature.[44] Some authors in this period would identify Rome or a Roman emperor with the Antichrist, the first beast of Rev 13, or the "restraining forces" of 2 Thess 2:6.[45] When persecution was decreased and in times of peace, Christians tended to adapt to the imperial lifestyle and set their hopes on earthly expectations because of the delay of Christ's second coming. The external response of the church, as Cunningham points out, consisted of a passive retreat in recognition of God's sovereign ordination of worldly rulers and Christians' obligation

---

land Coxe (Grand Rapids, MI: W.B. Eerdmanns, 1989), 5:272-273.

[42] Murphy, 39; Ralph Martin Novak, Christianity and the Roman Empire: Background Texts (Harrisburg, PA: Trinity Press International, 2001), 33.

[43] For further information on early Christians' relations with Jews and the Roman Empire, see: Gillian Clark, Christianity and Roman Society, Key Themes in Ancient History (Cambridge: Cambridge University Press, 2004); Everett Ferguson, Church and State in the Early Church, Studies in Early Christianity, vol. 7 (New York: Garland, 1993); Erwin Ramsdell Goodenough, The Church in the Roman Empire (New York: H. Holt and Company, 1931), 3-39; Frederick C. Grant, The Early Days of Christianity (New York: Abingdon Press, 1922), 223-310; Ernest George Hardy, Christianity and the Roman Government: A Study in Imperial Administration (London: G. Allen & Unwin, 1925); Paul Keresztes, Imperial Rome and the Christians (Lanham: University Press of America, 1989); Murphy, 6-114; Novak, 10-138; William Mitchell Ramsay, The Church in the Roman Empire before A.D. 170, [5th] ed. (Grand Rapids: Baker Book House, 1954), 171-374; Marta Sordi, The Christians and the Roman Empire (Norman: University of Oklahoma Press, 1986), 3-132.

[44] Cunningham, 6

[45] According to Collins, the Sibylline Oracles identifies Nero as the Antichrist. Hippolytus identifies Rome as the first beast of Rev 13 and affirms that the Antichrist would not come until the Roman Empire had been divided into 10 democracies. Tertullian is the first one to identify the Roman Empire with the "restraining forces" of 2 Thess 2:6. For the Sibylline Oracles see: J. J. Collins, "The Sibylline Oracles," in The Old Testament Pseudepigrapha, ed. James H. Charlesworth (Garden City, NY: Doubleday, 1983). For information on Hippolytus see: Hippolytus, Antichrist, ANF, ed. Alexander Roberts, James Donaldson, and A. Cleveland Coxe (Grand Rapids, MI: W.B. Eerdmanns, 1989); Hippolytus, Kommentar Zu Daniel, ed. G. Nathanael Bonwetsch and Marcel Richard, 2d ed., Griechischen Christlichen Schriftsteller Der Ersten Jahrhunderte, vol. 7 (Berlin: Akademie Verlag, 2000). For further studies see: Bernard McGinn, Antichrist: Two Thousand Years of the Human Fascination with Evil (New York: Harper SanFrancisco, 1994), 35-78.

to submit to them, as well as the rise of apologists portraying Christians as good citizens and Roman persecution as unjust.[46]

Early Christians' passive attitude before the state was related to their independent way of living—Christians are foreigners in this world—and their resulting detachment from political institutions. Wood summarizes this point as follows:

> The early Christians emphasized that their citizenship was not on earth but in heaven. Like Abraham, they "looked forward to the city which has foundations, whose builder and maker is God." "For here we have no lasting city, but we seek the city which is to come." They looked upon political institutions with a spirit of inner detachment and independence since such institutions belonged to a perishing world and were everywhere steeped in paganism. Tertullian wrote, "As those in whom all ardor in the pursuit of honor and glory is dead, we have no pressing inducement to take part in your public meetings; nor is there aught any more entirely foreign to us than affairs of state." Consequently, there is almost no evidence of any Christians taking part in the political life during this period. But they sought to respect the State and show an attitude of deference toward it rather than an attitude of hostility. This position was given special emphasis by many of the early Apologists who claimed, "We are the best citizens of the Emperor." Even after the Neronian and Domitian persecutions, prayers continued to be offered for rulers, even the Emperor, as divinely appointed officials.[47]

In spite of Christians' non-participation in the political life of the empire, the continued affirmation of God's supremacy over the empire and His ordination of earthly governments is mentioned by several Christian authors in the first three centuries.[48] This theological understanding of the sovereignty of God was the basis for their acceptance of the state and led some Christians to combine faith and patriotism.[49] Rahner argues that "the early Church's basically positive view of the state extended from a purely theological base to social and even political collaboration with the state."[50] The common understanding of Christian abstention from military services lost its strength, and more and more Christians became "prone to lapse, in persecution, to fraternize with the

---

[46] Cunningham, 6-11.

[47] Wood, Church and State in Scripture, 48-49.

[48] Polycarp states that Christians should render honor to appointed authorities. Athenagoras mentions that emperors received their power from above. Theophilus of Antioch affirms that emperors are appointed by God and Christians should honor, obey, and pray for them. Irenaeus accepts the state as ordained by God to promote justice as a result of human rejection of God. Michael Bauman and David W. Hall, God and Caesar (Camp Hill, PA: Christian Publications, 1994), 27-40. Clement of Rome prayed for the emperor and the welfare of the state, and recognized their sovereign authority as given by God. Rahner, 13.

[49] Rahner, 15.

[50] Ibid., 14.

world and to engage in war."[51] Aristides of Athens, Justin Martyr, Tertullian, Origen, and others claimed that Christians were not enemies of the empire or the emperor and that God sustained the empire because of Christians.[52] Origen even "contrasts the imperial officials with the bishops and leaders of the local churches, whom he regards as models of prudent government and political wisdom."[53] Taylor Innes argues that Cyprian popularized the idea that the unity of the church was in the leadership of the bishops, who were the successors of the apostles and the head of the living body of the church. He says, "Their dioceses generally coincided with the Roman districts and prefectures, and everywhere the Church had begun to run into the mould of the empire and to imitate its organization."[54] Gradually the early church began to seek equality with the empire, and its net of bishoprics was noticed by the empire as a great power.[55]

SUMMARY

In summary, the scriptural paradigm for a Christian political theology outlined in the NT would include (1) the existence of civil and spiritual leadership without an earthly theocratic concept of kingship; (2) the notion of messianic kingship and a kingdom of God headed by Jesus Christ, first in heaven and finally established on

---

[51] Roland Bainton, "The Christian and the War," The Christian Century 61 (1944): 560. This is a review of the book The Fall of Christianity by G. J. Heering. For more information on early Christianity and military service, see Cecil John Cadoux, The Early Church and the World: A History of the Christian Attitude to Pagan Society and the State Down to the Time of Constantinus (Edinburgh: T. & T. Clark, 1955); Cecil John Cadoux, Christian Pacifism Re-Examined (New York: Garland Publishing, 1972); idem, The Early Christian Attitude to War: A Contribution to the History of Christian Ethics (New York: Seabury Press, 1982); Adolf von Harnack, Militia Christi: The Christian Religion and the Military in the First Three Centuries (Philadelphia: Fortress Press, 1981); Guy F. Hershberger, War, Peace, and Nonresistance, 3d rev. ed. (Scottdale, PA: Herald Press, 1969); Archie Penner, The Christian, the State, and the New Testament (Scottdale, PA: Herald, 1959); Ernst Troeltsch and Olive Wyon, The Social Teaching of the Christian Churches, 1st Harper torchbook ed. (New York: Harper, 1960).

[52] Aristides of Athens in his apology argued that Christians' prayers kept the world alive. Aristides of Athens, The Apology of Aristides the Philosopher (Early Christians Writings, 125), http://www.earlychristianwritings.com/text/aristides-kay.html (accessed 15 October 2007). Justin Martyr stated that God was delaying the collapse of the world because of Christians. Justin Martyr, The Second Apology, ANF, ed. Alexander Roberts, James Donaldson, and A. Cleveland Coxe (Grand Rapids, MI: W.B. Eerdmanns, 1989), 1:191. He also argued that Christians were the best help for the empire. idem, The First Apology, ANF, ed. Alexander Roberts, James Donaldson, and A. Cleveland Coxe (Grand Rapids, MI: W.B. Eerdmanns, 1989), 1:167. Tertullian expressed the same idea in his apology and other works. Tertulian, The Apology, ANF, ed. Alexander Roberts, James Donaldson, and A. Cleveland Coxe (Grand Rapids, MI: Eerdmanns, 1989), 3:37, 43-47.

[53] Rahner, 17.

[54] A. Taylor Innes, Church and State: A Historical Handbook, 2d ed. (Edinburgh: T. & T. Clark), 16.

[55] Rahner, 18.

earth at His second coming; (3) the state as a temporal power with provisional settings until the final establishment of the kingdom of God; (4) the church and the state working in different realms, where the jurisdiction of the church is in the spiritual realm while the state is in the worldly realm; (5) the idea that Christians' first allegiance is to God; and (6) the charge that Christians, who are citizens of the world, should obey the authorities in everything that does not conflict with the law of God.

This overview of the development of church and state understanding in the first three centuries presented a concept of church-state relations in the primitive church grounded primarily in the NT. From this the following could be noted:

1 - Christians were living as an independent community inside the empire, without the boundaries of nationality.

2 - After Nero, the Roman Empire began to recognize Christianity as an independent religious group, not a Jewish sect.

3 - Christians' lack of national identity, their natural opposition to any other religious allegiance, and the political and social problems in Palestine around the first Jewish war contributed to Roman intolerance of Christians.

4 - In response to imperial persecution, Christians internally developed a theology of martyrdom and a renewed expectation of the coming kingdom of God, and externally displayed a passive attitude before the state because of their independence and detachment from political institutions.

5 - Christians' theological understanding of the sovereignty of God was the basis for their gradual acceptance of the state and led some Christians to join their faith with patriotism.

ROMAN RELIGIOUS POLICY[56]

The Roman Empire can be considered a type of pluralistic society where religion and state were intimately connected.[57] This broad definition is due to the complexity

---

[56] The analysis of Roman religious policy in this section will focus on the major principles that were present in Roman religion throughout its history.

[57] For more studies that emphasize the close relationship between religion and state in the Roman Empire, see Mary Beard and John A. North, Pagan Priests: Religion and Power in the Ancient World (Ithaca, NY: Cornell University Press, 1990); Elizabeth Rawson, Roman Culture and Society: Collected Papers (Oxford: Oxford University Press, 1991); Alan Wardman, Religion and Statecraft among the Romans (Baltimore, MD: Johns Hopkins University Press, 1982); Alan Watson, The State, Law, and Religion: Pagan Rome (Athens, GA: University of Georgia Press, 1992).

of traditional Roman paganism "in its priestly organization, in its range of divinities and in its relations with the religious systems of its neighbours."[58] From the earliest period of Roman history to the time of the empire, it is almost impossible to identify a pure Roman religion.[59] John Ferguson affirms that "in general ancient religions were accommodations."[60] However, in spite of the constant political changes in Rome, Roman religion always had a political tone. For the Romans, religious duties were connected with citizenship.[61] The Greek writer Polybius observed that Roman society was superior because "the very thing that among other peoples is an object of reproach, namely superstition, is what holds together the Roman state. At Rome religion plays this part in both public and private life: its significance is hardly conceivable."[62] Some of the major concepts in Roman religion will be delineated in this section.

The Romans had a different vision of the gods. Simeon L. Guterman points out that unlike other cultures, they did not humble themselves before the gods; their cult was a contract between them and the gods, in which the gods would provide protection and victory to the state and the state would provide the proper offerings and honors to the gods.[63] He continues that "the Romans up to the latest times ascribed their success as a people to the fidelity with which they observed the conditions of this contract with the gods."[64] This led the Romans to be very accurate in the formulae of prayers and vows. Beard, North, and Price say that "a slight error in performance, even a single wrong word, led to the repetition of the whole ritual."[65]

---

[58] Mary Beard, John A. North, and S. R. F. Price, Religions of Rome, vol. 1 (Cambridge: Cambridge University Press, 1998), xi.

[59] According to Scheid, there are some difficulties in determining the pure Roman religion and its origins. He argues that there are a limited number of sources to reconstruct the origins and the pure tradition of Roman gods. He questions Dumézil's theory of Roman religion origins from Indo-European cultures, the primivist theory of Deubner, and the common Etruscan theory of origins. For more information about the origins of Roman religion and prehistoric Roman religion, see Franz Altheim, History of Roman Religion (New York: E. P. Dutton, 1937); Cyril Bailey, Phases in the Religion of Ancient Rome (Westport, CT: Greenwood Press, 1972); Georges Dumézil, Archaic Roman Religion, with an Appendix on the Religion of the Etruscans, 2 vols. (Chicago: University of Chicago Press, 1970); William Reginald Halliday, Lectures on the History of Roman Religion from Numa to Augustus (Liverpool: The University Press of Liverpool, 1923); H. J. Rose, Ancient Roman Religion (London: Hutchinson's University Library, 1948); John Scheid and Janet Lloyd, An Introduction to Roman Religion (Bloomington: Indiana University Press, 2003); Georg Wissowa, Religion Und Kultus Der Römer (Munich: C.H. Beck, 1912).

[60] John Ferguson, The Religions of the Roman Empire (Ithaca, NY: Cornell University Press, 1970), 211.

[61] Scheid and Lloyd, 19.

[62] Polybius, The Histories, The Loeb Classical Library (Cambridge, MA: Harvard University Press, 1979), 7.53.

[63] Simeon L. Guterman, Religious Toleration and Persecution in Ancient Rome (London: Aiglon Press, 1951), 25.

[64] Ibid.

[65] Beard, North, and Price, Religions of Rome, 32.

Roman religion had its public and private sides. Ittai Gradel says that it is important to "strictly distinguish between public cults, which were always carried out and controlled by freeborn of high rank, and private worship, where the status of worshippers was more variable."[66]Sextus Pompeius Festus explains in his *De Verborum Significatu* that the *public sacra* were performed at public expense and the *privata sacra* were not.[67] The public cults were always headed by the magistrates or by the members of the *collegia*.[68] Gradel says that the distinction between public and private worship was not restricted to the place where the ritual was performed, but extended to the people for whom it was performed: "The state cult in Rome functioned on behalf of the whole Roman people" and "Roman state gods were simply and exclusively those which received worship in such state cult."[69]

The private side of Roman religion involved individual worshipers who would pay alms to different gods according to their needs: rain, crops, birth, marriage, and such.[70] Each family had its own religious traditions that were carried on by the *paterfamilias*.[71] Family affairs such as birth, marriage, death, and burial were within the family's religious responsibility.[72] However, these private cults had an effect only on those who were participating in the ceremonies. They could be held in public temples, but they were considered private because they were not presided over by magistrates and religious leaders appointed by the senate that functioned on behalf

---

[66] Ittai Gradel, Emperor Worship and Roman Religion, Oxford Classical Monographs (Oxford: Oxford University Press, 2004), 9.

[67] Sextus Pompeius Festus and Paul, Sexti Pompei Festi De Verborum Significatu Quae Supersunt Cum Pauli Epitome, ed. Marcus Verrius Flaccus, Emil Thewrewk, and W. M. Lindsay, Bibliotheca Scriptorum Graecorum Et Romanorum Teubneriana (Lipsiae: B.G. Teubneri, 1913), 284.

[68] Roman religious leaders were divided into colleges known as the Collegia Romanorum. These colleges were composed mainly of aristocratic patricians after the end of the Republic. The four major Roman religious colleges were the Augures, Pontifis, Quindecemviri, and Epulones. The public rituals in Roman religion were performed by people with authority in public life, not by consecrated priests. The election or appointment for a public function and the social role of the individual were what qualified him to perform religious sacrifices. There was no difference between public and religious life. For more information, see Beard, North, and Price, Religions of Rome, 18-30; Gradel, 10; Scheid and Lloyd, 129-146.

[69] Gradel, 12.

[70] For example, the worship of Juno, the goddess of menstruation, marriage, and birth, according to Robert E. A. Palmer, Roman Religion and Roman Empire: Five Essays (Philadelphia: University of Pennsylvania Press, 1974), 3-56. Van Gennep calls this attitude of bringing common phases of human life into the sacred sphere "Rites of Passage." For more information see Arnold van Gennep, The Rites of Passage (Chicago: University of Chicago Press, 1960).

[71] Beard, North, and Price, Religions of Rome, 49.

[72] Ibid.

of the whole Roman people.[73] Most of these rituals were led by the family leaders or local priests, but private cults could also be supervised very closely by public authorities who were responsible for *sacra privata* as well as *sacra publica*.[74]

Roman religion emphasized community more than the individual. The morality and virtue of each citizen was a public concern, and for the Romans virtue could be attained only through religious behaviors. John Scheid says that Roman religion "was a social religion, closely linked to the community, not to the individual. It involved individuals only in so far as they were members of a particular community."[75] Scheid states that Roman religion "aimed for the earthly wellbeing of the community, not for the salvation of an individual and his or her immortal soul in the after-life. The gods did help individuals, but primarily in so far as they were members of the community, and only secondarily as individuals *per se* rather than as people involved in community affairs."[76] It was a religion with a civic and true political character.

The main political aspect of Roman religion, according to Géza Alföldy, was its importance in maintaining the social and political stability of the Empire for most of the republican period and even afterwards.[77] He points out that in the republican system of government,

> the domination of the aristocracy over Roman society did not depend entirely upon its political power and manipulation in its favour. The senatorial aristocracy also stamped the identity of the Roman people with its own traditions: it convinced the free strata of the citizen body of the idea of a state that was the property of the whole of Roman society—the *res publica* that was a *res populi*. The ideological basis of this conception of the state was religion. . . . The aristocracy determined the nature of this *religio*, the correct relationship with the gods. It furnished the state priests, who were called upon to discover divine will and to determine religious regulations. Moreover, the traditions of the families of the aristocracy dictated the religious behaviour proper to the members of society in various situations. The

---

[73] Gradel, 12-13.

[74] The Roman historian Livy says, "All other public and private sacrifices he likewise made subject to the decrees of the pontifex, that there might be someone to whom the commons could come for advice, lest any confusion should arise in the religious law through the neglect of ancestral rites and the adoption of strange ones. And not merely ceremonies relating to the gods above, but also proper funeral observances and the propitiation of the spirits of the dead were to be taught by the pontifex as well, and also what prodigies manifested by lightning or other visible sign were to be taken in hand and averted." Livy, Livy, with an English Translation by B. O. Foster, trans. Benjamin Oliver Foster, 13 vols., The Loeb Classical Library, Latin Authors (Cambridge, MA: Harvard University Press, 1939), 1:71-73.

[75] Scheid and Lloyd, 19.

[76] Ibid., 19-20.

[77] Géza Alföldy, The Social History of Rome (Baltimore, MD: Johns Hopkins University Press, 1988), 35.

standard for thought and action was the *mos maiorum*, ancestral conduct as expressed in the great deeds of the past. The collective memory of these deeds and their emulation ensured the continuity of state ideology. . . . Moreover, the pattern of behaviour enshrined in these deeds was precisely the pattern of thought and action upheld by the senators. The men who had achieved the glorious deeds of the past—politicians, generals and priests—were their ancestors: the glory of the ancestors ensured, in turn, the prestige of the descendants.[78]

Eric M. Orlin also argues that in the Roman Republic, religion was a means of keeping a balance between the ambitions of individuals (generals and aristocrats) and the welfare of the state, allowing individuals' achievements to benefit not only them personally, but also the whole society.[79] He continues that "the principal purpose of the state religion was to safeguard the *pax deum*, the favor of the gods, and thereby to ensure the safety and prosperity of the community. By their very nature, therefore, religious actions had political overtones. The Senate, as *de facto* guardian of the state, exercised a close supervision of religious matters, which included the recognition and handling of prodigies, the resolution of disputes involving sacred matters, and on occasion the introduction or suppression of new cults."[80]

The expansion of the Roman Empire enlarged the pantheon of Roman gods with the Romanization of foreign gods. Even though Roman traditions were very important, and as Robert Turcan points out, "*religio* (national and authentic) was readily contrasted with *superstitio* (exotic and suspected),"[81] a college of specialists would integrate foreign gods by giving them Latin names (*interpretatio Romana*) through the consultation of "Sibylline books or the ritual of the *evocatio*."[82] Different nationalities were united by the empire's central government, which tolerated and in fact authorized hundreds of religious cults. The lost political independence of previous free states was balanced with the maintenance of many local primitive beliefs.[83] Almost all religions, no matter how peculiar, were tolerated and considered good for society in that they provided unity and purpose to the citizens of the empire.[84]

Regarding the addition of new gods to the Roman pantheon, Guterman also

---

[78] Ibid., 35-36.

[79] Orlin writes that Roman generals' custom of vowing to construct temples to specific deities after victorious military campaigns allowed those generals to have personal promotion and gloria without seeking despotic rulership. Eric M. Orlin, Temples, Religion, and Politics in the Roman Republic (Boston: Brill Academic, 2002), 1-9.

[80] Ibid., 4.

[81] Robert Turcan, The Cults of the Roman Empire (Oxford: Blackwell, 1996), 10.

[82] Ibid., 12.

[83] It is important to mention that some changes in the form of worship could occur in the Romanization of the new deity (Guterman, 27).

[84] Scheid and Lloyd, 28.

affirms that the senate—the organ responsible for the final decision on the recognition of new divinities—was very conservative in policy. He points out that even though "it was assumed in all cases that the god, by being admitted to Rome, lost his former nationality and became strictly Roman,"[85] "a distinction was made between the *Di novensiles*, the newly admitted divinities, and the *Di indigetes*, the old gods. Only the latter were to be admitted within the *pomoerium*, or sacred boundary, but the worship of both was permitted."[86]

Romans, however, were reluctant to integrate nontraditional religions, which they called *superstitio*. Turcan states that "anything that deviated from the ritual taught by the ancestors and legitimized by tradition smacked of *superstitio*, chiefly the fringe practices of prophecy and occultism, the techniques of mental exaltation, of direct contact with the supernatural and the sacred, where people ventured in times of moral crisis or epidemics, without the mediation of pontiffs, flamines and augurs."[87] This is why in the eyes of Pliny the Younger, Tacitus, and other Roman writers and authorities, Christianity was considered a "depraved superstition" and "disastrous."[88] The Romans' pluralistic view of religion assumed that peace with heaven was essential for the prosperity and security of the empire. Religious freedom was connected with the welfare of the state. Any religious movement that threatened the unity and peace of the commonwealth of the state was considered treason. Worshipers' allegiance to multiple divinities was not a problem if it did not conflict with the interest of the state.[89]

In the imperial Roman era, social circumstances gradually changed. Alföldy asserts that leading provincial families became more and more dominant in the higher strata of the empire.[90] The social composition of the aristocracy included more provincial citizens than Italians.[91] Turcan states that "the vast majority of Roman citizens did not live in Rome" and "were not ethnically or physically linked with Rome."[92] He continues that "The *Urbs* became the *Orbis*. Rome was the great political and legal fatherland, cosmopolitan and

---

[85] Guterman, 29.

[86] Ibid., 28-29.

[87] Turcan, 10.

[88] Pliny and John Delaware Lewis, The Letters of the Younger Pliny (London: Kegan, Paul, Trench, Trubner, 1890), 10.98.8; Cornelius Tacitus and Michael Grant, The Annals of Imperial Rome, Penguin Classics (Harmondsworth: Penguin, 1971), 15.44.5. Guterman argues that the main reasons for the persecution of Christianity were because (1) it was not an authorized religion and (2) Christians did not worship the traditional imperial cult. See Guterman, 158.

[89] Scheid and Lloyd, 28.

[90] Alföldy, 103.

[91] Ibid., 125.

[92] Turcan, 17.

generous, but it was no longer a 'city' properly speaking: it was an idea. The imperial regime released the ordinary citizens from their political obligations. They decided nothing, no longer voted (since Tiberius) for the election of magistrates, no longer deliberated on the affairs of the *Urbs*."[93]

These social and political changes in the imperial life affected religion in many ways. The religious control that was exercised by a college of pontiffs became more connected with the emperor after Augustus assumed the position of *pontifex maximus*.[94] The lack of participation in public life weakened the *religio* and led many to seek *superstitio*.[95] The maintenance of a standard for thought and action—the *mos maiorum*—was more in the figure of the emperor than in the traditions of aristocratic families,[96] which led to the divination and worship of the emperor.[97] The understanding of how to appease the gods' anger was no longer under the strict control of the magistrate and senate, who in the republic and early empire held the "power to converse with the gods, to request their advice and weigh it up—to be more precise—the power to speak for them," which "conferred an extraordinary prestige upon the Roman aristocracy."[98] The civic theology, "the religion inspired by the model of the city had run out of

---

[93] Ibid.

[94] Scheid and Lloyd, 142.

[95] Turcan, 17.

[96] Mark Silk affirms that at the end of the republic, the emperor became responsible for civil theology, following the model of Numa, the famous Sabine King who, according to tradition, ruled Rome after Romulus and established the Roman religious system. Mark Silk, "Numa of Pompilius and the Idea of Civil Religion in the West," Journal of the American Academy of Religion 72, no. 4 (2004): 868.

[97] For further studies on emperor worship, see Beard, North, and Price, Religions of Rome, 206-210, 348-363; Allen Brent, The Imperial Cult and the Development of Church Order: Concepts and Images of Authority in Paganism and Early Christianity before the Age of Cyprian, Supplements to Vigiliae Christianae, vol. 45 (Boston: Brill, 1999); Alexander Del Mar, The Worship of Augustus Caesar, Derived from a Study of Coins, Monuments, Calendars, Aeras, and Astronomical and Astrological Cycles, the Whole Establishing a New Chronology and Survey of History and Religion (New York: Cambridge, 1900); Steven J. Friesen, Twice Neokoros: Ephesus, Asia, and the Cult of the Flavian Imperial Family, Religions in the Graeco-Roman World, vol. 116 (Leiden; New York: E.J. Brill, 1993); Gradel; S. R. F. Price, Rituals and Power: The Roman Imperial Cult in Asia Minor (New York: Cambridge University Press, 1984); Daniel N. Schowalter, The Emperor and the Gods: Images from the Time of Trajan, Harvard Dissertations in Religion, vol. 27 (Minneapolis: Fortress Press, 1991); Kenneth Scott, The Imperial Cult under the Flavians (New York: Arno Press, 1975); Morten Lund Warmind, "The Cult of the Roman Emperor before and after Christianity," in The Problem of Ritual: Based on Papers Read at the Symposium on Religious Rites Held at Åbo, Finland, on the 13th-16th of August, 1991, ed. Tore Ahlbäck (Åbo, Finland: Donner Institute for Research in Religious and Cultural History, 1993); Stefan Weinstock, Divus Julius (Oxford: Clarendon Press, 1971).

[98] Scheid and Lloyd, 150.

steam . . . the Romans had given up on some of their gods and above all on a particular kind of relationship with them. . . . The new piety greatly stressed human inferiority and submission to the gods, underlining the importance of the knowledge of what happened *beyond* this world rather them efforts to establish and maintain good relations with the immortals *within* it and with a view to life in the here and now."[99]

Even though by the end of the third century, Romans had changed how they tried to please the gods and relate to them, some aspects of Roman religion remained the same from the time of the republic and early empire. They continued to place more value on practice than dogma; rituals were more important than theological understanding and belief.[100] The social aspects, the *pax deum*, and the well-being of society were more important than individual affairs. Proper worship of the gods was essential to win the favor of the gods.[101]

SUMMARY

In Roman society, religion was an integral part of the state. Romans' relationship to their gods was like a contract in which the gods provided protection and victory to the state in exchange for the proper offerings and honors. Romans emphasized the cultic aspects of religion over the theological aspects. Their public cults were carried out by high-ranking Roman officials, and their private ones by individual worshipers who would pay alms to different gods according to their needs: rain, crops, birth, marriage, and such. Roman religion emphasized the communitarian aspect more than the individual aspect of society. Religious behaviors were a public concern because they related to the morality and virtue of each citizen of the empire. Religion was a way of maintaining the stability of social and political life of the empire and safeguarding the favor of the gods. In the Roman Republic, the senate was the guardian of the State and supervised religion, while in the empire, the supervision of religion was linked to the person of the emperor, who became the *pontifex maximus*.

Roman territorial expansion led to the assimilation of foreign gods into the Roman pantheon, but not all foreign cults were recognized by the Romans. Cults that practiced prophecy and occultism, the techniques of mental exaltation, or direct contact with the supernatural and the sacred were considered *superstitio* and were not recognized as *religio licita*.

---

99   Ibid., 186.

100   Ibid., 173.

101   Ibid.

The social and political changes in the imperial life affected religion in many ways. Rome gradually lost its political influence because the aristocracy became dominated by provincial citizens rather than Italians. The lack of participation in public life during the empire weakened the *religio* and led many to seek *superstitio*. However, this weakening of tradition did not change the main tenets of Roman religion: (1) that proper worship was essential to achieve the favor of the gods, (2) that religion was an affair of the state, and (3) that the well-being of the state was more important than that of the individual.

Constantine and the Christian Church

The analysis of Constantine scholars is not a simple task. Historians, sociologists, politicians, and other writers give different accounts and focus on different aspects of what happened in Constantine's reign. Even when the focus is narrowed to the topic of church and state relationships, controversial and opposing opinions are presented. The traditional works of Constantine scholars present him as a great emperor and Christian who laid the foundation for the political system that dominated Europe in the Middle Ages and made Christianity the proper partner of the state for the benefit of society.[102] On the other hand, there are works from as early as the beginning of the Middle Ages that question Constantine's religious convictions and portray him more as a politician taking any advantage possible to gain power and promote imperial unity.[103]

For the present study, Constantine's sincerity in his acceptance of Christianity, the reliability of the miraculous events described by Constantine's contemporary biographers, and the historicity and/or proper chronology of these events will not be the center of the discussion. The focus of the analysis will be the political reasoning behind the interplay of church and state that led Constantine and the

---

[102] See for example: Baker; Barnes; Edward Lewes Cutts, Constantine the Great: The Union of the State and the Church, Home Library (London: Society for Promoting Christian Knowledge, 1881); Eusebius, HE; idem, The Life of the Blessed Emperor Constantine, NPNF2, ed. Philip Schaff and Henry Wace (Grand Rapids, MI: Eerdmans, 1983); idem, The Oration of Eusebius Pamphilus, in Praise of the Emperor Constantine. Pronounced on the Thirtieth Anniversary of His Reign, NPNF2, ed. Philip Schaff and Henry Wace (Grand Rapids, MI: Eerdmans, 1983); Holsapple; D. George Kousoulas, The Life and Times of Constantine the Great: The First Christian Emperor (Bethesda, MD: Provost Books, 2003); Lactantius, Of the Manner in Which the Persecutors Died, ANF, ed. Alexander Roberts, James Donaldson, and A. Cleveland Coxe (Grand Rapids, MI: W.B. Eerdmanns, 1989).

[103] See for example: Leslie W. Barnard, "Church-State Relations, A.D. 313-337," Journal of Church and State 24 (1982); Jacob Burckhardt, The Age of Constantine the Great (Garden City, NY: Doubleday, 1949); Zosimus, New History, trans. Ronald T. Ridley, Byzantina Australiensia, vol. 2 (Canberra: Australian Association for Byzantine Studies, 1982).

church leaders to action.[104] The important questions are (1) the nature of the relationships between church and state in Constantine's time, and (2) how the state influenced the church and the church the state.

THE EDICT OF MILAN (A.D. 313)

The Edict of Milan[105] was a proclamation whereby Constantine and Licinius (305-324) established a policy of freedom of worship.[106] The Edict was officially supposed to end any form of religious persecution, especially of Christians, since Christianity was given status as a legal religion alongside paganism.

The Edict of Milan was not proclaimed in a vacuum, and it was not the first proclamation of religious freedom for Christians. According to Eusebius, an edict (c. A.D. 260)[107] was proclaimed by Gallienus (A.D. 259-268) ending the persecu-

---

[104] I recognize that theology and politics were closely related and there was no clear notion of separation between church and state at the time of Constantine. Religion was part of the welfare of the state, like any other aspect of government. Also, the intent to focus on political aspects will not hinder this work from portraying theological points of view interrelated with political actions.

[105] The text of the Edict of Milan is found in a Latin version in Lactantius, De Mortibus Persecutorum, 48.2 (English translation Lactantius, 320-321), and in a Greek version in Eusebius, Historia Ecclesiastica, 10.5.4-11 (English translation Eusebius, HE, 1:379-380.). The Eusebius text is traditionally accepted as a translation of Lactantius. For the discussion of authorship, see Milton V. Anastos, "The Edict of Milan (313): A Defence of Its Traditional Authorship and Designation," in Conversion, Catechumenate, and Baptism in the Early Church, ed. Everett Ferguson, Studies in Early Christianity (New York: Garland, 1993); Otto Seeck and Manlio Sargenti, Die Zeitfolge Der Gesetze Constantins, Materiali Per Una Palingenesi Delle Costituzioni Tardo-Imperiali; vol. 2 (Milano: Giuffrè, 1983). For more details on the date when the edict was issued, see Salvatore Calderone, Constantino e il Cattolicesimo (Firenze: F. Le Monnier, 1962).

[106] The authorship of the Edict of Milan and the exact date when Catholic Christians received freedom of worship, the return of their property, and political privileges after Diocletian's resignation are not the topic of this section. However, it is important to mention that some historians like Thomas D. Barnes argue that the Edict of Milan was an extension of Constantine's policy of religious freedom (which had already been in place in the West since 306) to the eastern part of the empire. According to Barnes, Constantine was able to convince Licinius to adopt the same policies of religious tolerance and restitution of Christian property that he had already done in his territory. Timothy David Barnes, "The Constantinian Settlement," in Eusebius, Christianity, and Judaism, ed. Harold W. Attridge and Gohei Hata, Studia Post-Biblica (New York: E.J. Brill, 1992), 635-657.

[107] The exact date of this edict is unknown. Fergus Miller favors A.D. 260 as the date of the edict, because Eusebius reports that it was proclaimed soon after Gallienus became the sole emperor. Since the names of Valerian and Gallienus continue to appear on papyri as joint rulers up to A.D. 260, and the rescript sent to Dionysius enforcing the edict was almost certainly dated in A.D. 261/2, the edict was probably promulgated in A.D. 260. Fergus Millar, The Emperor in the Roman World: (31 Bc-Ad 337), 2nd ed. (London: Duckworth, 1992), 571. According to Keresztes, it is possible that at this time the Christian church was recognized as a religio licita. Paul Keresztes, "The Peace of Gallienus: 260-303 AD," Wiener Studien (1975): 174-185.

tion against Christians established by his father Valerian (A.D. 253-259), and by rescript, he gave freedom of worship to Christians.[108] Galerius (A.D. 305-311) proclaimed an edict in A.D. 311, in his last days of life, revoking all previous edicts of persecution against Christians.[109] As Charles Tompkins says, the Edict of Milan "is the culmination of a series of manifestoes each of which offered better terms to the despised slaves of Christ."[110]

The importance of the Edict of Milan does not lie in its being the first edict of religious freedom for Christians, but in the results it had for the future of the church as well as the state. For the state, the edict reaffirmed and amplified the Roman policy of religious pluralism.[111] The diplomatic wording of the edict granted freedom of worship to any religious group (including those sects that were not before recognized as legal religions), and it did not establish primacy among them.[112] According to Robert L. Wilken,[113] "the decree set forth a policy of religious freedom, not simply the toleration of a troublesome sect."[114] H. A. Drake points out three innovations[115] brought by the Edict of Milan that differentiate it from the previous ones: (1) "it is the first official government document in the Western world that recognized the principle of freedom of belief,"[116] (2) it does

---

[108] The text of this edict is not preserved. Part of the rescript is mentioned by Eusebius (HE, 1:7.13). According to Miller, this rescript was "probably a subscription granted to the bishops as a group of individuals, rather than an epistula" (571).

[109] Eusebius, HE, 1:8.17.

[110] Charles Tompkins, "Their Word to Our Day: Constantine, Secular Christian (c A.D. 280-337)," Expository Times 80 (1969): 179.

[111] See the above section: Roman Religious Policy.

[112] The analysis of the edict in this section will be confined to the time and wording of the edict. Constantine favored Christianity over paganism during his reign. However, the edict itself did not establish supremacy of religion. The mention of Christianity in the edict is clearly understood by the fact that Christianity was the illicit religion and it was now receiving the same status as paganism. The benefits enjoyed by pagan temples and priests were now extended to Christians.

[113] Robert L. Wilken at the time of this dissertation was the William R. Kenan, Jr., Professor of the History of Christianity, University of Virginia.

[114] Robert L. Wilken, "In Defense of Constantine," First Things, no. 112 (2001): 37.

[115] Going against the idea of any innovation brought by the Edict of Milan, Jacob Burckhardt says that "Constantine introduced nothing altogether new, nor did he use the question of toleration as a weapon against the other Emperors, but rather persuaded Licinius, who had in the meanwhile married into his family, to participate in the decrees at Milan (winter of 312-313), and both together negotiated with Maximinus Daia to join in the obligation and obtained his qualified consent." Burckhardt, 273.

[116] H. A. Drake, by the time of this publication, was a professor of history at the University of California at Santa Barbara. Drake, Constantine and the Bishops, 196.

not specify any "supreme divinity" as grantor of Roman well-being,[117] and (3) it presents an official recognition that religion should not be coerced.[118]

Constantine's religious policy expressed in the Edict of Milan reflects the process of change that was happening in the Roman Empire. The Roman Empire had always followed the maxim that the prosperity of the empire was a result of the favor of the gods.[119] The political and military crisis of the empire in the third century shattered the traditional views on how to be a prosperous empire. Unlike Diocletian (284-305), who had sought the favor of the gods following the traditional pagan Roman religious policy, Constantine did not restrict the welfare of the state to a specific religious form; any deity could be worshiped and all were important for the prosperity of the empire.[120]

The decree also opened the door for any person to be an active citizen. Citizenship was no longer connected with religion (the sacrifice to the emperor). Constantine did not lose the support of pagans and added to the state the support of Christians. As Wilken said, "Constantine not only forged a new policy, he acquired a new constituency."[121]

It is important to mention also that in the Edict of Milan, even though Constantine manifested a preference for Christianity over paganism, he continued exerting the same judicature as the previous pagan Roman emperors. He was Augustus, the divine ruler: emperor, the supreme commander of the army, consulate, and juridical system, which empowered him as the final, inviolable, and omnipotent authority in the empire.[122] In addition to that, he

---

[117] Ibid., 197.

[118] Ibid. Even though the edict clearly grants freedom of beliefs, this policy was not strictly followed by Constantine. He promoted persecution both for political and religious reasons. He limited pagan worship and persecuted dissident Christians. Barnes affirms that Constantine forbade pagan public sacrifices and quoted Eusebius to establish that Constantine had launched a program of persecution against paganism. Beard, North, and Price, however, argue that Constantine's laws against paganism are dubious because of the use of the word superstitio. They say that Constantine did not forbid the traditional religio of the Romans, but suppressed only what was considered superstitio. See Barnes, "The Constantinian Settlement," 649-650; Mary Beard, John A. North, and S. R. F. Price, Religions of Rome, vol. 1 (Cambridge: Cambridge University Press, 1998), 369-375; Eusebius, HE, 1:2.44-54.

[119] See the above section, Roman Religious Policy.

[120] During Constantine's reign, Catholic Christianity was the prominent religion of the empire. Constantine extended freedom of belief to religio licita, not to superstitio. Some of Constantine's laws on religion banned different aspects of pagan superstitio, heresies, and schematics. For more information, see Beard, North, and Price, 169-175; CT 16.5.5, 16.10.1.

[121] Wilken, 38.

[122] Victor Saxer, "L'église et L'empire Chrétien au IVe Siècle: La Difficile Séparation des Compétences devant les Problèmes Doctrinaux et Ecclésiologiques," Revue des sciences religieuses 77, no. 1 (2003): 13-14.

was the *pontifex maximus*, the supreme religious leader of the empire. It is important to mention that this specific title, *pontifex maximus*, conferred such responsibilities as the oversight of any religious affair that would threaten the peace of the state, the final word on marriage, divorce, testaments, exhumation, and other such matters that from a Christian perspective were the sole responsibility of the church.[123]

The edict introduced the Christian church to the political life of the empire. From A.D. 312/313 on, Constantine's concessions to the Catholic church began to shape the role of the Catholic church as an institution in the social and political framework of the empire.[124] The church not only received back its confiscated properties, but also received significant donations from the imperial treasury.[125] Bishops were exempted from taxation,[126] public services,[127] and other benefits; they also were recognized as prelates and their courts as legal jurisdictions of appeal.[128] This new situation led the leadership of the church to incorporate the Hellenistic view of kingship, in which the empire became part of the kingdom of God on earth; the emperor was not only appointed by God to promote peace and justice in the secular world, he was the representative of the godhead on earth.[129]

---

[123] Ibid.

[124] Barnes, "The Constantinian Settlement," 646.

[125] Regarding Constantine's donations for the building of churches, the Liber Pontificalis presents an extensive list of cities where basilicas were built using Constantine's donations. Raymond Davis, The Book of Pontiffs (Liber Pontificalis): The Ancient Biographies of the First Ninety Roman Bishops to AD 715, rev. ed., Translated Texts for Historians, vol. 6 (Liverpool: Liverpool University Press, 2000), 16-27. See also Richard Krautheimer, Early Christian and Byzantine Architecture, 3d ed. (Harmondsworth: Penguin Books, 1979), 39-70; Richard Krautheimer, Rome, Profile of a City, 312-1308 (Princeton, NJ: Princeton University Press, 1980), 3-31. From now on the Liber Pontificalis will be abbreviated as LP and all quotations on this dissertation to the Liber Pontificalis up to A.D. 715, will be taken from Davis translation.

[126] Pharr, 441.

[127] Ibid.

[128] Ibid., 477.

[129] For more information on the political theology described by Eusebius in his works Historia Ecclesiastica and Vita Constantino, and on the political and theological discussion about Christian society in a Christian Roman Empire, see: Norman Hepburn Baynes, Byzantine Studies and Other Essays ([London]: University of London Athlone Press, 1960), 168-172; Ferdinand Edward Cranz, "Kingdom and Polity in Eusebius of Caesarea," Harvard Theological Review 45 (1952): 47-66; Erik Peterson and Giuseppe Ruggieri, Il Monoteismo Come Problema Politico, Giornale Di Teologia, vol. 147 (Brescia: Queriniana, 1983); Jean Marie Sansterre, "Eusèbe De Césarée Et La Naissance De La Théorie 'Césaropapiste'," Byzantion 62, no. 1 (1972): 131-195.

THE DONATIST CRISIS[130]

The Donatist controversy was the first religious crisis that occurred in the aftermath of Constantine's promotion of Christianity to *religio licita*. It was the first major Christian issue that a Roman emperor had to settle.[131] The controversy had its root in the northern African Christian tradition of spiritual virtue and severe discipline.[132] The core of the controversy, as Maureen A. Tilley describes it, was "a dispute over the proper way to be a Christian in a changing world."[133]

After almost fifty years of peace, Christianity suffered under Diocletian's persecution. As a result, two major parties arose in North Africa: (1) Christians who would stand for their beliefs in the face of imprisonment, loss of social position, or death, and (2) Christians who would keep away from any unnecessary conflict with the state by adopting political measures to avoid persecution.[134] In

---

[130] In this section, the historical events of the Donatist controversy are not the center of the discussion. They are provided as a background for the problem and to help explain the church and state issues related to them. For more information on the history of the Donatists, see: Timothy David Barnes, "Beginnings of Donatism," Journal of Theological Studies, no. 26 (1975): 13-22; L. Duchesne, Early History of the Christian Church, from Its Foundation to the End of the Fifth Century, vol. 2 (London: J. Murray, 1911); W. H. C. Frend, The Donatist Church: A Movement of Protest in Roman North Africa (Oxford: Clarendon Press, 1952); W. H. C. Frend and K. Clancy, "When Did the Donatist Schism Begin," Journal of Theological Studies, no. 28 (1977): 104-109; Paul Monceaux, Histoire Littéraire De L'afrique Chrétienne Depuis Les Origines Jusquä L'invasion Arabe, 7 vols. (Brussels: Culture et civilization, 1966), vols 5-7; Maureen A. Tilley, Donatist Martyr Stories: The Church in Conflict in Roman North Africa, Translated Texts for Historians, vol. 24 (Liverpool: Liverpool University Press, 1996); idem, The Bible in Christian North Africa: The Donatist World (Minneapolis: Fortress Press, 1997); Geoffrey Grimshaw Willis, Saint Augustine and the Donatist Controversy (London: S. P. C. K., 1950).

[131] This is not the first time an emperor intervened in a church dispute. Eusebius talks about the appeal made by the church at Antioch to Aurelian in the case of Paul of Samosata (272). Aurelian attended the church's petition, drove out Paul of Samosata, and delivered the building to Domnus, the new bishop of Antioch. See Eusebius, HE, 1:7.30.

[132] Around 50 years before the Donatist problem, at the great council of Carthage (A.D. 256), the African Episcopacy under the leadership of Cyprian had established not only the question of rebaptism, but also the whole concept of readmission of the lapsed and the validity of the sacraments based on the virtue of the officiant. The Cyprian formula contrasted with the one adopted by the leadership of the Roman church, which was more tolerant with lapsed persons and did not accept rebaptism. For more information on the background of the Donatist controversy, see: Frend, The Donatist Church, 1-140; Tilley, Donatist Martyr Stories, xix-xxxiv; idem, The Donatist World, 9-52.

[133] Tilley, The Donatist World, 11.

[134] At the end of the third and beginning of the fourth century, martyrdom was seen differently by these two groups. Among the most conservative, it was culturally considered a privilege to die as a martyr. Many Christians gave themselves up for martyrdom. Tertullian advised that martyrdom should not be avoided, but

the aftermath of persecution, under Constantine's policy of religious freedom, the subjects of purity, apostasy, and discipline became a big problem again for the church in North Africa. The major issues were (1) determining who would be considered a *traditor*[135] and (2) dealing with lax Christians who had cooperated with the civil authority in the time of repression.[136]

The four edicts of Diocletian against Christians were not executed in the same way all over the empire.[137] In some parts of North Africa, the persecution was more intense. Bishops at Carthage used subterfuge to overcome the pressure: When under investigation of the authorities they submitted secular books instead of Christian books.[138] Bishops in Numidia and other parts of Africa did not hand out Christian books and even acted boldly in defiance of the authorities, following the example of Cyprian, the great Christian martyr of North Africa.[139]

---

for the moderate party, it was considered excess; it provoked a counter-reaction among some bishops, who discouraged even the supplying of food to prisoners who had voluntarily given themselves up as martyrs. According to The Acts of the Abitinian Martyrs, "In the city of Carthage in the year 304, there was a riot outside the entrance to the prison. Christians coming in from the countryside to visit their friends and relatives in prison were pushed, shoved, whipped, and prevented from bringing consolation to the confessors confined in dark cells and tortured to the shedding of blood. The food and drink they brought for those in the dungeons were knocked from their hands and scattered where the dogs could lap them up. Parents, both fathers and mothers, were beaten into the gutters." Tilley, Donatist Martyr Stories, xi. "The Christians coming in from the countryside where beaten not by the Roman officers, but by a troop following the orders of Mensurius bishop of Carthage and Caecilianus his deacon." "Acta Martyrum Saturnini, Felicis, Dativi, Ampelii Et Aliorum," in PL, ed. J. P. Migne, vol. 8 (Paris: J.-P. Migne, 1844), col. 689-715.

[135] The word traditor "became a technical expression to designate those who had given up the Sacred Books, and also those who had committed the worse crimes of delivering up the sacred vessels and even their own brethren." John Chapman, "Donatists," The Catholic Encyclopedia; an International Work of Reference on the Constitution, Doctrine, Discipline, and History of the Catholic Church, ed. Charles George Herbermann et al. (New York: Encyclopedia Press Incorporation, 1913), 121.

[136] After the end of persecution, many of the traditors had returned to their positions of authority in their sees. The Donatists believed that those who obeyed the state rather than becoming martyrs should not be allowed to hold church offices, and they proclaimed that any sacraments celebrated by these priests and bishops were invalid.

[137] The first edict (A.D.303) ordered the destruction of Christian temples and religious books. The second (A.D. 303) ordered that all Christian bishops should be thrown to the beasts. The third (A.D. 303) ordered that religious leaders should offer sacrifices to pagan gods. The fourth (A.D. 304) ordered that any Christian should offer sacrifices to the gods. Henry Chadwick, The Early Church, rev. ed., Penguin History of the Church (London, New York: Penguin Books, 1993), 121-122.

[138] This is the case of Mensurius, who handed over sacred books to the magistrate trying to manage the ongoing persecution. Augustine says that the books he handed over were heretics' writings. See Augustine, "Breviculus Collationis Cum Donatistis," in PL, ed. J. P. Migne, vol. 43 (Paris: J.-P. Migne, 1865), col. 638.

[139] Tilley, Donatist Martyr Stories, xiii-xv.

The conflict between the two parties did not fully emerge until the consecration of Caecilianus as bishop of Carthage.[140] Some members of the Carthaginian church refused to acknowledge Caecilianus as bishop because his consecrator, Felix of Aptunga, was charged with being a *traditor*.[141] The opposition sought support from Secundus, bishop of Tigisis, and in a council elected Majorinus as bishop of Carthage. The issue became stronger because Constantine's monetary clergy support was granted only to the Catholic bishop Caecilianus.[142] The conservative party, led by Donatus,[143] sought state recognition as the legitimate bishopric of Carthage. Because the proconsul Anulinus did not respond positively to their request, they appealed to Constantine.[144]

---

[140] The problem of dating the origin of the Donatist schism is controversial. There are two main dates: (1) from A.D. 306 to 307, and (2) from A.D. 311 to 312. For more information on the origin of the Donatists, see: Barnes, "Beginnings of Donatism"; Duchesne; Frend and Clancy, "When Did the Donatist Schism Begin?"; Monceaux; Otto Seeck, Geschichte Des Untergangs Der Antiken Welt (Darmstadt: Wissenschaftliche Buchgesellschaft, 1966).

[141] According to Optatus, Caecilianus was chosen with the unanimous vote of the people and without the influence of bishops of other cities. The group opposing him was influenced by a rich woman named Lucila who had had problems with Caecilianus before: he had forbidden her from bringing her martyr relic to church and kissing it. Optatus, "S. Optati Milevitani Libri VII," in Contra Parmenianum Donatistam, ed. Karl Ziwsa, CSEL, vol. 26 (Vindobonae: F. Tempsky, 1893), 19-21.

[142] Eusebius mentions a letter from Constantine addressed to Caecilianus about the monetary support he was giving to the church. Eusebius, HE, 1:10.6. There is some contention regarding the date of this letter among scholars, but most of them place the letter between A.D. 312-313. See Baynes, Constantine the Great and the Christian Church, 10, 68-69; Monceaux, 3.39; Otto Seeck, Regesten Der Kaiser Und Päpste Für Die Jahre 311 Bis 476 N. Chr. Vorarbeit Zu Einer Prosopographie Der Christlichen Kaiserzeit (Stuttgart: J.B. Metzler, 1919), 151, 160. Also, in Anulinus's letter to Constantine addressing the problem brought to him against Caecilianus, he declares that everything that Constantine had asked him to give to the Catholic Church in his previous "heavenly letter" he had given, and afterwards that a group approached him accusing Caecilianus and asking for his deposition as bishop and recognition of their own appointed bishop. The way Anulinus wrote to Constantine implies that only Caecilianus received the benefits of Constantine's new policy of financial support to the Catholic Church. See Optatus appendix 4: Optatus, 206-208. It is important to notice also that Constantine's own letter to Anulinus refers to "the Catholic church of the Christians." Why would Constantine use this terminology if he did not mean that an exclusive group of Christians would receive the financial benefit?

[143] Majorinus died and Donatus was chosen bishop in his place for the conservative party.

[144] This issue of who appealed first to the emperor was a matter of contention in the dispute between Donatists and Catholics afterwards. Optatus quotes a letter sent by Donatist bishops asking Constantine to send bishops from Gaul to judge their case. Yet B. Kriegbaum mentions that Optatus could have been unaware of the proper date of the Donatist petition; this would place Caecilianus's petition to Constantine before the Donatists'. See B. Kriegbaum, "Ein Neuer Lösungsverschlag Fur Ein Altes Problem: Die Sogennanten Preces Der Donatisten (Optatus 1.22)," in Studia Patristica, Papers Presented to the 10th International Conference on Patristic Studies Held in Oxford, 1987, ed. Elizabeth A. Livingstone (Leuven: Peeters Press, 1989), 279; Optatus, 25-26.

Constantine referred the matter to the bishop of Rome, Melchiades.[145] He also ordered that other bishops from Gaul should help in the judgment of the issue.[146] The synod of Rome[147] (313) headed by Melchiades favored Caecilianus and condemned the Donatists. The Donatists did not accept their decision, and the issue was brought up again at the council of Arles (314), where Caecilianus and Felix were found innocent of the Donatist charges.[148] The Donatists, not happy with the results of the council, appealed again to the judgment of the emperor himself. Constantine confirmed Caecilianus as bishop of Carthage and condemned those who refused to accept him to be punished and their churches to be confiscated.[149] After a time of persecution, Constantine tolerated the Donatists, and their churches remained strong in North Africa until the middle of the fifth century.[150]

Some points are relevant on the church and state relationships at the beginning of the Donatist controversy. The Catholic church was forced to reevaluate its views on church and state.[151] The prior view of the state as appointed by God to promote peace and order in civil affairs broadened to give the state responsibility for the promotion of Christian moral values.[152] This included using the

---

[145] Also known as Miltiades.

[146] Eusebius, HE, 1:10.5.21.

[147] This synod was held at the Lateran, the residence of the Empress Fausta, in October 2, 313. Optatus, 26-27.

[148] Constantine's letter to Chrestus, bishop of Syracuse, implies that the Donatist problem would be solved in the council of Arles, but the Donatist issue was not the main topic of the meeting Eusebius, HE, 1:10.6. In the canons of the council, there is no specific mention of the Donatist problem. Some canons (VIII—On baptism; XIII—On the problem of traditor; and XIV—On false accusations) refer to the Donatist problem. However, in the letter addressed to Silvestre, bishop of Rome, there is a clear mention that the Donatist issue was discussed in the council. The letter says that if Silvestre had been in person in the council, more severe judgment would have been given to the accusers of Caecilianus. For the canons of the council, see: Sacrorum Conciliorum, Nova et Amplissima Collectio, ed. Philippe Labbe and Giovan Domenico Mansi, 54 vols. (Graz: Akademische Druck- u. Verlagsanstalt, 1960), 2:470-474. and Karl Joseph von Hefele, A History of the Councils of the Church: From the Original Documents, 5 vols. (Edinburgh: T. & T. Clark, 1883), 1:184-198. For the letter, see: Sacrorum Conciliorum, 2:469.

[149] Augustine, Letters, Fathers of the Church, vol. 18 (New York: Fathers of the Church, 1951), 24.

[150] For more details on the Donatists, see: Barnard; Barnes, "Beginnings of Donatism"; John L. Boojamra, "Constantine and the Council of Arles : The Foundations of Church and State in the Christian East," Greek Orthodox Theological Review 43, no. 1-4 (1998); John Chapman, "Donatists"; Frend, The Donatist Church; Frend and Clancy, "When Did the Donatist Schism Begin?"; Kriegbaum; Monceaux; Zablon Nthamburi, "The Donatist Controversy as a Paradigm for Church and State," Africa Theological Journal 17, no. 3 (1988): 196-206; Optatus; Saxer; Tilley, Donatist Martyr Stories; idem, The Donatist World; Willis.

[151] See the section "The Christian Church and the State before Constantine" in this chapter.

[152] For more information on Christians' views of church and state relationships before Constantine, see the section "The Christian Church and the State before Constantine."

political and military power of the state to suppress anyone who threatened the sound doctrine of the Catholic church.

The Catholic church had to reevaluate her role in society. Some years before the Donatist controversy, the leadership of the church was more inclined to accommodate itself to the social order around it. As Drake points out, some of the canons of the council of Elvira[153] indicate a Christian community willing "to define the boundaries of acceptable behavior at any given moment."[154] The Catholic church trends were "to reduce the tensions that originally separated their organization from the surrounding culture."[155]

On the other hand, the proximity between church and state brought about by Constantine's conversion contrasted with the vision of church and state separation developed by the Donatists. This was the first attempt to clearly define the roles of the church and the state in society.[156] The Donatists continued to stress the common North African view of the state as an oppressor and a symbol of the Antichrist.[157] Later on, the Donatist crisis also became a social crisis. Zablon Nthamburi says that the Donatists identified themselves with the poor people, and the schism was more a social and national movement than a religious one.[158] The Donatists believed there should not be any union between church and state: The state should not interfere in the business of the church and vice versa.[159]

On the side of the state, the Donatist crisis revealed Constantine's understanding of church and state relationships. Constantine's main concern was the welfare of the state and the continued support of the supreme God in his enterprises.[160] Ecclesiologi-

---

[153] The council of Elvira is considered the first council held in Spain. The exact year of the council is unknown. Scholars date the council from A.D. 300 to 313. Its eighty-one canons were mainly on disciplinary issues. For the date and canons of the council, see: Hefele, 1:131-172.

[154] Drake, Constantine and the Bishops, 224.

[155] Ibid., 229.

[156] At the beginning of the controversy, when the church's properties were granted only to Caecilianus's party by the order of Constantine, the Donatists asked for church judgment over state intervention. They asked for neutral parties—bishops from Gaul—to judge the case. However, after being condemned by Catholic church leaders twice, they appealed to Constantine's judgment—state intervention over church decision—contradicting the position they adopted afterward on church and state relationships. Optatus condemned them because of that. See Optatus, 25, 27.

[157] Tilley, Donatist Martyr Stories, xii-xiii.

[158] He even stresses that the disintegration of the Donatist movement weakened the ties between the Berber population and Christianity. This made it easier for the Berbers to move from Christianity to Islam after the Muslim invasion of North Africa. Nthamburi, 201.

[159] This idea is clearly stated in the Donatist phrase "Quid christianis cum regibus? Aut quid episcopis cum palatio?" (What have Christians to do with kings? Or what have bishops to do with palaces?). Optatus, 25.

[160] In almost all the letters sent by Constantine to bishops and other political leaders related to the Donatist

cal or theological differences could exist, since they would not threaten the unity and welfare of the state. Dissidents and troublemakers could cause not only civil disorder, but also the disfavor of divinity over the empire.[161] His policy, writes Drake,

> was the concept that a viable coalition could be forged by emphasizing the points of agreement between monotheists of whatever persuasion, a vision of a new kind of commonwealth in which stability, peace, and unity could be achieved by officially ignoring sectarian or theological differences—"small, trivial matters," as Constantine later would call them—and emphasizing the beneficent Providence of a single, Supreme Being, represented on earth by his chosen representative, the Roman emperor.[162]

Constantine's procedures for dealing with ecclesiastical problems took shape throughout the Donatist crisis.[163] First, his appointment of Melchiades, the bishop of Rome, to solve the schism might be an indication that he thought the church should solve its own problems. Also, as a good politician, he was passing the burden of decision-making. However, in the letter he sent to Melchiades, he made clear that he was in favor of unity and against any schismatic party.[164] Second, imperial commissions investigated the charge against Felix of Aptunga. Even though Constantine expressed his thought that this should not be necessary, he had to fulfill his duty to bring justice to all his subjects.[165] Third, the summoning of a council (Council of Arles, 314) was another step in the attempt to solve the problem. He not only summoned the clergy and gave financial support for them to attend the council, but also sent letters to participants in the council outlining the results he expected from it.[166] Finally, the decisions of the council were imposed by imperial power.

Constantine's policy on church and state relationships was not created because of the Donatist crisis. He had already chosen which group to support; he would not be "limited to a small body of pristine elect."[167] He was seeking a common ground; a way to favor peace and harmony, smoothing the differences to achieve

---

and other controversies, the issue of unity and the support of the supreme God are present. See: Eusebius, HE, 1:10.5-7; idem, VC 1:2.22, 2.72, 3.29-31, 3.51-53, 3.61, 4.13.

[161] A. H. M. Jones, Constantine and the Conversion of Europe (New York: Macmillan, 1949), 96.

[162] Drake, Constantine and the Bishops, 199.

[163] Both Drake and Boojamra see in Constantine's response to the Donatist crisis the foundation for the future actions of Constantine and other emperors before ecclesiastical problems. For further information, see: Boojamra; Drake, Constantine and the Bishops, 212-221.

[164] See the letter from Constantine to Melchiades in Eusebius, HE, 1:5.5.18.

[165] See Constantine's letter to Aelafius: Optatus, 204-206.

[166] See the letter from Constantine to Crestus in Eusebius, HE, 1:5.5.21-24.

[167] H. A. Drake, "Constantine and Consensus," Church History 64 (1995): 2.

a policy of consensus.[168] Constantine realized through the Donatist controversy that the use of military power would not always be the best option to solve religious conflicts. On the other hand, as Leslie W. Barnard says, "The way was thus prepared for the use of imperial synodal power, i.e., councils summoned by the emperor to heal religious dissension in the Empire. This was Constantine's master stroke, and his successors were to follow his example."[169]

The Council of Nicaea

The Arian controversy was the most important religious crisis dealt with by Constantine. The Council of Nicaea was at the center of the crisis, but it continued to cause problems for Constantine until his death. The historical and theological aspects of the controversy have been discussed extensively in scholarly materials and will not be the center of the present discussion. Historical and theological data will be given in this section to elucidate the church and state relationships at that time.[170]

---

[168] Ibid., 3.

[169] Barnard, 344.

[170] On theological and historical discussions about Arianism and the Council of Nicaea, see: Ephrem Boularand, L'hérésie d'Arius et la "Foi" de Nicée, 2 vols. (Paris: Letouzey & Ané, 1972); A. E. Burn, The Council of Nicaea: A Memorial for Its Sixteenth Centenary (London: Society for Promoting Christian Knowledge, 1925); Henry Chadwick, "Faith and Order at the Council of Nicea: A Note on the Background of the Sixth Canon," Harvard Theological Review 53, no. 3 (1960): 171-195; Mark J. Edwards, "The Arian Heresy and the Oration to the Saints," Vigiliae christianae 49, no. 4 (1995): 379-387; Thomas G. Elliott, "Constantine's Preparation for the Council of Nicaea," Journal of Religious History 17, no. 2 (1992): 127-137; Jack Forstman, "Nicene Mind in Historical Perspective and Its Significance for Christian Unity," Encounter 38 (1977):213-226; Robert C. Gregg and Dennis E. Groh, "Centrality of Soteriology in Early Arianism," Anglican Theological Review 59, no. 3 (1977): 260-278; Jaakko Gummerus, Die Homousianische Partei: Bis Zum Tode Des Konstantius : Ein Beitrag Zur Geschichte Des Arianischen Streites in Den Jahren 356-361 (Leipzig: A. Deichert'sche, 1900); Henry Melvill Gwatkin, The Arian Controversy (London: Longmans Green, 1908); Günther Christian Hansen, "Eine Fingierte Ansprache Konstantins Auf Dem Konzil Von Nikaia," Zeitschrift für antikes Christentum 2, no. 2 (1998): 173-198; Richard P. C. Hanson, The Search for the Christian Doctrine of God: The Arian Controversy, 318-381 (Grand Rapids: Baker Academic, 2005); idem, "The Doctrine of the Trinity Achieved in 381," Scottish Journal of Theology 36, no. 1 (1983): 41-57; Adolf von Harnack, Outlines of the History of Dogma, trans. Edwin Knox Mitchell (New York, London and Toronto: Funk and Wagnalls, 1893), 235-280; J. N. D. Kelly, Early Christian Creeds, 3d ed. (New York: D. McKay, 1972), 215-230; Hans Lietzmann, Symbolstudien I-XIV, Sonderausg. ed. (Darmstadt: Wissenschaftliche Buchgesellschaft, 1966); Alistair H. B. Logan, "Marcellus of Ancyra and the Councils of A.D. 325: Antioch, Ancyra, and Nicaea," Journal of Theological Studies 43 (1992): 428-446; Friedrich Loofs and Kurt Aland, Leitfaden Zum Studium Der Dogmengeschichte, 6, durchgesehene Aufl. ed. (Tübingen: M. Niemeyer, 1959), 169-190; Henryk Pietras, "Le Ragioni Della Convocazione Del Concilio Niceno Da Parte Di Constantino Il Grande: Un'investigazione Storico-Teologica," Gregorianum 82, no. 1 (2001): 5-35; Eduard Schwartz, Gesammelte Schriften, vol. 3 (Berlin: W. de Gruyter, 1956); idem, Kaiser

The divergent views of Arius and Alexander on the divinity of Christ resulted in a crisis of contention among opposing sees in the fourth century. Arius's propositions extrapolated the theological field to reach the political field.[171] Barnard says, "Very quickly the Christian East became embroiled with bishops either taking different sides or maintaining mediating positions."[172] Constantine could not suffer a controversy between Alexander and Arius that would spread discord in the church and empire. His action was required to maintain his ideal of unity of the empire through the favor of the Sovereign God of the Christians.[173]

The political steps taken by Constantine in the Arian controversy were very similar to those he took in the Donatist crisis. As in the Donatist crisis, he first sent a church representative, Bishop Hosius,[174] to put an end to the conflict.[175] Since Hosius did not accomplish much, Constantine summoned a

---

Constantin Und Die Christliche Kirche: Fünf Vorträge, 3, unveränderte Aufl. ed. (Stuttgart: B. G. Teubner, 1969); Oskar Skarsaune, "A Neglected Detail in the Creed of Nicaea (325)," Vigiliae christianae 41, no. 1 (1987): 34-54; Jörg Ulrich, "Nicaea and the West," Vigiliae christianae 51, no. 1 (March 1997): 10-24.

[171] At the same time that Arius sought the support of bishops in Palestine and Antioch, Alexander sent letters to eastern churches exposing his side of the problem, justifying his attitude toward Arius, and seeking political support for his position. See Socrates, Historia Ecclesiastica, NPNF2, ed. Philip Schaff and Henry Wace (Grand Rapids, MI: Eerdmans, 1983), 2:3-5; Sozomen, Historia Ecclesiastica, NPNF2, ed. Philip Schaff and Henry Wace (Grand Rapids, MI: Eerdmans, 1983), 2:251-252; Theodoret, Historia Ecclesiastica, NPNF2, ed. Philip Schaff and Henry Wace (Grand Rapids, MI: Eerdmans, 1983), 3:33-34.

[172] Barnard, 345.

[173] There is some contention among scholars about whether Constantine really understood and was concerned with the theological aspects of the Arian problem. Those who follow Jacob Burckhardt's views on Constantine argue that he had no religious interest in the case, only political. Others, like Thomas G. Elliott, argue that Constantine had a deeper understanding of and interest in the theological issues. For further studies, see: Barnes, Constantine and Eusebius; Baynes, Constantine the Great and the Christian Church; Burckhardt; Drake, Constantine and the Bishops; Thomas G. Elliott, "Constantine's Early Religious Development," Journal of Religious History 15 (1989): 283-291; idem, "Constantine's Preparation for the Council of Nicaea," Journal of Religious History 17, no. 2 (1992): 127-137; Øyvind Norderval, "The Emperor Constantine and Arius: Unity in the Church and Unity in the Empire," Studia theologica 42, no. 2 (1988): 113-150.

[174] Also known as Bishop Ossius.

[175] Eusebius, VC, 1:2.63-64. Even though Eusebius did not identify the emissary, there is now general agreement that the peacemaker was Bishop Hosius. For more information see: Athanasius, Apologia Contra Arianos, NPNF2, ed. Philip Schaff and Henry Wace (Grand Rapids, MI: Eerdmans, 1983), 4:139-140; Victor C. De Clercq, "Hosius of Cordova; a Contribution to the History of the Constantinian Period" (Ph.D. diss., Catholic University of America Press, 1954), 165-166; Elliott, "Constantine's Preparation for the Council of Nicaea," 127; Socrates, 2:6; Sozomen. Warmington believes that the emissary was Marianus B. H. Warmington, "The Sources of Some Constantinian Documents in Eusebius' Ecclesiastical History and Life of Constantine," in Studia Patristica (Kalamazoo: Cistercian Publications, 1985), 95-97.

council to solve the matter.[176] He also used imperial funds to finance bishops' travel expenses and used the military power of the state to enforce the council resolutions. On the other hand, Constantine's involvement was greater in the Arian controversy than in the Donatist crisis. He was present at the church council, directly influenced the final result, and acted more strongly to solve the council's problems in the aftermath.[177]

Constantine's first action was to solve the problem by diplomacy. His letter to Alexander and Arius expressed his policy of unity, calling them toward conciliation and harmony.[178] Even though he said eleven times in the letter that the contention was about (politically) trivial questions, he did not minimize the theological importance of the issue.[179] As Norderval said, "Constantine evaluates the whole controversy as a question about things which lie outside human ability of comprehension, and which are not at all suitable for discussion."[180] In this letter, he underlines again his understanding that divergent opinions can coexist together if on the whole there are more common points than divergent ones, and both parties are directed toward unity and the welfare of society.[181]

---

[176] Eusebius, VC, 1:3.6; Socrates, 2:8; Sozomen, 2:253.

[177] Robert McQueen Grant, "Religion and Politics at the Council at Nicaea," Journal of Religion 55, no. 1 (1975): 6-9.

[178] There is some contention regarding the authenticity of this letter. Some scholars like P. Batiffol regard it as a forgery. Pierre Batiffol, La Paix Constantinienne et le Catholicisme, 2nd ed. (Paris: Librairie Victor Lecoffre, 1914), 314-317. Others question its content, arguing that part of it is false or that it does not reveal the real picture that Constantine had in mind when he wrote the letter. For more information see: Elliott, "Constantine's Preparation for the Council of Nicaea"; W. Telfer, "When Did the Arian Controversy Begin?" The Journal of Theological Studies 47 (1946): 129-142. For a sample of the letter, see Eusebius, VC, 1:2.71. For information on the authenticity of the documents in Eusebius's Life of Constantine, see A. H. M. Jones, "Notes in the Genuineness of the Constantinian Documents in Eusebius's Life of Constantine," Journal of Ecclesiastical History 5, no. 2 (1954): 196-200.

[179] Rahner argues that Constantine never comprehended the real theological issues involved in the Arian controversy (47). However, Constantine expresses in the letter that his purpose is to "bring the diverse judgments formed by all nations respecting the Deity to a condition, as it were, of settled uniformity." This is a demonstration of his concern with the importance of the theological issue. At the same time, he points out that those were trivial questions because they were more speculative than part of the sounding doctrines of the church, as he said, "the divine law." Constantine said "those points of discussion which are enjoined by the authority of no law, but rather suggested by the contentious spirit which is fostered by misused leisure, even though they may be intended merely as an intellectual exercise, ought certainly to be confined to the region of our own thoughts" (Eusebius, VC, 1:2.71).

[180] Norderval, 119.

[181] "You know that philosophers, though they all adhere to one system, are yet frequently at issue on certain points, and differ, perhaps, in their degree of knowledge: yet they are recalled to harmony of sentiment by the uniting power

Constantine's diplomatic efforts were not effective. He and the Catholic bishops had different views on topics like the role of the church in the state and the definition of heresy and its theological implications. As Norderval said, Constantine had a "pragmatic external evaluation of the Church as both a religious fellowship and as a political factor."[182] He also stated that for Constantine, church and state were two sides of the same coin and no good would come from theological disagreements.[183] For the majority of the bishops, their understanding of what should be the sound doctrine of the church was more important than unity and peace in the empire. For them, there was a battle between truth and lies, where no heresy could be part of the true church. Their struggle was with how to properly manage the power of the state for "the universal validity of each of their various particular truths, but subject to the rule of emperors who prized unity, stability, and consensus above all."[184] The bishops also fought for ecclesiastical supremacy. A Christian emperor was important if they could have his support for what they thought to be orthodoxy. The struggle between bishops for the political support of the emperor was the novelty of the Donatist and Arian controversies.

Constantine sought consensus by playing the theological game. Theological controversies were common within the church, but never before had non-ecclesiastical authorities defined orthodoxy.[185] Yet, as in the Donatist crisis, Constantine assumed the authority to arbitrate the Arian controversy. He convened the council of Nicaea, and even though he was not a bishop and had not even been baptized yet,[186] he presided over the council and was present at most of the sessions.[187]

Constantine's political ability was clearly seen at the council of Nicaea. He began the council by burning the accusations brought to him from both sides,[188] a political move that removed his obligation to point out which side was right.

---

of their common doctrines. If this be true, is it not far more reasonable that you, who are the ministers of the Supreme God, should be of one mind respecting the profession of the same religion? . . . Open then for me henceforward by your unity of judgment that road to the regions of the East which your dissensions have closed against me, and permit me speedily to see yourselves and all other peoples rejoicing together, and render due acknowledgment to God in the language of praise and thanksgiving for the restoration of general concord and liberty to all" (Eusebius, VC, 1:2.71).

[182] Norderval, 120.

[183] Ibid.

[184] David Nirenberg, "Truth and Consequences," New Republic 235, no. 24 (2006): 36. See also: Michael Gaddis, There Is No Crime for Those Who Have Christ: Religious Violence in the Christian Roman Empire, The Transformation of the Classical Heritage (Berkeley: University of California Press, 2005).

[185] In the first three centuries the distinction between orthodoxy and heresy was made through theological writers like Irenaeus, Hypollitus, etc.; and synods or councils headed by bishops. See Hefele, 1:77-118.

[186] Constantine was baptized by Eusebius in A.D. 337, close to his death.

[187] Eusebius, VC, 1:3.10-14.

[188] Socrates, 2:9.

According to Eusebius, he called the bishops to unity in his first speech, and afterwards acted strongly to achieve this unity by leading the bishops to a compromise.[189] Eusebius stresses that it was the emperor's leadership that brought the opposite views into conciliation:

> As soon as the emperor had spoken these words in the Latin tongue, which another interpreted, he gave permission to those who presided in the council to deliver their opinions. On this some began to accuse their neighbors, who defended themselves, and recriminated in their turn. In this manner numberless assertions were put forth by each party, and a violent controversy arose at the very commencement. Notwithstanding this, the emperor gave patient audience to all alike, and received every proposition with steadfast attention, and by occasionally assisting the argument of each party in turn, he gradually disposed even the most vehement disputants to a reconciliation. At the same time, by the affability of his address to all, and his use of the Greek language, with which he was not altogether unacquainted, he appeared in a truly attractive and amiable light, persuading some, convincing others by his reasonings, praising those who spoke well, and urging all to unity of sentiment, until at last he succeeded in bringing them to one mind and judgment respecting every disputed question.[190]

Constantine's opening address to the council, his letters to the churches and people in general respecting the council of Nicaea, and his meeting with the bishops after the council show the importance of and connection between religion and his policy of unity in the empire. In his opening address, he said that the major blessing he received from God was to have all the bishops "united in a common harmony of sentiment."[191] He continued by saying, "I feel that my desires will be most completely fulfilled when I can see you all united in one judgment, and that common spirit of peace and concord prevailing amongst you all."[192] He also pleaded with them "to discard the causes of that disunion which has existed among you, and remove the perplexities of controversy by embracing the principles of peace."[193] After the council, in his letter to the churches, he linked the prosperity of the empire with the unity of faith: "Having had full proof, in the general prosperity of the empire, how great the favor of God has been towards us, I have judged that it ought to be the first object of my endeavors, that unity of faith, sincerity of love, and community of feeling in regard to the worship of Almighty God, might be preserved among the

---

[189] Eusebius, VC, 1:3.12.

[190] Ibid.

[191] Ibid.

[192] Ibid.

[193] Ibid.

highly favored multitude who compose the Catholic Church."[194] Even on the issue of Easter, he argued that keeping it on the same day would bring unity.[195] In his final meeting with bishops before the council was dissolved, Constantine confirmed his policy of unity: "That unity of judgment at which they had arrived in the emperor's presence continued to prevail, and those who had long been divided were bound together as members of the same body."[196]

Constantine did not achieve the successes he was waiting for. After the council of Nicaea, he had to deal with much dissension among bishops because of the Arian theological controversy. Yet Constantine's policy of unity was open enough to accommodate those who were willing to accept the Nicaean formula even though they did not strictly agree with its content. Extremist actions from both the orthodox and Arian sides were reprimanded by the emperor. A classical case of that is the deposition of orthodox bishops who adopted a hard line against Arians after Nicaea, like Eustathius (A.D. 326 or 328).[197] "If the Eustathians had promptly used the doctrinal decision at Nicaea as a basis for disruptive purge, Constantine might well have made haste to demonstrate that he regarded the decisions of Nicaea as a basis for the peaceful burial of the heresy, not for a war on those who had once entertained (or even espoused) it."[198] The same happened in the case of Athanasius's first exile. He was not exiled because of his religious beliefs, but because of his political moves, which conflicted with Constantine's policy of consensus.[199] Also, Arius's return to Alexandria was followed by an imperial order for him to leave the city as soon as Constantine realized the trouble it had caused.[200]

---

[194] Ibid.

[195] Ibid.

[196] Ibid., 1:3.20.

[197] For further studies in Eustathius, see: R. W. Burgess, "The Date of the Deposition of Eustathius of Antioch," Journal of Theological Studies 51, no. 1 (2000): 150-160; Henry Chadwick, "The Fall of Eustathius at Antioch," Journal of Theological Studies 49 (1948): 27-35; Thomas G. Elliott, "Constantine and 'The Arian Reaction after Nicaea," Journal of Ecclesiastical History 43 (1992): 169-194; Richard P. C. Hanson, "The Fate of Eustathius of Antioch," Zeitschrift für Kirchengeschichte 95, no. 2 (1984): 171-179; Rudolf Lorenz, "Die Eustathius Von Antiochien Zugeschriebene Schrift Gegen Photin," Zeitschrift für die neutestamentliche Wissenschaft und die Kunde der älteren Kirche 71, no. 1-2 (1980): 109-128; Felix Scheidweiler, "Ein Glaubensbekenntnis Des Eustathius Von Antiochien," Zeitschrift für die neutestamentliche Wissenschaft und die Kunde der älteren Kirche 44, no. 3-4 (1953): 237-249; Michel Spanneut, "Position Théologique D'eustathe D'antioche," Journal of Theological Studies 5 (1954): 220-224; Joseph W. Trigg, "Eustathius of Antioch's Attack on Origen: What Is at Issue in an Ancient Controversy?" Journal of Religion 75, no. 2 (1995): 219-238.

[198] Elliott, "Constantine and 'The Arian Reaction after Nicaea," 179.

[199] Barnard, 353-354.

[200] See: H. A. Drake, "Athanasius' First Exile," Greek, Roman and Byzantine Studies 27 (1986): 193-204; Elliott, "Constantine And 'The Arian Reaction after Nicaea," 169-194.

Even though Constantine had an open policy of unity, he chose to give his patronage to Christianity, namely Catholic orthodoxy. As his political power and control over the territory of the Roman world enlarged, he gradually withdrew support from pagans, Jews, and schismatic individuals and transferred it to the Catholic orthodoxy.[201] His efforts to suppress heresy and promote unity after the council of Nicaea—sometimes through intolerant imperial legislation and popular violence—reaffirm that, for him, unity was important to maintain the favor of the Supreme God and Catholic orthodoxy was the means to achieve it. Jones states that the reason for "Constantine's persistent efforts to heal schism in the church" was that "schism would provoke God's anger against the empire and particularly against himself, to whose care the empire had been committed."[202] The success of Christianity was crucial to affirm his political change in imperial religious policies. Religion for Constantine was an affair of the state, even though the notion of Christianity as the religion of the state had not developed yet.[203]

On the side of the church, the council of Nicaea stirred up a political struggle to gain the favor of the emperor and ecclesiastical supremacy. Unlike the Donatists, those who disagreed with the Nicaean formula did not rebel against the state or compare the state's intervention with a manifestation of the Antichrist. Religious leaders on both sides made it clear to the emperor that their theological understanding was in accord with the Nicaean creed and that the theological understanding and private or public lives of their adversaries were a threat to the stability of the empire.[204]

Constantine, the Bishops, and the Church

According to most historians, the relationship between the emperor and leadership of the church, which in the fourth century was in the hands of the bishops, is important for understanding Constantine's policy of church and state relationships. They disagree on Constantine's true religious allegiance to either Christianity or paganism, but they see a strong connection between Constantine's choice to support Catholic Christianity and his choice to introduce bishops into aristocratic life.

---

[201] It is important to mention that Constantine's laws in suppression of paganism were connected with the category of superstitio. The traditional Roman cults continued their rituals during his reign and even afterwards. Catholic Christianity after Constantine proclaimed itself as the religio and everything else as superstitio, but there is not clear evidence that Constantine saw only Christianity as a religio. For further information, see Baynes, Constantine the Great and the Christian Church; Beard, North, and Price, 369-375.

[202] A. H. M. Jones, "Church and State from Constantine to Theodosius," Journal of Theological Studies 5, no. 2 (1954): 270.

[203] Saxer, 13.

[204] See Barnard.

Constantine introduced the bishops to the political life of the empire, which produced a gradual integration between church and state. His choice did not eliminate the traditional pagan aristocracy, but affected it in such a way that from Constantine on, the aristocracy became more and more Christian.

The results of Constantine's choices and actions in favor of Christianity and bishops have led historians to debate the true nature of Constantine's policy of church and state relationships.

CONSTANTINE'S CHOICE

Even though Burckhardt rejects the idea of Constantine's conversion to Christianity, he acknowledges that bishops received special favors from Constantine. For him, Constantine's choice was a natural one, since "Constantine found the clergy already so suitably organized for power and so elevated by the persecution" that he had basically two options: "either rule through this corporation and its high credit or acquire its irreconcilable enmity."[205] Burckhardt, however, affirms that Constantine's use of clergy as an administrative power was more beneficial to the church; he says it "was of immeasurable importance for the whole development of the church."[206]

Jones argues that just as previous emperors had consulted *haruspices*, Sibylline oracles, and such for expert advice, now Constantine consulted only bishops.[207] He states as an example that "when the Donatists appealed to him, he appointed the bishops of Rome, Cologne, Autun and Arles to investigate the facts and report to him. . . . In dealing with the Arian controversy, in the hope of securing an absolutely unquestionable verdict, he took the unprecedented step of summoning a universal council of the whole church at which he himself presided."[208]

Barnes argues that Christianity was a powerful community at the time of Constantine and that bishops had political influence not only over Christians, but also over the non-Christian communities in their bishoprics. He says, "Throughout the East, the Christian bishop had become a respected figure of the urban establishment

---

[205] Burckhardt, 306.

[206] Ibid.

[207] A weak point in Jones's argument is that Constantine's consultations of bishops, as quoted by him, were related only to church problems. Even after his conversion to Christianity, he took special guidance from divination, as in the battle against Licinius (through dreams); he had both pagans and Christians as personal advisors, and sometimes he consulted diviners, according to Zosimus. For more information, see: ibid., 292-335; Zosimus, New History, 2.29.

[208] A. H. M. Jones, The Later Roman Empire, 284-602: A Social Economic and Administrative Survey, 2 vols. (Baltimore, MD: Johns Hopkins University Press, 1986), 1:94.

whom provincial governors treated with respect or deference, and bishops acted as judges in legal disputes within the local Christian community."[209]

In his book *Constantine and the Bishops: The Politics of Intolerance*, Drake writes extensively on Constantine's relationship with bishops. He sees Constantine's choice of bishops as a political move, a way to achieve a religious force of coherency and a new constituency. He points out that the office of a Roman emperor had two important aspects: *auctoritas* and *potesta,* meaning "prestige" and "coercive force."[210] He continues by arguing that the emperor's authority derived not only from the army—coercive force—but also from the legitimacy granted by his constituency—prestige. In the case of Octavian, his gesture of laying down his power before the Senate and the Senate convincing him to stay and endowing him with the title of Augustus granted him legitimacy as a ruler. Drake says that this "gesture had the effect of transferring Octavian's title, so to speak, from the armies to the Senate, for in giving him the name *Augustus,* the Senate also gave Octavian an alternative sanction for his rule, one that was stronger and more stable than the armies could provide."[211]

Drake continues by saying that later developments in the Roman Empire led emperors to find another source of legitimacy, because the Senate no longer represented the people.[212] The Senate was still the traditional center of Roman values, but because the magistrates were no longer elected by the people after Tiberius, they lost their constituency and influence in political decisions.[213] He also states that "no matter what the period of Roman history, access to the corridors of power, along with the patronage that access brought, was the driving force. . . . Emperors and aristocrats were driven into each other's arms by their need for legitimacy and administrators on the one hand, patronage and access on the other."[214] He argues that just as Augustus chose to rely on the senators for support, Constantine relied on the bishops. His patronage of the Catholic church, in the persons of the bishops, provided him not only with a new monotheistic and heavenly force of coherency to the empire, but also with a new constituency. [215]

Drake also discusses the great influence bishops exerted over believers and argues that by the time of Constantine, bishops were a strong political force in their milieu.

---

[209] Barnes, Constantine and Eusebius, 191.

[210] Drake, Constantine and the Bishops, 40.

[211] Ibid., 39.

[212] Ibid., 54-56.

[213] Cornelius Tacitus, The Annals, trans. Clifford Herschel Moore and John Jackson (London: W. Heinemann, 1931), 1.15.

[214] Drake, Constantine and the Bishops, 59.

[215] Ibid., 42-44.

After the Apostolic age, more and more, bishops became the centers of their Christian communities. They were not restricted to cultic activities, as the pagan priests were; they oversaw the financial, spiritual, juridical, and social needs of the community.[216] Bishops were the strong point in the maintenance of unity in the Christian church because they were the ones who determined the orthodoxy. Drake states:

> Their effect on Christian faith can be debated, but bishops were absolutely crucial to the strength of Christianity as a movement. They grew in importance precisely because of the ease with which the Christian message could be distorted. By defining the Christian canon and the criteria for sainthood, appropriating to themselves the prestige of the martyrs and the skills of the apologists, they made the church a fact as well as a theory, representing their local traditions to the universal body and the hinge that united the one to the other. Though rarely as charismatic as martyrs or as eloquent as apologists, bishops were more significant than either, because they constituted the effective power of the church. The bishops were the players.[217]

Commenting on Drake's book *Constantine and the Bishops: The Politics of Intolerance*, Paula Fredriksen argues that Constantine's conversion to Christianity and his choice to patronize bishops was part of his effort to deal with political challenges. She describes the bishops as a very organized urban power network with "long experience in organizing opinion and administering resources. Thus they represented a new and enormous pool of administrative talent. Constantine, disgusted and frustrated by the clogged and corrupt mechanisms of imperial governance, turned gladly to this new cadre of talented men."[218]

Fredriksen continues:

> The bishops were too powerful to be mere pawns in an imperial game. They had a program of their own. Constantine's initiatives [interesting choice of words] served only to enhance their power. Constantine wanted to use the bishops as one foundation of his empire-wide coalition of moderates, but the bishops wanted to use him. They wanted him, first of all, to settle issues of internal cohesion. That is, they wanted the emperor to enforce party discipline. Thus the very first victims of the new Christian government were other Christians—in the view of the bishops, "false" Christians, or heretics.[219]

---

[216] Ibid., 103-108.

[217] Ibid., 109.

[218] Paula Fredriksen, "Lambs into Lions," The New Republic (2001), 37.

[219] Ibid., 109.

CONSTANTINE AND THE BISHOPS

Constantine's choice of bishops brought a new status to the office of bishop. According to Barnes, Constantine increased the bishops' power through judicial authority, autonomy, immunity, and patronage. The imperial munificence was distributed through metropolitan bishops to local bishops, and through them to widows, orphans, the poor, and anybody else the bishops considered to be in need, even the clergy's families and servants. He argues that most of the administration of the imperial welfare system turned over to the Christian clergy, a new type of patronage where the bishop became the center of a network of local distribution of resources which consequently bestowed upon them political and social power.[220] Burckhardt argues that Constantine's patronage of the bishops led to the enrichment of the bishopric, bestowed a distinctive power and prestige on the bishops, raised the clergy "above society," and made the position of bishop more a political than a spiritual one.[221]

The reaction of the bishops to Constantine's religious policy is another point analyzed by historians. They began to incorporate heavenly aspects of the kingdom of God into earthly imperial affairs. Lactantius's and Eusebius's works connect Constantine's successes to his close ties with the God of the Christians. Lactantius referred to Constantine as the "most holy emperor," the one raised by God "for the restoration of the house of justice, and for the protection of the human race; for while you rule the Roman state, we worshippers of God are no more regarded as accursed and impious."[222] For Lactantius, Constantine's ascendance to the throne was God's providence "to rescind the injurious decrees of others, to correct faults, to provide with a father's clemency for the safety of men—in short, to remove the wicked from the state, whom being cast down by pre-eminent piety, God has delivered into your hands, that it might be evident to all in what true majesty consists."[223] He linked human rulership with God's providence. Constantine was not only supposed to vindicate God's people on earth—Christians—to restore the true worship, but also, as a ruler of the Roman state, to promote justice and to be a model emperor for future generations.

Eusebius also saw God's hand at work in Constantine's government. According to Rudolph Storch, Eusebius used four major points to support the idea of divine providence in Constantine's life: "(1) all success and benefit derive from the favor of the divinity; (2) only the pious receive divine favor; (3) the most important indi-

---

[220] Timothy David Barnes, Athanasius and Constantius: Theology and Politics in the Constantinian Empire (Cambridge, MA: Harvard University Press, 1993), 177-179.

[221] Burckhardt, 309.

[222] Lactantius, Divine Institutes [book on-line] (New Advent, 2007); http://www.newadvent.org/fathers/07017.htm (accessed 24 February 2008).

[223] Ibid.

cation of divine favor for a pious ruler is military victory; and (4) with the victory secured, divine favor will produce peace and unity for the realm."[224]

Another point to be mentioned is that most of the bishops shared the views of Lactantius and Eusebius on church and state relationships, because at that time the majority of Christians were deeply indebted to Constantine for their freedom.

CONSTANTINE AND THE ARISTOCRACY

Constantine's favoring of Christianity over paganism and his close relationship with the bishops did not mean that he despised the pagan aristocracy. His reasons for patronizing Catholic Christianity and giving special favors to bishops could have been grounded in religion or politics, as argued by historians, but he operated within the traditional emperor-aristocracy Roman system of government. Michele R. Salzman says that emperors "need to gain the legitimating support of the aristocracy, a class in possession of significant resources and prestige as well as expertise of the sort needed to maintain the imperial bureaucracy. Indeed, it was precisely because the aristocracy was key to imperial rule and legitimacy that emperors from Diocletian on worked to incorporate them into the service of the state."[225] Constantine's choice of bishops brought new status to the clergy and introduced Catholic Christianity to the political life of the empire. "Thus through law the emperors gave prestige and honors to the church and its clergy, which in themselves made Christianity appealing to aristocrats imbued with the values of their status culture."[226] As a result, from Constantine on, the aristocracy gradually became more Christian.

CONSTANTINE AND THE CHURCH

There is no consensus among scholars, historians, and theologians on the issue of church and state relationships and religious policy at the time of Constantine. Before Gibbon, Christians and pagans, secular rulers and clergy had different perspectives on Constantine's policy of church and state relationships, according to their allegiance. However, Gibbon and scholars after him, even though they sought to give unbiased historical accounts by using Catholic and non-Catholic sources, miscel-

---

[224] Rudolph H. Storch, "Eusebian Constantine," Church History 40, no. 2 (1971): 145-146. Eusebius's understanding of Constantine's religious policy will be discussed further in the next section, "Constantine and the Church."

[225] Michele Renee Salzman, The Making of a Christian Aristocracy: Social and Religious Change in the Western Roman Empire (Cambridge, MA: Harvard University Press, 2002), 179.

[226] Ibid., 195.

laneous documents, and archaeological materials, still had contradictory views on many issues. The reasons for Constantine's support of Christianity, his suppression or non-suppression of paganism, the level of independence of the church from the state, and the state's influence over the church are some of these controversial issues. In this section I will probe Constantine's policy of church and state relationships after exploring some ancient and contemporary views on the topic.

The political analysis of Constantine started with Eusebius. Scholars such as Erik Peterson, K. M. Setton, F. Edward Cranz, Storch, H. Berkhof, Francis Dvornik, Michael Azkoul, Drake, and others refer to Eusebius more as a politician than a theologian.[227] Barnes, Robert M. Grant, B. H. Warmington, Gerhard Ruhbach, Michael J. Hollerich, and others portray him more as a theologian than a politician.[228] Even though the two groups do not agree on Eusebius's final intent, they recognize that in his works Eusebius linked monarchy and monotheism, and as Dvornik says, he "laid the foundations for the political structure and for Eastern [Constantinople] policies on the relationship between church and state."[229]

Eusebius presented two sides on the relationship of church and state. First, he commented on the role of the state in religious matters. In his *Ecclesiastical History*, *Laus Constantine*, and *Vita Constantine*, he wrote that Constantine's empire was divinely favored by God and the fulfillment of God's purpose for the church in history. He described Constantine as the model of a good emperor, replacing the one provided by the Senate, and setting the basis for future Christian emperors.[230] He validated Constantine's religious actions through extensive description of his genuine conversion to Christianity and his close relationship with the Logos, and described

---

[227] Azkoul, 431-464; H. Berkhof, Die Theologie des Eusebius von Caesarea (Amsterdam: Uitgevers-maatschappij Holland, 1939); Hendrik Berkhof, Kirche und Kaiser. Eine Untersuchung der Entstehung der Byzantinischen und der Theokratischen Staatsauffassung im Vierten Jahrhundert: Aus dem Holländischen Übers. von Gottfried W. Locher (Zollikon-Zürich: 1947); Cranz; Drake, Constantine and the Bishops; Dvornik, Early Christian and Byzantine Political Philosophy; Peterson and Ruggieri; Kenneth Meyer Setton, Christian Attitude Towards the Emperor in the Fourth Century, Especially as Shown in Addresses to the Emperor (New York, London: Columbia University Press; P.S. King & Son, 1941); Storch.

[228] Barnes, Constantine and Eusebius; Robert McQueen Grant, "Religion and Politics at the Council at Nicaea," Journal of Religion 55, no. 1 (1975); Michael J. Hollerich, "Religion and Politics in the Writings of Eusebius: Reassessing the First 'Court Theologian,'" Church History 56, no. 3 (1990): 309-325; Gerhard Ruhbach, "Euseb Von Caesarea," in Alte Kirche (Stuttgart: Verlag W Kohlhammer, 1984); B. H. Warmington, "The Sources of Some Constantinian Documents in Eusebius' Ecclesiastical History and Life of Constantine," in Studia Patristica (Kalamazoo: Cistercian Publications, 1985).

[229] Dvornik, 2:617. On the influence of Eusebius's works on Byzantine political philosophy, see also: Azkoul; Storch.

[230] Drake, Constantine and the Bishops, 384-392.

his military success followed by a period of prosperity and peace as a confirmation of Constantine's rulership by divine favor.[231] He also validated Constantine's monarchy by comparing it with God's monarchy. For him, a divine monarchy was superior to all other forms of government if it was based on the monotheistic principle.[232] Drake says that for Eusebius, "monotheism equals monarchy, morality, and Christianity, whereas polytheism equals polyarchy, depravity, and paganism."[233]

Second, Eusebius set the proper place occupied by the church in worldly affairs. He upheld the role of the church in God's unveiling of history.[234] For him the church was the "godly polity," "the city of God," and "the primary fulfillment of Isaiah's prophecy," and the key element of church authority was the bishop.[235] Hollerich, analyzing Eusebius's *Commentary on Isaiah,* says, "The godly polity is firmly episcopal in its authority structure: according to Eusebius, numerous passages in Isaiah anticipated the Christian bishop's monopoly of authority."[236] Constantine, whom Eusebius considered to be a pious Christian and model of a good emperor, received his imperial authority and victories over his enemies from God.[237] Constantine's support of Catholic Christianity, his suppression of paganism and heresies, and his promotion of the Catholic Christian faith were a normal result of his submission to the will of God and God's response to Christian persecution.[238] In his sphere, Constantine was supposed to fulfill God's plan for him, the promotion of the godly polity, God's church. In his promotion of the godly polity, the church, Eusebius magnified the importance of the bishops. As leaders of the Catholic church, he stated that bishops should replace the Senate as the imperial college. Drake argues,

> Eusebius has, in fact, set up the bishops not only to take the place of the Senate in judging the good king but to act with an independence that the imperial Senate never had ... Eusebius wanted a means to judge and, if necessary, condemn imperial conduct. He found this means in the bishops.[239]

---

[231] See Eusebius, HE, 1:9.9-11; idem, VC, 1:1.3-4.75; idem, LC, 1:1-18.

[232] See Eusebius, VC, 1:2.20, 4.29; idem, OC, 1:3; Eusebius and W. J. Ferrar, The Proof of the Gospel Being the Demonstratio Evangelica of Eusebius of Caesarea (London: Society for Promoting Christian Knowledge, 1920), 141, 349-351, 393.

[233] Drake, Constantine and the Bishops, 380.

[234] See Hollerich, "Religion and Politics in the Writings of Eusebius," 312.

[235] Ibid., 313.

[236] Ibid., 313-314. For the prestige of the bishops in Eusebius, see Craig Warryn Clifford Ginn, Prestige of the Bishop in Eusebius' "Ecclesiastical History" (University of Lethbridge, 1999).

[237] Throughout his Vita Constantine and Laus Constantine, Eusebius referred many times to Constantine's piety and great moral behavior.

[238] Barnes, Constantine and Eusebius, 254.

[239] Drake, Constantine and the Bishops, 391.

From this perspective, Eusebius and probably most of the bishops of his time did not have any objections to Constantine's actions upholding Christianity and suppressing paganism and heresies.

Most of the material produced on Constantine's religious policy before the Renaissance did not introduce significant new notions beyond those presented by Eusebius, except the work of such pagan authors as Zosimus.[240] Modern scholars, however, have broadened the discussion by questioning Constantine's allegiance to Christianity and interpreting his religious policy more as a political movement.

Burckhardt presents Constantine essentially as an unreligious man, an astute politician who knew how to use the power of Christian faith to promote his political plan for unity of the empire. According to Burkhardt, Constantine used the church to achieve his political ambitions, and the church, which received the most benefit from this relationship, became involved not only in spiritual, but also in political matters.[241]

Contradicting Eusebius's description of Constantine, but not denying his acceptance of Christianity as Burckhardt does, Leslie Barnard affirms that there is no such thing as "Constantinian Church-State" in the time of Constantine. According to Barnard, even though Constantine became a Christian, his religious thinking was ambiguous and confusing. He argues that Constantine never assumed the role of the divine logos as portrayed by Eusebius. For Barnard, the church under Constantine was "a religious institution on equal footing with pagan cults."[242] He continues by saying, "The emperor's own attitude, although he claimed to be a Christian, is ambiguous. He found it very difficult, almost impossible, to break from the classical past."[243] He sums up his point by saying, "Church-state relations between 313 and 337 present a checkered picture. The bishops of the church were unprepared for the risks involved in Christianity's becoming a *religio licita*. Moreover, Constantine himself had no fixed plan for dealing with the church, beyond a vague aspiration for unity, and his actions, at times, verge on total bewilderment."[244]

For Norderval, Constantine's religious policy was a policy of continuity. He points out that Constantine did not differ much from the previous Roman emperors. Like those of Aurelius and Diocletian, his imperial policies leaned toward religious and political unity. Norderval argues that the major difference is that "this was connected to a monotheistic program, and he thereby put an end to a development which had been in progress within the polytheistic cult of state. Polytheism,

---

[240] Zosimus, New History.

[241] Burckhardt, 292-335.

[242] Barnard, 337.

[243] Ibid., 340.

[244] Ibid., 355.

for Constantine, was the cause of political division."[245] He continues by saying that Constantine's policy was only one transition "from the *principate* in which 'the great leader' had his power from the people to the *dominate* where the power of the Emperor was given by Heaven."[246] This transition, however, represents a continuity of the old Roman political policy of power drawn from the constituency.

Barnes believes Constantine's conversion to Christianity was genuine. He argues that Constantine's actions were coherent with his religious policy—to convert the Roman Empire to Christianity.[247] He points out that Constantine's promotion of Christian orthodoxy was more intense at the end of his rulership because his political power had increased and there was less resistance from paganism in the eastern part of the empire. For Barnes, Constantine was a man like any other, but a good politician who knew the best time to act to achieve his goals.[248]

Drake does not confirm or deny Constantine's conversion to Christianity. He argues that Constantine's religious policy was a policy of unity: The unity of the empire was more important than theological discussions, but the unity of the church was important to promote the unity of the empire and retain the favor of God. He summarizes Constantine's policy by saying, "He thought of Christianity as an 'umbrella' organization, able to hold a number of different wings or factions together under a 'big tent' of overarching mutual interest."[249] Constantine thought the Christian church and his leadership were more suitable than paganism to achieve his plan of unity in the empire. However, as a good politician, he did not despise paganism or the adherents of paganism; he only forbade some of its practices. Drake argues that Constantine's intent in banning some pagan practices was "to create a neutral public space in which Christians and pagans could both function, and that he was far more successful in creating a stable coalition of both Christians and non-Christians in support of this program of 'peaceful co-existence' than has generally been recognized."[250]

Baynes argues that relation between church and state at the time of Constantine was not a concordat but a unilateral act. Constantine, as emperor, adopted the Christian faith and supported it. He issued laws empowering bishops, but they never set terms of allegiance with the emperor: "The emperor defined the terms of that and the church accepted them."[251] Armstrong, in line with Baynes, argues

---

[245] Norderval, 116.

[246] Ibid.

[247] Barnes, Constantine and Eusebius, 247.

[248] Ibid., 224-275.

[249] Drake, "Constantine and Consensus," 3.

[250] Ibid., 4.

[251] Norman Hepburn Baynes, "Idolatry and the Early Church," in Byzantine Studies and Other Essays (London: University of London Athlone Press, 1955), 126.

that "Constantine was an absolutist emperor who had no intention of letting the Church operate independently of the State."[252]

The analysis of primary and secondary sources indicates that Constantine had an established religious policy that developed throughout his time as emperor. His religious policy was a policy of unity in which the welfare of the state was more important than that of the church. As Drake pointed out, for Constantine, unity was more important than theology. Thus, sectarian theology and theologians did not have the support of the emperor and had to be suppressed.[253] Theological matters and the proper way of worship were important for the sake of maintaining the favor of the divine power for the emperor and empire. Thus, one of Constantine's duties as emperor was to legislate on religious matters that would affect the well-being of the empire. In this sense, Constantine's religious policy resembles the old Roman religious system. As Norderval said, it was a policy of continuity[254] with one new element, the support of Christianity as *religio licita*.

Constantine's attitude toward paganism and Christianity has provoked an ongoing discussion. Eusebius, Lactantius, Barnes, and others believe that Constantine was a genuine Christian and his policy was to convert the Roman world to Christianity. Burckhardt, Barnard, and others argue that Christianity and paganism were on equal footing during his reign.

Constantine affirmed religious freedom for all in the edict of Milan, but throughout his rulership, he promoted Catholic Christianity and suppressed paganism and non-Catholic churchmen. As Glen L. Thompson said "Already in 315, a law forbade Christian conversion to Judaism (CT 16.8.1). In 321, the army was commanded to pray each Sunday to 'the only God . . . as king . . . [and] as ally' (Eus. VC 4.19). Soon after, Constantine prohibited private assembly of various Christian splinter groups— the Novatians, Valentinians, Gnostics, Marcionites, Samosatans, and Montanists (Eus. VC 3.64 5)."[255] Constantine's attack on paganism was gradual and more intense after he had been established as the sole ruler of the empire. His first action was to prohibit private divination.[256] He also, according to Eusebius, prohibited sacrifices, closed pagan temples, confiscated their properties, and used imperial influence to promote the conversion of pagans to Christianity through the power of the army.[257]

---

[252] Armstrong, "Church and State Relations: The Changes Wrought by Constantine," 6. See also S. L. Greenslade, Church and State from Constantine to Theodosius (London: SCM Press, 1954), 12-13.

[253] Drake, "Constantine and Consensus," 1.

[254] Norderval, 116.

[255] Glen L. Thompson, Trouble in the Kingdom: Church and State in the Fourth Century [Essay], http://www. wlsessays.net/authors/T/ThompsonKingdom/ ThompsonKingdom.rtf (accessed 29 May 1999). See also CT, 16.5.1.

[256] CT, 16.10.1.

[257] See Eusebius, VC, 1:3.54-55, 3.64-65; Barnes, Constantine and Eusebius, 51-61, 245-253.

Constantine's suppression of paganism did not extend to eradication. Even though he forbade some pagan rituals and closed pagan temples, confiscating their properties, at the same time, he continued his financial support of pagan priests, and even supported the rebuilding of pagan temples.[258] On the other hand, he incorporated Christian principles in his imperial edicts and donated extensively to the construction of church buildings.[259]

Throughout his time as emperor, Constantine demonstrated his religious and political preference for Catholic Christianity, but did not overlook the political importance of the pagan aristocracy and individual pagan leaders who could help him achieve his goal of political supremacy and unity.[260] When unity was jeopardized, Constantine acted promptly to eliminate the threat, no matter whether it involved Christianity or paganism.

Constantine's legislation favoring Catholic Christianity, like the edict of Milan (313), the concession of tax exemption (313), the juridical empowerment of bishops as a civil court of appellation (316), and the Sunday law of 321,[261] set Catholic Christianity on a higher level than paganism. As Victor Saxer said, the church was not yet a state church, but it was granted greater privileges than other contemporary religious institutions.[262]

Under Constantine's religious policy, the leadership of the church could independently legislate on ecclesiastical matters, if those issues did not threaten the unity of the empire. When Constantine had to deal with church problems that affected the unity of the state, first, he began by urging church leaders to find a solution for their own problems.[263] Second, he summoned a council that might or might not include state representatives. Third, he used state power to impose that council's canons, even if it meant the opposing church leaders would be exiled. In a sense, Armstrong is right in affirming that Constantine, as an absolutist, would not allow the church to operate

---

[258] See Burckhardt, 302-302.

[259] See Davis, 16-27.

[260] See Drake, "Constantine and Consensus," 3-6.

[261] Constantine's Sunday law of 321 does not describe Sunday as the Lord's Day. The decree mentions only the venerable day of the sun. Robert Leo Odom states that worship to Mithra was held on Sunday in the Roman empire, and Allan S. Hoey mentions that the only deity prescribed for the army was the Sol Invictus. However, after this law for the first time Sunday should be kept as a day of rest in all cities and towns. See: Robert Leo Odom, Sunday in Roman Paganism: A History of the Planetary Week and Its 'Day of the Sun' in the Heathenism of the Roman World During the Early Centuries of the Christian Era (Brushton, NY: TEACH Services, 2003), 156. Allan S. Hoey, "Official Policy Towards Oriental Cults in the Roman Army," Transactions and Proceedings of the American Philological Association 70, no. (1939): 456.

[262] Saxer, 13.

[263] This can be seen in the case of both Donatism and Arianism. For more information, see the above sections: "The Donatist Crises," and "The Council of Nicaea."

independently of the state.[264] However, the available sources indicate that Constantine intervened in church affairs on major issues that could affect the state, but did not bother with trivial issues or very small localized problems.[265] At the same time, Baynes is right in affirming that the relationship between church and state at the time of Constantine was not a concordat, but a unilateral act of the emperor in choosing Catholic Christianity.[266] However, as demonstrated by Eusebian theology and the Donatist and Arian controversies, the bishops were not passive in accepting all imperial propositions; the game was to gain the favor of the emperor, play ecclesiastical politics, and, for many, to continue fighting even in the face of persecution and exile.

SUMMARY

Constantine's first action toward Christianity was the issuing of the Edict of Milan (A.D. 313). In a diplomatic wording, the Edict of Milan granted freedom of worship to any religious group (including sects that were not previously recognized as legal religions) and did not establish primacy among them. However, in the Edict of Milan, Constantine did manifest a preference for Christianity over paganism. The decree also opened the door for any person to be an active citizen. Thus, Constantine was able to acquire a new constituency, and the church was incorporated into the political life of the empire.

After Constantine issued the Edict of Milan, he became involved in a long and difficult controversy between two rival factions in North Africa: the Donatists and the orthodox Catholics. In this controversy, Constantine's way of handling church issues took shape. First, he asked church leaders to solve the problem themselves. Second, he asked for an imperial commission's investigation. Third, he summoned a council to solve the issue. Finally, he used imperial power to impose the council's decisions.

Through the Donatist crisis, Constantine clearly supported only Catholic Christianity, and his policy was to promote unity over theological differences. On the side of the church, it demonstrated a tendency for the leadership of the church to reevaluate its role in society and accommodate the social order around it.

The second major religious crisis faced by Constantine was the Arian controversy, which culminated with the Council of Nicaea. Constantine handled this in a way similar to the Donatist controversy, except that he was more directly involved in solving the problem. Constantine was part of the council and

---

[264] Armstrong, "Church and State Relations: The Changes Wrought by Constantine," 6.

[265] Drake, "Constantine and Consensus," 1-3.

[266] Baynes, "Idolatry and the Early Church," 126.

influenced its final result. For the first time in Christian history, civil authority helped to define Christian orthodoxy. Constantine sought to affirm unity through Christianity, which would be crucial for his political change in religious policy. For him, religion was an integral part of the state.

Constantine favored Catholic Christianity over paganism and other non-Catholic Christians; introduced the Catholic Church to the political life of the empire; empowered bishops financially, judicially, and politically; chose to rely on bishops as Augustus did on the Senate; and incorporated Christian principles into state legislation. Constantine did not ally with Christianity through a concordat, but did it through a unilateral act; however, he did not make Catholic Christianity the state church.

CONCLUSION

From the beginning, the Christian church did not deny the authority of the state in temporal matters. The NT and the primitive church recognized the state as an institution established by God to promote justice in the civil and political sphere. However, in the spiritual sphere the allegiance of Christians was directed only to God.

On the other hand, Roman society believed that religion was an integral part of the state. The success of the state was related to the favor of the gods and proper worship. Roman religion was more communitarian; the welfare of the state was more important than that of the individual. Religious behaviors were a public concern because religion was related to the morals and virtues of each citizen. In Roman society, religion was connected with citizenship.

The primitive church's understanding of religious policy differed from the Roman religious policy on the issue of citizenship. Christian citizenship was related to obedience to the state's authority in any civil obligation except regarding religion. Christians' allegiance was directed to God. They were living in the world, but were citizens of the heavenly kingdom.

After Constantine issued the Edict of Milan (A.D. 313), the state embraced Christianity. Constantine gave preferential treatment and full freedom of worship to Catholic Christians. In this context of change, the majority of Christians were deeply indebted to Constantine for their freedom, and did not question state intervention in ecclesiastical issues. The leadership and the laymen of the church chose to live in this Christianized society despite their previous persecution. Many bishops, lured by the new status and financial benefits granted to the church by the emperor, returned Constantine's favor by recognizing him as a pious man sent by God to promote Catholic Christianity.

For Constantine, Christianity was more effective than paganism for the unity of the empire. He chose to rely on the bishops to promote political changes. The Catholic Christian church was an empire within the empire, headed by the bishops.

Even though the Catholic church was not a united bloc in theological matters, its monotheistic and exclusivist attitude against other religions, even before persecution, gave outsiders the impression that it was a united bloc.

Whether he was a true convert to Christianity or not, Constantine chose Catholic Christianity and suppressed other forms of religion and even dissident Christians. However, his religious policy was similar to that of previous pagan emperors. Religion was an integral part of the state, and the welfare and unity of the empire were more important than individual beliefs. Constantine always sought consensus, but if it was not achieved, those who threatened unity were sent into exile or suffered other punishments. His religious policy was to allow the church to solve its problems as much as possible, to supervise the solving of ecclesiastical problems through political games, then directly intervene in church affairs by summoning council to reach ecclesiastical and theological unity, and finally, to use political power to impose the council's decisions.

The effects of Constantine's acceptance of Christianity on the state included the broadening of the emperor's constituency, the introduction of Christianity into the aristocracy, the incorporation of Christian values into Roman legislation, the gradual substitution of the Catholic church for the Senate as a source of political legitimacy, and the establishment of the concept of divine kingship based on Christian principles.

The effects of Constantine's acceptance of Christianity on the Catholic church included the introduction of the Catholics into the political life of the empire; the favoring of Catholicism over paganism; the gradual conversion of the aristocracy to Catholic Christianity; the browadening of the influence of bishops beyond ecclesiastical boundaries, bestowing upon them political and judicial power; the empowering of bishops through a politics of munificence centered in the bishopric; the enrichment of the church; the introduction of pagan customs into the church; the adoption of a politics of compromise to accommodate the new status of the church; and the expansion of Christianity through imperial support.

At the time of Constantine, the Catholic church was not the state church, but it was greatly favored by the emperor; it replaced paganism as the basis for the prosperity of the empire, even though it did not eliminate it. Constantine's conversion to Christianity laid the foundation for the future dominance of Catholic Christianity in late antiquity and the Middle Ages.

CHAPTER III

ANALYSIS OF ANCIENT AND CONTEMPORARY
VIEWS ON CHURCH-STATE RELATIONSHIPS FROM
CONSTANTINE'S SONS TO JUSTINIAN

INTRODUCTION

After Constantine's death, the Catholic Church and the state became closer and closer.[1] Christianity's influence over the social, cultural, and religious life of the empire expanded, and it was made the official religion of the Roman Empire by Theodosius in A.D. 380. All the emperors were Christians, except Julian (361-363), and most of the aristocracy had become Christian. This scenario (where Constantine favors Catholic Christianity) did not mean that the Catholic Church was free from problems. A large number of aristocrats, mainly in Rome, were still pagans, and Christian emperors were always interfering in church affairs. Bishops fought for preferment, and brotherhood was often replaced by violence and mutual condemnation for the sake of supremacy. In addition, theological differences hindered the unity of the church and the establishment of Catholic orthodoxy, and affected the relationships between church and state. Not only did the emperors position themselves for or against Catholic orthodoxy, they also contended with bishops for supremacy in religious matters.

The barbarian invasions imposed a new system of political administration on the western part of the Roman Empire.[2] The eastern and western parts of the Roman

---

[1] It is important to note that the Arian controversy continued to exist, and some of the emperors were more in favor of Arian bishops than Catholic orthodox bishops. It was only after Valens's death that emperors from both East and West recognized the Nicaean creed as the proper Catholic faith and ruled out Arianism. For more information on the history of this period, see David Woods, "Three Notes on Aspects of the Arian Controversy c. 354-367 CE," Journal of Theological Studies 44 (1993): 604-619.

[2] Much of today's scholarship replaces the Latin term "barbarian invasions" with "migration period." They see the occupation of the western part of the Roman Empire by Germanic people not as a hostile invasion, but as normal migration or accommodation of tribes occupying territories that were already sparsely populated. This trend was propagated mainly after Peter Brown's reevaluation of Late Antiquity. As R. W. Burges says, historians "realized

Empire developed different policies concerning church and state relationships. Since the eastern part of the empire did not suffer the same barbarian attacks as the western part, emperors in the East exerted more control over church affairs. In the West, bishops increased their political power by helping to defend their cities from barbarian attacks and the disintegration of the frontier defenses. The threat of barbarian Arianism affected the political and religious life of the western part of the Roman Empire.

The period from the end of the fourth century through the beginning of the sixth century, as Chris Wickham describes it, is by far the most obscure of the late Roman centuries[3] Since most of the actions of post-Constantine emperors did not bring about new policies on church and state relationships, this chapter will analyze only the main events in which emperors adopted religious policies similar to those of Constantine and point out new or significant differences in attitude that led to a closer union between church and state. The first part will analyze the emperors' religious policies from Constantine's sons to Justinian. The second part will analyze bishops' responses for or against imperial intervention in church affairs, and the ascendancy of the bishop of Rome as the supreme head of the church. The third part will focus on the relationship between Romans and barbarians, analyzing their policies on church and state relationships and the effect of the barbarian invasion on the political and religious life of the western part

---

that Late Antiquity was chiefly discussed in negative terms, usually in relation to the glorious classical past, and so they gradually stopped using such terms as decline, fall, degeneration, ignorance, barbarism, and irrationalism. The new watchword became 'transformation' rather than decline and fall." He indicates that there has been a change of focus in the study of Late Antiquity where "culture, religion, ethnicity, and economics have become the paramount indicators of change, replacing political, military, and geographical definitions." R. W. Burgess, "The Fall of Rome and the End of Civilization," review of The Fall of Rome and the End of Civilization, by Bryan Ward-Perkins, Canadian Journal of History/Annales Canadiennes d'Histoire 42 (2007): 83-84. For more information, see Peter Robert Lamont Brown, The World of Late Antiquity, A.D. 150-750 (New York: Harcourt Brace Jovanovich, 1971); Wendy Davies and others, People and Space in the Middle Ages, 300-1300, Studies in the Early Middle Ages, vol. 15 (Turnhout: Brepols, 2006); Walter A. Goffart, Barbarians and Romans, A.D. 418-584: The Techniques of Accommodation (Princeton, NJ: Princeton University Press, 1980); Guy Halsall, Settlement and Social Organization: The Merovingian Region of Metz (Cambridge; New York: Cambridge University Press, 1995); Guy Halsall, Warfare and Society in the Barbarian West, 450-900, Warfare and History (London; New York: Routledge, 2003); Guy Halsall, Barbarian Migrations and the Roman West, 376-568, Cambridge Medieval Textbooks (Cambridge: Cambridge University Press, 2007); Walter Pohl, Die Volkerwanderung: Eroberung Und Integration (Stuttgart: Kohlhammer, 2002); Walter Pohl and Max Diesenberger, Integration Und Herrschaft: Ethnische Identitäten Und Soziale Organisation Im Frühmittelalter, Denkschriften / Österreichische Akademie Der Wissenschaften, Philosophisch-Historische Klasse (Vienna: Verlag der Österreichischen Akademie der Wissenschaften, 2002); Bryan Ward-Perkins, The Fall of Rome: And the End of Civilization (Oxford; New York: Oxford University Press, 2005).

[3] Chris Wickham, "The Other Transition: From the Ancient World to Feudalism," Past and Present 103 (1984): 3.

of the Roman Empire. The fourth part will analyze Justinian's (527-565) policies regarding church and state relationships and his special interest in religious and political affairs in the western part of the Roman Empire.

RELIGIOUS POLICIES FROM CONSTANTINE'S SONS TO JUSTINIAN

Imperial religious policies adopted after Constantine were in line with Constantine's support of Catholic Christianity. Religious legislation was most often issued in response to local or general theological problems. Theological controversies like Donatism, Arianism, and Nestorianism reached the imperial courts through magisterial inquiries or bishops' requests. Emperors' responses were through direct legislation or synod or council convocations mediated by imperial magistrates. In the majority of cases, the will of the emperor was established as orthodoxy, which could clash with bishops' theological understandings.[4] Bishops who would not abide by the imperial will were usually removed from their sees and sent into exile.

RELIGIOUS POLICIES RELATED TO CHURCH AFFAIRS

Most of the emperors in the fourth and fifth centuries followed and deepened Constantine's policy of church and state relationships.[5] They summoned councils and interfered in church affairs, such as the choice of bishops,[6] church synods,[7] banishment of bishops,[8] and support of Catholic orthodox theology or opposite views. They issued more and more laws regulating church affairs, and these laws became an integral part of the Roman legal system, affecting the social, political, juridical, and economic life of the empire and the church. The same control exercised by the emperors over the pagan state religious system was continued in the Catholic Christian system. Some historians call this inter-

---

[4] Normally emperors legislated in ecclesiastical affairs, but not in theological ones. Theological controversies would be settled through councils summoned by emperors and then enforced by law. Some emperors would work through the councils to impose their understanding as Catholic orthodoxy, like Constantius in the synod of Rimini. One of the emperors who added some innovation to this Constantinian policy of legislating theological concepts through council decisions was Zeno with his Henotikon.

[5] For chronological list of Roman emperors see appendix A.

[6] After Constantine, almost all the emperors chose the bishops of Constantinople. This practice was not common in other cities of the empire. See Jones, Later Roman Empire, 1:96.

[7] See for example Sardica (347), Milan (355), Rimini (359), Aquileia (381), Ephesus (449), and others.

[8] For example, Constantius, who sent into exile Athanasius, Pope Liberius, Hilary of Pontiers, Lucifer of Cagliari, and Rhodanius of Toulouse. See W. H. C. Frend, The Rise of Christianity (Philadelphia: Fortress Press, 1984), 521-552; Theodoret, 3:2.13, 17.

vention of the state over the church Caesaropapism[9]—religious control under the guidance of the state headed by emperors.[10]

The intervention of the state in church affairs did not mean disregard for the church. In their own view, emperors were working to establish orthodoxy and unity in the church. As Jones comments on Constantius's policies against the Catholic bishops, he was only performing "his imperial duty and giving unity to the church."[11] Whether they supported Catholic orthodoxy or not, the emperors issued laws that expanded the privileges of bishops and suppressed heresies and pagan worship.[12] Catholic Christianity not only became the official church of the state, but also gradually became part of the state. As Burckhardt comments, after Constantine, the church had turned into the state and the state into the church.[13]

Even though there were many laws promulgated by emperors outside the Theodosian and Justinian Codes,[14] the core of the legislation related to church

---

[9] There is a current discussion of whether the term "Caesaropapism" is proper to define the Byzantine style of church and state relationships. For more information, see Richard F. Costigan, "State Appointment of Bishops," Journal of Church and State 8, no. 1 (1966): 82-96; Gilbert Dagron, Emperor and Priest: The Imperial Office in Byzantium (Cambridge; New York: Cambridge University Press, 2003), 282-312; Wilhelm Ensslin, "Gottkaiser Und Kaiser Von Gottes Gnaden: Staat Und Kirche," in Byzantinische Herrscherbild (Darmstadt: Wissenschaftliche Buchgesellschaft, 1975), 54-85; Wilhelm Ensslin, "Konstantin D Grossen Bis Theodosius D Grossen: Cäsaropapismus," in Byzantinische Herrscherbild (Darmstadt: Wissenschaftliche Buchgesellschaft, 1975), 193-205; Deno John Geanakoplos, "Church and State in the Byzantine Empire: A Reconsideration of the Problem of Caesaropapism," Church History 34, no. 4 (1965): 381-403; Deno John Geanakoplos, "Church Building And 'Caesaropapism' A.D. 312-565," Greek, Roman and Byzantine Studies 7 (1966): 167-186; Edward A. Johnson, "Constantine the Great: Imperial Benefactor of the Early Christian Church," Journal of the Evangelical Theological Society 22, no. 2 (1979): 161-169; McGuckin, "The Legacy of the 13th Apostle," 251-288; Vatro Murvar, "Max Weber's Concept of Hierocracy: A Study in the Typology of Church-State Relationships," Sociological Analysis 28, no. 2 (1967): 69-84; Alvaro d Ors, "La Actitud Legislativa Del Emperador Justiniano," Orientalia Christiana Periodica 13, no. 1-2 (1947): 119-142; Charles Pietri, "La Politique De Constance II: Un Premier "Césaropapisme" Ou L'imitatio Constantini," in Église et L'empire au Ive Siècle (Geneva Fondation Hardt, 1989), 113-172; Schmemann, 5-22.

[10] For some historians, a classical example of Caesaropapism can be seen in Constantius's rulership. They use Athanasius's arguments as proof of this; Athanasius said in his Historia Arianus that Constantius's wishes should be regarded as canon law (Athanasius, 3). These historians also mention the Synod of Rimini (359), where Constantius sent a letter saying that no church decree would have force of law if he thought it would deny its (synod) importance and obligation. See Hilary of Poitiers, Collectanea Antiariana Parisina, ed. Alfred Leonhard Feder, CSEL, vol. 65 (Vienna: F. Tempsky, 1916), A.8.2. For more information on Caesaropapism, see the previous footnote.

[11] Jones, Later Roman Empire, 1:118.

[12] Ibid.

[13] Burckhardt, 308.

[14] All quotations from the Justinian Code and Novels will be abbreviated as CJ and taken from Samuel Parsons Scott and others, The Civil Law: Including the Twelve Tables, the Institutes of Gaius, the Rules of Ulpian, the Opinions

issues is found in these two codes. This section will first survey the religious legislation related to church affairs in the Theodosian Code,[15] then analyze the major theological crises mediated by emperors at the end of the fourth century and throughout the fifth century.

For the present discussion, it is important to note that at this time there was no clear notion of separation between church and state. Religion was part of the welfare of the state, like any other aspect of government. Rulers were expected to legislate on religious matters just as they did on economic, political, military, and social issues.[16] Also, religion was seen by most of the emperors as a tool to unite the state and to secure the favor of God. Since for Catholic Christians, there was only one God and one way to reach him (Christianity), all other religious manifestations were wrong and should be suppressed. Thus, it is natural to expect that a Catholic emperor would legislate in favor of Catholic Christianity and try to establish the proper way to be a Catholic Christian according to his own convictions.

RELIGIOUS LEGISLATION RELATED TO CATHOLIC CHURCH AFFAIRS

Religious legislation related to church affairs was mainly related to privileges bestowed upon the Catholic Church and its clergy. These laws were connected to the legal issues of the state related to the church. However, after Gratian (367-383), emperors gradually started to legislate in internal church affairs related to matters of faith and praxis.

Constantine and emperors after him, following the economic changes promoted by Diocletian, legislated in favor of state control of industry, centralization of government, and hereditary obligations to local administrative responsibilities.[17] Alföldy argues, "Compulsion and centralization were the only responses that the imperial monarchy could offer to the growing economic difficulties, the social and political problems and the ideological conflicts of Late Antiquity." He adds that "an enormous and expensive machinery of power was required to apply these responses" and the state "could only find methods of force in order to oblige decurions, traders, craftsmen and agricultural

---

of Paulus, the Enactments of Justinian, and the Constitutions of Leo (Cincinnati: Central Trust Company, 1973).

[15] The religious laws of the Justinian Code will be analyzed in the section of this chapter titled "Justinian's Ecclesiastical Policies."

[16] See Hill, viii-ix. He even argues that in the reality of those living before A.D. 1300, there was no contradictory jurisdiction between church and state and the terms "state" and "church" did not apply.

[17] For more information see Alföldy, 187-220; William Kenneth Boyd, The Ecclesiastical Edicts of the Theodosian Code (New York: Columbia University Press, 1905), 71-73; Jones, Later Roman Empire, 1:321-763, 2:767-872.

labourers to deliver the requisite taxes and services."[18] A few professions that were considered to serve the welfare of the state, such as teachers, rhetoricians, physicians, and priests, were exempt from this oppression. Constantine added Catholic Christian clergy to this privileged class, and with the exception of Julian (360-363), all other emperors reaffirmed and expanded the clerical exemption from taxes and compulsory public service.[19]

Even though Constantius II (337-361) favored Arianism instead of Catholicism for most of his life, he followed his father's policies, exempting young and poor sons of clergy from curial duties; expanding clergy special levies, exempting them and their properties from taxes; regulating that they could be tried only by other clergy; exempting monks from state obligations and church properties from taxation; and making it a crime to rape or marry holy "maidens" and widows.[20]

Jovian (363-364) was a Catholic Christian, but his influence was limited because his reign was so short. However, besides reinstating Catholic Christianity as the empire's religion, he declared raping holy maidens and widows or soliciting them into marriage to be a capital crime.[21] His successors Valentinian I (364-375) and Valens (364-378), the former a Catholic and the latter the last emperor to support Arianism, legislated in favor of Catholic Christianity. They expanded bishops' authority as ecclesiastical judges, excluding only criminal cases from their jurisdiction. They exempted clergy of the first rank of the church, such as priests, deacons, subdeacons, exorcists, lectors, and doorkeepers, from compulsory public service; stated that Christians could not be sent to the arena, appointed as custodians of pagan temples, or sued on Sunday; and exempted women devoted to the church from taxes.[22]

After Gratian, emperors issued many laws favoring Catholic Christianity and regulating church discipline and other internal church affairs. Sunday worship was upheld and Christians received many special privileges: actresses who converted were freed from employment in drama production, Christians could not be sentenced to the arena, widows who dedicated their life to the church were exempt from taxes, clerics' lives were regulated, and divine law was considered civil law.[23]

Emperors following Gratian reinforced the role of bishops as judges and the

---

[18] Alföldy, 187.

[19] See CT, 16.2.1, 2, 3, 5, 6, 7, 8, 9 10, 11, 14, 15, 19, 21, 24, 26, 36, 38.

[20] CT, 16.2.11, 16.2.8 and 9, 16.2.10, 16.2.12, 16.2.16, 11.1.1, 9.25.1.

[21] CT, 9.25.2.

[22] CT, 16.2.23, 16.2.24, 9.40.8, 16.1.1, 8.8.1, 13.10.6.

[23] CT, 9.40.8, 8.8.1, 2.8.18, 19, 20, 15.5.2, 2.8.23, 2.8.25, 9.3.7, 15.5.5, 15.7.1, 13.10.6, 15.7.4, 15.7.8-9, 15.7.12, 16.2.20, 16.2.25, 8.5.46, 9.17.7; CJ, 7.38.2; CT, 16.2.27, 16.3.1, 16.4.3, 16.2.29; CJ, 1.4.5; CT, 16.7.6, 16.2.30, 11.16.21-22, 16.2.32-36; CJ, 1.3.16; CT, 16.5.51, 16.2.40-44, 11.1.33, 16.2.46; CJ, 1.8.1; CT, 16.5.45, 16.5.51, 15.3.6.

sacredness of church property as a place of refuge for criminals. Clergy were judged in ecclesiastical courts; if litigants agreed, a bishop might serve as a civil judge and his verdict would be enforced by the civil authorities.[24] However, the church could hire lawyers to seek its rights, and they would be put into effect. Also, criminals who took refuge in a church could not be taken [25]out by force or violence. Bishops could plead the case of the criminal, even if he or she was already in prison, but if the offense was a debt to the state, the bishop had to pay the debt.[26]

Theodosius I (379-395) had great zeal for the Catholic faith; his edict of February 28, 380, made Catholicism the official religion of the empire and outlawed paganism and heretical movements. He said:

> It is our will that all the peoples who are ruled by the administration of Our Clemency shall practice that religion which the divine Peter the Apostle transmitted to the Romans, as the religion which he introduced makes clear even unto this day. It is evident that this is the religion that is followed by the Pontiff Damasus and by Peter, Bishop of Alexandria, a man of apostolic sanctity; that is, according to the apostolic discipline and the evangelic doctrine, we shall believe in the single Deity of the Father, the Son, and the Holy Spirit, under the concept of equal majesty and of the Holy Trinity.[27]

Boyd mentions that these privileges raised two major problems: (1) "the expansion of church membership increased the number of the clergy, over whose choice the emperor exercised no control" and (2) "many *curiales* [members of the curia, ruling nobles] sought refuge from their economic burdens by entering the ecclesiastical orders."[28] One of the responses of Constantine and other emperors to these problems was to regulate the order *curiale* and even other professionals who were willing to enter into ecclesiastical orders. Valentinian I and Valens legislated that all tradesmen were required to pay the tradesmen's tax, including Christian clergy; they forbade the wealthy and bread-makers from becoming clergy, and ordered that members of the curial class should give their property to either a relative or the state if they became clergymen. They ordered tradesmen to use some of their excess money to aid Christians, paupers, and the needy.[29] However, Valens, Gratian, Valentinian II (375-392), and Theodosius I confirmed exemption from

---

[24] Collectio Avellana, ed. Karl Ziwsa, CSEL, vol. 35 (Vindobonae: F. Tempsky, 1893), p. 52-54; CS, 2; CJ, 1.4.7 271; CT, 1.27.2, 16.11.1, 16.2.23, 16.2.41.

[25] CT, 16.2.38.

[26] CT, 9.40.16, 9.45.1, 9.45.3; CS, 13; Sacrorum Conciliorum, Nova et Amplissima Collectio, 5:437-445.

[27] CT, 16.1.2.

[28] Boyd, 75.

[29] CT, 13.1.5, 14.3.11; CJ, 1.4.1; CT, 16.2.17, 12.1.59; CJ, 1.55.8.

public services for priests, deacons, exorcists, lectors, and other church ministers, and exemption from merchants' taxes if their profit was low.[30]

Curiales and those who were able to perform as *curiales* were forbidden to enter ecclesiastical orders; by the time of Emperor Arcadius (377/378–408), *curiales* working as bishops, deacons, or presbyters were required to provide substitutes to their curia.[31] Even senators who held municipal positions had to surrender their properties if they wanted to serve the church or find a replacement to carry on the responsibilities.[32]

The practical result of the legislation bestowing privileges and immunities on Christianity was the political and economic empowering of the clergy, mainly bishops, and the Catholic Church. The clergy was added as a new order in the social system of the Roman Empire, and the church was given the right to accept bequests—a privilege not extended to any other pagan religion[33]—which made the "wealth of the churches grow enormously between the beginning of the fourth century and the sixth."[34] A new avenue of power was opened into the aristocratic life of the empire, where the senatorial order had previously been the highest rank.[35] In many cities, bishops were more influential than public magistrates.[36] Many entered ecclesiastical service not for spiritual reasons, but seeking political power or to avoid civic obligations.[37]

This change in Roman society also affected its concern for tradition—the *mos maiorum*. The intellectual, moral, and spiritual guidance based in the political ethics and pagan religion of the empire fostered by the Neo-Platonist senate was gradually replaced by the Christian tradition, which had assimilated many aspects of natural philosophy and fewer of the biblical elements of the Jewish theological tradition.[38] In the West, the Catholic church became the stronghold of Roman tradition, due to the military and political disintegration of Roman power in the fifth and sixth centuries. Christianity became the link of integration between Roman traditions and Christian

---

[30] CT, 16.2.24, 13.1.11, 11.16.15.

[31] CT, 12.1.59, 12.1.63, 12.1.122-123, 12.1.163, 12.1.172, 14.3.11, 13.1.5, 16.2.3, 6, 15, 17, 19, 21, 22, 39.

[32] CT, 12.1.104, 115, 121.

[33] CT, 16.2.4; Boyd, 82-83.

[34] Jones, Later Roman Empire, 2:904.

[35] According to Alföldy, in the late Roman Empire the differences between the upper and lower strata of society were marked more by economic power then social order. This does not mean that the senatorial order lost its prestige, but it did not have the same political influence as it had in the early Roman Empire. Alföldy, 186-220.

[36] This is the case of Ambrose, bishop of Milan. See more about Ambrose in the section "Bishop Responses to Imperial Intervention in Church Affairs."

[37] Boyd, 77.

[38] See Jaroslav Jan Pelikan, The Emergence of the Catholic Tradition (100-600), ed. Jaroslav Jan Pelikan, 5 vols., Christian Tradition, vol. 1 (Chicago: University of Chicago Press, 1971), 11-67.

morality with the invader barbarians.[39] As Dill said, "in the age when Roman institutions were tottering . . . the Church carried on the tradition of pagan Rome."[40]

Another point to be mentioned about religious legislation between Constantius and Anastasius (491-518) is the way Emperor Zeno (474-475, 476-491) dealt with church unity and theological controversy. After the council of Chalcedon (451), the Monophysite party became a problem for the emperor, who tried to promote unity by issuing a theological decree—the *Henotikon*. Even though the theological content was prepared with the help of Patriarch Acacius (471-489) of Constantinople, Zeno published and enforced as law his definition of faith without basing it in any church council.[41]

RELIGIOUS LEGISLATION REGARDING HERETICS AND SCHISMATICS

After Constantine, the Catholic Church was still fighting to establish the Nicaean definition of faith as orthodoxy. Arianism and Donatism were the two major schools of thought challenging the Catholic Church. In the East, Arianism had the support of emperors like Constantius (337-350) and Valens (364-375), and many bishops up to the three Cappadocian fathers—Gregory of Nissi, Gregory Nazianzus, and Basil of Caesarea—advocated an Arian or semi-Arian definition of faith. In North Africa, Donatism survived until the beginning of the fifth century, when it was suppressed by the emperors Honorius (A.D. 393-423) and Theodosius II (A.D. 408-450) and bishops such as Augustine.

Other heretic groups such as the Manicheans, Eunomians, and Apollinarians suffered persecution from the civil authorities; most of the laws punished heretics with such penalties as exile, confiscation of property, making inheriting property impossible, and even capital punishment. These laws were issued mainly after Gratian. All heresies were forbidden; heretics could not have public or private meetings, teach their theology to others, inherit property, or leave wills, they were banned from cities and prohibited from joining the society of holy persons, and special courts were set up to judge these cases where judges and other officials had to enforce these laws.[42]

By the time of Arcadius (A.D. 383-408) and Honorius (A.D. 393-423), anyone who disagreed with the Catholic Church even on a minor point of doctrine was considered a heretic. All previous laws passed regarding heretics were reviewed,

---

[39] Alföldy, 219.

[40] Samuel Dill, *Roman Society in the Last Century of the Western Empire*, 2nd rev. ed. (London: Macmillan, 1926), 5.

[41] For more information, see the section below, "Background of the Theological Controversies Inherited by Justinian."

[42] CT, 16.5.3-24.

heretics could not hold imperial office, their beliefs were considered public crimes on the grounds that crime against religion was detrimental to all, and Donatism suffered its final persecution.[43]

After Theodosius II (A.D. 408-450), the previous laws against heretics were renewed and new ones were added: Legal action related to religion and heresies had to be taken before bishops rather than secular judges, all churches occupied by heretics had to be returned to the Catholic Church, and heretics' books were banned and required to be burned. The penalties for heresy included exile, confiscation of properties, inability to work in public office (except in the defense of a city), inability to leave or receive inheritance, and even execution.[44]

Even though heretics were persecuted under Christian emperors, some laws were issued that gave them rights. Eunomians were considered heretics and forbidden to hold meetings or bequeath and accept property in 389 by a rescript of Valentinian II, Theodosius I, and Arcadius, but this law was rescinded in 394, then restored and rescinded again in 395; in 399, even though the law confirmed them as heretics, it allowed them to have property and donate their property in life. After Arcadius's death, however, Honorius and Theodosius II revoked all rights previously granted to Eunomians.[45] Another example is Emperor Marcio's (A.D. 450-457) law allowing heretics to be buried according to orthodox and ordinary practice.[46]

RELIGIOUS POLICIES REGARDING NON-CHRISTIANS

The emperors' laws suppressing paganism did not extinguish paganism, but diminished its influence throughout the empire in the fourth and fifth centuries. The persecution of pagans was not equally intense throughout the empire. Even though the majority of the aristocracy had become Christian at the end of the fourth century, in many cities the magistrates were still pagans and did not push for the suppression of paganism. Some pagan ceremonies survived Christianization and were incorporated into Christian traditions or became traditional cultural festivals. However, the suppression of paganism increased the political influence of bishops. Bishops were not the ones directly responsible for the execution of legislation suppressing paganism, but they actively participated

---

[43] CT, 16.5.25-58, 16.6.3-5; CS, 12, 14; CT, 16.2.31, 16.11.3, 16.6.7

[44] CT, 16.5.59-66; CS, 6; CT, 16.2.47; CJ, 1.5.8, 1.5.10; J. B. Pitra, Juris Ecclesiastici Graecorum Historia Et Monumenta (Rome: Typis Collegii Urbani, 1868), 2:556.

[45] CT, 16.5.17, 23, 25, 36, 49, 50.

[46] CJ, 1.5.9.

in the destruction of pagan temples and converting pagans.[47] Even though the legislation empowered only magistrates to suppress paganism, the weakening of political power in the western part of the empire broadened the bishops' political influence in the area of suppressing paganism.

Religious Legislation against Pagans

Constantius increased anti-pagan legislation. He decreed that pagan superstition and sacrifices were completely forbidden, in accord with the law set forth by Constantine, and that pagan temples should be closed to worship and sacrifice and transformed into places of amusement. Violators would have their property given to the state treasury, and governors who failed to carry out this punishment would be punished. Christians who converted to paganism would lose their property; nocturnal sacrifices were forbidden; pagan worship was made a capital offense; and those involved with these sacrifices should "be struck down with the avenging sword" and their properties should "be forfeited to the fisc." He even added that "governors of the provinces shall be similarly punished if they should neglect to avenge such crimes." Anyone who consulted a soothsayer on account of curiosity about the future would suffer capital punishment, and torture was decreed for diviners or magicians discovered in the imperial service.[48]

Trials of persons of the senatorial order for practicing magic might be entrusted to the prefect of the city; however, if a judgment could not be ascertained, the trial would be transferred to the imperial court.[49]

Besides making laws suppressing paganism, Gratian, Theodosius I, and emperors after them issued laws forbidding Christians to return to paganism. However, the analysis of these laws demonstrates that anti-pagan legislation did not remove pagan influence from people's hearts. Newly converted Christians were in most cases still attached to their old religious practices, and returning to pagan practices was as easy as their conversion to Christianity had been.[50]

At the time of Valentinian I, Valens, and Gratian, divination and sacrifice to demons were forbidden during the night hours, but since divination had no con-

---

[47] The religious sections of the Codex Theodosianus, book 16, address all articles related to suppression of heresy and paganism to magistrates, proconsuls, and other political Roman authorities. The only mention of bishops holding authority in connection to the eradication of paganism is in an edict of A.D. 407, where bishops were granted to use ecclesiastical power to prohibit convivial banquets (convivia). However, the term for ecclesiastical power (ecclesiastica manus) does not make it clear how bishops would do this. See Garth Fowden, "Bishops and Temples in the Eastern Roman Empire A.D. 320-435," Journal of Theological Studies 29, no. 1 (1978): 53-78.

[48] CT, 16.10.2-6, 16.8.7, 9.16.6.

[49] CT, 9.16.10.

[50] CT, 16.7.1.

nection to magic, it could be practiced as long as the purpose was not harmful.[51] However, laws made by Gratian, Valentinian II, and Theodosius I forbade divination; the punishment for examining the livers and entrails of sacrifices was torture. These laws also invalidated wills made by Christians who converted to paganism and penalized performers of pagan sacrifices with the loss of property, but they allowed local rulers to appoint high priests for pagan temples.[52]

The laws of Theodosius making Christianity the official religion of the empire caused persecution against pagans to escalate. Even though bishops and clerics were not empowered to persecute pagans, they participated in the destruction of pagan temples and holy sites in Gaul, Syria, Carthage, Alexandria, Gaza, and Egypt.[53]

By the time of Arcadius and Honorius, magic was considered a crime, pagan sacrifices and worship in pagan temples were forbidden, pagan festivals were no longer considered holidays (although festivals without pagan sacrifices or superstition could be celebrated), and governors who did not enforce these laws were punished. They also abolished privileges granted to pagan priests and leaders and ordered the destruction of pagan temples in rural areas. However, temples not containing illegal objects (idols and altars) were not destroyed.[54]

Honorius and Theodosius II reinforced anti-pagan legislation by transferring taxes directed toward pagan temples to the army, ordering the destruction of pagan altars and removal of images from pagan temples and making them places for secular use, and ordering other pagan property to be given to the church. Also, astrologers who did not convert to Christianity and burn their books in the presence of a bishop were exiled; pagans who tried to enter the imperial services were exiled and had their possessions confiscated, and could even face execution.[55]

After Theodosius II, Justinian was the next emperor to reissue laws suppressing paganism. The lack of legislation during this period does not mean that paganism was completely dead; Beard and North point out that Gelasius "found necessary both to argue against the efficacy of the cult [Lupercalia] (as some Christians writers had done for three hundred years) and to ban Christian participation"[56] in this pagan ritual, which shows that paganism was still alive. As Beard and North argue, "it

---

[51] CT, 9.16.7, 9.

[52] CT, 16.10.9, 16.7.1, 16.10.7, 12.1.112.

[53] Edward Gibbon and William Youngman, The History of the Decline and Fall of the Roman Empire (London: William Ball, 1839), 205-215; Ramsay MacMullen, Christianizing the Roman Empire: A.D. 100-400 (New Haven: Yale University Press, 1984), 86-101; Sulpitius Severus, On the Life of St Martin, NPNF2, ed. Philip Schaff and Henry Wace (Grand Rapids, MI: Eerdmans, 1983), 11:11; Socrates, 2:5.16.

[54] CT, 9.16.11, 16.10.10, 2.8.22, 16.10.13-18.

[55] CT, 16.10.19-25, 9.10.12.

[56] Beard, North, and Price, Religions of Rome, 388.

was not simply a question of 'paganism' successfully resisting Christianity"—many pagan festivals were incorporated into Christian tradition or remained as cultural festivals, "more than some Christian bishops would have liked to allow."[57]

RELIGIOUS LEGISLATION AGAINST JEWS

Jews had always enjoyed recognition and protection from Roman emperors as a *religio licita*. However, after Constantine, laws were issued restraining Jewish freedom. Constantius ordered that Jews could not hold slaves from any other people and should let them go free. Also, Jews could not circumcise non-Jewish slaves; if they did, they would be executed, and all their slaves would be taken away and freed if they owned Christian slaves. He forbade Jews from proselytizing on pain of death and confiscation of properties for the converted one.[58]

Gratian, Valentinian II, and Theodosius I reaffirmed the previous laws, adding that Christians who converted to paganism would lose the right to make a will.[59] By the time of Arcadius and Theodosius I, Jews and Christians were forbidden to intermarry, but Jewish religion was protected by law, with their leaders having authority to administer their religious laws and communities.[60] Emperors Arcadius and Honorius issued many laws granting Jews both civil and religious rights, even giving them the same privileges of exemption from municipal services as the Christian clergy, but forbidding them from enrolling as members of the secret service of the empire. Also, local governors were charged with protecting synagogues and Jewish communities from being harassed or attacked.[61]

By the time of Honorius and Theodosius II, the previous prohibitions were confirmed, yet Jewish rights were preserved; Sabbath observance in Jewish communities was respected, but they could not build new synagogues.[62] Theodosius II also forbade Jews and Samaritans from excluding their children from their wills if they became Christians.[63]

Even though the emperors after Constantine issued anti-Jewish legislation, Jews did not have as hard a time under them as they did in the time of Justinian. In the fifth century and the beginning of the sixth century, as Rachel Hachlili said, the Jewish "economy flourished, and agricultural settlements were established

---

[57] Ibid.

[58] CT, 16.9.2, 16.8.6-7.

[59] CT, 3.1.5, 16.7.3.

[60] CT, 3.7.2, 16.8.8-9.

[61] CT, 16.8.10-17, 9.45.2.

[62] CT, 16.8.18-27, 16.5.44, 16.9.3-5, 16.10.24.

[63] CT, 16.8.28.

in the south of the country [land of Israel]" and this "was a quieter and more relaxed period for the Jews."[64] However, there were some violent clashes between Christians and Jews where synagogues were destroyed by Christian clergy, even though they had the protection of the law.[65]

Summary

Constantine's sons and the emperors after them followed Constantine's policies on church and state relationships. They legislated and set policy concerning such ecclesiastical issues as church property, tax exemption for clerics, the role of the bishop in society, rules for those who wanted to enter ecclesiastical life, electing bishops in some cities, and so on. Also, they intervened in theological matters in various ways, such as making Catholic orthodoxy the official religion of the state, summoning and confirming church council decisions as the law of the state, outlawing heresy and persecuting heretics, directing church councils through imperial representatives, exiling members of the clergy who opposed their religious decisions or condemning them as heretics, and issuing laws establishing definitions of faith without summoning church councils, as Emperor Zeno did with his *Henotikon*.

During this period, the Catholic church and the Roman state became closer and closer, paganism was outlawed but did not die out completely, the majority of the aristocracy converted to Christianity, Jews saw their religious and civil rights limited, bishops became more influential in the political life of the empire, and some bishops acted violently against non-Christian places of worship even though they did not have legal sanction for it.

Bishops' responses to imperial intervention in church affairs

This imperial intervention in ecclesiastical and theological issues aroused questions among the clergy as to what should be the limits of state interference in church affairs. The controversy between emperors and orthodox bishops produced various theological responses to the problem of church and state relationships. Bishops were not fighting for a separation of church and state, but for the proper role that each institution should exert in society.

---

[64] Rachel Hachlili, Ancient Jewish Art and Archaeology in the Land of Israel (Leiden; New York: E. J. Brill, 1988), 6.

[65] Peter Robert Lamont Brown, "Christianization and Religious Conflict," in The Cambridge Ancient History: The Late Empire, A.D. 337-425, ed. Averil Cameron and Peter Garnsey (Cambridge: Cambridge University Press, 1998), 647-649.

Even at the time of Constantine, many bishops rose up against his positions on ecclesiastical and theological matters. Athanasius was the boldest one facing Constantine and his sons in defense of the Catholic Trinitarian interpretation of the Nicaean canons.[66]

Another theologian who confronted the state was Bishop Ambrose of Milan. Based on the spiritual authority of the priest, he upheld the institutional side of the Catholic Church and stated that any believer, even the utmost authority of the state—the emperor—should be under the church's spiritual authority. Ambrose did not write a specific treatise or book on ecclesiology. However, based on his actions and quotations throughout his writings, his view was that church and state were independent institutions working together in their own spheres of action.[67] Even though Ambrose emphasized the church's spiritual authority more than its juridical authority, his boldness before Emperors Valentinian, Theodosius, Valentinian II, and other political authorities helped the Catholic Church triumph over paganism and set the ground for the medieval political theories of church and state relationships.[68] Ambrose's acts do not

---

[66] Barnes, Athanasius and Constantius: Theology and Politics in the Constantinian Empire; Drake, "Athanasius' First Exile," 193-204; Elliott, "Constantine and 'The Arian Reaction after Nicaea,'" 169-194; Richard P. C. Hanson, "The Doctrine of the Trinity Achieved in 381," Scottish Journal of Theology 36, no. 1 (1983): 41-57; Charles Kannengiesser, "Athanasius of Alexandria vs. Arius: The Alexandrian Crisis," in The Roots of Egyptian Christianity, ed. Birger A. Pearson and James E. Goehring, Studies in Antiquity and Christianity (Philadelphia: Fortress Press, 1986), 204-215; Norderval, 113-150.

[67] Most of Ambrose's works on church and state relations are found in De Officiis Ministrorum and Hexaemeron. See for example Ambrose, "Hexaemeron," in PL, ed. J. P. Migne, vol. 14 (Paris: J.-P. Migne, 1840), 2.3.12, 5.15.52, 5.21.67-73; idem, "De Officiis Ministrorum," in PL, ed. J. P. Migne, vol. 16 (Paris: J.-P. Migne, 1844), 1.28.130-135, 2.7.31-34.

[68] Campenhausen, in his work Ambrosius von Mailand als Kirchenpolitiker, argues that in most cases Ambrose did not seek juridical dominance of the church over the state. He was basically advocating the ultimate sovereignty of God, a spiritual leadership of the church, where all Christians, irrespective of rank, should be subservient to this spiritual body. On the other hand, Morine, in his work Church and State in the Teaching of St. Ambrose, argues that Ambrose regarded the church more as an organization with a primarily juridical reality. These two positions are the dominant ones on the scholarly debate over Ambrose's understanding of church and state relationships. For more on Ambrose's life, ecclesiology, and church and state relationships, see Hans Freiherr von Campenhausen, Ambrosius Von Mailand Als Kirchenpolitiker (Berlin, Leipzig: W. de Gruyter, 1929); Pierre Paul Courcelle, Recherches Sur Saint Ambroise: "Vies" Anciennes, Culture, Iconographie (Paris: Études augustiniennes, 1973); F. Homes Dudden, The Life and Times of St. Ambrose, 2 vols. (Oxford: Clarendon Press, 1935); Yves-Marie Duval, Ambroise De Milan: Xvie Centenaire De Son Élection Épiscopale (Paris: Études augustiniennes, 1974); Gunther Gottlieb, Ambrosius Von Mailand Und Kaiser Gratian (Göttingen: Vandenhoeck und Ruprecht, 1973); Raymond Johanny, L'eucharistie, Centre De L'histoire Du Salut, Chez Saint Ambroise De Milan (Paris: Beauchesne et ses fils, 1968); Andrew Lenox-Conyngham,

indicate a desire for political supremacy, but as Andrew Lenox-Conyngham says, "the fact is that Ambrose   . . . contributed more than any other man in the Roman Empire to the strengthening of the Church as an institution which was, in effect, to take over from the crumbling Empire as the only organization capable of imparting order to the increasingly disorientated world of a collapsing civilization."[69]

It was not Augustine's main purpose to address the roles of church and state in his work, and he did not challenge the emperors' positions, but his works, mainly *The City of God,* greatly influenced secular and church leaders in their struggle for supremacy. According to Frederick William Loetscher, *The City of God* was not "intended as a manual on the problem of the relation of church and state, though for a thousand years emperors and popes were to exploit it as an arsenal in their struggle for supreme power; the former to maintain their independence in secular affairs, and the latter to establish their dominion over all other earthly rulers, whether temporal or spiritual."[70]

Augustine's work influenced the understanding of church and state after him because of the way he tried to harmonize the conflict between the secular and religious realms. In a time where the theory of Hellenistic kingship in a Christian empire—the merging of secular and religious power in one—as proposed by Eusebius and others was flourishing as the answer for the ideal form of government on earth,[71] Augustine presented a different solution to the conflict between the future implementation of God's kingdom on earth and the present imperial theology of the Empire—the kingdom of God and the kingdom of Caesar.

"The Church in St. Ambrose of Milan," International Journal for the Study of the Christian Church 5, no. 3 (2005): 211-225; Goulven Madec, Saint Ambroise et la Philosophie (Paris: Études augustiniennes, 1974); Neil B. McLynn, Ambrose of Milan: Church and Court in a Christian Capital (Berkeley: University of California Press, 1994); Jean Mesot, Die Heidenbekehrung Bei Ambrosius Von Mailand (Schöneck-Beckenried, Schweiz: Neuen Zeitschrift für Missionswissenschaft, 1958); Claudio Morino, Church and State in the Teaching of St. Ambrose, trans. M. Joseph Costelloe (Washington, DC: Catholic University of America Press, 1969); Angelo Paredi, Saint Ambrose, His Life and Times, trans. M. Joseph Costelloe (Notre Dame: University of Notre Dame Press, 1964); Boniface Ramsey, Ambrose (London, New York: Routledge, 1997); Thomas Gerhard Ring, Auctoritas Bei Tertullian, Cyprian und Ambrosius (Würzburg: Augustinus-Verlag, 1975); Robinson Thornton, St. Ambrose: His Life, Times, and Teaching (London: Society for Promoting Christian Knowledge, 1898); J. W. C. Wand, The Latin Doctors (London: Faith Press, 1948).

[69] Lenox-Conyngham, 215.

[70] Frederick William Loetscher, "Augustine's City of God," Theology Today 1, no. 3 (1944): 317-318.

[71] Not all Christians accepted this solution proposed by Eusebius. Donatists in North Africa and others saw the state as a demonic power, Babylon, in which Christianity should have no part. See section "Constantine, the Bishops, and the Church" in chapter 2 above.

He presented the existence of two cities, an earthly—*civitas terrena*—and a heavenly—*civitas Dei*. Even though he identified the *civitas terrena* with empires like those of Assyria and Rome,[72] he did not equate the *civitas terrena* with earthly empires and the *civitas Dei* with the visible church. For him, the two realms encompassed both men and angels, good and bad. He wrote, "It is not incongruous and unsuitable to speak of a society composed of angels and men together; so that there are not four cities or societies—two, namely, of angels, and as many of men—but rather two in all, one composed of the good, the other of the wicked, both angels and men."[73]

Until the final separation of these two cities on the day when the *civitas Dei* would prevail, both cities would live together in this world and people would move from one to the other side. In this view, secular power was not bad per se and could be used by God to promote the welfare of human beings, if it did not become a tool for evil in the hands of an absolute power. As Rosemary Radford Ruether says, for Augustine, "the empire can also be viewed as a strictly secular realm organized for legitimate secular purposes. It has to do with the supplying of the temporal material needs of food, shelter, and law and order; all essential for material existence. The Christian can and must fully support the empire and takes his place as a citizen within it so long as it pursues this legitimate secular function."[74]

Augustine made space for the state in a Christian society, but limited its functions to the secular realm. Secular power, even in a Christian empire, would serve strictly secular ends. "He sees the empire as legitimate in its own secular realm, but as serving strictly the lower material needs of man. These are good within their own sphere, as long as they are kept strictly subordinate to the higher goods of the spirit, but of a lower and finitely limited good."[75] Thus, for Augustine there was space for the state, but it was at a lower level than the church, since the church dealt with eternal realities and the state with ones limited to time and space. "The battle, it must be remembered, is between the two communities, not necessarily between the Church and the state, save as these embody the antagonistic spirits of the communities. For the state is a natural and also, like the Church, a divinely sanctioned institute of society."[76]

Another important issue that later influenced church and state relationships was Augustine's understanding of universal history in which the saints would enjoy their Sabbath on earth, which for him was the present millennium where Christ was reigning in the Catholic Church, the kingdom of heaven already being established

---

[72] Augustine, The City of God (New York: Modern Library, 1950), 13.2.

[73] Ibid., 12.1.

[74] Rosemary Radford Ruether, "Augustine and Christian Political Theology," Interpretation 29, no. 3 (1975): 260.

[75] Ibid., 261.

[76] Loetscher, 321.

on earth. He wrote, "Therefore, the Church even now is the kingdom of Christ and the kingdom of heaven. Accordingly, even now His saints reign with Him."[77]

THE DEVELOPMENT OF THE ECCLESIASTICAL SUPREMACY OF THE BISHOP OF ROME

According to some historians, one of the first references to the Roman bishop's supremacy over other sees is found in the Sixth Nicaean Canon (325).[78] The canon mentions that the bishops of Alexandria should have authority over Egypt, Libya, and Pentapolis, as this was also customary for the bishop of Rome. It refers to the authority of the bishop of Rome, but does not specify what kind of authority or supremacy it was or how far it extended.[79] However, Roman bishops' fight for supremacy and intervention in church problems outside Rome can be traced throughout history. Bishop Clement of Rome (c. 91-101) claims in his letter to the Corinthians that if anyone were to "disobey what has been said by Him through us, let them understand that they will entangle themselves in transgression and no small danger."[80]

Irenaeus, bishop of Lyon (c. 202), talking about the Roman church in his treatise *Adversus Haereses*, writes that "the universal Church, that is, the faithful everywhere, must be in agreement with this Church [Rome] because of her outstanding superiority."[81] Firmilian (died c. 269), bishop of Caesarea, complained to Cyprian that Stephan, bishop of Rome, "so boasts of the place of his episcopate, and contends that he holds the succession from Peter, on whom the foundations of the Church were laid." He also said that Stephen "announces that he holds by succession the throne of Peter."[82]

---

[77] Augustine, The City of God, 20.9. Augustine dedicated Book 20 of The City of God to the topic of the millennium, where he expanded his idea of universal history in ages of a thousand years, arguing for the seventh millennium as the final age where the saints would enjoy their Sabbath on earth.

[78] See: James F. Loughlin, "The Sixth Nicene Canon and the Papacy," American Catholic Quarterly Review 5, no. (1880): 220-239; Stephen K. Ray, Upon This Rock: St. Peter and the Primacy of Rome in Scripture and the Early Church, Modern Apologetics Library (San Francisco: Ignatius Press, 1999), 195-196. For a chronological list of Roman bishops from Constantine to Charlemagne see appendix A.

[79] Hefele, 1:388-399.

[80] Clement, The Epistles of St. Clement of Rome and St. Ignatius of Antioch, trans. James Aloysius Kleist (Westminster, MD: Newman Bookshop, 1946), 45.

[81] Irenaeus, Against Heresies, ANF, ed. Alexander Roberts, James Donaldson, and A. Cleveland Coxe (Grand Rapids, MI: Eerdmans, 1989), 1:3.3.2-3.

[82] Firmilian, Firmilian, Bishop of Caesarea in Cappadocia, to Cyprian, against the Letter of Stephen, ANF, ed. Alexander Roberts, James Donaldson, and A. Cleveland Coxe (Grand Rapids, MI: Eerdmanns, 1989), 5:394.

In the Donatist controversy, Constantine remitted the cause to be judged by the bishop of Rome, Miltiades (311-314). His judgment was against the Donatists.[83] Later on, in the Arian controversy, pro-Arian bishops asked Bishop Julius of Rome (337-352) to summon a council to decide the problems discussed in the council at Tyre.[84] Julius, in the synod of Rome, decided in favor of Athanasius.[85] Ambrose said also that Athanasius sought the judgment of the church of Rome.[86] In the time of Julius, the council of Sardica (347) decided that bishops who felt that they were treated unjustly in their sees could appeal to the bishop of Rome.[87] In the letter sent to Bishop Julius (not present at the council of Sardica), the church of Rome is identified with the head and the chair of St. Peter.[88] "It was best and fittest that the priests [bishops] from all the provinces should make their reports to the head, that is, the chair of St. Peter."[89]

Years later, Pope Liberius's (352-366) support of Athanasius and his refusal to sign Emperor Constantius's semi-Arian formula resulted in his exile by the emperor.[90] At this time, the bishop of Rome was seen as a great defender of orthodoxy. Liberius also exerted authority over eastern churches; he reinstated Eustathius as bishop of Sebaste, and Basil the Great accepted it even though he recognized that Eustathius was still a semi-Arian. Basil said,

> On being ejected from his episcopate, on the ground of his former deposition at Melitine, he [Eustathius] hit upon a journey to you as a means of restitution for himself. What propositions were made to him by the blessed bishop Liberius, and to what he agreed, I am ignorant. I only know that he brought a letter restoring him, which he shewed to the synod at Tyana, and was restored to his see. He is now defaming the very

---

[83] Eusebius, HE, 10.5.18, 19.

[84] The council of Tyre was summoned by Constantine with the purpose of appraising the charges brought against Athanasius, bishop of Alexandria. For more information see Hefele, 2:19-25; J. P. Kirsch, "Julius I," The Catholic Encyclopedia: An International Work of Reference on the Constitution, Doctrine, and History of the Catholic Church, ed. Charles George Herbermann and committee, Knights of Columbus Catholic Truth (New York: Encyclopedia Press, 1913), 561.

[85] Sozomen, 2:3.8.44-48.

[86] Ambrose, "Epistolae XIII," in PL, ed. J. P. Migne, vol. 16 (Paris: J.-P. Migne, 1844), col. 950-952.

[87] See canons 3-5; Hefele, 2:112-129.

[88] Several scholars consider this part of the text to be a later insertion because it interrupts the flow of the text's thought. See: Archibald Bower and Samuel H. Cox, The History of the Popes: From the Foundation of the See of Rome to A.D. 1758, 3 vols. (Philadelphia: Griffith & Simon, 1844), 1:192; Hefele, 2:163-166.

[89] Philip Schaff and Henry Wace, Nicene and Post-Nicene Fathers Series 2, 14 vols. (Grand Rapids, MI: Eerdmans, 1983), 14:434.

[90] Liberius signed a formula of semi-Arian belief and came back from exile, but according to Baronius, he was barred from Catholic communion.

creed for which he was received; he is consorting with those who are anathematizing the Homoousion, and is prime leader of the heresy of the pneumatomachi. As it is from the West that he derives his power to injure the Churches, and uses the authority given him by you to the overthrow of the many, it is necessary that his correction should come from the same quarter, and that a letter be sent to the Churches stating on what terms he was received, and in what manner he has changed his conduct and nullifies the favour given him by the Fathers at that time.[91]

At the time of Bishop Damasus I (366-384), the Roman See grew in religious and secular authority. Writing to bishops present at the council of Antioch in 379, Bishop Damasus was the first to call the Roman bishopric the "Apostolic See." He called the other bishops sons, not brothers, and demanded that they be in accordance with his Apostolic See. In his words, "Most honorable sons, in that your charity accords to the Apostolic See the reverence due, you confer the greatest honor upon yourselves."[92] According to Giovan Domenico Mansi, Bishop Damasus provided the theological basis for papal supremacy. He said that the authority of the Roman See was not based in councils or synods, but in the Lord's command given to Peter in Matt 16:18[93]—"You are Peter; and upon this rock I will build my church."[94]

---

[91] Basil, Epistolae, NPNF2, ed. Philip Schaff and Henry Wace (Grand Rapids, MI: Eerdmans, 1983), 8:163.3.

[92] "Quod vestra charitas debitam sedi apostolicae reverentiam tribuit, fillii honoratissimi, vobis ipsis quoque maximo sane honori est." Damasus, "Epistolae," in PL, ed. J. P. Migne, vol. 13 (Paris: J.-P. Migne, 1840), col. 370.

[93] The patristic exegesis of the Rock of Matt 16:18 is almost unanimous in presenting Christ as the Rock upon which the church was built and Peter as the apostle who had primacy over all other apostles. The traditional understanding that Peter and Paul were the founders of the church of Rome and that they and many others died as martyrs in Rome led some to see the church of Rome as a stronghold for doctrine and faith. These things led Roman bishops after Damasus to claim more and more supremacy for Rome as the Apostolic See. For information see the following sources describing Augustine's exegesis of Matt 16:28: Augustine, The Teacher. The Free Choice of the Will. Grace and Free Will, vol. 59 (Washington, DC: Catholic University of America Press, 1968); Augustine, The Works of Saint Augustine: A Translation for the 21st Century, trans. Edmund Hill and John E. Rotelle, vol. 3.1 (Brooklyn, NY: New City Press, 1990), 195, 197, 269, 282-283; idem, The Works of Saint Augustine: A Translation for the 21st Century, trans. Edmund Hill and John E. Rotelle, vol. 3.3 (Brooklyn, NY: New City Press, 1991), 117-119, 311-313, 426; idem The Works of Saint Augustine: A Translation for the 21st Century, trans. Edmund Hill and John E. Rotelle, vol. 3.4 (Brooklyn, NY: New City Press, 1992), 21; idem, The Works of Saint Augustine: A Translation for the 21st Century, trans. Edmund Hill and John E. Rotelle, vol. 3.7 (New Rochelle: New City Press, 1993), 48, 95-96, 148-149, 289, 320-321, 327, 343; idem, The Works of Saint Augustine: A Translation for the 21st Century, trans. Edmund Hill and John E. Rotelle, vol. 3.9 (Hyde Park: New City Press, 1994), 144, 197-199, 211, 271; idem, The Works of Saint Augustine: A Translation for the 21st Century, trans. Edmund Hill and John E. Rotelle, vol. 3.10 (Hyde Park: New City Press, 1995), 193.

[94] The Roman synodal canon about the primacy of the Roman bishopric based on the prominence of the Apostle Peter was issued in response to the first council of Constantinople (381). The following text, a part of this canon, was quoted from the prologue of the Lucense Codex (from Lugo, Spain) council's manuscript of the Pseudo-Gelasin Decretum de libris recipiendis et non recipiendis. "Sancta tamen Romana Ecclesia nullis synodices

Saint Jerome calls Damasus "the chair of Peter" and writes in many letters that because of the confusion in the eastern church, the chair of Peter should be consulted.[95] He wrote in a letter to Damasus the following words that confirm this designation: "Therefore I have decided that I must consult the chair of Peter and the faith that was praised by the lips of the Apostle. . . . Following none but Christ as my primate, I am united in communion with Your Beatitude—that is, with the chair of Peter. Upon that rock I know the Church is built. . . . Whoever is not in Noe's ark will perish when the flood prevails."[96]

Even though Bishop Damasus was not pleased with the honors granted to the bishop of Constantinople at the council of Constantinople in 381, the council affirmed the primacy of the bishop of Rome, granting honor to the bishop of Constantinople only after the bishop of Rome.[97]

Bishop Siricius (384-399), Damasus' successor, furthered the theological understanding of Rome as the Apostolic See based in the authority of the Apostle Peter. He was the first to apply the term "pope" to himself and the first to issue a papal decretal[98] on disputes in the church, making papal authority equal to synodal canon;[99] he applied Paul's words that the bishop should bear "the care of all the

---

conflitutis caeteris Ecclesiis praelata est, sed Evangelica voce Domini and Salvatoris Nostri primatum obtiniut: Tu es Petrus, inquiens, super hanc petram aedificabo Ecclesiam meam." See Sacrorum Conciliorum, 8:151-158.

[95] Jerome wrote two letters to Bishop Damasus when he was in the East. In these letters he seeks guidance on which of the three claimants of the patriarchal see of Antioch Viatalis, St. Meletius, and Paulinus he should communicate with. See José de Sigüenza and Mariana Monteiro, The Life of Saint Jerome, the Great Doctor of the Church, in Six Books (London: Sands, 1907), 198.

[96] Jerome, The Letters of St. Jerome, trans. Thomas Comerford Lawler (New York: Newman Press, 1963), 70, 71.

[97] Sacrorum Conciliorum, 573; Walter Ullmann, Gelasius I. (492-496): Das Papsttum an Der Wende Der Spätantike Zum Mittelalter (Stuttgart: Hiersemann, 1981), 21, 22.

[98] "A letter containing a papal ruling, more specifically one relating to matters of canonical discipline, and most precisely a papal rescript in response to an appeal." Charles Duggan, "Decretals," New Catholic Encyclopedia, ed. Editorial Staff of the Catholic University of America (New York: McGraw-Hill, 1967), 707.

[99] There is some contention over whether the Canones Synodi Romanorum ad Gallos episcopos frequently attributed to Damasus is the first papal decretal. Detlev Jasper sees in Siricius's rescript the first indisputable papal decretal. He states that the reasoning of Caspar and Wojtowytsch that the lack of decretals from Damasus is due to chance "is not satisfactory, since other important documents from Damasus' pontificate which do survive, such as his Tomus fidei (ed. Turner, EOMIA 1.281ff.) or the Explanatio fidei (ed. Ibid., 155ff.) are widely distributed, cf. Maassen, Geschichte § 274.2 and 5." Detlev Jasper and Horst Fuhrmann, Papal Letters in the Early Middle Ages, History of Medieval Canon Law (Washington, DC: Catholic University of America Press, 2001), 11. For further studies, see: Erich Ludwig Eduard Caspar, Geschichte Des Papsttums Von Den Anfängen Bis Zur Höhe Der Weltherrschaft (Tübingen: J.C.B. Mohr, 1930), 247-255; Myron Wojtowytsch, Papsttum Und Konzile Von Den Anfängen Bis Zu Leo I. (440-461): Studien Zur Entstehung Der Überordnung Des Papstes Über Konzile (Stuttgart: A. Hiersemann, 1981), 431.

churches"[100] to Rome and presented Rome as the head and all other churches as the body.[101] He also argued that the validity of the episcopal office and the apostolic succession were derived from Peter its founder.[102] Detlev Jasper argues that Pope Siricius's papal letters (decretals) shifted from Rome's epistolary style, characterized by a brotherly pastoral style, to a commanding style used in imperial rescripts.[103]

Pope Innocent I (402-416) introduced the concept of "primacy of jurisdiction," which supported the idea of papal supremacy. His claims to papal supremacy before the sack of Rome by the Goths were not authoritarian, as they were after this event. At the beginning of his reign, he acted more as a judge in a court of appeal. In his response to the letters of Gallican bishops Victricius of Rouen and Exsuperius of Toulouse, he stated that his claim to authority was based on the synod's decision (Sardica), not on the apostolic succession.[104] Even in the case of John Chrysostom, he did not order restitution (even though he favored Chrysostom's cause), but said that the issue should be settled in a council.[105]

On the other hand, after the sack of Rome, his claims became stronger, basing his supremacy in Peter and the apostolic succession.[106] Commenting on the weakening of Roman institutions at the time of Innocent I, William E. Beet writes, "Amid the wreck of old institutions the Christian Church alone stood firm; her Bishop became, in consequence, the foremost citizen of Rome, in the person of whom, if at all, her imperial traditions must henceforth find expression."[107] In the Pelagian controversy, Innocent I praised the African bishops who had appealed to papal authority to suppress the Pelagian heresy and asserted his ecclesiastical supremacy, affirming that the

---

[100] 2 Cor 11:28.

[101] Siricius, "Epistulae et Decreta," in PL, ed. J. P. Migne, vol. 13 (Paris: J.-P. Migne, 1845), col. 1133, 1138, 1164, 1146. See Bettenson and Maunder, 90.

[102] "Dilectissimis fratribus et coepiscopis per Africam Siricius. Diuersa quamuis cum in unum plurimi fraters conuenissemus ad sancti apostolic Petri reliquias, per quem et apostolatus et episcopates in Christo coepit exordium, placueritque propter emergentes plurimas causas, quae in aliquantis non errant causae sed criminal, de cetero sollicitudo esset unicuique in ecclesiam curam huiusmodi habere, sicuti apostolus praedicat Paulus talem Deo ecclesiam exhibendam, non habentem maculam aut rugam, ne per alicuius morbidae ouis afflatum conscientia nostra contaminate uideretur. Siricius, "Incipit Consilium Thelense Super Tractoriam Sancti Sirici Episcopi Urbus Romae Per Africam," in Concilia Africae, A. 345-A. 525, ed. Charles Munier (Turnholti: Brepols, 1974), 59.

[103] Jasper and Fuhrmann, 18-19.

[104] See Innocent I, "Epistolae et Decreta," in PL, ed. J. P. Migne, vol. 20 (Paris: J.-P. Migne, 1845), col. 474, 495-502, 505, 511; Sozomen, 2:415-417.

[105] John Chrysostom was banned from Constantinople by the influence of Eudoxia, wife of emperor Arcadius. Innocent I asked for his restitution as bishop of Constantinople but did not demand it. See: Wendy Mayer and Pauline Allen, John Chrysostom (London: Routledge, 2000), 3-16.

[106] See Innocent I, "Epistola et Decreta," cols. 547-551.

[107] William Ernest Beet, The Rise of the Papacy: A.D. 385-461, 1st ed. (London: C. H. Kelly, 1910), 39.

bishops of the east had taken the right decision in consulting him before promulgating the canons of the councils. He said that "nothing which was done even in the most remote and distant provinces should be taken as finally settled unless it came to the notice of this See, that any just pronouncement might be confirmed by all the authority of this See, and that the other churches might from thence gather what they should teach."[108] In the East, he also extended his claim of supremacy in letters to Bishop Alexander of Antioch and Bishop John of Jerusalem.[109]

During his reign, the influence of the church in political life was great, and this was manifested in the selection of clergy headed by Innocent as diplomatic agents in the Gothic crisis. Even the barbarians had a special consideration for the church. In the sack of Rome by Alaric, the church was the only institution spared by the Goths pillaging the city.[110] As Beet says,

> Thus did the sack of Rome, while it sent a thrill of awe throughout the length and breadth of the empire, serve to reveal, under the most impressive circumstances, the elements of real stability and unconquerableness possessed by the Christian Church in general and that of Rome in particular. The Bishop of the stricken city, now without a rival in real power and public estimation in the widowed and dishonoured Queen of the World, rightly enjoyed the largest share in what was really a victory wrested out of defeat. . . . The Bishop of Rome was saved by Alaric from becoming a mere court chaplain and the nominee or victim of some dark palace intrigue, as his brother the bishop of Constantinople was too often destined to become.[111]

Bishop Zosimus (417-18), Innocent I's successor, also affirmed the supremacy of the papacy in his letter to African bishops telling them to reinstate Coelestius and Pelagius. He declared his authority as "the authority of the Apostolic See, to which the decrees of the Fathers have, in honour of St Peter, sanctioned a peculiar reverence."[112]

The conflict between African bishops and Bishop Zosimus of Rome extended to the reign of Pope Boniface I (418-22). The bishops of Africa complained to Boniface I that in the Nicaean canons they could not find any register of the supposed authority claimed by Pope Zosimus to overrule the synod's decision regarding excommunication.

---

[108] Innocent I, 583; quoted in Bettenson and Maunder, 88.

[109] See Innocent I, 547-551, 600-602.

[110] Augustine boasts about that in his defense of Christianity. See Augustine, The City of God, 7-10.

[111] Beet, 40-41.

[112] Zosimus, "Epistolae II: Ad Epistolae Africanus," in PL, ed. J. P. Migne, vol. 20 (Paris: J.-P. Migne, 1845), col. 649. In this letter Zosimus quoted two canons of the council of Sardica as part of the Nicaea to justify his authority. The bishops of Africa, in a synod at Carthage in January 418, resolved to follow the decision of Pope Innocent I and appealed again to Zosimus for reconsideration, reminding him that they could not find such canons in the Nicaea council. Zosimus did not answer them, but condemned Pelagius in Epistola Tractaria.

Boniface I did not acknowledge any Roman "mistake" and answered that "it was never lawful to discuss again anything that had once been decided by the Apostolic See."[113]

Pope Celestine I (422-32) claimed universal authority for his office as the successor of Peter in his letters to Perigenes of Corinth and other bishops concerning his ecclesiastical supremacy over the eastern Illyricum see.[114]

At the time of Celestine I's reign, other appeals were sent to Rome. He not only upheld his ecclesiastical supremacy, but as Augustine said, he used magisterial and military power to accomplish the sentences of the Apostolic See.[115] Also, the African bishops complained in a letter to Celestine about the errors in the Roman copy of the council of Nicaea, but Celestine also never admitted the Roman "mistake."[116]

Celestine was consulted regarding the Nestorian heresy. He issued a letter in favor of Cyril of Alexandria and condemned Nestorius. The issue was resolved in the council of Ephesus (431) and the decision of Pope Celestine was confirmed by the council. The emperor deposed Nestorian and sent him to exile in Egypt. The importance of the event is that it was the "opening of a new chapter in the dogmatic action of the popes. For the first time a pope had undertaken to determine, by his sentence, the orthodox position in respect of a doctrine which was a matter of controversy."[117] Celestine gave strict orders to his legates to "carry out what has formerly been decided by us, . . . and watch over the authority of the Apostolic See."[118]

Most historians consider Leo I (440-461) to be one of the greatest pontiffs of Rome and the builder of the papacy.[119] Through his writings and practice, he fully adopted the idea of primacy of jurisdiction.

In his theology, Leo formulated papal authority by claiming that all the other apostles received the apostolic authority not directly from Christ, but through Peter;[120] that all

---

[113] Boniface I, "Epistolae et Decreta," in PL, ed. J. P. Migne, vol. 20 (Paris: J.-P. Migne, 1845), col. 776.

[114] Celestine I, "Vita Operaque," in PL, ed. J. P. Migne, vol. 50 (Paris: J.-P. Migne, 1845), col. 427-429.

[115] Augustine, "Epistolae," in PL, ed. J. P. Migne, vol. 33 (Paris: J.-P. Migne, 1845), col. 955-956. Socrates says that he "extended itself beyond the limits of ecclesiastical jurisdiction, and degenerated into its present state of secular domination." Socrates, 2:158.

[116] According to Edward Denny, several popes down to Gregory the Great maintained these two canons in the Nicaean creed. Edward Denny, Papalism. A Treatise on the Claims of the Papacy as Set Forth in the Encyclical Satis Cognitum (London: Rivingtons, 1912), 105-112.

[117] Beet, 129.

[118] Acta Conciliorum Et Epistolae Decretales, Ac Constitutiones Summorum Pontificum, ed. Jean Hardouin, Philippe Labbe, and Gabriel Cossart (Parisiis: Ex Typographia Regia, 1714), 1:1347,1467; Celestine I, 503, 511-512.

[119] See, for example, Beet, 161; Hector Burn-Murdoch, The Development of the Papacy (London: Faber and Faber, 1954), 229; Robert B. Eno, The Rise of the Papacy (Wilmington, DE: M. Glazier, 1990), 102; Philip Hughes, A History of the Church, rev. ed. 1948, 3 vols. (London: Sheed & Ward, 1960), 2:68.

[120] Pope Leo I, "Epistolae," in PL, ed. J. P. Migne, vol. 54 (Paris: J.-P. Migne, 1845), col. 628-636.

other churches should recognize that *orderly* manner in a spirit of *love* came from Peter in Peter's see;[121] that his decrees were based on Peter's authority, because "he is not only the president of this see but also the primate of all bishops";[122] and that the Roman See was appointed by God to preside over all others.[123] As Beet said, for him, "Peter was directly appointed by Christ as Prince of the Universal Church, the primate to whose authority all bishops must defer. As for Rome, she is a holy and elect people, a priestly and royal city, which Peter's chair has raised to be the first city in the world."[124]

Leo's claim of primacy of jurisdiction was reinforced when Emperor Valentinian issued a law in 445 proclaiming the authority of the bishop of Rome as the law for all under his jurisdiction: "We decree, by a perpetual edict, that nothing shall be attempted by the Gallican bishops, or by those of any other province, contrary to the ancient custom, without the authority of the venerable pope of the Eternal City. But whatsoever the authority of the Apostolic See has enacted, or shall enact, let that be held as law for all."[125]

In the Euthician controversy, Leo acted boldly to uphold his ecclesiastical supremacy. He condemned the Ephesian council of 449 where his *Tome* was disregarded, confronted the emperor's confirmation of the acts of the council, and asked for the convocation of a new council to be held in Italy.[126] Even though Emperor Theodosius ignored Leo's request, in this controversy Leo assumed the role of convening a council to settle theological matters, which was traditionally assigned to emperors after Constantine. This controversy also fortified the position of the Roman See, since the main sees of the East—Constantinople, Antioch, and Alexandria—were divided and sought in Rome the proper court of appeal on theological issues.[127]

Leo's rejection of the council of Ephesus set the stage for papal power over the Episcopal College, addressed in the *Encyclical of Pope Leo XIII on the Unity of the Church,* which declared that it was "the office of the Roman Pontiffs to ratify or to

---

[121] Pope Leo I, "Sermones in Praecupuis Totius Anni Festivitatibus Ad Romanam Plebem Habiti," in PL, ed. J. P. Migne, vol. 54 (Paris: J.-P. Migne, 1845), col. 144.

[122] Ibid., col. 146-147. The Encyclopedia Britannica asserts that Leo assumed the title of pontifex maximus, or chief priest. However, it does not give the source for this information. From the sources available to this search, Leo calls himself the "primate of all bishops," as quoted above. See "Papacy," Encyclopedia Britannica [Encyclopedia On-line], http://www.britannica.com/EBchecked/topic/441722/papacy (accessed August 05, 2008).

[123] Pope Leo I, "Epistolae," col. 1047.

[124] Beet, 171. See also Pope Leo I, "Sermones in Praecupuis Totius Anni Festivitatibus Ad Romanam Plebem Habiti," col. 146-147, 150-154, 309, 351, 395, 423, 430.

[125] Pope Leo I, "Epistolae," col. 636.

[126] Ibid., col. 829, 892.

[127] Trevor Jalland, The Life and Times of St. Leo the Great (London: Society for Promoting Christian Knowledge, 1941), 242.

reject the decrees of Councils."[128] At the council of Chalcedon (451), Pope Leo I worked to ratify the definition of faith previously expressed in his *Tome*.[129]

Leo expanded his influence in the political sphere. In 442, Leo was sent by the senate and imperial authorities as an ambassador to negotiate with Attila the Hun. His diplomatic work saved Rome from being attacked and sacked. Three years later, negotiating with the Vandals, he did not avoid the sack of Rome, but prevented the burning of the city. Besides diplomacy with barbarian leaders, Leo performed other political and civil duties in Italy. In his letter to Emperor Marcian (450-457), he implies that his absence from Rome could threaten the public peace, saying that temporal necessities would not allow him to leave Rome.[130]

Popes Hilarus (461-468), Simplicius (468-483), and Felix III (483-492) upheld the supremacy of the Roman See in their writings, following the theological arguments laid down by their predecessors.[131] It is important to mention that even though Pope Hilarus affirmed that all decrees of the Roman See should be strictly observed, he recognized that the authority bestowed upon him derived from imperial legislation. He said, "It has been decreed by law of the Christian princes that whatever the high-priest of the Apostolic See has deliberately appointed for the Churches and their rulers, for the peace of all the Lord's priests and the observance of discipline, is to be reverently received and strictly observed. . . . Nothing fixed by decree both ecclesiastical and regal can ever be uprooted."[132]

At the time of Pope Simplicius, the raising of barbarian rulership in Italy and the end of the western imperial power affected not only the political but also the ecclesiastical life of the empire. East and West took different routes in both political and ecclesiastical policies. Chadwick comments on this:

> The immigration of the Germanic tribes transformed the empire and in the West substituted several small barbarian kingdoms—which Augustine thought a much more satisfactory form of organization for government than the huge unwieldy Ro-

---

[128] Pope Leo XIII, "Encyclical Satis Cognitum of Leo XIII," http://www.vatican.va/holy_father/leo_xiii/encyclicals/documents/hf_l-xiii_enc_29061896_satis-cognitum_en.html (accessed August 05, 2008).

[129] With the exception of the 28th canon rejected by Leo, which positions Constantinople as the overseer of the east in the same way Rome was for the West, all the other canons are in accord with Leo's Tome. According to Leo, the 28th canon of Chalcedon conflicts with the sixth canon of Nicaea. See Burn-Murdoch, 249-254; Pope Leo I, "Epistolae," col. 991-1009.

[130] Pope Leo I, "Epistolae," col. 930-931.

[131] Sacrorum Conciliorum, Nova et Amplissima Collectio, 8:1138; Felix III, "Epistolae," in PL, ed. J. P. Migne, vol. 58 (Paris: J.-P. Migne, 1862), col. 972; Hilarus, "Epistolae," in PL, ed. J. P. Migne, vol. 58 (Paris: J.-P. Migne, 1862), col. 15, 30-31; Simplicius, "Epistolae," in PL, ed. J. P. Migne, vol. 58 (Paris: J.-P. Migne, 1845), col. 40.

[132] Hilarus, "Epistolae," col. 30-31, quoted in Burn-Murdoch, 255.

man Empire. The Christians did not think the barbarians fell outside the kingdom of God. But incorporation in the *ecclesia catholica* was also integration into a society respectful of Roman law. As civil authority declined under the hammer blows of barbarian invasion, bishops emerged as the defenders of their flock and so of their cities. Bishops, Augustine once remarked, are becoming *principes super omnem terram,* in an international Church which embodied unity and universality through the episcopate that transcended all frontiers whether ethnic or imperial.[133]

For the Greek East, the linchpin of order and the embodiment of unity and universality were seen in the emperor at Constantinople, and that ideal is already present in Themistius's pages in the 370s. In the Latin West, the stronger sense of reserve toward government interference in the independence of the church left the path open for the authority of the Roman See, which was enhanced further as barbarian invasion and the dangers of travel made episcopal synods harder to hold. The Eusebian and Constantinian dream of a universal society acknowledging a single law and one authority came to be realized in the western church in a manner distinct from that of the East.[134]

The strong leadership role the emperor took in the East in order to establish ecclesiastical order and theological unity clashed with the sovereign jurisdiction claimed by the papacy. Popes Felix III (483-492), Gelasius I (492-96), Anastasius II (496-498), and Symmachus (498-514) could not impose their theological and ecclesiastical demands on eastern emperors.[135] Even though bishops of the East accepted the council of Chalcedon, the issue of sovereign jurisdiction caused a split between East and West for 35 years.

Bishops of Rome, in their turn, enlarged and strengthened their understanding of the papacy's supremacy of jurisdiction. In his correspondence with the emperor during the Acacian schism,[136] Pope Felix III stated that the emperor "is son and not ruler of the church." He also said that in religious matters the emperor had to learn and not to teach, and his power was derived from God for public administration.[137]

Pope Gelasius I further explored this topic, bringing forth the theory of the two swords. In a letter to Emperor Anastasius, he conveyed a dualist structure of power as spiritual and temporal, the former headed by the pope and the latter by the emperor.

---

[133] Chadwick, The Early Church, 41, 42.

[134] Ibid.

[135] A classical example of that is Felix III's letter to Emperor Zeno commanding him to submit to the authority of the church of Rome in humble obedience. See Felix III, col. 934-944.

[136] The Acacian Schism was a break in communion between the Churches of Constantinople and Rome after the Council of Chalcedon, in regard to the publication of the Emperor Zeno's formula of consensus on the Monophysist controversy, the Henoticon.

[137] Ibid., col. 1077.

As a member of the church, the emperor should humbly be subordinated to the authority of the church in ecclesiastical and theological matters, as the clergy was to the emperor in civil matters. Both powers had received their authority from God, and as any faithful member of the church submitted to all priests, more obedience should be shown to the pope as the head of the see appointed by God to be over all others.[138]

Scholars have debated how far Gelasius went in claiming supremacy of the church over the empire.[139] In his two treatises on the subject, Gelasius did not claim secular supremacy of the church over the emperor, but he clearly pointed out that the church was above the state due the nature of its responsibility—the salvation of the souls of men—and stated that the emperor "is the church's son, not sovereign."[140] He did not deny that secular powers also worked for the salvation of souls, but he affirmed that the church was God's representative on earth for spiritual matters, guided by him, the vicar of the Apostolic See.[141] Gelasius also expanded Pope Julius I's views on the validity of ecumenical councils, asserting that the only valid ecumenical councils were those recognized as such by the papacy.[142]

Until Justinian's recognition of the bishop of Rome as the head of the Catholic Christian church, popes asserted the supremacy of the Roman See over all other sees, but did not bring new insights to the table.[143]

---

[138] Gelasius, "Epistolae et Decreta," in PL, ed. J. P. Migne, vol. 59 (Paris: J.-P. Migne, 1862), col. 42.

[139] One of the points of discussion is Gelasius's distinction between the imperial potestas and ecclesiastical auctoritas. For the Romans, the executive power was the potesta and the legislative and moral power was the auctoritas. Auctoritas would have a higher prestige than potesta, but potesta would hold the power to execute the laws. Some authors, such as Stein, do not see this distinction of Gelasius's as important for his theory of power, dismissing his use of these words as only a rhetorical antithesis. Others, like Dvornik, see a clear purpose in the pope's words to remind the emperor of the rights exclusive to the priests. See Caspar, 65, 753; Dvornik, 2:804-809; Trevor Jalland, The Church and the Papacy; an Historical Study, Being Eight Lectures Delivered before the University of Oxford, in the Year 1942, on the Foundation of the Rev. John Bampton, Canon of Salisbury (London: Morehouse-Gorham, 1949), 326-329; Ernest Stein, review of Geschichte des Papsttums von den Anfängen bis zur Höhe der Weltherrschaft, by Erich Ludwig Eduard Caspar, The Catholic Historical Review 21 (1935): 129; Ernest Stein and Jean-Rémy Palanque, Histoire Du Bas-Empire (Amsterdam: A. M. Hakkert, 1968), 112-114; Ullmann.

[140] "Filius est non praesul ecclesiae." Gelasius, 95. Gelasius's treatises mentioned above are his Epistulae VIII and XV. Gelasius, 41-47, 90-99.

[141] He was the first to take the title "Vicar of the Apostolic See." Gelasius, 41.

[142] Gelasius, "Decretalis De Recipiendis Et Non Recipiendis Libris. Epistolae 42," in Epistolae Romanorum Pontificum Genuinae Et Quae Ad Eos Scriptae Sunt: Tomus 1. A S. Hilaro Usque Ad Pelagium II, ed. Andreas Thiel (Hildesheim; New York: Olms, 1974), 456. He recognized as ecumenical councils only the councils of Nicaea (324), Constantinople (381), Ephesus (431), and Chalcedon (451). Julius had affirmed that it was not the convocation of a council by the emperor which validated a council as universal, but the confirmation of the whole church in the promulgation of the council's canons. Athanasius, 4:113.

[143] For more information on popes' statements on Roman supremacy after Gelasius, see Dvornik, 2:809-814.

SUMMARY

Catholic clerics after Constantine gladly accepted the imperial recognition of Catholic Christianity as the official religion of the empire, but did not give blind support to emperors' religious decisions. Many bishops, like Athanasius and Ambrosius, confronted emperors' religious and ecclesiastical decisions that they considered to be against the Catholic definition of faith. Also, such bishops as Augustine and Gelasius proposed distinct roles for emperors and bishops in a Christian empire. In his book *The City of God*, Augustine explained his idea of two kingdoms, heavenly and earthly; he believed the heavenly kingdom that had already started with the Christian church was superior to the state, since the state was a simple secular power used by God to maintain peace and order until Jesus' final implementation of his heavenly kingdom on earth. Augustine's ideas fostered the debate over ecclesiastical or political supremacy that came after him.

During the fourth century and the beginning of the sixth century, the bishops of Rome developed a theory of primacy of jurisdiction over other sees and tried to exert ecclesiastical leadership in the eastern and western parts of the Roman Empire. Also, they set up theories on the proper roles for emperors and bishops in the Roman Empire. By the end of the sixth century, the jurisdiction of the bishops of Rome was recognized in the West, but they were facing problems reaching the same recognition with eastern emperors and clergy. However, throughout this period, the authority of the bishop of Rome was acknowledged in the solving of ecclesiastical and theological issues by both eastern and western clerics.

THE CHURCH IN THE WEST AND THE BARBARIAN INVASION

Historians have produced scholarly works trying to unfold the impact of the barbarian invasion on the western part of the Roman Empire.[144] In most cases, these works present contradictory information. Some call it a catastrophic devastation of Roman society and a near-death of civilization; others say there was continuity of Roman civilization, but with a Germanic flavor.[145] No matter what approach is adopted by historians, the barbarian invasion was an integral part of the establish-

---

[144] For maps on the Roman Empire and Barbarian invasions see appendix B.

[145] For a more catastrophic approach to barbarian invasion, see: Gibbon and Youngman; Halsall; Ward-Perkins. For a more positive view of the barbarian invasion, see: Heather; Henri Pirenne, From the End of the Roman World in the West to the Beginnings of the Western States, A History of Europe (Garden City, NY: Doubleday, 1958); Lynn Townsend White, The Transformation of the Roman World: Gibbon's Problem after Two Centuries (Berkeley: University of California Press, 1966).

ment of the new European civilization. It provoked political, economic, and social changes in the Roman Empire. The western part of the empire, where the political and military structures were changed by the barbarians, was more affected than the eastern part. However, much of the Roman style survived the barbarian invasion and became part of the political system established by the barbarians in the West.

The economic and social changes brought by the barbarian invasion in the West modified the structure of the state, and city life lost its strength as the unifying force of the late Roman Empire. As Wickham said, "The empire had always been a cellular structure based on cities and their territories."[146] The ideological structure of the state based in Roman traditions, and a senatorial aristocracy centralized in the cities, had been the dominant force in the political, religious, and social life of the empire. "Its money underpinned every cultural activity—learning, religion, rhetoric, the leisure necessary for the *belles-lettres* culture of Ausonius and his circle, the gigantic buildings of the late empire."[147] The constant incursions of barbarians into Roman territory exhausted the resources of the army and the capacity of the land to raise enough taxes to pay for more soldiers. The *pax Romana* was broken, and the aristocracy, who had already incorporated most of the small landowners under their patronage, were more willing to be under a barbarian government (which had the army and taxes based more on landowning) than a Roman one. At the same time, many senators had left the cities and retired to their rural proper-ties.[148] These factors weakened the cities and their political power. In many cities, the administration was left in the hands of the bishops, who were already caring for the poor. Bishops, as administrators of great properties, could provide political and economic support for the population in times of need.

Italy, and especially Rome, as the center of civilization, was greatly affected by the barbarian invasion. The first incursions of barbarian tribes in Italy brought devastation and weakened the political and military composition of the country. In the fifth century, a barbarian army and barbarian kings replaced the Roman army and emperors. Even before the fall of the western Roman Empire, the Roman army in Italy was in the hands of such Germanic generals as Aetius and Ricimar.[149]

In this section, the barbarian invasion will be analyzed, focusing on its impact and the changes it produced in the state, economy, society, and church, mainly in Italy.[150]

---

[146] Wickham, 14.

[147] Ibid.

[148] For more information see Alföldy, 210-220; Bertrand Lançon, Rome in Late Antiquity: A.D. 313-604, trans. Antonia Nevill (New York: Routledge, 2001), 45-56; Wickham.

[149] Ernest Barker, "Italy and the West, 410-476," in The Cambridge Medieval History, ed. J. B. Bury et al. (New York: Macmillan, 1926), 409-425.

[150] As stated above, the focus of this section is the impact of the barbarian invasion on Italy, not the cause of

THE POLITICAL SITUATION IN ITALY AFTER THE BARBARIAN INVASIONS

The civil administration of the Roman Empire was affected by the barbarian invasion, mainly in the West. Since Diocletian's political reforms, the empire had been divided into four great administrative sections: Gauls, Italy, Illyricum, and the East. Bury explains the territorial extension and political administration of these sections as follows:

> The Gauls, which included Britain, Gaul, Spain, and the north-western corner of Africa, and Italy, which included Africa, Italy, the provinces between the Alps and the Danube, and the north-western portion of the Illyrian peninsula, were subject to the Emperor who resided in Italy. Illyricum, the smallest of the Prefectures, which comprised the provinces of Dacia, Macedonia, and Greece, and the East, which embraced Thrace in the north and Egypt in the south, as well as all the Asiatic territory, were subject to the Emperor who resided at Constantinople. Thus each of the Praetorian Prefects had authority over a region which is now occupied by several modern States. The Prefecture of the Gauls was composed of four Dioceses: Britain, Gaul, Viennensis (Southern Gaul), and Spain; Italy of three: Africa, the Italies, and Illyricum; Illyricum of two: Dacia and Macedonia; the East of five: Thrace, Asiana, Pontus, Oriens, and Egypt. Each of the diocesan governors had the title of Vicarius, except in the cases of Oriens where he was designated *Comes Orientis*, and of Egypt where his title was *Praefectus Augustalis*. It is easy to distinguish the Prefecture of the Oriens from the Diocese of Oriens (Syria and Palestine); but more care is required not to confound the Diocese with the Prefecture of Illyricum.[151]

By the end of the sixth century, the political administration in two of these sections was completely changed. The Gauls and Italy were under barbarian control. Since

---

the fall of the western part of the Roman Empire, of which the barbarian invasion was a part. For information on the fall of the Roman Empire, see: Arthur Edward Romilly Boak, Manpower Shortage and the Fall of the Roman Empire in the West, The Jerome Lectures (Ann Arbor: University of Michigan Press, 1955); Mortimer Chambers, The Fall of Rome: Can It Be Explained? (New York: Holt, Rinehart and Winston, 1970); Michael Grant, The Fall of the Roman Empire (New York: Collier Books, 1990); Richard Mansfield Haywood, The Myth of Rome's Fall (New York: Crowell, 1958); Solomon Katz, The Decline of Rome and the Rise of Mediaeval Europe (Ithaca, NY: Cornell University Press, 1968); Ferdinand Lot, The End of the Ancient World and the Beginnings of the Middle Ages (London: Routledge & Kegan Paul, 1966); Ramsay MacMullen, Corruption and the Decline of Rome (New Haven: Yale University Press, 1988); Klavs Randsborg, The First Millennium A.D. in Europe and the Mediterranean: An Archaeological Essay (New York: Cambridge University Press, 1991); R. W. Southern, The Making of the Middle Ages (New Haven: Yale University Press, 1953); Lynn Townsend White.

[151] J. B. Bury, History of the Later Roman Empire: From the Death of Theodosius I to the Death of Justinian (New York: Dover, 1958), 1:26.

Valentinian II, emperors in Ravenna had not been able to face the barbarian incursions effectively. The barbarian plundering in the fourth century had caused towns to shrink, mainly in the frontiers of the western part of the Roman Empire. By the time of Honorius, the empire had lost part of its territory to the settlements of the Visigoths in Gaul and the Vandals and Sueves in Spain during 415–423.[152] Britain was lost to the empire when Honorius recognized that he was financially incapable of defending their cities and sent a rescript abrogating the *Lex Julia* in Britain and transferring the responsibility for city defense to individual citizens.[153] Years later, the Vandals took control of Africa (A.D. 435), the Heruli of Italy (A.D. 476), and the Burgundians (A.D. 444) and Franks (A.D. 481) of Gaul.[154] The Gauls and Italy's prefectures were divided into independent political entities headed by Germanic kings, with a mixed population of Romans and barbarians, which still in many ways felt as if they were part of the Roman Empire. But the *pax Romana* was broken, the political unity of the empire in the West was destroyed, and its urban administrative institutions were shattered.[155]

Even before the political disintegration of the western part of empire, the number of barbarian soldiers and officials had increased in the Roman army. Barbarians were admitted to Roman territory as federates (*foederati*) and charged with the defense of the Roman frontiers.[156] At the end of the fourth century and throughout the fifth century, the security of the empire became more and more dependent on Germanic *federates*. Roman generals such as Stilicho, Aetius, and Ricimer had more barbarians than Romans in their armies. Even these three famous Roman generals, who were considered Roman citizens and exerted political power as well as military power, were of Germanic descent.[157]

---

[152] Ibid., 1:202-208; Antonio Santosuosso, Storming the Heavens: Soldiers, Emperors, and Civilians in the Roman Empire (Boulder, CO: Westview Press, 2004), 187.

[153] Zosimus, New History, 4.10.

[154] Bury, 1:248, 254, 346, 405; Santosuosso, 187.

[155] For maps on the political situation of the Roman Empire after the barbarian invasions see appendix B.

[156] Foederati is a Latin term used to describe tribes who lived in Roman territory but who were not granted Roman citizenship. They were expected to contribute to the power of Rome by providing military force in exchange for being able to live in Roman territory. This was the case with the Franks in northern Gaul. For more information about foederati, see George Long, "Foederatae Civitates," A Dictionary of Greek and Roman Antiquities, ed. William Smith (London: John Murray, 1875), 542-543. For more information about the Franks, see chapter 4.

[157] For information about Stilicho, see Bury, 106-173; Claudius Claudianus, Claudian, ed. Maurice Platnauer, 2 vols., The Loeb Classical Library (London; New York: W. Heinemann; G.P. Putnam's Sons, 1922), 1:364-392, 2:3-70; Gibbon and Youngman, 398-416. For information about Aetius, see Arnold Hugh Martin Jones, John Robert Martindale, and J. Morris, The Prosopography of the Later Roman Empire A.D. 395-527, vol. 2 (Cambridge: Cambridge University Press, 1980), 21-29. For information about Ricimer, see Guy Lacam, Ricimer: Un Barbare Au Service De Rome (Paris: Atelier National Reproduction des Theses, Universite Lille III, 1986).

The disruption of the political unity of the empire affected the official hierarchy of the aristocracy. The Roman administration was a network of honorary offices appointed by the emperor, which provided much more status in society than financial gain. However, under barbarian leadership, some of these positions were eliminated. The office of praetorian prefect and other higher offices had historically not been filled by natives of a province, but under barbarian rulership, these positions were occupied by provincial landowners.[158] The cities had decreased in size and economic power, and the political influence of senatorial aristocrats in most places became restricted to their provincial domains.[159] The settler barbarians retained the military power and the Roman civilians the public administration.

Especially in Italy, the old institutions that had shaped the life of the empire for centuries suffered transformation under the barbarian threat. After Maxentius (306-307), Rome ceased to be the seat of the Roman emperors, but it retained its prestige as the political center of the empire and the house of the senate.[160] The senate was the keeper of Roman tradition with its structured urban administration and traditional magistracy. After Constantine, senators were not in control of the army as they had been in the time of the republic, but the main body of the political administration of the empire was drawn from the senatorial rank.[161] However, the barbarian invasion in the West limited the political influence of the senate, and it became an institution governing little more than the city of Rome. Some senators, as landowners, left the political life of Rome and retired to their provincial domains to escape the barbarian military threat.[162] Others who had property in different

---

[158] This law seems to have its origins with Marcus Aurelius; however, it was not always observed. See CJ 1.41.1, 9.29.3.

[159] There were differences of rank within the senatorial order. Salzman points out that not all members of the senatorial aristocracy were members of the senate or participated in the civic senatorial career. She also states that emperors appointed military leaders from non-senatorial families to administrative positions previously reserved for the senatorial aristocracy. Some of these leaders were incorporated into the senatorial aristocracy, but were not part of the senate of either Rome or Constantinople. For more information, see Salzman, 19-68.

[160] There were differences of rank within the senatorial order. Salzman points out that not all members of the senatorial aristocracy were members of the senate or participated in the civic senatorial career. She also states that emperors appointed military leaders from non-senatorial families to administrative positions previously reserved for the senatorial aristocracy. Some of these leaders were incorporated into the senatorial aristocracy, but were not part of the senate of either Rome or Constantinople. For more information, see Salzman, 19-68.

[161] Between A.D. 312 and 326, Constantine promoted equestrian families to the senatorial order, and from then on, provincial governors, praetorian prefects, and council members were recruited from the senatorial order. Bertrand Lançon, Rome in Late Antiquity: A.D. 313-604, trans. Antonia Nevill (New York: Routledge, 2001), 48.

[162] Katherine Fischer Drew, The Barbarian Invasions: Catalyst of a New Order (New York: Holt, Rinehart, and Winston, 1970), 20; Jones, Later Roman Empire, 1:552-554, 2:1059-1060.

regions of the empire such as North Africa and Gaul had their wealth diminished when their land came under barbarian control. This exodus of aristocratic families from Rome and other cities to rural properties, and the disappearance of some imperial offices after the fall of the western empire in 476, isolated many senators from the political life of the empire, impoverished the political administrations of cities, and reduced the political power of the senate in Rome.[163]

The fragmentation of the western part of the Roman Empire into political units headed by barbarian kings did not alienate the aristocracy from the eastern part of the empire or eliminate the senate. Some of the barbarian leaders sought political recognition from eastern emperors, and senators in the West still had properties in the eastern part of the empire. The barbarian kings saw themselves as inside the empire, not outside it.[164] They preserved most of the Roman political and financial administration and continued to appoint members of the senate "to traditional offices and to hold the western consulship even under the Ostrogoths."[165] Especially in the time of Theodoric, "the Italians and the Goths together, in fact, were seen as living in a thriving Roman Empire, the *res publica*. The valor of the Goths was to contribute military security to a mutually beneficial relationship."[166]

Even though some administrative positions had disappeared under barbarian leadership, most of the urban administration was still in the hands of senatorial families. Theodoric had Cassiodorus, a senator, as his prime minister, and acted as a Roman benefactor by sponsoring games at the circus, rebuilding the aqueducts in Rome, and sponsoring other embellishments in Ravenna and

---

[163] Chris Wickham, Framing the Early Middle Ages: Europe and the Mediterranean 400-800 (Oxford; New York: Oxford University Press, 2005), 84-89.

[164] Some of the new barbarian leaders were granted their power by Roman emperors. The western Roman emperor Honorius commissioned the Visigoth king Ataulf to settle, restore order in, and govern the Iberian Peninsula in return for defending it. See R. C. Blockley, "Barbarians Settlement in the West, 411-418," in The Cambridge Ancient History. Empire and Successors, A.D. 425-600 Vol. 14, Late Antiquity (Cambridge: Cambridge University Press, 2000), 130-131. Theodoric invaded Italy and defeated Odoacer, encouraged by Emperor Zeno. See Richards, 65. Even Odoacer, after his victory over Romulus Augustus, sent the insignia of emperor to the eastern emperor and declared himself Patrician of the West under the empire. John Higginson Cabot and Charles Merivale, Italy, Including Merivale's Rome, 44 B.C.-476 A.D. (Philadelphia: J.D. Morris, 1906), 155. During the conquest of the Vandals in North Africa and the Gothic war, senators sought refuge in Constantinople from the oppression of the wars. See Fouracre, The New Cambridge Medieval History, 131.

[165] Averil Cameron, The Mediterranean World in Late Antiquity, A.D. 395-600, Routledge History of the Ancient World (London; New York: Routledge, 1993), 41.

[166] Patrick Amory, People and Identity in Ostrogothic Italy, 489-554, Cambridge Studies in Medieval Life and Thought (Cambridge; New York: Cambridge University Press, 2003), 45. Cassiodorus in the Variae supports the idea of Theodoric's kingdom as the res publica, and even as the western part of the empire. Cassiodorus, Variae, ed. T. Mommsen, MGH Scr. AA, vol. 12 (Berlin: Weidmannos, 1894), 1.20.1, 3.18.2, 1.1.4, 2.1.4.

Rome.[167] The reigns of Odoacer and Theodoric marked a revival of power for the senate. Unlike Constantine and the emperors after him, these barbarian leaders sought legitimacy for their claims of sovereignty in the senate and not in the church. However, the end of the Gothic kingdom also marked the end of the political power of the senate of Rome. It did not disappear, but became a puppet in the hands of the papacy.[168]

After the barbarian invasions, the political, social, and economic changes in the western part of the Roman Empire also affected the relationship between church and state. Even though most of the barbarian invaders were Arian Christians, they did not adopt a policy of persecuting Roman Catholics.[169] John Meyendorff even says that in Italy under Gothic dominion, the barbarians "were not only tolerant of the Catholic Church, but also interested in using it as a diplomatic link with the empire in Constantinople."[170] Sharing the same Christian background became a link between the barbarians and Romans. As Pirenne says, "the Germans, like the Romans, were Christians; and while they entered the

---

[167] Pirenne, 16.

[168] More information about the end of the senate's political power will be provided in the section "The Political Implications of the Gothic War."

[169] Excepting the Franks, who had converted from paganism or Arianism to Catholicism at the time of Clovis and favored Catholicism over Arianism, the other Arian barbarians—the Vandals, Visigoths, Burgundians, and Ostrogoths—in general adopted policies of religious tolerance. Some cases of intolerance have been reported, like the policy of the Visigoth king Euric, who according to Sidonius Apollinaris forbade the consecration of bishops in the vacancy sees; the missionary work of Ajax among the Suevis; Odoacer's intervention in the succession of Pope Simplicius; Theodoric's intervention in the election of Symanchus as pope; and Victor Vitensis's account of Vandal persecution of Catholics in North Africa. More information about the Franks will be given in the next chapter. For more information on other barbarian kings, see Alberto Ferreiro, "Braga and Tours: Some Observations on Gregory's De Virtutibus Sancti Martini," Journal of Early Christian Studies 3 (1995): 195-210; Ralph W. Mathisen, "Barbarian Bishops and the Churches 'in Barbaricis Gentibus' During Late Antiquity," Speculum 72, no. 3 (1997): 664-697; Sidonius Apollinaris, The Letters of Sidonius: Translated with Introduction and Notes, trans. Ormonde Maddock Dalton (Oxford: Clarendon Press, 1915), 7.6; Stein and Palanque, Bas-Empire, 2:134-189; E. A. Thompson, "The Conversion of the Spanish Suevi to Catholicism," in Visigothic Spain: New Approaches, ed. Edward James (Oxford; New York: Clarendon Press; Oxford University Press, 1980); idem, "Barbarian Collaborators and Christians," in Romans and Barbarians: The Decline of the Western Empire (Madison: University of Wisconsin Press, 1982); idem, "Spain and Britain," in Romans and Barbarians: The Decline of the Western Empire (Madison: University of Wisconsin Press, 1982); Victor Vitensis, "Historia Pesecutionis Africanae Provinciae, Temporibus Geiserici Et Hunirici Regum Wandalorum," in PL, ed. J. P. Migne, vol. 58 (Paris: J.-P. Migne, 1845); Herwig Wolfram, History of the Goths (Berkeley: University of California Press, 1988), 175-181.

[170] John Meyendorff, Imperial Unity and Christian Divisions: The Church, 450-680 A.D. (Crestwood, NY: St. Vladimir's Seminary Press, 1989), 158.

empire as conquerors, they submitted themselves to the church, which, under her authority, merged the Germans with the Romans."[171]

Under barbarian control, the Catholic Church, headed by the bishop of Rome, kept her ecclesiastical unity in the West and sought to exert her leadership in the East. In Italy, especially in the reign of Theodoric, the Catholic Church experienced a time of almost complete independence from the state. Theodoric did not interfere in church affairs as Roman emperors had done in the East.[172] This independence strengthened the church's political power and position of ecclesiastical supremacy in both the East and West, and contributed to its independence from eastern imperial interference in ecclesiastical affairs. Meyendorff argues that the bishops of Rome, as the heads of the Catholic Church, "being themselves convinced that they were performing an essentially apostolic mission towards the Western Barbarians, while also standing up, whenever necessary, against imperial abuse and heresy coming from the East, they boldly began to describe their own function in the universal Church as one of *government*."[173]

The Catholic Church also increased in political power due to the bishops' incorporation of city administrative functions into their pastoral care functions. In many places, church leadership filled the political vacuum of the cities. Wallacy-Hadrill argues that even though many biographical studies on the Gallo-Roman bishops' reactions to the barbarian invasion constitute propaganda, there is no reason "to doubt the substantial accuracy of their common contention—that the Catholic bishops rose to the occasion, adversity being the Christian's proper element. They led where the civil authorities failed."[174] Bishops gained political power and adopted a more active civic role, participating in the organization of the defense of the cities against barbarian invasion.[175] The bishops of Rome, in particular, became in the West "the symbol of *Romanitas*. They were in constant touch with Constantinople, and acted as transmitters of imperial laws and decrees."[176] P. J. Heather also says that without the collapse of the Roman Empire the papacy would not have risen "as an overarching authority for the whole western Christendom."[177]

---

[171] Pirenne, 11.

[172] John Moorhead, Theodoric in Italy (Oxford; New York: Clarendon Press; Oxford University Press, 1992), 114-139.

[173] Meyendorff, 129.

[174] Wallace-Hadrill, The Barbarian West, 400-1000, 29.

[175] Claire Sotinel, "Emperors and Popes in the Sixth Century," in The Cambridge Companion to the Age of Justinian, ed. Michael Maas (Cambridge; New York: Cambridge University Press, 2005), 268.

[176] Meyendorff, 128.

[177] P. J. Heather, The Fall of the Roman Empire: A New History of Rome and the Barbarians (Oxford; New York: Oxford University Press, 2007), 442.

The weakening of the political institutions of the empire also strengthened the church's political influence. Under the barbarians, cultural development decreased outside ecclesiastical circles, and gradually the duties of formal education and government moved more and more into the hands of the church because the clergy were more qualified to manage higher administration; some of the best minds of the aristocracy, such as Sidonius, Cassiodorus, and others, had been incorporated unto the clergy.[178] Also, the production of literary work at the end of the fifth and beginning of the sixth century was centered on defense of the Catholic faith, even among the aristocracy, who had now converted to Christianity.[179] Sotinel argues that the independence enjoyed by Italian bishops under the Ostrogoths promoted a new balance of power "between the clergy and the senatorial aristocracy, partly because of disagreements about how to deal with the emperor."[180] And since the influence of paganism had declined among senators, Wallace-Hadrill affirms that "just as the senators had once striven in the face of the imperial opposition to preserve their religious rites as the dearest part of their heritage, so now they stood for the full Catholic tradition of St. Augustine, or at least for as much of it as they could assimilate."[181] As a result, the Catholic Church became the center of the senatorial life, the most solid institution in society; it promoted the continuity of Roman traditions and kept alive the ideology of the Christian Roman Empire, and senators considered the pope as one of themselves.[182]

SUMMARY

The barbarian invasions of Roman territory affected the relationship between church and state. It brought economic and social changes in city life, breaking the ideological structure of the state based in Roman traditions and a senatorial aristocracy centralized in the cities. It exhausted the resources of the army, diminishing it and breaking the *Pax Romana*. The administration of the cities changed as most of the aristocracy retired to their rural properties and the bishops assumed new political and economic positions in support of the population.

In Italy, there was a revival of the senate with the barbarian administration, but the Catholic Church enjoyed ecclesiastical freedom, replaced the senate as preserver of Roman tradition, became the most solid institution in society and

---

[178] Ibid., 440-442.

[179] Wallace-Hadrill, The Barbarian West, 400-1000, 35.

[180] Sotinel, "Emperors and Popes," 269.

[181] Wallace-Hadrill, The Barbarian West, 400-1000, 35.

[182] Ibid., 34-37.

the center of senatorial life, and kept alive the ideology of the Christian Roman Empire. The bishops of Rome began to describe their functions as extending beyond the religious realm, into that of governance.

Justinian's Policies on Church-State Relationships

The issue of church and state relationships at the time of Justinian could not be covered by a simple ecclesiastical policy. Justinian's religious understanding and relationships with clergy developed and differed according to necessity and occasion.[183] The responses from bishops were also different depending on the issue and ecclesiastical, regional, and ideological interest.[184] The emperor and the bishops agreed that they shared responsibilities in the establishment of orthodoxy, but they diverged on the authoritative role of each part.[185] Since Constantine, the empire had been portrayed by such Christian theologians as Eusebius as a divine providence destined to uphold

---

[183] See for example Justinian's submission to the demands of Popes John and Agapetus, and his demands of Pope Vigilius.

[184] Vigilius gladly promoted Justinian's rulership in Italy at the beginning of his reign, but had a hard time opposing the emperor afterwards in the controversy of the three chapters. The bishops of Africa who praised Justinian for the deliverance of the Vandals and the reestablishment of Catholic orthodoxy in North Africa later compared him to Ozias, the impious king who usurped priestly functions. See Facundus, "Pro Defensione Trium Capitulorum Concilii Chalcedoniensis Libri XII," in PL, ed. J. P. Migne, vol. 67 (Paris: J.-P. Migne, 1862), col. 838.

[185] M. V. Anastos argues that Justinian was an independent thinker on religious matters and imposed his own understanding of Catholic orthodoxy through legislation. See Milton V. Anastos, "Justinian's Despotic Control over the Church as Illustrated by His Edicts on the Theopaschite Formula and His Letter to Pope John II in 553," in Melanges Georges Ostrogorsky (Belgrade: Institut d'Etudes Byzantines, 1963), 1-11. Moorhead states that for Justinian, the establishment of Catholic orthodoxy was a matter of state, but he regarded the Roman see as the defenders of Catholic orthodoxy and sought their support; see John Moorhead, Justinian, The Medieval World (London; New York: Longman, 1994), 116-143. Sotinel argues that Justinian recognized the authority of the pope and sought his approval for his theological formulas, but at the same he did not need Rome to teach him what Catholic orthodoxy was. See Claire Sotinel, "Autorité Pontificale Et Pouvoir Impérial Sous Le Règne De Justinien: Le Pape Vigile," Mélanges de l'école française de Rome 104, no. 1 (1992): 439-469; Sotinel, "Emperors and Popes," 272-273. Meyendorff sees Justinian as a despotic ruler and states that his policies on church and state relationships can be better defined as Caesaropapism. John Meyendorff, "Justinian, the Empire and the Church," in Dumbarton Oaks Papers (Washington, DC: Dumbarton Oaks Center for Byzantine Studies, 1968), 43-60; idem, Imperial Unity and Christian Divisions: The Church, 450-680 A.D., 211-221. Dvornik presents Justinian working in close connection with the church, and explains his despotic policies during the Three Chapters Controversy as a momentary error that he regretted afterwards (815-823). David M. Olster argues that Justinian's actions, sometimes despotic and other times in submission to the church clergy, were related to his political diplomacy to achieve unity of the empire. He also argues that in the letters of Justinian and Pope John in the Justinian Code, there are two distinctive proposals about the authoritative role on the establishment of Catholic orthodoxy. David M. Olster, "Justinian, Imperial Rhetoric, and the Church," Byzantinoslavica 50 (1989): 165-176.

Christianity and spread the gospel message.[186] However, the different responses of emperors to the Arian heresy in the fourth century and to the Nestorian and Monophysite crises of the fifth and sixth centuries led bishops and church writers to ascribe different roles to the king and clergy on ecclesiastical matters.[187]

Justinian's policies were not introduced in a vacuum. He inherited more than 30 years of conflict between East and West on the definition of Catholic orthodoxy. This breach between East and West, along with the western church's independence from political interference during the rulership of Theodoric, strengthened the bishop of Rome's position as the defender of Catholic orthodoxy and his political and ecclesiastical supremacy. Justinian recognized the importance of the bishop of Rome in his *renovatio*—the unity of the church and the eastern and western part of the empire. Justinian's ecclesiastical policy promoting theological unity between East and West and his military enterprises in the West created new horizons for church and state relations after him.

The analysis of Justinian's policies regarding church and state relationships in this section will have a brief introduction discussing the background of the theological controversies inherited by Justinian. Then, Justinian's relationships with bishops and the implications of the barbarian invasions and Gothic war for the church and state relationships in the West will be analyzed. Next, the Justinian code, the ecclesiastical changes he promoted, and his ideology of governance in a Christian empire will be discussed. Finally, a summary and conclusion will be given.

THEOLOGICAL CONTROVERSIES INHERITED BY JUSTINIAN - CHALCEDON AND THE ACACIAN SCHISM

Justin I (518-527), Justinian's uncle, came to power having to deal with more than thirty years of religious controversy between East and West. He was Catholic Orthodox and sought the union of the church, abiding by the terms of the bishop of Rome, Pope Hormisdas.[188] After the council of Chalcedon, eastern bishops challenged the western doctrinal understanding of orthodoxy headed by the bishop of

---

[186] See Eusebius's theories of kingship above.

[187] See the section "The Development of the Ecclesiastical Supremacy of the Bishop of Rome" above and the section "The Corpus Juris Civilis" below.

[188] According to Procopius, Justinian was the leading force behind the reunion of the eastern and western churches. He presents Justin in the Secret History as a donkey obedient to Justinian, who was pulling the reins. However, as Moorhead points out, Justinian was not so powerful as Procopius pointed out; otherwise, he would not have made so many innovations and political changes when he assumed the empire. See Moorhead, Justinian, 21; Procopius, The Secret History of Procopius (New York: Covici Friede, 1934), 8.3.

Rome on the two natures of Christ. They supported a Monophysite or Miaphysite theory of Christ's nature.[189] Acacius, bishop of Constantinople, proposed to Emperor Zeno a formula of unity for the eastern churches known as Henotikon, condemning Eutyches and Nestorius while accepting the twelve chapters of Cyril of Alexandria; these chapters described Jesus Christ as the only begotten Son of God and as one and not two natures, but did not mention the teaching of Chalcedon, with no explicit reference to the two natures.[190] The formula was implemented in the East but not in the West. Pope Simplicius and his successor Felix III condemned the Henotikon; Felix III sent letters to Acacius and Emperor Zeno demanding the acceptance of the Chalcedonian formula and summoning Acacius to answer before Rome. Since his demands were not accepted, Felix III excommunicated Acacius and deposed him as bishop, but the emperor in the East did not follow suit.[191] Acacius did not accept the charges made by Felix III and erased his name from the diptychs, and most of the bishops of the East kept communion with him; as a result, a schism between the eastern and western church began.

In spite of the schism, communications between Rome and Constantinople were not interrupted. Popes Felix III, Gelasius, Symmachus, and Hormisdas maintained open communication with emperors in the East, finding "new ways to legitimate their disagreement with the religious policy of the East and to uphold the authority of the Roman See. They never discussed religious matters with the emperor, but they never broke communion, either."[192] Some attempts were made to heal the schism, but emperors in the East would not take orders from the bishop of Rome.[193] Since

---

[189] Monophysitism is the Christological position which holds that Christ has only one nature: the fusion of the divine and the human. Miaphysitism is the Christological position which holds that in Jesus Christ divinity and humanity are united in one nature without separation, confusion, or alteration. See Roberta C. Bondi, Three Monophysite Christologies: Severus of Antioch, Philoxenus of Mabbug and Jacob of Sarug, Oxford Theological Monographs (London: Oxford University Press, 1976); W. H. C. Frend, The Rise of the Monophysite Movement: Chapters in the History of the Church in the Fifth and Sixth Centuries (Cambridge: University Press, 1972); Mebratu Kiros Gebru, "Miaphysite Christology, a Study of the Ethiopian Tewahedo Christological Tradition on the Nature of Christ" (M.A. thesis, University of Toronto, 200); Iain R. Torrance, Christology after Chalcedon: Severus of Antioch and Sergius the Monophysite (Norwich: Canterbury Press, 1988); Philip John Wood, "Foundation Myths in Late Antique Syria and Mesopotamia: The Emergence of Miaphysite Political Thought, 400-600 A.D." (Ph.D. diss., University of Oxford, 2007).

[190] Evagrius, The Ecclesiastical History of Evagrius Scholasticus, trans. Michael Whitby, Translated Texts for Historians, vol. 33 (Liverpool: Liverpool University Press, 2000), 127-151.

[191] Felix III, 1, 2, 6, 9 10, 12; Simplicius, 18, 19.

[192] Sotinel, "Emperors and Popes," 269.

[193] See, for example, the attempts of Popes Hormisdas and Anastasius to put an end to the schism: Paul Robinson Coleman-Norton, Roman State & Christian Church: A Collection of Legal Documents to A.D. 535 (London: S.P.C.K., 1966), no. 964.

the bishops of Rome were not under imperial control after Odoacer's conquest of Rome in 476 and enjoyed ecclesiastical freedom under barbarian reign, they were independent in religious matters and sought ecclesiastical supremacy. Wallace-Hadrill argues that at the end of the fourth century and throughout the fifth century, the bishop of Rome had already slowly achieved political predominance in Rome and ecclesiastical primacy over other sees.[194]

This ecclesiastical independency and primacy of jurisdiction can be seen at the end of the schism at the time of Emperor Justin I. Pope Hormisdas did not answer the emperor's demands and set the conditions for the reconciliation in his *libellus*; they were accepted by John, bishop of Constantinople, under pressure from the emperor.[195] Sotinel says that "the union was made according to Rome's agenda: not only Acacius' name, but the names of all Constantinopolitan bishops after him, as well as the names of emperors Zeno and Anastasius, were to be erased from the diptychs."[196] It was the end of the schism and the triumph of Rome and Chalcedon.

The victory of the pope was not complete. Justin and Justinian did not force all the eastern bishops to sign the *libellus*, but asked for more time for the East to conform to the claims of the Roman See, which never happened. Justin and Justinian, like other Roman emperors before them, had a vision of religion as part of the state, not as an independent institution.[197] For them, the union of East and West in 518 represented the integration of the church of Rome "in the imperial system, in which the secular and sacred spheres coincided,"[198] and not the full recognition of the authority of Rome over ecclesiastical matters by the emperor, as seen by the pope. Constantine's conversion had incorporated Christianity under the umbrella of the state, and he made it part of the legislation of the empire. Dvornik points out that after Constantine, council decisions became a way of proposing definitions of faith that would be incorporated into imperial legislation.[199] In the Theodosian Code, a whole section was dedicated to regulating the new religion and determining what it meant to be a Catholic orthodox faith.

Meyendorff comments that the ecumenical councils of Nicaea, Constantinople, Ephesus, and Chalcedon were summoned by emperors to describe the true Catholic

---

[194] Wallace-Hadrill, The Barbarian West, 400-1000, 30-31.

[195] Dioscorus to Hormisdas, "Letter 167," in Collectio Avellana, ed. Karl Ziwsa, CSEL, vol. 35 (Vindobonae: F. Tempsky, 1893), 2:618-621; Hormisdas, "Exemplum Libelli," in Collectio Avellana, ed. Karl Ziwsa, CSEL, vol. 35 (Vindobonae: F. Tempsky, 1893), 2:521.

[196] Diptych was a double catalogue, containing in one part the names of living, and in the other of deceased, ecclesiastics and benefactors of the church. Sotinel, "Emperors and Popes," 271.

[197] See chapter 2 above.

[198] Sotinel, "Emperors and Popes," 271.

[199] Francis Dvornik, "Emperors, Popes, and General Councils," in Dumbarton Oaks Papers (Washington, DC: Dumbarton Oaks Center for Byzantine Studies, 1951), 1-23.

Orthodox definition of faith, but did not achieve consensus among the most dominant ecclesiastical sees: Rome, Constantinople, Antioch, Alexandria, and Jerusalem. Rome would head the West, accepting most of the canons of the four councils except canon 3 of Constantinople, which would be repeated in 28 of Chalcedon. In the East, different parties would challenge the definitions of those four councils, and at the end of the fifth century and beginning of the sixth only Nicaea would have general acceptance among all sees.[200] This formula that Constantine introduced of drawing definitions of faith through councils and incorporating them into the Roman legal system would be a problem for such emperors as Zeno and Anastasius, who sought unity of faith through imperial legislation with a formula of Concordia.[201]

On the other hand, unlike paganism, Christianity did not merge into the state. Christian leaders did not reject the idea of Christianity as the official religion of the empire and gladly accepted the conversion of emperors, but they supported Christian emperors only if their religious decisions would agree with their understanding of faith. Catholic Christianity saw itself more and more as an institution independent from the state, although closely connected to it.[202]

These two hundred years during which Christianity was incorporated into the life of the state and sought to define Catholic orthodoxy through council decisions left some challenges for Justinian to face. First, he had to find a way to promote union of the empire and unity of faith. Second, he had to decide which method would be used to define Catholic orthodoxy. Third, he had to set religious policies that created harmony among the different religious factions. Finally, he had to define the status of the church and its leadership (especially the role of the pope) in relation to the state. Through his legislation and dealings with ecclesiastical leaders and religious crises, we can reach an understanding of Justinian's religious policies.

Justinian's Ecclesiastical Policies

Justinian's ecclesiastical policies continued the previous emperors' attitudes toward religious matters, but granted the emperor more control over issues that he would find crucial for the unity of the empire and the church. At the beginning of his government, he strongly promoted Catholic Christianity and issued laws against non-Christians and non-Catholic heretics.[203] His relationship with clerics fluctuated from partial

---

[200] Meyendorff, "Justinian, the Empire and the Church," 47.

[201] This was the case with the Henotikon of Emperor Zeno, which became law on matters of faith from A.D. 482 to 518 as formula of Concordia.

[202] For more information, see Meyendorff, "Justinian, the Empire and the Church," 45-49.

[203] For more information on the Justinian code, see the sections below.

tolerance of opposition to total imposition to his will, and no other emperor deposed and nominated bishops as he did.[204] He believed that proper reverence for God would bring peace and prosperity to the state and that Catholic Christianity was the means to reach it.[205] Christianity, then, was part of the state, and the state's concern should be upholding the sound doctrine and moral values that derived from it.[206]

Justinian differed from other emperors before him in that he acted as a theologian, issued laws legislating Christian doctrine, and wrote theological treatises.[207] For him, Christian values and the church canons were not restricted to the ecclesiastical milieu and Roman law; they were the foundation of any law system. Moorhead says, "While the legal code issued by Theodosius II in 438 concluded with a statement of belief, the code of Justinian opened with one."[208]

Justinian, like Constantine, worked through clergy and summoned councils to solve theological and ecclesiastical problems, but he also promulgated personal formulas of faith through imperial legislation such as Emperor Zeno's Henotikon.[209] But whether he was a sincere Christian or not, he worked from the beginning of his reign on the unity of the church and the establishment of the proper Catholic Christian faith. As a good politician, he sought compromise between the different theological positions on the nature of Christ—the adherents of the Chalcedonian Creed and the Monophysites—to reach unity in the empire, but satisfied neither.

JUSTINIAN AND THE BISHOPS OF ROME ON CHURCH-STATE RELATIONSHIPS

Justinian worked closely with bishops to promote the welfare of the state and the Catholic Church. Even under his uncle's rulership, his first move was to establish the supremacy of the bishop of Rome over all other sees, since the Roman See was the cornerstone in the defense of Chalcedon and he had sided with the

---

[204] Moorhead, Justinian, 136.

[205] In his Novel 133.5 he asks monks to pray for the state, since their closeness to God would assure prosperity for the empire.

[206] Many of the moral laws of the Justinian code reflect Christian values, as will be seen below.

[207] There are two complete works ascribed to the emperor—the Letter to the Alexandrian Monks and On the Right Faith—and two incomplete ones—the Epistle to Zoilus and the Dialogue with Paul of Nisibis. Jeffrey Lee Macdonald supports Justinian's authorship of these works and expresses the importance Justinian bestowed upon theological issues in his works. Jeffrey Lee Macdonald, "The Christological Works of Justinian" (Ph.D. diss., The Catholic University of America, 1995).

[208] Moorhead, Justinian, 119.

[209] More information below in this section.

Chalcedonian faith.[210] After the suppression of the Monophysite controversy by his uncle Justin, Justinian sought a path of conciliation with the Monophysite bishops while maintaining a close connection with the bishop of Rome. However, unlike Constantine, who sought to solve theological and ecclesiastical problems through the leadership of the church, Justinian acted more independently based on his own personal convictions, or as many have suggested, through the influence of his wife Theodora.[211] He issued many laws regarding theological and ecclesiastical issues throughout the two major theological controversies that he faced—the Theopaschite and the Three Chapters—which mark two major phases in the history of his dealings with church problems and his theological understanding.

The first phase, for the purpose of this dissertation, will cover the period from Pope Felix IV (526-530) to Pope Agapetus (527-536), and the second the reigns of Popes Silverius (536-537), Vigilius (537-555), and Pelagius I (556-561).

JUSTINIAN AND POPES FELIX IV, BONIFACE II (530-532), JOHN II (533-535), AND AGAPETUS

Justinian started his reign with a renewed interest in religious matters, but he followed the basic principles already in place from the time of his uncle Justin—the Chalcedonian definition of faith as Catholic orthodoxy and the Roman See as its defenders. In his first years, he also incorporated the Theopaschite formula into his definition of faith and saw it as a way of reconciliation with the Monophysites.

Justinian's dealings with the Theopaschite controversy started before he had taken the throne. The Theopaschite formula was proposed by a group of Chalcedonian monks in 513 with the purpose of upholding the Chalcedonian creed against Monophysite attacks, bringing forth an Christological formula drawn from Cyril of Alexandria that stated, "One of the Trinity suffered in

---

[210] See the case of the healing of the Acacian schism with Pope Hormisdas, and his later legislation on papal supremacy: CT,1.1.8 and Novel 131.

[211] See Averil Cameron, Procopius and the Sixth Century, The Transformation of the Classical Heritage, 10 (Berkeley: University of California Press, 1985), 67-83; Averil Cameron, "Religious Policy: The Three Chapters and the Fifth Oecumenical Council," in The Cambridge Ancient History. Empire and Successors, A.D. 425-600 (Cambridge: Cambridge University Press, 2000), 79-82; Leo Donald Davis, The First Seven Ecumenical Councils (325-787): Their History and Theology, Theology and Life Series, V. 21 (Collegeville, MN: Liturgical Press, 1990), 225-239; J. A. S. Evans, The Empress Theodora: Partner of Justinian (Austin: University of Texas Press, 2004), 85-97; Lynda Garland, "Byzantine Empresses: Women and Power in Byzantium, A.D. 527-1204," Routledge; Wilhelm Möller and others, History of the Christian Church (London; New York: S. Sonnenschein; Macmillian, 1892), 422-432.

the flesh."[212] At first Justinian rejected the monks' formula; then he gave his approval to it, even though Pope Hormisdas had rejected it.[213] Justinian ordered the monks to go back to Constantinople, but the pope, free from the political influence of Constantinople, acted independently and disregarded the emperor's demand, holding the monks until he had condemned their formula as heresy.[214] The procedures Justinian adopted at the beginning of the Theopaschite controversy, even though he was not yet enthroned as emperor, provide some clues about his future policies on religious matters, according to Sotinel. She argues that even though Justinian had recognized the authority of the pope and asked his authoritative opinion on the matter, he did not need the pope's opinion to know what Catholic orthodoxy was; he just "needed the authority of Rome to back his own religious policy but did not allow Rome any autonomy in religious policy."[215] However, Dvornik sees Justinian's actions as those of a man who not only recognized the authority of the bishop of Rome, but worked as a close partner of the Catholic Church.[216] These two distinct understandings of the roles of the state and the church in the religious and political life of the empire marked the first phase of the history of church and state relationships in the reign of Justinian.

Justinian's actions demonstrated the common understanding that the prosperity and unity of the empire were dependent on the approval of God or the gods, and his first measure was to fully integrate religion as part of the state.[217] A new code was prepared in which religion was set as the basis for all other legislation, and the definition of Catholic orthodoxy was set as the first article, including an attack on heresies and non-Christian religions.[218] For Justinian, he was not advocating a new definition of faith, but only fulfilling his duties as representative of God in leading the subjects of the Catholic Christian empire in the proper way of worshiping God and defending

---

[212] For more information on the Chalcedonian monks, also called the Scythian monks, see Patrick T. R. Gray, "The Legacy of Chalcedon: Christological Problems and Their Significance," in The Cambridge Companion to the Age of Justinian, ed. Michael Maas (Cambridge; New York: Cambridge University Press, 2005), 215-238.

[213] See Anastos, "Justinian's Despotic Control over the Church as Illustrated by His Edicts on the Theopaschite Formula and His Letter to Pope John II in 553," 1-11; John A. McGuckin, "The 'Theopaschite Confession' (Text and Historical Context): A Study in the Cyrilline Re-Interpretation of Chalcedon," Journal of Ecclesiastical History 35, no. 2 (1984): 239-255.

[214] Hormidas to Justinian, "Letter 236," in Collectio Avellana, ed. Karl Ziwsa, CSEL, vol. 35 (Vindobonae: F. Tempsky, 1893), 2:716-722.

[215] Sotinel, "Emperors and Popes," 273.

[216] Dvornik, 824-828.

[217] For more information, see the section "The Corpus Juris Civilis" below.

[218] For more information, see the section "The Corpus Juris Civilis" below.

the faith. His definition of faith was the same one taught by the bishops and fathers of the church and upheld in the previous ecumenical councils. He wrote:

> Since the true and unchangeable faith which the holy Catholic and Apostolic Church of God declares[,] does not admit of any innovation, we following the precepts of the holy apostles and of those who after them became renowned in the holy churches of God [and] believe it proper to make manifest to all what we think of the faith which is in us, following the tradition and consensus of opinion of the Holy Catholic and Apostolic Church of God.[219]

Other edicts with Theopaschite content and letters to bishops were incorporated into the legislation, aiming for reconciliation between Monophysites and Chalcedonians, and also to draw bishops' support for Justinian's religious policies. After Pope John's visit to Constantinople as ambassador of Theodoric in 526, the next two popes, Felix IV and Boniface, did not have much contact with the East; however, when Pope John II was pope, Justinian wrote him a letter reaffirming the supremacy of the Roman See and seeking approval of the religious formula in the constitutions of 527 and 533.[220] He also sent other letters to eastern bishops and sponsored theological debates between Monophysites and Chalcedonian bishops.[221]

The reconciliation Justinian sought had a setback with Pope Agapetus's visit to Constantinople in 536. Under the influence of Theodora, clergy from the Monophysite party were elevated to higher positions in the episcopate, such as Theodosius to the see of Alexandria and Anthimus to the see of Constantinople.[222] When he came to Constantinople, Pope Agapetus learned of the appointment of Anthimus to the patriarchal chair, and without delay, cut communion with Anthimus and ordered his deposition. The pope was received by Emperor Justinian with the same honor as Pope John in 525 and obtained from the emperor the deposition of Anthimus. He consecrated Menas as his successor. This is a "remarkable confirmation of the Roman prestige,"[223] as Meyendorff says, even though other scholars attributed Justinian's subjection to papal authority to his political ambitions in campaigning for the reconquest of the West, his search for unity between East and West, and Roman support for his theological Theopaschite formula of unity.[224]

---

[219] CJ 1.1.5.

[220] CJ 1.1.5, 6, 8.

[221] See CJ 1.1.6 and 7, and Innocent of Maroneia, "Innocentii Maronitae Epistula de Collatione Cum Severianis Habita," in ACO, ed. J. Straub and Eduard Schwartz, vol. 4.2 (Berlin: de Gruyter, 1914), 169-184.

[222] Evagrius, 4.10; Theophanes, The Chronicle of Theophanes Confessor: Byzantine and Near Eastern History: AD 284–813, trans. Cyril A. Mango and Roger Scott (Oxford: Clarendon Press, 1997), 152.

[223] Meyendorff, Imperial Unity and Christian Divisions: The Church, 450-680 A.D., 226.

[224] See Sotinel, "Emperors and Popes," 277-279.

From Pope Felix IV to Pope Agapetus, Justinian's relations with bishops were generally to get support or to impose his theological legislation. He had chosen the Chalcedonian definition of faith plus the Theopaschite formula and the Roman See as the proper representation and defenders of the Catholic orthodoxy. His relations with the pope during this phase consisted of almost full concessions to the papacy, seeking unity of the empire and the church.

JUSTINIAN AND POPES SILVERIUS, VIGILIUS, AND PELAGIUS I

Justinian's relations with popes after Agapetus were greatly related to Pope Vigilius. Justinian was fighting to recover Italy from the Ostrogoths; Silverius, who had been appointed by Theodahad, king of the Ostrogoths, did not have much contact with Justinian. Under the leadership of Belisarius at Rome, Vigilius replaced Silverius as bishop of Rome in A.D. 537. Sotinel is correct in affirming that of all the popes in the sixth century, Vigilius' biography is the most complicated.[225] Most of his acts are described in connection to the Gothic war or the Three Chapters Controversy.[226]

Vigilius was the pope's representative in Constantinople at the time of Pope Agapetus. Agapetus, as we have seen above, deposed Anthimus and ordained Menas as bishop of Constantinople. After Agapetus's death, Silverius was chosen by Theodahad as pope. Theodora, a supporter of Monophysitism, asked him to reinstate Anthimus as bishop of Constantinople. When Silverius denied her request, she offered Vigilius the papacy if he would reinstate Anthimus as bishop of Constantinople and support Theodosius and Severus.[227] Under the influence of his wife Antonina, Belisarius deposed Silverius and appointed Vigilius as pope. There are some divergences in both primary and secondary sources about the dates of the deposition of Silverius and ascendance of Vigilius to the Roman chair. According to Procopius, Silverius

---

[225] Sotinel, "Autorité Pontificale," 439.

[226] Well-known biographical accounts of Pope Vigilius or works that mention parts of his life are: LP, 58-61; Facundus, Facundi Episcopi Ecclesiae Hermianensis Opera Omnia, 519 vols., Corpus Christianorum Series Latina, vol. 90a (Turnholti: Brepols, 1974); Liberatus Carthaginensis Diaconus, "Breviarium Causae Nestorianorum Et Eutychianorum," in PL, ed. J. P. Migne, vol. 68 (Paris: J.-P. Migne, 1848); Procopius, Procopius, trans. Henry Bronson Dewing, vol. 3 (New York: Macmillan, 1914).

[227] LP, 57. Liberatus even affirmed that after Vigilius's ascension to the papacy, he wrote a letter to Anthimus, Theodosius, and Severus, promising to fulfill his agreement with Theodora and his agreement with them in the matters of faith, and asking them only to keep silent about it until he had the opportunity to accomplish what he had promised. Liberatus Carthaginensis Diaconus, 1041. Baronius and others argue that this letter is a Monophysite forgery. However, Antonio Pagi sees it as authentic and justifies Vigilius's acts, asserting that he was at this time a pseudo-pope. See Cesare Baronio and others, Annales Ecclesiastici, Denuo Excusi Et Ad Nostra Usque Tempora Perducti Ab Augustino Theiner (Barri-Ducis: L. Guerin, 1864), 532-534, 550-551; Sotinel, "Autorité Pontificale," 449-50.

was deposed in March of 537, at the beginning of the siege of Rome by the Goths.[228] Mansi points out that in the *Catalago Blanchiniano,* Vigilius was ordained on March 29, 537.[229] According to Anastasius, Pagi, and Blanchini, calculating from the number of years and days of Silverius's reign as pope in the *Liber Pontificalis,* Vigilius was ordained on November 22, 537.[230] There is also a disagreement on Silverius's death. The accepted date of his death today is December of 537.[231] However, Anastasius, Pagi, Blanchini, and others, based on the *Liber Pontificalis,* pointed out that Silverius died on June 20, 538, and only after his death would the Roman clergy recognize Vigilius as pope.[232] In spite of the conflict in the primary sources and scholars, the records of Vigilius's activities as pope in Rome start only in 538, both inside and outside of Rome.[233] This point strengthens the argument that Vigilius was recognized as pope by the church only in 538 after Silverius's death.

The other important point is that the appointment of Vigilius as pope marked the end of Ostrogothic political ideology.[234] Silverius, set up in power by the Gothic king Theodahad, was replaced by Vigilius, the real representative of the

---

[228] He does not give a specific date, but he mentions it happening before April 13, 537. Procopius, Procopius, 65-67.

[229] This is the date that contemporary scholars think to be the best one for Vigilius's ordination. See Davis, The Book of Pontiffs (Liber Pontificalis): The Ancient Biographies of the First Ninety Roman Bishops to A.D. 715, 58; Richards, 132-133; Sotinel, "Autorité Pontificale," 445-449. Besides the Catalago Blanchiniano, Duchesne mentions Rossi's reconstitution of the manuscript of the Church of St. Pancras at Rome from June of 537, in which Vigilius is mentioned as the "Blessed Pope," but as Sotinel well mentioned, even though the manuscript is lost, it was hard to affirm with certainty the reconstitution of the name of Vigilius, because it was so mutilated. See M. l'abbé Duchesne, "Vigile Et Pélage, Étude Sur L'histoire De L'église Romaine Au Milieu Du VI Siècle," Revue des Questions Histo- riques 19, no. 36 (1884): 376; Giovanni Battista de Rossi, Inscriptiones Christianae Urbis Romae Septimo Saeculo Antiquiores (Rome: Ex Officina Libraria Pontificia, 1857), 1:481-483; Sotinel, "Autorité Pontificale," 449.

[230] Silverius held the see for one year, five months, and eleven days, according to the LP. Since he was or- dained on June 8, 536, this means he was deposed on November 18, 537, and Vigilius was ordained on November 22. See Anastasius bibliothecarius, "Historia De Vitis Romanorum Pontificum," in PL, ed. J. P. Migne, vol. 128 (Paris: J.-P. Migne, 1880), col. 563, 571-573, 588-589; Baronio and others, 550-551; Davis, The Book of Pontiffs. According to Thomas Hodgkin, the return of Procopius and Antonina at the end of October makes this latter date the most suitable one for the ordination of Vigilius. Theodora interceded before Justinian to speed military help to Belisarius in exchange for the deposition of Silverius and the appointment of Vigilius as pope in Rome. The account of the LP presents Silverius before Antonina when he was deposed by Belisarius. See LP, 57; Thomas Hodgkin, Italy and Her Invaders: 535-553, 2d ed., vol. 4 (Oxford: Clarendon Press, 1896), 220.

[231] See LP, 55; Sotinel, "Autorité Pontificale," 448.

[232] Anastasius bibliothecarius, 571-575; LP, 55-56.

[233] Vigilius's first letter from March 538 was addressed to Caesarius of Arles, trying to ensure his leadership in the West and demonstrating his concerns with Arianism. See Vigilius, "Epistolae et Decreta," in PL, ed. J. P. Migne, vol. 69 (Paris: J.-P. Migne, 1845), col. 21.

[234] For more information, see Amory.

Roman law. Even though Totila regained control of Rome in 546, he was not able to control the papacy, which was outside Rome at this time. After 538, the papacy never came back under the control of the Ostrogothic kings. After the destruction of Rome by Totila in 546, the senate and all other political institutions disappeared from Rome for forty days.[235] The papacy was the only institution that outlived Totila's destruction. Vigilius also changed the papacy's policy on political matters. For the first time since the fall of the Roman emperor Romulus in 476, the pope was actively supporting the emperor's religious and military policies and had withdrawn his loyalty from the Gothic kings.[236]

After the successful resistance of Belisarius and the end of the siege of Rome in 538, the reorganization of the political administration of the city of Rome conferred political authority on the bishop of Rome, according to Alonzo T. Jones.[237] Rome was back under imperial legislation, and by 540, almost all of Italy was linked to the empire. During these years, Vigilius enjoyed political and ecclesiastical stability and did not have problems with the emperor, even though he had denied Theodora's request to reinstate Anthimus to the Constantinople see. His major problem started when Justinian requested his presence at Constantinople to support a new imperial move for the unity of the church—the condemnation of the "Three Chapters."[238]

In the Three Chapters Controversy, Justinian used his common method of dealing with ecclesiastical affairs. He issued a decree with a theological definition of faith based in the council of Chalcedon and also condemning the person and works of Theodore of Mopsuestia, some writings of Theodoret of Cyrus, and the letter of Ibas of Edessa to Maris.[239] Afterward, he wrote letters to bishops and promoted theological discussions, aiming their support to his theological formula.[240] At this

---

[235] Totila sacked and controled Rome three times between 546 and 552. Sotinel, 282.

[236] Amory, 158.

[237] Alonzo Trévier Jones, The Two Republics; or Rome and the United States of America (Battle Creek: Review and Herald, 1891), 552.

[238] The Three Chapters were the condemnation by Justinian of the person and works of Theodore of Mopsuestia, some writings of Theodoret of Cyrus, and the letter of Ibas of Edessa to Maris, in an attempt to remove the resistance of Monophysite theologians from the council of Chalcedon. For more information see: Pauline Allen, "Justin I and Justinian," in The Cambridge Ancient History, Empire and Successors, A.D. 425-600 Vol. 14, Late Antiquity (Cambridge: Cambridge University Press, 2000), 820-828; Cameron, "Religious Policy: The Three Chapters and the Fifth Oecumenical Council," 79-82; Alois Grillmeier and Theresia Hainthaler, Christ in Christian Tradition, 2 vols. (London; Louisville, KY: Mowbray; Westminster John Knox, 1995), 411-462.

[239] This edict of 544/545 is completely lost. Some of it is found in Facundus's Pro Defensione Trium Capitulorum. Facundus, "Defensione," col. 527-852.

[240] Justinian, "Adversus Nonnullos, Impium Theodorum Atque Iniqua Ejus Dogmata," in PL, ed. J. P. Migne, vol. 69 (Paris: J.-P. Migne, 1845), col. 273-328.

stage, he summoned Pope Vigilius to Constantinople, intending to have his support and that of the whole West. Justinian also adopted measures to eliminate resistance to his theological formula of unity by deposing bishops and clerics who opposed his views.[241] Then he promulgated a confession of faith and made it law, claiming it to be a true apostolic faith and always defended by the fathers and church councils.[242] However, after opposition from both East and West, he summoned an ecumenical council together with Pope Vigilius to settle the issue.[243] At the council, the Justinian confession of faith was recognized as Catholic orthodoxy, and those who refused to abide by the council's decision were afterwards removed from their sees.[244]

Justinian's religious policy did not reach its goal. The focal points of contention were still strong in both East and West. Many Monophysites did not adhere to the theological formula proposed by the council of Constantinople (553), and ecclesiastical leaders in the West were reluctant to adhere to the Three Chapters proposed by the council. The Three Chapters Controversy was also problematic to the reign of Pope Vigilius, since his decisions during the controversy—condemning, promising approval, approving, retracting, and finally approving the council's decisions—made both the emperor and ecclesiastical leaders in Africa and Europe express dissatisfaction with his attitudes.[245] His successor, Pope Pe-

---

[241] See for example the deposition of Reparatus of Carthage and Zoilus of Alexandria. Facundus, "Adversus Mocianum," in PL, ed. J. P. Migne, vol. 67 (Paris: J.-P. Migne, 1862), col. 853-868; Facundus, "Defensione," col. 527-582.

[242] Justinian, "Confessio Rectæ Fidei Adversus Tria Capitula " in PG, ed. J. P. Migne, vol. 86 (Paris: J.-P. Migne, 1857), col. 994-1095.

[243] William George Smith and John Murray, A Dictionary of Christian Biography, vol. 3 (Whitefish, MT: Kessinger Publishing, 2000), s.v. "Justinianus I."

[244] Henry Chadwick, East and West: The Making of a Rift in the Church: From Apostolic Times until the Council of Florence, Oxford History of the Christian Church (Oxford; New York: Oxford University Press, 2005), 56.

[245] Vigilius's first reaction against the emperor's edict was influenced by western bishops who were refugees at Constantinople and by Stephen, his apocrisarius—pope's representative—at Constantinople, who had cut communion with Menas, bishop of Constantinople, after he had signed Justinian's edict in 543/544 condemning the Three Chapters. These men saw in the emperor's edict condemning the Three Chapters a formal condemnation of the council of Chalcedon. After negotiations with the emperor, Vigilius submitted a Judicatum that formally condemned the Three Chapters but upheld the council of Chalcedon. His arguments in the Judicatum were challenged by many of the clerics who had accompanied him to Constantinople, who accused him of having betrayed the council of Chalcedon, and even in North Africa he was excommunicated in a council in Carthage. He then took back his Judicatum, and made arrangements with the emperor for the summoning of a council to settle the issue, but soon after, he felt betrayed by the emperor when Justinian published his confession of faith in 551 and broke communion with the emperor and Menas. Since the council was not held in Sicily as the pope requested and only a small number of clerics from the West were present, Vigilius refused to attend the council and submitted a Constitution after the council had met six times already, signed by sixteen bishops and three clerics and condemning

lagius I, also had many troubles because of the Three Chapters Controversy and Vigilius's ways of dealing with the issue. However, he established his political and ecclesiastical supremacy largely without the emperor's support.[246] Even though the papacy continued to be linked to the empire centuries after Justinian, more and more popes would seek independence of action from the empire.[247]

Although Vigilius is seen by most of the historians as a weak pope and a puppet in the hands of Justinian due to his dealings with the Three Chapters Controversy, he can be considered a great politician for the church. Justinian was struggling to heal the religious division between Chalcedonians and Monophysites, and according to Meyendorff, he thought that if he had the support of the pope, he would have the support of the whole western church. Meyendorff says, "Justinian could not fail to realize that the further progress of his policies depended upon one person—Pope Vigilius—and that the enhancing of papal authority . . . could be effective again: the pope's role was now to 'deliver' Western compliance with the condemnation of the

---

parts of the works of Theodore of Mapsuestia, but not him personally. His Constitution was not read at the council, and the council proposed to delete his name from the diptychs and separate him from communion with the church. After the council, Vigilius changed his mind again and submitted a new Judicatum that accepted the decisions of the council of Constantinople. See Carmelo Capizzi, Giustiniano I Tra Politica E Religione, Accademia Angelica Costantiniana Di Lettere Arti E Scienze. Saggi, Studi, Testi; 1 (Soveria Mannelli: Rubbettino, 1994), 68-74; Carmelo Capizzi, "La Politica Religiosa Ed Ecclesiastica Di Giustiniano," in Christian East. Rome: Pontificio Ist Orientale (1996), 55-84; "Concilium Universale Constantinopolitanum Sub Iustiniano Habitum," in ACO, ed. J. Straub and Eduard Schwartz, vol. 4.2 (Berlin: W. de Gruyter, 1914), 11-12; "Gesta Concilii," ACO, ed. J. Straub and Eduard Schwartz, vol. 1 (Berlin: W. de Gruyter, 1914), 3-234; "Sententia Dogmatica," in ACO, ed. J. Straub and Eduard Schwartz, vol. 4.1 (Berlin: W. de Gruyter, 1914), 239-240; Horst Fuhrmann, "Justinians Edictum De Recta Fide (551) Bei Pseudoisidor," in Melanges G Fransen (Rome: Libreria Ateneo Salesiano, 1976), 217-223; Meyendorff, "Justinian, the Empire and the Church"; idem, Imperial Unity and Christian Divisions: The Church, 450-680 A.D, 237-245; Vincenzo Poggi, "La Controverse Des Trois Chapitres," Istina 43, no. 1 (1998): 99-110; Sotinel, "Autorité Pontificale," 439-463; idem, "Emperors and Popes," 280-284; Stein and Palanque, Bas-Empire, 386-417; Pope Vigilius, "Constitutum De Tribus Capitulis," in Collectio Avellana, ed. Karl Ziwsa, CSEL, vol. 35 (Vindobonae: F. Tempsky, 1893), 1:230-234; idem, "Epistula ad Rusticum et Sebastianum," in ACO, ed. J. Straub and Eduard Schwartz (Berlin: W. de Gruyter, 1914), 236-239; idem, "Ex Tribus Capitulos," in ACO, ed. J. Straub and Eduard Schwartz, vol. 4.2 (Berlin: W. de Gruyter, 1914), 245-248; idem, "Vigilii Epistula I ad Eutychium," in ACO, ed. J. Straub and Eduard Schwartz, vol. 4.1 (Berlin: W. de Gruyter, 1914), 198-199; idem, "Vigilii Epistula II Ad Eutychium," in ACO, ed. J. Straub and Eduard Schwartz, vol. 4.1 (Berlin: W. de Gruyter, 1914), 138-168; idem"Vigilii Iuramenti Testificatio," in ACO, ed. J. Straub and Eduard Schwartz, vol. 4.1 (Berlin: W. de Gruyter, 1914), 188-194; idem, "Epistola IV," in Sacrorum Conciliorum, Nova et Amplissima Collectio, ed. Philippe Labbe and Giovan Domenico Mansi, vol. 9 (Graz: Akademische Druck- u. Verlagsanstalt, 1960), 35-38.

[246] See Sotinel, "Emperors and Popes," 284-286.

[247] For more information, see chapter 6 on Charlemagne.

'Three Chapters.'"[248] Vigilius then was summoned to Constantinople, and due to the siege of Rome by Totila, he was escorted by Justinian's guard out of Rome and received with honors at Constantinople.[249] His situation was very delicate. Clerics from Europe and Africa were against Justinian's proposal, and the emperor was counting on Vigilius to bring them to his side. Even though most of these opposing clerics did not know Greek or understand the content of the documents anathematized by Justinian, they saw in it the negation of Chalcedon and expected the pope to uphold Chalcedon and condemn the emperor's edict. In these circumstances, Vigilius's actions demonstrated that he was more a politician than a religious leader. He adopted measures that could please both sides in his *Judicatum*—the emperor condemning the Three Chapters and the clerics upholding the council of Chalcedon. Playing this political game, sometimes favoring the emperor's position, sometimes pleasing the clerics, he was able to survive politically in Constantinople—since he could not return to Rome, which was under Totila's control—and at the end, he sided with the emperor, receiving from him political supremacy and the right to appoint political leadership in Italy.[250]

The problems that Vigilius faced throughout the Gothic war and before Justinian's intervention and intransigence on matters of faith led the church to reevaluate the relations between empire and church. Amory comments that "Vigilius's pontificate was a 'fundamental caesura' in church history—inseparably the caesura of Justinian's momentous reign. This time of synthesis marked the beginning of the consolidation of the notion that the pope led a distinctively western and Latin Christian community."[251] Beginning in 538, Vigilius's pontificate then marks the consummation of the legal recognition of papal primacy on ecclesiastical matters and the beginning of the notion of papal political independence and leadership in the West out of the Constantinian, Eusebian, and Justinian views of the priestly function of the king.[252]

---

[248] Amory, 238.

[249] The Liber Pontificalis and other western historians from the time of Vigilius say the he was taken by force from Rome and led to Constantinople as almost a prisoner. The Marcellinus Chronicle says that Vigilius went to Constantinople as the result of an invitation from Justinian. See LP, 59; Marcellinus, The Chronicle of Marcellinus: A Translation and Commentary: (with a Reproduction of Mommsen's Edition of the Text), trans. Brian Croke, Byzantina Australiensia, 7 (Sydney: Australian Association for Byzantine Studies, 1995), 546.1.

[250] In A.D. 554, Justinian issued a Pragmatic Sanction that bestowed the control of weights and measures upon the papacy and the senate and gave the Catholic Church rights in the new government in Rome. Corpus Iuris Civilis, Paul Krueger et al. (Berlin: Weidmannos, 1895), 799-803.

[251] Amory, 233.

[252] For the Constantinian and Eusebian views on the priestly function of the king, see chapter 2. For Justinian's view, see the below section "The Corpus Juris Civilis."

The political implications of the Gothic war for church-state relationships in Italy

Justinian's military expansion affected political, economic, social, and religious life in Italy. Under Gothic leadership, Italy had peace and prosperity for almost a half-century. Even though Ravenna was still the capital of the Gothic kingdom, the Roman senate ascended to political power in the Gothic court. The Arian barbarians did not interfere in the Roman church's religious and ecclesiastical decisions. The bishops of Rome enjoyed independence from political interference on religious matters and deepened their theory of religious supremacy. The Catholic leadership in Rome and the emperor in the East still had open correspondence, but there was no political and religious interference from the emperor in the West.

Justinian's ascendance to the throne began new trends for the political and religious life of Italy. Carole M. Cusack comments, "When Justinian became Emperor in the East in 527 he had many plans. He was concerned to retrieve the Western Empire from the Barbarians, and by doing so to eliminate the Arian heresy."[253] Justinian did retrieve part of the western empire, but instead of returning the old glory to the Italian peninsula, he weakened it economically, socially, and politically.

The Gothic war had weakened the political institutions in Italy and the old aristocratic families, which basically disappeared with the Lombard invasion. "The arrival of the Lombards therefore caused the total replacement of the dominant social classes. What was left of the Roman senatorial aristocracy—after the disasters of the Gothic war (535-53)—was eliminated and the greater majority of the lands passed into the hands of the invaders."[254]

During the Gothic war, many senators had sought asylum in Constantinople because some of them still had properties in the eastern part of the empire; others were killed in the war,[255] which devastated Rome economically and impoverished the traditional senatorial Roman families.

After the siege of Rome, when the eastern empire took total control of the city, the senate did not disappear immediately, but it lost its power and significance in the political life of the city and empire.[256] Lançon argues, "The long Gothic war,

---

[253] Carole M. Cusack, The Rise of Christianity in Northern Europe, 300-1000, Cassell Religious Studies (London; New York: Cassell, 1999), 50.

[254] Philippe Levillain, The Papacy: An Encyclopedia (New York: Routledge, 2002), 957.

[255] Vitiagis killed almost all the senators he was holding hostage in Ravenna after he could not come to terms with Belisarius.

[256] Gregorovius even argues that the senate's last assertion of life was the letter sent to Emperor Justinian praying for peace at the beginning of the Gothic war. After that, the senate lost its importance as a political force in Italy. Ferdinand Gregorovius and Annie Hamilton, History of the City of Rome in the Middle Ages (London:

which devastated Italy for nearly thirty years in the mid-sixth century, delivered some hard blows to the Senate, leading to its inevitable decline."[257] However, the war fostered the setting up of the papacy as the political power of Rome. The Roman church was the only institution that outlived the war.[258]

After the end of the first siege of Rome in 538, the city was sacked by the Goths, headed by Totila, who left no one living there for about three months. During this time, the papacy was the only political institution that survived and was not under Gothic control. Pope Vigilius was in Constantinople at this time. And even after the city had been repopulated, the senate no longer represented the political power of Rome; it was under the authority of the papacy. As Lançon says, "The vast senatorial order of the fourth and fifth centuries had become a small assembly dominated by the figure of the pope."[259]

Another important change brought about by the Gothic war was the change in people's allegiance to the Catholic Church and local communities. The years of prosperity and peace under Gothic rulership gave new identity to the inhabitants of the Italian peninsula. Amory explains that Theodoric created an ideology of mutual coexistence of Romans and Goths, with specific roles for each part for the prosperity of the Roman Empire—Romans leading the civil government and Goths defending the Roman state.[260] However, the instability brought by the war led the Roman population to move from one to the other side according to moment and convenience. In this pool of instability, the Catholic Church became the only pole of unity for the Italian population. The written and monumental works of Vigilius and other members of the clergy, as Amory points out, show a loyalty of the people more to the local Rome and the function of the pope in the *Roma Eternae* than to the eastern Roman Empire.[261]

THE CORPUS JURIS CIVILIS

The *Corpus Juris Civilis* (Body of Civil Law) is very important in understanding Justinian's position on religious and ecclesiastical affairs. It was a collection of works of Roman law from the classical times to the time of Justinian, composed of three parts: the *Digesta*, the *Institutions*, and the *Codex*. Later, the compilation of Justinian's legislation called *Novellas*[262] was added as a fourth book.[263]

G. Bell, 1894), 358.

[257] Lançon, 52-53.

[258] Ibid.

[259] Ibid.

[260] Amory, 46-85.

[261] Ibid., 186.

[262] Hereafter the English translation novel/s will be used to refer to Constantine's Novellas

[263] For more information on the composition of the Corpus Juris Civilis and the history of Roman law, see

For the Romans, religion had always been a matter of state. After Constantine, the empire gradually shifted from paganism to Christianity, and Christian emperors incorporated Christian principles into the Roman law system. After Catholic Christianity had been recognized as the official religion of the state, ecclesiastical affairs were incorporated into the Roman legal system. In the Theodosian Code, a whole book—book sixteen—was dedicated to the Catholic faith.

However, Justinian not only incorporated Christian values into his legislation and legislated on theological and ecclesiological matters, but he made the Catholic Christian creed the basis of Roman law. At this point, it is important to mention that even though Justinian's legislative works and letters were connected and directed to the different problems he was facing, some basic assumptions can be drawn from them independently of the events they were a response to. A careful analysis must be made, since as Olster points out, the events and the actions that followed them are different, but there is a "rhetorical uniformity" in Justinian's writings. He complements that by saying, "We find that not only were different topoi often applied to different situations and audiences, but the same topoi have a different meaning when set in a particular political context."[264]

The first point to be mentioned is Justinian's understanding of God, law, order, and the function of the emperor. In his writings can be seen a "deep-rooted desire for order, and his firm belief that the Empire was God's agent for bringing divine order to an otherwise chaotic world."[265] His *Institutions* started by affirming that "learning in the law entails knowledge of God and man,"[266] and he went on to explain in his *Codex* what it meant to have the knowledge of God, starting with a Trinitarian formula that affirmed the Catholic religion as the only religion of the empire, outlawed paganism and heresy, and made the church canons the law of the state.[267] He also maintained that unity of Christians in the true faith and the lack of dissension in the holy church as a result was the best way to please God.[268] In this way he linked law, God, and religion—not just any kind of religion, but the Catholic religion.

Barry Nicholas, An Introduction to Roman Law, Clarendon Law Series (Oxford: Clarendon Press, 1962); J. L. E. Ortolan, The History of Roman Law from the Text of Ortolan's Histoire De La Legislation Romaine Et Generalisation Du Droit (Edition of 1870) (London: Butterworths, 1871); Seeck and Sargenti, Die Zeitfolge Der Gesetze Constantins; Hans Julius Wolff, Roman Law: An Historical Introduction (Norman: University of Oklahoma Press, 1951).

[264] Olster, 166.

[265] Ibid.

[266] Justinian, Justinian's Institutes, trans. Peter Birks and Grant McLeod (Ithaca, NY: Cornell University Press, 1987), 37.

[267] CJ 1.1.5, 6, 7.

[268] Justinian, "Confessio Rectæ Fidei Adversus Tria Capitula," 993.

Based on this understanding of God, law, and religion, he addressed the concept of empire and order, stating that the empire was established by God to promote justice and preserve order. He writes, "God has sent us [the emperor and the empire] from heaven so that it might remedy difficulties through its perfection, and adapt the laws to the varieties of nature."[269] He set the empire in the person of the emperor as the one responsible for establishing order through legislation. The emperor received this "power from God in order to establish laws."[270] These laws were not the fruit of the emperor's mind, but eternal precepts handed out by God and preserved by emperors through centuries. "Each worthy act must receive sovereignty as the will of God, either from us, or if some corruption has stained our predecessors' good acts, it is necessary that we restore the law and bring it back to its original state, so that we might hurry on to have eternal communion either with performing the deed, or in its renewal to noble activity."[271] According to Justinian, the emperor did not bring forth new laws, he just restored and preserved them for the maintenance of order in society. Since religious and secular laws were integrated as one in his code, the emperor's duty was to help in the defense of the true faith and the welfare of the church. This is clear in much of his religious legislation, as in the decree addressed to the Patriarch Epiphanius:

> Since we constantly exercise every care for the holy churches, by which, we are confident, our empire is sustained and the common welfare is, through the grace of God, protected, and since we look out, no less for our own souls as for the souls of all, and therefore are very solicitous that the rights beneficial to the holy churches in the various cities shall not in any manner be abridged; that the sacred rites shall not, by the absence of the pious bishops, be impeded or less becomingly performed . . . therefore we deemed it necessary to employ this letter to Your Blessedness.[272]

Then, he set the roles of the emperors and the clergy and the proper relationship between church and state. He began his sixth novel by stating, "There are two greatest gifts which God, in his love for man, has granted from on high: the priesthood and the imperial dignity. The first serves divine things, while the latter directs and administers human affairs; both, however, proceed from the same origin and adorn the life of mankind."[273]

There are divergent analyses of the roles of the emperor and the clergy as presented in the novels and legislation of Justinian. Meyendorff sees Justinian granting

---

[269] Novel 73.

[270] Novel 72.

[271] Novel 59.

[272] CJ 1.3.42.

[273] Novel 6.

the emperor sole responsibility for the care of both secular and religious affairs, while the clergy's role is only to pray for the emperor and empire, excluding any political activity. Meyendorff says that "Justinian's attitude toward the Bishop of Rome is to be understood in this framework." Justinian followed the popes' demands at the beginning of his reign as a means of gaining their support for his policies of expansion, until he had political and military control over Italy.[274]

Dvornik presents the great support Justinian received from the clergy as the reason for Justinian to act more boldly on religious issues, but at the same time, Justinian was aware of his role as emperor in ecclesiastical affairs; he summoned councils and legislated in doctrinal matters that had been previously decided by the clergy to rebut heresies and uphold the councils' decisions and apostolic traditions.[275]

Capizzi opines that is difficult to establish a clear line on Justinian's understanding regarding the roles of the emperor and the clergy. According to him, Justinian had a polyvalent and often contradictory personality. He put religion at the center of his legislation, but would choose different solutions according to who was influencing him—Theodora or the clerics. Capizzi writes that his actions look like they were driven by the problems he was facing.[276]

According to Stein's analysis of the roles of the emperor and clergy, Justinian had the clergy under his authority both politically and religiously, but at the same time, he reinforced their power to help with the political leadership in their cities, defending the poor, orphans, children, foreigners, and women. Yet he exempted the clergy from all civil and criminal jurisdictions, stating that the church would judge only spiritual cases.[277]

For Olster, the controversy regarding the roles of emperor and clergy in church affairs is not related to what Justinian meant by applying the phrase "divine things" to the clergy and the phrase "human affairs" to the emperor in the sixth Novel, but to Justinian's understanding of who was the guardian of the true faith. He argues that for Justinian, the church, in the person of the apostles and fathers, was responsible for defining truth, but the emperor was responsible for enforcing it. Olster writes, "Justinian's justification for intervening in ecclesiastical life was not based on any claim to rule the church, but rather, the imperial *potestas* guarded it. Ecclesiastical law took its place as part of the universal, imperial law that aimed at maintaining order and harmony in the world, and thus came within

---

[274] Meyendorff, "Justinian, the Empire and the Church," 49-50.

[275] Dvornik, "Early Christian and Byzantine Political Philosophy: Origins and Background," 2:815-828

[276] Capizzi, "La Politica Religiosa Ed Ecclesiastica Di Giustiniano," 55-84.

[277] Stein and Palanque, Bas-Empire, 395-402.

the compass of imperial power."[278] He continues, "Justinian distinguished between the responsibility of the church to define doctrine, and 'the hope placed' in the imperial office to defend the church, clarify doctrine and guard the faith: he claimed both the suppression and refutation of heresy as imperial duties."[279] He adds that Justinian thought the church should follow his lead in the defense of the Catholic faith, and finally writes, "Justinian went beyond supporting ecclesiastical authority with imperial power. His claims that the imperial power clarified the faith and expelled heretics assimilated the dogmatic authority of the church into the imperial power. Justinian used the imperial model of law, the imperial duty to clarify and enforce, to blur the distinction between church and state."[280]

Justinian's religious policy consummated the marriage between church and state that Constantine had started. Through the apostolic tradition, the works of the fathers, and the ecumenical councils, the church would define what true Catholic Orthodox Christianity meant, and the emperor would enforce it and punish those who professed other beliefs as orthodoxy.

The relationship between the emperor and the bishop of Rome was another topic addressed by Justinian. In his legislation, he asserts the hierarchical authority of the bishop of Rome over ecclesiastical matters. Two letters from the correspondence between Justinian and Pope John II in 533/534 were included in the code, in which both emperor and pope present their perspectives on their roles in church and state relationships.[281] It is interesting to note why Justinian added the letter from Pope John to the code, since even though it confirms Justinian's Theopaschite formula as orthodox, it presents a distinct view of the role of the pope in theological and ecclesiastical matters as if correcting Justinian's own understanding of the topic.

A good analysis of these two letters is given by Olster. According to him, Justinian used his usual rhetorical style of leading with ecclesiastical authorities, not affirming, but asking approval for the definition of Catholic orthodox faith expressed in his edict. He started his letter by presenting his intention of preserving the unity of the church under the spiritual leadership of the pope. "The Pope was unequivocally 'the head of all the holy churches,' and Justinian's duty was to maintain the unity of the churches by firmly establishing Papal leadership over the church."[282] Then, Justinian explained that he put forth religious

---

[278] Olster, 169-170.

[279] Ibid., 172.

[280] Ibid.

[281] These letters are found in book 1, chapter 1.8 of Justinian's Constitutions.

[282] Olster, 174.

legislation only to suppress "those who have dared to raise a disturbance."[283] According to Olster, even though Justinian had already recognized the authority of the pope, not only as the source of doctrine but of its preservation, when he said that faith "has been ever and firmly guarded and preached by all priests according to the doctrine of your Apostolic See,"[284] he claimed in a most respectful way that "civil disturbance left a place for the imperial *potestas* to intervene."[285] Olster summarized his comments on Justinian's letter by saying, "Justinian did not entirely resign all authority to the church; underlying even this most respectful address was the imperial prerogative to enforce order and law that left open the door to imperial intervention in the church."[286]

To Olster, the pope's answer to Justinian was crafted not only to affirm his authority over the church, as Justinian had said, but to demonstrate his independence on theological and ecclesiastical matters. The unity of the church was maintained by the pope and the emperor, but the emperor had a part in it because he was connected to the church. Unity in the church would happen only through the maintenance of papal supremacy by the emperor. The emperor would earn Christ's protection by uniting all churches under the leadership of the Roman See. As Pope John said, "We pray to God, and Jesus Christ, our Savior, that He may deign to guard you through long and peaceful years, in this true religion and in your agreement with and veneration for this apostolic seat, whose preeminence you guard in a Christian and pious spirit."[287]

Olster argues that the pope made a clear distinction between his authority and the emperor's:

> The Pope at all times maintained a distinction between the authority that he possessed, and the power that the emperor possessed. The Pope contrasted the authority through which he approved Justinian's confession of faith, to the imperial power that preserved the unity of the church and the imperial harmony. He contrasted 'that edict you have proposed to the faithful populace out of love for the faith, with the desire to suppress the heretics,' to that confirmation of its orthodoxy that could only be given by the Pope, 'which, because it accords with the apostolic doctrine, we confirm by our authority.' He further reserved the right to define heresy and judge heretics solely to the Papacy.[288]

The most interesting point brought up by Olster in his analysis of Pope John's letter is how the pope asserted his authority on religious matters:

---

[283] CJ 1.1.8.10

[284] CJ 1.1.8.13.

[285] Olster, 174.

[286] Ibid.

[287] CJ 1.1.8.36.

[288] Olster, 175.

The Pope's distinction between the emperor's right to forgive the heretic's criminal trespass, and his own permission to rejoin communion illustrates how the Papacy could use Justinian's own arguments to exclude the emperor from ecclesiastical intervention. Justinian had argued that the duty to maintain order meant the clarification, and therefore the exposition and judgment of doctrinal orthodoxy. The Pope, however, argued that the suppression of civil disorder did not impinge on the sacerdotal monopoly of doctrinal judgment, but rather the two remained entirely distinct. The one was a matter of civil disorder, which was in the imperial sphere; the other was a matter of doctrinal truth, which was in the sacerdotal sphere. Justinian had blurred the distinction between the civil and religious aspects of heresy, and had used the former to bring the latter within the imperial compass. The Pope, using the same distinction divided the imperial and sacerdotal spheres to exclude Justinian from any action independent of the Papacy.[289]

During his reign, Justinian used his *potesta* and his own judgment to guard the Catholic Christian church and prevent deviation from the apostolic teachings, which, according to him, were expressed in the fathers' writings and church councils preserved through the leadership of the Roman See. However, he did not deny the ecclesiastical and religious authority of the church. As Olster says, "the addition of a Papal letter into the *Codex* with the force of imperial law is itself an interesting example of Justinian using the ecclesiastical *auctoritas* within the undoubted sphere of imperial authority."[290] With the publication of his code in 534, Justinian defined canon law as imperial law and established the supremacy of the pope over the Catholic Christian world. However, this took fully effect only after 538 when Justinian officially recognized Italy as part of the empire,[291] and Vigilius, having been recognized by the empire and clergy as pope, started a campaign against Gothic leadership that was contrary to the part of the senate still supporting the Goths.[292] As Alexander Hunter said, "Greater than a shifting territorial supremacy were the influence and the authority of the Church in supporting and fostering the Justinian legislation. For the Popes and the pontifical courts ranked the Roman civil law only a little lower than the canon law, and consistently upheld its authority; their influence penetrating far beyond the borders of the States of the Church, wherever an ecclesiastic found his way."[293]

---

[289] Ibid., 175-176.

[290] Ibid., 176.

[291] The first mention of Justinian as lord of Italy is found in Novel 69, addressed to the people of Constantinople on June 1, 538.

[292] See the above section "Justinian and Popes Silverius, Vigilius, and Pelagius."

[293] William Alexander Hunter, Gaius, and J. Ashton Cross, A Systematic and Historical Exposition of Roman Law in the Order of a Code (London: Sweet & Maxwell, 1897), 98.

The code, which had been written in Latin since the beginning, and the novels, which were translated to Latin and enforced as law in Italy in 554, became the Roman law in Italy until the 12th century Bologna revival of Roman law studies.[294]

JUSTINIAN'S POLICIES REGARDING PAGANS, JEWS, SAMARITANS, AND HERETICS

Justinian's laws against heresy and non-Christian religions were made up of a collection of previous laws on the subject plus some of his own. The significance of this legislation was in the way Justinian enforced it. After A.D. 527, he promoted strong persecution of heretics and non-Christians. As Capizzi comments, Justinian's religious legislation had more coherence and violence than that of any other emperor before him.[295] He worked hard for the conversion of pagans and heretics, but did not hesitate to exile or put to death those who did not become Christians.[296]

He started his code with a Catholic definition of faith and ruled out any other form of religion, denying them rights to hold meetings, offer private teachings, and receive or give property, and even for most of them the common rights of citizenship.[297] He dedicated whole titles to each problem related to those outside Catholic Christianity, and he added new laws, known as novels, as needed during his reign.

Even though emperors after Constantine had summoned councils to promote unity of faith throughout the Roman Empire, as Stephen Mitchell says, "in practice, the empire was a maelstrom of diverse religious communities."[298] Jews, Samaritans, and non-Catholic Christian sects survived even after having their citizenship rights limited or being completely banned from society.

If Manicheans and other heretics did not convert to Catholic orthodoxy, they would lose their property and citizenship rights, could not hold any imperial office, and could even be put to death.[299] Stein mentions that some Manicheans in Constantinople who held imperial offices and other intellectual positions were persecuted and put to death.[300] In the case of Arians, after destroying the Vandal kingdom of North Africa, Justinian persecuted them like other heretics and ordered them to return their churches to Catholics.[301] For the Goths, after 538 Justinian disregarded his law granting them religious

---

[294] Charles Phineas Sherman, Roman Law in the Modern World (Boston: Boston Book Co., 1917), 199-202.

[295] Capizzi, Giustiniano I Tra Politica e Religione, 41.

[296] John Malalas and others, Ioannis Malalae Chronographia, Corpus Scriptorum Historiae Byzantinae (Bonnae: Weber, 1831), 423.

[297] Even though they had limited rights, Jews and Samaritans kept their citizens' rights. CJ 1.1.1-5, 1.5.12.

[298] Stephen Mitchell, A History of the Later Roman Empire, A.D. 284-641: The Transformation of the Ancient World, Blackwell History of the Ancient World (Malden, MA: Blackwell, 2007), 130.

[299] CJ 1.5.12-21.

[300] Stein and Palanque, Bas-Empire, 370.

[301] Gibbon and Youngman, book 4, chapter 41.

freedom[302] and persecuted them throughout the empire, destroying their churches and enforcing the penalties set by his previous legislation on them.[303] Cusack comments that the decline of Arianism was a direct result of the Justinian religious policy. She says, "Under Justinian, Christian historians gloried in the defeat of Arianism by Catholicism," and adds that Isidore of Seville connected the conversion of the Visigoth king of Spain in 587 to Justinian's enterprises against Arianism.[304] Procopius points out that one of the justifications for Justinian's conquest of Italy was Arianism; the Goths were Arians and an Arian king could not rule under the umbrella of the empire.[305]

Samaritans were also included in the law against Manicheans of 527; their civil and religious rights were also limited by Justinian.[306] According to Procopius, this legislation led to the revolt of the Samaritans in 529, where thousands of insurgents were put to death by military force.[307]

For the Jews, Justinian not only reissued old legislation against them, but also took away some of the protections created by previous emperors. In his code, he ordered that Jews could not have Christian slaves and that if a Jewish slave had become Christian, she or he should be liberated.[308] He also issued five novels from 535 to 553 that inflicted severe religious limitations on Jewish communities.[309] In these novels, Justinian forbade Jews and heretics from North Africa to perform religious rites, and announced that their places of worship and synagogues should be confiscated and given to Catholic Christians.[310] It denied to Jews, Samaritans, and heretics any exemption from the decurionate, but also denied them the privileges enjoyed by the holders of this office.[311] Also, Jews were forbidden from buying ecclesiastical property, which could be confiscated. Even the Jewish liturgy was regulated, with the prohibition of the reading of the Bible in Hebrew and the use of the Mishnah.[312]

---

[302] CJ 1.5.12.17.

[303] J. A. S. Evans, The Emperor Justinian and the Byzantine Empire, Greenwood Guides to Historic Events of the Ancient World (Westport, CT: Greenwood Press, 2005), xxxii.

[304] Cusack, 50.

[305] Procopius, Procopius, 3:5.3.1-7.

[306] CJ 1.5.12, 18-19.

[307] Procopius, The Secret History of Procopius, 11.26-27.

[308] CJ 1.10.2.

[309] Justinian Novels on the Jews: 37 of 1st August 535, 139 of 535 or 536, 45 of 18th August 537, 131 of 18th March 545, and 146 of 13th February 553.

[310] Novel 37.

[311] Novel 45. The decurionate was a service with heavy financial burdens, but also a few privileges, such as immunity from corporal punishment or exile.

[312] Novels 131 and 146.

Among all non-Christian religions, paganism received the harshest treatment. From 527 to 529, Justinian reinforced previous anti-pagan legislation and issued new laws that delivered a deadly blow against paganism. Besides losing their civil rights, pagans who refused to be baptized would lose all property, be left in penury, and be punished until they became Christian. For those who professed to be Christians but still held to pagan practices, the punishment was death.[313] Teaching of paganism was forbidden, the school of philosophy in Athens was closed down, and pagan books were burned.[314] Justinian's anti-pagan policy was intended to convert pagans to Catholic Christianity, as was his missionary campaign in Asia headed by John of Ephesus, but it was hard enough to arraign and put to death academics such as rectors or lawyers.[315]

After the recognition of Catholic Christianity as the official religion of the empire and the suppression of paganism, no other emperor worked so hard to eliminate paganism as Justinian. As Evans says, "even though pockets of paganism survived, Justinian's reign can rightly be regarded as the period when the last embers of pagan vitality were finally extinguished."[316]

SUMMARY

The beginning of the reign of Justin I marked the end of the Acacian schism and the ascendance of Catholic orthodoxy headed by the bishop of Rome. However, Monophysitism was not dead, and Justinian had to deal with it throughout his reign. Justinian's first attempt to solve the problem of Monophysitism was the adoption of the Theopaschite formula. Through letters, he sought approval from bishops in the East and the bishop of Rome for his definition of faith. He recognized the supremacy of the bishop of Rome over other sees and made concessions following the ecclesiastical wishes of Popes John and Agapetus, but Popes Vigilius and Pelagius had a hard time negotiating the Three Chapters with the emperor. Since Justinian did not reach a consensus through his legislation and negotiations with the clergy for the approval of the condemnation of the Three Chapters, he and Pope Vigilius summoned a council to settle the issue. The Council of Constantinople condemned the Three Chapters, and both Popes Vigilius and Pelagius afterwards confirmed the decision of the council.

---

[313] CJ 1.11.9, 10.

[314] The date for the closing of the Athens School is placed today between A.D. 529 and 531. See Malalas and others, 491; Giovanni Reale, History of Ancient Philosophy: The Schools of the Imperial Age (Albany: State University of New York Press, 1990), 447-450.

[315] F. Nau, "L'histoire Ecclesiastique De Jean D'asie," Revue de l'Orient chrétien 2, no. 1 (1897): 481-482.

[316] Evans, The Emperor Justinian and the Byzantine Empire, xxx.

Pope Vigilius was ordained bishop of Rome in 537, but, in actuality, his reign as pope—as recognized by the clergy—did not begin until 538. The reign of Pope Vigilius was marked by conflict between the emperor and the clergy. Vigilius adopted a policy that supported the eastern empire and the elimination of Arianism, differing from his immediate predecessors in the Roman See. However, he did not yield to pressure to reinstate Anthimus as bishop of Constantinople to compromise with the Monophysites. He had a hard time reconciling his leadership in the West with imperial demands to condemn the Three Chapters. Even though in his reign the recognition of the ecclesiastical supremacy of the papacy was consummated, his reign marked the beginning of the papacy's fight for political independence.

From Justinian's legislation and letters, and analysis from secondary sources, it can be determined that Justinian's religious policies varied according to the audience and the problem he was facing, but they were built on these basic presuppositions: God was the lawgiver and the Catholic Church had the true definition of faith that expressed the will of God; unity of the church was essential for the prosperity of the empire; unity of the church could only exist through the supremacy and leadership of the Roman See; Christ's blessings on the empire and emperor came through the church and proper defense of the Catholic orthodoxy; the emperor was to use his *potesta* to unify all churches to the see of Rome and to suppress heresy and non-Christian religions; and the emperor was the guardian of the church and promoter of order.

Justinian adopted a policy of religious persecution stronger than that of any other Christian emperor before him. His legislation on paganism can be considered the last blow to the fading pagan religions. Jews and Samaritans saw their civil and religious rights diminished and were faced with death or forced conversion in some places. Heretics were to be completely eliminated, and after 538, with the defeat of the Ostrogoth force by Justinian, all the Arians would also be eliminated.

The yaer 538 can be singled out as a significant year in Justinian's reign because it marks a division point in the relations between the papacy and the emperors. Justinian officially recognized Italy as part of the empire in 538, making it possible for his legislation to be fully implemented in the West; it limited religious liberties, made the Roman Empire a Catholic state, made canon law state law, and made the pope the supreme ecclesiastical authority in the empire. After 538, the papacy became the strongest political institution in Italy, since the Roman senate had been decimated in the Gothic war during the first siege of Rome and part of the survivors' aristocratic families had sought refuge in Constantinople. The papacy did not come under Gothic control again after 538, and it became the sole local institution representing the interests of the population of Italy.

After 538, Pope Vigilius started a campaign for the empire and against the Gothic rulers, but the sufferings caused by the Gothic war in Italy and the theological differences between East and West pushed the allegiance of the people in the West toward the Catholic Church. Because of the political and economic conflicts between the local population of Italy and the representatives of the eastern empire and the theological crisis between East and West, Pope Vigilius's pontificate represented a caesura—a change of paradigm—between East and West, with the formation of a new western and Latin Catholic Christian society headed by the pope. The winner of the Gothic war was the papacy; after 538, its ecclesiastical supremacy was recognized throughout the empire and it had an open door to exercise political supremacy in the West.

CONCLUSION

Analysis of church and state relationships from the time of Constantine's sons to Justinian demonstrates an increasing proximity between the two, but at the same time, an increasing differentiation of authority and roles for religious and political powers in the Roman Empire.

The emperors deepened the traditional Roman understanding of the function of the state to legislate in religious matters; since the welfare of society depended on the benevolence of God toward the state, the state had to regulate any aspect related to the proper worship of God—definition of faith, church property, ecclesiastical life, moral values, and suppression of non-Christians. The Catholic Church changed from a church sponsored by the state to the sole official church of the state. At the time of Constantine's sons, the empire was more a pluralistic empire with an emperor who supported Catholic Christianity, but by the time of Justinian it was a Catholic Christian empire where the emperor's function was to rule out any other form of religion. The state that at the time of Theodosius II would issue laws on religious matters, by the time of Justinian, became a state where Catholic Christian principles were the basis of any law. The acts, laws, and writings of Justinian demonstrate that in his time there was a complete integration of the Catholic Church and the state.

Justinian also went beyond previous emperors because he not only consummated the marriage between church and state, but also expanded the emperor's function in theological and ecclesiastical matters. He recognized the role of the Catholic Church through the apostolic tradition, the works of the fathers, and the ecumenical councils as the definition of true Catholic Orthodox Christianity, and the role of the pope as the glue that kept the church together and confirmed council decisions. However, in his works he gave the emperor the heavenly mission of legislating on religious matters to preserve faith and punish those who professed other beliefs as orthodoxy.

Justinian differed from previous emperors in the way he dealt with ecclesiastical authority. He had the old vices of previous emperors regarding appointing, deposing, and exiling bishops. However, he increased ecclesiastical authority, gave canon law the same force as civil law, expanded bishops' authority juridically and politically, and put control of the Catholic Christian church in the hands of the bishop of Rome, even making one of the pope's letters law.

For the church, the increasing conflict between clergy and emperors in the theological crisis of the period helped develop clearly defined roles for the ecclesiastical leadership of the church and the emperor in the empire. The church fought for its autonomy in the definition of Catholic orthodoxy. Clerics pointed out the importance of the emperor in the defense of the true faith, but stressed the limits of his power in internal affairs of the church. They recognized the existence of two powers on earth—ecclesiastical and secular—but maintained that they had different roles in society and should act harmoniously without crossing the borders of their influence.

Throughout the empire, bishops gained political influence in cities due to the proper nature of their work, their defense of moral values, and their protection of those less economically favored. Ecclesiastical functions also became respected positions in Roman society that the new Christian aristocracy would fight for—especially in Rome, which as the moral capital of the empire would develop a theory of primacy over other ecclesiastical sees and seek an ecclesiastical and theological leadership role.

The fall of the Roman Empire in the west and the policy of religious freedom adopted by Theodoric in Italy helped develop the independence of the Roman See from imperial, political, and ecclesiastical intervention. By the time of Justinian, this ecclesiastical primacy was confirmed by the emperor, who made the pope the head of the Catholic Church, but was not willing to recognize all the claims of the pope, such as the superior role of bishops in relation to emperors stated in the two-sword formula of Pope Gelasius.[317] Vigilius's reign is significant, not only because he was the first pope to enjoy Justinian's decree making the pope the head of the Catholic Church in both east and west, but also because he made the papacy aware of the independence it would need to have from imperial control. Vigilius's reign marked the beginning of the papacy's fight for political and ecclesiastical independence from state control. This did not mean that the papacy was fighting for separation of church and state, but for the church to have independence in its sphere of action and have the empire fight its battles according to its agenda. Popes after Vigilius, such as Pelagius, would use the force of Roman law to enforce their wishes, but would act without the emperor to settle their own primacy and resolve ecclesiastical problems.

The conquest of Italy by barbarians, Justinian's reconquest of the West, his legislation, and the relationship between pope and emperor in the pontificate

---

[317] For more information on Pope Gelasius's theory of two swords see section "The Development of the Ecclesiastical Supremacy of the Bishop of Rome" in chapter 3 above.

of Vigilius present important aspects of the church-state relationship and the political and temporal power of the papacy in the West. First, barbarian rule in Italy propelled the desire for political independence of the papacy. Second, Justinian's legislation made the Roman state Catholic, finalized the replacement of paganism by Christianity, replaced Roman law with Catholic orthodoxy, made the pope the supreme head of the Catholic Church, made canons of church councils law of the state, and eliminated religious tolerance. Third, after 538 the papacy became the most powerful political institution in Italy; the senate had been decimated during the first siege of Rome and became a group of aristocrats controlled by the papacy, the Goths lost their political and military power after the first siege of Rome, and the allegiance of the Italian population was transferred to the Catholic Church instead of the government in Constantinople. After 538, never again did the papacy come under Gothic control, even during 546 and 552 when Totila sacked and controlled Rome three times and Italy was impoverished. Fourth, Vigilius's pontificate represented a new paradigm of relations between the eastern empire and the papacy. The "music" continued—the church and the state continued to be united—but the theme had changed: Now the papacy was fighting for political independence. It would stay connected to the empire until the popes could find a better army to defend the interest of the church, which they found in the Frankish kings.[318] For all these reasons, 538 can be considered the dawn of the political power of the papacy.

---

[318] See chapter 5 on Charlemagne below.

CHAPTER IV

ANALYSIS OF ANCIENT AND CONTEMPORARY VIEWS ON CHURCH-STATE RELATIONSHIPS DURING CLOVIS' REIGN (A.D. 481-511)

INTRODUCTION

The Franks,[1] out of all the Germanic tribes, were the most successful barbarian group in Europe after the fall of the Western Roman Empire. Barbarian tribes such as the Vandals, Huns, and Ostrogoths had periods of great expansion and political and military power, but they gradually lost their influence or were completely eliminated.

The Franks experienced an extraordinary expansion of power from A.D. 450 to 511. In A.D. 451, they inhabited only the delta lands at the mouths of the Rhine and Scheldt rivers, but by 511 they controlled a great part of the Western Roman Empire.[2]

Clovis, son of Childeric, king of the Salic Franks, was responsible for this Frankish expansion. He not only unified all the Frankish tribes, but also

---

[1] In this chapter, if not specified clearly, the name Franks refers to all the different ethnicities (Salians, Ripuarians, or other groups) that lived in areas where any known Frankish king had control. M. Guizot and Guizot de Witt, The History of France from the Earliest Times to 1848, trans., Robert Black(New York: J. B. Alden, 1885), 102-108. For a general overview of the History of France, see Guillaume de Bertier de Sauvigny and David H. Pinkney, History of France, rev. and enl. ed. (Arlington Heights, IL: Forum Press, 1983); Crowe; Guizot and Guizot de Witt; W. Scott Haine, The History of France, The Greenwood Histories of the Modern Nations (Westport, CT: Greenwood Press, 2000). For a background on Late Antiquity and early Middle Ages in Gaul see: Peter Robert Lamont Brown, The World of Late Antiquity, AD 150-750; M. Wallace-Hadrill, The Barbarian West, 400-1000; Edward James, The Origins of France: From Clovis to the Capetians, 500-1000 (New York: St. Martin's Press, 1982). For contemporary works on the Franks and Frankish rulers, see: James, The Franks; Lot, Naissance De La France; Patrick Périn and Laure-Charlotte Feffer, Les Francs: A La Conquête De La Gaule, vol. 1 (Paris: A. Colin, 1987); Wood, The Merovingian Kingdoms.

[2] Raymond Van Dam, "Merovingian Gaul and the Frankish Conquest," in The New Cambridge Medieval History 1, C. 500–C. 700, ed. Paul Fouracre (Cambridge: Cambridge University Press, 2006), 193-197. For maps on the Frankish territory expansion see appendix C.

conquered significant parts of other emergent kingdoms in the territory that formerly belonged to the Western Roman Empire.[3]

Different reasons are presented as the key points for Clovis's success. Yet, like Constantine, Clovis had a story of miraculous conversion to Catholicism, which Gregory of Tours presented in his *History of the Franks* as the decisive point in Clovis's military success.

Analyzing the history of the Franks and particularly the period of Clovis's reign raises some questions related to church and state relationships. Were there any religious factors in the Frankish expansion? Which entity benefited most from Clovis's adoption of Catholicism—the Catholic Church or the Frankish kingdom? Did the Catholic Church have any political influence in the Frankish Kingdom? What was the impact of Clovis's adoption of the Catholic faith on the future history of the Catholic Church and the Frankish people?

The purpose of this chapter is to examine ancient and contemporary sources on the history of the Franks in order to analyze the relationship between the Catholic Church and the state from A.D. 481 to 511 (the dates of Clovis's ascendancy to the throne and of his death).

In order to accomplish this task, the first section of the chapter will discuss the political and religious background prior to Clovis's reign. The second section will describe historical events in Clovis's kingdom. The third section will analyze the impact of Clovis's conversion on the Catholic Church and on Clovis's kingdom. The fourth section will analyze how historians, theologians, and clergymen described the importance of Clovis's conversion to Catholicism. Finally, a summary will be given and conclusions drawn.

GAUL BEFORE CLOVIS

The inhabitants of Gaul before and during Clovis's reign were a mix of different barbarian tribes and ancient groups such as the Celts, Greeks, Aquitanians, and others. They did not all share one religion, even though they had a strong Catholic diocesan organization. They were organized at the *civitas* level, and had kept the basic Roman political system.

The Franks were not well organized and did not have centralized political and military power as did other Germanic tribes. They were independent tribes that acted more like hunters or harassers and were part of the Roman armies on many occasions. They were the first Germanic tribe to settle permanently in Roman territory.

---

[3] Jean-Benoît Nadeau and Julie Barlow, The Story of French (New York: St. Martin's Press, 2006), 23-24.

DEMOGRAPHIC BACKGROUND

Gallo-Roman civilization grew out of several groups: the Iberians or Aquitanians, Phoenicians, Greeks, Kymrians, and Gauls or Celts. Except for the Greeks, the dates when these groups settled in what is today French territory are unknown.[4] Roman military expansion wiped out some of the Gallic tribes, and Gaul became a consular province of Rome.[5] "From the conquest of Gaul by Caesar, to the establishment there of the Franks under Clovis, she [Gaul] remained for more than five centuries under Roman dominion; first under the Pagan, afterwards under the Christian empire."[6]

Even under Roman dominion, Gaul was invaded by other barbarian tribes from time to time. A group of Germanic tribes known as Franks[7] occupied the north of Gaul and was recognized by the Romans as a federacy; this was part of the Roman strategy for protecting Gaul against the other Germanic tribes.[8] The origin of these tribes is uncertain.[9] Tacitus, the Roman historian of the second century, in his

---

[4] Guizot presents one of the most extensive descriptions of the beginning of Gallo-Roman civilization. Most of what is known today about the birth of Gallo-Roman civilization, as presented by Guizot in his book, comes from Roman and Greek historians. These Roman and Greek accounts are considered inaccurate by some because they reflect Greek and Roman perspectives, not the reality of what would be the barbarian civilization. For further studies on the birth of Gallo-Roman civilization, see Guizot and Guizot de Witt, 9-10; Joël Schmidt, Lutèce: Paris, Des Origines À Clovis: 9000 Av. J.-C.--512 Ap. J.-C (Paris: Librairie Académique Perrin, 1986).

[5] Guizot and Guizot de Witt, 37-65.

[6] Ibid., 65.

[7] According to Malcolm Todd the meaning of the name Franks is unclear. After Gregory of Tours (538-9–593-4) the meaning was attributed as "free," since all Frankish citizens were born freemen. Malcolm Todd, "The Germanic People and Germanic Society," in The Cambridge Ancient History, ed. I. E. S. Edwards (Cambridge; New York: Cambridge University Press, 1970), 444. Sigebert of Gembloux (c.1035-1112) says that in the Latin language the name Franks is translated as brave, warlike; "quod in Latina lingua interpretatur feroces." Gemblacensis Sigebertus, "Sigeberti Gemblacensis Monachi Chronica," in PL, ed. J. P. Migne, vol. 160 (Paris: J.-P. Migne, 1857), col. 60b.

[8] Samuel Dill, Roman Society in Gaul in the Merovingian Age, 7.

[9] Gregory of Tours, Fredegar, Sigebert of Gembloux, and some others accept the Trojans as the real ancestors of the Franks. See Fredegar, The Fourth Book of the Chronicle of Fredegar, with Its Continuations, trans. J. M. Wallace-Hadrill (Westport, CT: Greenwood Press, 1981), 3.2; Gregory, The History of the Franks, trans. Ormonde Maddock Dalton, vol. 2 (Oxford: Clarendon Press, 1927), 2.9; Sigebertus, col. 59-61. Henrich Bebel (1472-1518), Count Hermann of Neuenar (1492-1530), and most of the modern historians posit a German origin for the Franks. See Widukind and others, Rerum Ab Henrico Et Ottone I Impp. Gestarum Libri III, Unà Cum Alijs Quibusdam Raris & Antehac Non Lectis Diuersorum Autorm Historijs, Ab Anno Alutis D. Ccc. Usq. Ad Praesentem Aetatem (Basileae: Apvd Io. Hervagivm, 1532), 99-105; Wood, The Merovingian Kingdoms, 33-38.

description of the barbaric tribes, did not mention any one that could be identified as the Franks who invaded the Roman Empire in the third century.[10]

According to M. Guizot, the first reference to the name "Franks" in history appears in the songs of the Roman soldiers commanded by Aurelian around A.D. 241-242. However, Guizot did not cite any source to confirm this information.[11] After the third century, the words "Franks" and "Francia" (the region inhabited by the Franks) became common in Roman literature. Roman geographers started to describe the limits of Francia as going along the West bank of the Rhine from Nimegen to Coblentz.[12]

In the third and fourth centuries, more and more Frankish tribes settled in the empire. In the fifth century, the most important of these Frankish tribes were the Chatti, the Ripuarians, and the Salians.[13] Most of these tribes that settled in Gaul were mainly focused mainly on farming. They were basically an agricultural civilization in small clans without a clear kingship dynasty, but they were also recognized as intrepid warriors who did not fear death.[14]

In spite of the fact that Gaul was a mix of different ethnicities, the traditional Roman culture was well accepted by all of them. All the tribes that were assimilated into the empire became a part of Roman civilization and culture. Barbarians and Gallo-Romans alike enjoyed the comfort provided by Roman civilization: schools, public

---

[10] Tacitus (c. 55–c. 117) mentions in his Annals the Sugambri or Sicambrians. Some historians classify this barbarian tribe as part of the Franks, because Gregory of Tours in his account of the baptism of Clovis put into Remigius's mouth the words "Meekly Bow thy Proud head, Sicamber," implying that Clovis had a Sicambrian ascendancy. See Gregory, The History of the Franks, 1:69. For further information, see Guizot and Guizot de Witt, 102-105; Lewis D. Sergeant, The Franks from Their Origin as a Confederacy to the Establishment of the Kingdom of France and the German Empire (London, New York: T. Fisher Unwin; G. P. Putnam's Sons, 1898), 11-20; Cornelius Tacitus, The Annals and the Histories, trans. Alfred John Church and William Jackson Brodribb, vol. 15 (Chicago: Encyclopædia Britannica, 1952), 28-30, 72.

[11] Guizot and Guizot de Witt, 102-103.

[12] Dill, 6.

[13] Guizot and Guizot de Witt, 102-108; James, 38-58; Jean Verseuil, Clovis, Ou, La Naissance Des Rois, L'histoire En Tête, Série Les Grandes Familles (Paris: Criterion, 1992), 17-54.

[14] The bishop of Clermont, Sidonius Apollinarius (c. 430-487) describes the Franks in the following way: "They excels launching in space their fast axes, without never missing their blow, and roll their shield like playing; they accompany by a jump the flight of their javelin, doing it before the coming of the enemy; their children have already the passion of the war. If they are crushed under the number or by the hazard of the position, death can cut them down, but never fear. They deny the defeat and their courage seems to survive death" (excussisse citas vastum per inane bipennes et plagae praescisse locum clipeosque rotare ludus et intortas praecedere saltibus hastas inque hostem venisse prius; puerilibus annis est belli maturus amor. si forte premantur seu numero seu sorte loci, mors obruit illos, non timor; invicti perstant animoque supersunt iam prope post animam). Sidonius Apollinaris, Carmen 5, ed. C. Luetjihann, MGH Scr. AA, vol. 8 (Berlin: Weidmannos, 1887), 193.

baths, entertainment, theaters, temples, and such. The civilized life of the cities was a point of attraction for any population inside or outside the empire that had contact with it. Even far away from the city of Rome, the cities in Gaul had all the essential amenities of the capital. Patrick J. Geary describes these cities in the following way:

> these cities had their own local public life centering on the local senate or *curia*, composed of the leading men of the municipality from whose ranks magistrates, called *decurions*, were elected to fill public offices. The municipal government was directly responsible for little other than maintenance of roads and bridges, while individual curials shouldered a variety of other public services (*munera* such as the collection of taxes and fees, maintenance of post animals for the imperial post service, and the entertainment of visiting Roman magistrates).[15]

In addition to the facilities offered by the cities, the Roman structure and administrative system were maintained in almost all the cities of Gaul, and Roman traditional values were preserved and cultivated by civil and religious authorities. Geary points out that

> these values included first and foremost Roman justice and law. They included a strong adherence to traditional Roman *pietas*, or subordination and dedication to family, religion, and duty. And they included a love of Latin (if not Greek) letters which were cultivated and supported by the leisured elites of the provinces both as a way of participating in the essence of Roman civilization and, increasingly, as a way of convincing themselves that the essence of this civilization would never slip away. None of these values would ever be entirely abandoned in the western provinces of the Empire.[16]

The cities of Gaul, even though they were not at the center of the empire, had a good agricultural structure, a very active social life, an effective educational system for the elite, and a strong military presence for security in the borderlands.[17]

POLITICAL BACKGROUND

The Franks ascended to political power in Gaul before Clovis because of their military strength and their coalition with the Romans. Rome's political and military power had changed gradually to meet the new reality of the barbarian threat. The legions, which in the beginning had been formed only of Italian peasants, began to

---

[15] Patrick J. Geary, *Before France and Germany: The Creation and Transformation of the Merovingian World* (New York: Oxford University Press, 1988), 7.

[16] Ibid., 6.

[17] Ibid., 7-10.

accept both Roman and barbarian soldiers. The Roman armies were controlled more and more by the barbarians and by regional leaders with Roman ascendancy, than by the Italian aristocracy. The senate, so powerful at the beginning of the empire, lost its political influence as the need for military power to keep the borders secure increased. Generals were gaining more power than the emperor and aristocracy, and this shift from political to military led to political decentralization and higher taxes.

After Julius Caesar's devastating conquest, political power in Gaul was totally in Roman hands. The Romans left legions in strategic cities to control the new territory. Italian peasants were sent to Gaul from time to time as soldiers to fill the vacancies left by those who retired or got better positions in other places. Aristocratic life was the most important goal for military and civil citizens of the Roman Empire.[18]

The settlement of retired army leaders as landlords in the territories where they had served and the lack of Italian peasants to fill the positions in the cities far from Rome resulted in a military force more connected with these particular regions than with Rome. Rome itself could not provide the necessary military force to contain the barbarian invasions and had to rely on local peasants and contracted barbarian soldiers to defend its territory.[19]

In the third century, the generals of these armies started to have great power in the empire. The local citizens were loyal to them, and many of them started to dispute for the emperor's title. The empire became fragmented, with multiple individuals claiming to be the emperor. The senate was no longer in charge of these frontier armies, and had to submit to this new reality of military supremacy.[20]

The emperor Diocletian tried to reunify the Roman Empire. He reorganized the empire economically and administratively to maintain a strong military organization connected with a centralized political power. "He accomplished this by reorganizing the Empire into several prefectures for the East and the West and then further subdividing the Empire into approximately 100 provinces, by separating the military and civil bureaucracies, and by enlarging the latter to handle the increasing load of judicial and financial affairs."[21]

Diocletian introduced a new tax system under which all citizens of the empire had to pay an *annona*.[22] The central government was responsible for collecting this

---

[18] Frank Burr Marsh, The Reign of Tiberius (New York: Barnes & Noble, 1959), 335.

[19] Geary, 15.

[20] See Lynn Avery Hunt, The Making of the West: Peoples and Cultures, a Concise History (Boston: Bedford/ St. Martin's, 2007), 205-210; Michael Ivanovitch Rostovtzeff, The Social and Economic History of the Roman Empire (Oxford: Clarendon Press), 416-448.

[21] Geary, 11.

[22] The annona was a land-tax determined by the quality of the land and the manpower available to work it, normally connected in kind (grains), instituted by Septimius Severus, and systematized by Diocletian as a way

tax from the landlords and their peasants. Rather than being based on the annual production of each landowner, the tax was a fixed amount based on how many subjects lived on the owner's land.[23]

In times when agriculture declined in productivity, many small landowners had to hand over their lands to pay the tax. The taxes were collected directly from the magistrates, and if they were not able to collect from small landowners, they had to pay from their own funds. There was a high demand for funds to pay the military as barbarian invasions became more frequent, and even some magistrates who were responsible for collecting taxes did not have the necessary money. This made provincial administration of the cities an unpopular occupation; many aristocratic landlords did not want to lose their properties and avoided public administration.[24]

These changes in local administration contributed to a growing regionalism and produced a vacuum in civic government that was filled in Gaul by the church. The office of the bishop did not assume responsibility for tax collection, but in many places it assumed the responsibility for civil government of the cities. The bishops had control over hospitals, cemeteries, judicial power, and even military power when it was needed for defense of the city.[25]

In the fourth and fifth centuries, the bishops in Gaul became powerful not only in the spiritual realm, but also in worldly affairs. This new political influence made the office of bishop a desirable position. Traditional moral values were no longer taken into consideration when a new bishop was appointed to the office, and more and more bishops were men from powerful aristocratic families.[26] "Bishops tended to come from the senatorial class and were selected, not from among the clergy, but usually from the ranks of those with proven records of leadership and administration. Election to Episcopal office became the culmination of a career pattern or *cursus honorum* which had nothing to do with the Church."[27]

Even before the political power of the western Roman Empire faded, the sees of Gallic cities began to display what became the main characteristic of the fallen western empire: an "Episcopal lordship."[28] Political control of the state was in the hands of the

---

to pay the soldiers in kind. See: Peter Garnsey and Richard P. Saller, The Roman Empire: Economy, Society, and Culture (Berkeley: University of California Press, 1987), 93-94.

[23] Stephen Williams, Diocletian and the Roman Recovery (New York: Methuen, 1985), 117-119.

[24] Rostovtzeff, 460-465.

[25] Geary, 34-35; Jean Heuclin, "Un Premier Concordat en 511," Notre Histoire Sommaire, April 1996, 9; Wood, The Merovingian Kingdoms, 73-79.

[26] For more information on the election of bishops, see Henry G. J. Beck, The Pastoral Care of Souls in South-East France During the Sixth Century (Rome: Aedes Universitatis Gregorianae, 1950), 15-18.

[27] Geary, 33.

[28] Martin Heinzelmann, Bischofsherrschaft in Gallien: Zur Kontinuität Römischer Führungsschichten Vom 4.

same powerful senatorial families who now controlled the bishops. "So closely did the office of bishop come to be identified with the Gallo-Roman aristocracy that in the fifth century, as these new values altered the Western concept of Episcopal office, so too did they permeate the idea the aristocracy held of itself. Thus the aristocracy increasingly focused on the episcopacy as its central institution, and in so doing began slowly to redefine itself and its *Romanitas* in terms of Christian values."[29]

Religious Background

The religion of Clovis's kingdom arose out of theological and eschatological trends that existed before the fall of the Western Roman Empire and a Catholic diocesan system strongly rooted in cities (*civitas*) and the office of the bishop. Since the strengthening of the diocesan system happened as a result of the theological and eschatological changes, those changes will be analyzed first.

Theological Trends

Gaul had a history of defending the orthodox faith and a tendency toward independence. One of the best known theologians of Gaul was Iraneaus of Lyon, whose theological works formed much of the basis of today's Catholic orthodoxy. Unlike the eastern part of the Roman Empire, the church in Gaul normally followed the theological decisions of the Catholic Church headed by the bishop of Rome.[30]

Early Christianity had a strong eschatological message focusing on the second coming of Jesus, the judgment, the Antichrist, and the resurrection. Apocalyptic imagery and eschatological language were very common in Christian writings during the first few centuries, but the delay in Jesus' second coming gradually changed the message of the imminent return of Christ. The *parousia* was no longer a future event, but a reality, since Jesus had become the Incarnate Logos.[31] A historical second coming of Jesus was not necessary. A new place was given to the church in the plan of salvation. [32]

Bis Zum 7. Jahrhundert: Soziale, Prosopographische Und Bildungsgeschichtliche Aspekte (Munich: Artemis, 1976).

[29] Geary, 35.

[30] Frederick William Kellett, Pope Gregory the Great and His Relations with Gaul (Cambridge: University Press, 1889), 20-26.

[31] Fritz Buri in his book Clemens Alexandrinus und der paulinische Freiheitsbegriff said that Clement understood the parousia not as "an event of the immediate future, as Paul did, but something that has already been fulfilled with the coming of Jesus as the Logos made flesh." Fritz Buri, Clemens Alexandrinus Und Der Paulinische Freiheitsbegriff (Zürich: M. Niehans, 1939), 50.

[32] Pelikan, 1:128.

From Constantine onward, the eschatological hope of a historical second coming of Jesus was gradually transferred to the final triumph of the church of God on earth. First Eusebius and later Augustine promoted a new role for the church in eschatology and the plan for salvation. Past, present, and future were embraced in the history of the church. Jesus, the church's supreme head, had endowed it with all power on earth regarding salvation. Only through the church could heavenly gifts be bestowed on the human race, and overcoming all other religions and philosophical ways of thinking was the only hope for humanity. As Pelikan said:

> Augustine set the standard for most catholic exegesis in the West when he surrendered the millenarian interpretation of Revelation 20, to which he had held earlier, in favor of the view that the thousand years of that text referred to the history of the church. Nor is it altogether irrelevant to note that Eusebius and Augustine represented, in their interpretations of the future of the world as in their views of its past, the church's new affirmation of the place of universal history in the economy of salvation.[33]

Augustine's reflections on society in his book *City of God (De civitate dei)* shaped religious and political enterprises throughout the fifth century and afterward. Even though Augustine did not stress any earthly political power connected with the church, his description of the earthly and heavenly cities encouraged many of those who read it to strive for the formation of a new model Christian society.[34] The appropriate time had come for the church to fulfill the prophecy and take the lead in shaping the destiny of the world.[35] Christian literature began to advocate the necessity of state action on behalf of the moral values of the Catholic Church.[36]

CHRISTIAN WRITERS AND MILITARY AFFAIRS

The barbarian invasions in the Western Roman Empire in the fifth century brought about a transition from unwarlike Christianity to a positive view of military intervention for morality's sake. The threat to traditional Roman virtues and the fear of barbarian heresies became compelling enough for some Christian writers to apply Augustine's ideas on the supremacy of the church in society.

---

[33] Ibid., 1:129.

[34] For more information on Eusebius, see chapter 2, and for Augustine, chapter 3.

[35] See Isabel Moreira, Dreams, Visions, and Spiritual Authority in Merovingian Gaul (Ithaca: Cornell University Press, 2000), 39-76.

[36] See Thomas J. J. Altizer, History as Apocalypse, SUNY Series in Religion (Albany: State University of New York Press, 1985), 79-96.

Five of the Germanic tribes that settled in Roman territory in the fifth century were Arian. This was a great threat to the Catholic orthodoxy. Part of Gaul had surrendered to these Arian rulers and the rest was governed by either weak Roman aristocrats or pagan barbarians. To some Catholic writers, the use of military power was the only way to reverse the Arian supremacy.[37]

The anonymous Gallic Chronicler of 452 and Hydatius, bishop of Chaves (468 d.), wrote historical accounts stressing that "military strength in the right hands might make a tremendous difference" and putting forward an "identification of Roman order with orthodoxy, and heresy or unbelief with barbarism, that would not seem out of place in later Byzantine works."[38]

Not all Catholic writers of the fifth century advocated the use of military power to promote moral values, even though they believed Christian moral values were essential for a healthy society. For them, where political and military leadership had failed in preserving the stability of the empire, a strong spiritual leader could do so, as in the case of Pope Leo,[39] who saved Rome from Attila and Geiseric.[40]

Whether they supported using military intervention to promote moral values or not, both groups of writers argued that the absence of strong political leadership with a moral agenda was a tragedy for the empire. As Steven Muhlberger says, "Had impressive and pious emperors dramatically restored a healthy and orthodox Empire through their military efforts, the clerical attitude might have been different."[41] Writers were looking to the past and not to the present for ideal military or spiritual leaders. Contemporary rulers did not match their expectations of political and ecclesiastical

---

[37] Heuclin, 14. See for example the writings of the anonymous Gallic Chronicler of 452 and Hydatius, bishop of Chaves (468 d.), as mentioned in fn. 38.

[38] Alexander C. Murray and Walter A. Goffart, After Rome's Fall: Narrators and Sources of Early Medieval History: Essays Presented to Walter Goffart (Toronto: University of Toronto Press, 1998), 86. The text of the anonymous Gallic Chronicler of 452 is found in Chronica Minora Saec. IV, V, VI, VII, ed. Theodor Mommsen and Johannes Lucas, MGH Scr. AA, vols. 11 (Berlin: Weidmannos, 1892), 2:615-666; and the Chronicle of Hydatius is found in Chronica Minora, 2:13-36.

[39] When Attila invaded Italy in 452, Pope Leo I in his diplomatic work was able to convince him of not sacking Rome. However, he did not prevent Genseric the Vandal of sacking Rome, but at least prevented the pillage of church properties. See: Thomas Hodgkin, Italy and Her Invaders, 2d ed., vol. 2 (Oxford: Clarendon Press, 1896), 2:158-160, 283-285; Patrick Howarth, Attila, King of the Huns: Man and Myth (New York: Barnes & Noble Books, 1995), 130-136.

[40] Prosper of Aquitaine's Chronicle is a classical example of this kind of literature. He wrote around 433 to 455 defending the use of the spiritual power in defense of moral values rather than the use of military power. See "Chronica Minora," 1:341-499. For further studies, see Steven Muhlberger, The Fifth-Century Chroniclers: Prosper, Hydatius, and the Gallic Chronicler of 452, Arca, Classical and Medieval Texts, Papers, and Monographs, 27 (Leeds: F. Cairns, 1990).

[41] Murray and Goffart, 89.

leadership. They did not predict the ascension of an orthodox king to counteract the barbarians and Arian heretics, but agreed that such king would be of great value for the defense of orthodoxy and preservation of Roman virtue.

THE CATHOLIC DIOCESAN SYSTEM

The Gallic dioceses were organized in a Roman administrative structure. "It was based on dioceses which for much of the kingdom were the ecclesiastical counter-parts of the *civitates*, with which they were conterminous."[42] The main power of the diocese was vested in the office of the bishop, who had theological, ecclesiological, hagiological, sociological, judicial, and political functions.[43]

Each bishop had the responsibility to preserve orthodoxy in his diocese. The bishops of Gaul had a long tradition of high respect for the orthodoxy of the church centralized in the authority of the bishop of Rome. Wallace describes this connec-tion in the following way:

> The pope was seen by Gallo-Romans as a fatherly figure, *Papa Urbis*, from whom advice on many matters could be sought. It was a warm relationship, especially with the churches of province, and correspondence survives to illustrate it. Cases of eccle-siastical discipline were referred to him, the initiative lying with those who sought guidance. This could result in the statement or re-statement of what we call papal prerogatives, as, for example, in the celebrated row between Pope Leo and Hilary of Arles; but what brings this about is not a papal desire to advance new claims over western churches but the need to explain the papacy's traditional authority to war-ring parties that have invoked papal intervention. The pope remained, as he had long been, the ultimate judge in *causae majores*, major issues, often concerning the be-haviour of difficult bishops. The pope, then, was a judge and acknowledged as such. He was also the guardian of orthodox doctrine. The churches of southern Gaul, and especially of Provence, saw in him their natural shield against heresy.[44]

Bishops sought to control the holy places and the possession of relics. The lack of living examples of virtue encouraged the bishops and the population to seek dead

---

[42] Wood, The Merovingian Kingdoms,71.

[43] Peter Robert Lamont Brown, The Rise of Western Christendom: Triumph and Diversity, A.D. 200-1000, The Making of Europe (Malden, MA: Blackwell Publishers, 2003), 78-79, 106-115; S. T. Loseby, "Gregory's Cities: Urban Functions in Sixth-Century Gaul," in Franks and Alamanni in the Merovingian Period: An Ethnographic Perspective, ed. I. N. Wood, Studies in Historical Archaeoethnology, vol. 3 (Woodbridge; Rochester, NY: Boydell Press, 1998), 252-256; Chris Wickham, Early Medieval Italy: Central Power and Local Society, 400-1000 (Ann Arbor: University of Michigan Press, 1989), 87.

[44] J. M. Wallace-Hadrill, The Frankish Church (Oxford: Clarendon Press, 1983), 110.

specimens to venerate. The superstitious people, whether converted to Christianity or not, identified the veneration of saints with similar pagan ritual practices, and Christian missionaries and bishops who could not eliminate pagan ritual sites transformed them into places of veneration for saints.[45]

Local councils and synods where the Gallo-Roman bishops discussed local affairs were common in Gaul. These provincial councils demonstrate how bishops in Gaul before Clovis had total control over ecclesiological affairs in their dioceses. There is no historical evidence of abbots—overseers of the monasteries—being associated with bishops in these councils.[46] While baptisms, burials, and other minor ceremonies were performed by both bishops and local priests, the main feasts of the church—Christmas, Easter, and Pentecost—were conducted only by the bishops in the cathedral cities.[47]

Caring for the flock was an integral part of the Gallo-Roman church: The bishops took care of the sick, the poor, widows, prisoners, and so on. In the context of the barbarian invasions of the fifth century, pastoral care was a significant tool for the empowerment of bishops. As Wood says, "Many bishops emerged as the saviours of their cities as they arranged for famine relief and secured the ransom of prisoners during the years of crisis. The great saint bishops of fifth-century Gaul were provided with an unequalled opportunity for the exercise of pastoral care, which they seized with open arms. At the same time, in some towns at least, bishops came to take over the duties of such late Roman officers as the *defensores*, who had been expected to defend the weak."[48]

Toward the end of the fifth century, the bishops accumulated judicial and political functions in the *civitas*, becoming more than mere shepherds of the flock. Civil administrators were often chosen to occupy the office of bishop.[49]

---

[45] One example is the cult of Benignus in Dijon; see Gregory, Glory of the Martyrs (Liverpool: University Press, 1988), 50. Wood analyzes this in the following way: "The devotion of the people of Dijon to an obscure tomb in one of the cemeteries outside the town was frowned on by the local bishop, Gregory of Langres, who regarded it as an act of pagan superstition. He may well have been right. Nevertheless on failing to extirpate this superstition, Gregory 'learned' in a vision that the tomb was that of the martyr Benignus, and he incorporated the site in a new church. Some years later, we are told, travelers brought back from Italy an account of the saint's life, about which nothing had been known previously. The Life itself looks remarkably like a version of the Passion of the Byzantine 'megalomartyr' Menignos, relocated in Dijon, and the whole Benignus dossier is probably best interpreted as the response of a bishop to a non-Christian cult which he had not been able to stamp out." Wood, The Merovingian Kingdoms, 74.

[46] Wallace-Hadrill, 94-109.

[47] Wood, The Merovingian Kingdoms, 72-73.

[48] Ibid., 75.

[49] Good examples in Gaul are Germanus of Auxerre, Gregory of Langres, and Sidonius Apollinaris. Like Ambrose of Milan, they were notable civil servants who became bishops. See Alban Butler, David Hugh Farmer,

They worked as judges not only in cases involving churchmen, but also in secular affairs.[50] The office of bishop became a high position in the late years of the fifth century. They were administrators of great properties and were leading figures in the community and in relations with the kings. As Samuel Dill says, "the real leader of the municipal community in the fifth century, alike in temporal and in spiritual things, was often the great Churchman."[51]

HISTORICAL BACKGROUND

Many historians considered the existing accounts of the Franks before Clovis and even during the period of Clovis's kingdom as more mythological than truly historical. According to them, most of the primary and secondary sources mix legend with history, and historians need to screen the oldest secondary sources to find what should be the true historical events. However, whether mythological or not, these secondary sources contain the most information available on the history of the Franks. Archaeological findings have helped archaeologists and historians understand different aspects of the Frankish society, but they have not revealed new events from the past.

One of the first incursions of the Frankish tribes into Roman territory was around A.D. 250; the Franks attacked many cities of Gaul and their territory extended beyond the borders of present-day Spain for about a decade before they were defeated and expelled from Roman territory.[52] At the end of the third century, Roman forces had to face Frankish attacks on the shipping lanes to Britain. Even though the Romans were able to pacify the region, they failed to drive out the Franks from the Scheldt region.[53]

---

and Paul Burns, Butler's Lives of the Saints (Tunbridge Wells, Kent; Collegeville, MN: Burns & Oates; Liturgical Press, 1995), 32; F. R. Hoare, The Western Fathers: Being the Lives of Ss. Martin of Tours, Ambrose, Augustine of Hippo, Honoratus of Arles, and Germanus Auxerre (New York: Sheed and Ward, 1954), 283-320; Courtenay Edward Stevens, Sidonius Apollinaris and His Age (Oxford: Clarendon Press, 1933).

[50] For further studies, see Heinzelmann; Edward James, "Beati Pacifici: Bishops and the Law in Sixth-Century Gaul," in Disputes and Settlements: Law and Human Relations in the West, ed. John Bossy (Cambridge: Cambridge University Press, 1983), 25-46.

[51] Samuel Dill, Roman Society in the Last Century of the Western Empire, 215.

[52] Eutropius, Eutropii Historiae Romanae Breviarium: Cum Versione Anglica, in Qua Verbum De Verbo Exprimitur: Notis Quoque & Indice: Or Eutropius's Compendious History of Rome; Together with an English Translation, as Literal as Possible, Notes and an Index, trans. John Clarke (London: J. F. and C. Rivington and T. Evans, 1793), 9.8-9; Paulus Orosius, The Seven Books of History against the Pagans; the Apology of Paulus Orosius, trans. Irving Woodworth Raymond, Records of Civilization, Sources and Studies, No. 26 (New York: Columbia University Press, 1936), 7.22.

[53] Zosimus, New History, trans. Ronald T. Ridley, vol. 2 of Byzantina Australiensia (Canberra: Australian Association for Byzantine Studies, 1982), 1.71.

In the middle of the fourth century, Julius the apostate inflicted a great defeat on the Franks. From then on, the Franks lived in relative peace with the empire, and on many occasions fought with the Romans against other barbarian tribes. They settled in the north of Gaul and became federates of the Roman Empire.[54]

The Frankish dynasties before Clovis are uncertain. Clovis's ancestors were called the Merovingians, and their dynasty probably began with Pharamond (?409-427). The first recognized chieftain of the Franks was Chlodio (?428-451) who was driven back by Aetius after he attempted to invade Roman territory around 430. He, his son Merovech (451-458), and his grandson Childerich (458-481) were on relatively friendly terms with the Romans and fought with the Roman armies against barbarian invasions in the fifth century.[55]

SUMMARY

The Franks before Clovis did not have a significant role in the political and military control of Gallo-Roman territory; they were assimilated as Roman *federates* and inhabited the north part of Gaul. The people of Gaul were of many different nationalities and religions. Gaul had a very organized diocesan system, but in the fifth century it was military and politically dominated by Arian and pagan barbarians.

In spite of this Arian supremacy and barbarian dominance, the church increased in prestige in the *civitas*. The pastoral care performed by the bishops elevated them to administrative and military positions in defense of their communities. A new relationship between church and state emerged in Gaul in the fifth century that became the model for the formation of the future Holy Roman Empire. As Laurent Theis says:

> L'administration des grandes cités, ainsi que des territories don't elles constituent la métropole, passé insensiblement aux mains des évêques. Pourquoi? Parce que ces grands clercs ont d'abord l'avantage de ne pas être trop tributaires des aléas poli-

---

[54] Marcellinus Ammianus, The Roman History of Ammianus Marcellinus: During the Reigns of the Emperors Constantius, Julian, Jovianus, Valentinian, and Valens, trans. Charles Duke Yonge (London; New York: G. Bell, 1894), 3.3; Périn and Feffer, 29-72; Sozomen, 2:3.7; Zosimus, 3.3-5.

[55] Jacques Barzun, The French Race: Theories of Its Origins and Their Social and Political Implications Prior to the Revolution (Port Washington, NY: Kennikat Press, 1966), 80; David B. Boles and Harold W. Boles, Withers-Davis Ancestry: With the Families of Abraham, Babb, Bachiler, Chandler, Collet, David, Davies, Hollingsworth, Hussey, Jefferis, Lewis, Martin, May, Nash, Nowell, Perkins, Powell, Ree, Roberts, Sloper, Tarrant, Wise, Wood, and Woolaston (Decorah, IA: printed for Anundsen Pub. Co., 1998), 390; Vincent-Claude Châlons, The History of France: From the Establishment of That Monarchy under Pharamond, to the Death of Lewis XIII (Dublin: printed by George Faulkner, 1752), 1-6; David Hughes, The British Chronicles (Westminster, MD: Heritage Books, 2007), 152-154; Richmal Mangnall, Historical and Miscellaneous Questions (New York: D. Appleton, 1866), 146-147.

tiques: quels que soient les partis, les clans, les clientèles, les renversements dálliance, l'épiscopat reste en place. Constat historique frappant : on ne tue pas les évêques. Leur personne est perçue comme sacrée. L'alliance entre les chefs germains parvenus et la vieille aristocratie gallo-romaine a donc créé le vivier où s'alimente le réseau des nouveaux responsables à la fois de l'Eglise et de l'Etat. La fusion, dans le cadre encore très solide de la romanité christianisée, des élites gauloises, romaines et germaniques va ainsi permettre l'irrésistible ascension du royaume franc.[56]

The church of Gaul was theologically orthodox and very well rooted in apostolic succession. It was faithful to the Catholic leadership of Rome and sought in Rome the authority for local decisions. It embraced the Augustinian vision of society and the traditional Roman virtues.

Clovis's Kingdom

Introduction

The Frankish leader Clovis, considered the founder of the Merovingian dynasty of Frankish kings,[57] expanded his kingdom not only in Gaul but also throughout central and western Europe. He united the Frankish tribes, conquered various Germanic tribes, and defeated the last Roman ruler in Gaul. He married a Catholic princess named Clotilda, and according to traditional accounts, he took an oath to become a Catholic after a successful battle against another Germanic tribe. After Clovis's conversion, the Frankish kingdom was established as a Catholic nation. The Salic Law and the canons of the national church council he summoned at Orleans would set the basis for future legislative actions in France and other parts of Europe.

The primary literature about the church-related historical events that took place in Clovis's kingdom is not as extensive as that of other periods in the history of the rise of Christianity, such as the fourth or ninth centuries. Nevertheless, what is considered today as primary literature by historians is a collection of documents, the most important of which are: three letters of the bishop Reims Remigius; the letter sent by Clovis to the Bishops on Visigoth dominions (507); the two major documents produced in Clovis's reign, the *Lex Salic* and the Canons of council of Orleans (511); the six letters sent by Theodoric the Great on the war between Clovis and Alaric II; bishop Avitus letter to Clovis after his baptism; and the book *The Life of Genevieve.*

---

[56] Heuclin, 9.

[57] Due to the uncertainty about Clovis's ancestors, historians considered Clovis as the founder of the Merovingian dynasty. See Haine, 29.

The majority of historians rely on Gregory of Tours's *History of the Franks* for an account of the events of Clovis's reign. However, many historians question the order adopted by Gregory of Tours.[58] According to Gregory of Tours's chronology, the events happened in the following order: beginning of rulership (481-482), war against Syagrius (486), war against the Thuringians (491), Clovis's marriage (492-493), war against the Alamanni and baptism (496), war against the Visigoths (507-508), unification of all Frankish tribes under his power, and the Council of Orléans (511).[59]

Beginning of Reign (481 or 482)

Clovis, Childeric's son, inherited his father's kingdom of Tournai in A.D. 481 or 482. Childeric, a tribal chieftain of the Salian Franks, had defeated the Visigoths at Orléans as an ally of the Romans around A.D. 463.[60] After that, he was recognized by the Romans as governor of the Roman district Belgica Secunda. However, Childeric did not have control over all the Frankish tribes that lived in the area along the Rhine River.[61]

Outside of Gregory of Tours's accounts, the beginning of Clovis's rulership is not clearly documented. The only document existing today from this period is a letter from Saint Remigius, archbishop of Reims, congratulating Clovis on his ascension as leader of the Franks. Remigius's letter confirms Clovis's rulership over Belgica Secunda, but does not attribute to him the title of king.[62]

The title of king attributed to Clovis by Gregory of Tours from the beginning of his rulership over Belgica Secunda is questioned by such contemporary historians as Geary. They argue that the political structure of the Franks in Clovis's

---

[58] Andre P. Van de Vyver and Rolf Weiss are the two major exponents of the revisionary chronology of the Frankish kingdom. Their works were widely accepted in the 1960s and 1970s, but today only a few of their appointed dates are considered to be the most probable ones (for example, the battle of Tobiac against the Alamanni in 506 and not in 496). For further information, see: A. Van de Vyver, "L'évolution du Comput Alexandrin et Romain du 3e Au 5e Siècle," Revue d'histoire ecclésiastique 52, no. 1 (1957); Rolf Weiss, Chlodwigs Taufe: Reims 508. Versuch Einer Neuen Chronologie für die Regierungszeit des Ersten Christlichen Frankenkönigs unter Berücksichtigung der Politischen und Kirchlich-Dogmatischen Probleme Seiner Zeit (Bern, Frankfurt/M: Herbert Lang, 1971).

[59] Gregory, The History of the Franks, 2.27-43.

[60] Ibid., 2.11-17; Fredegar, 3.11-12.

[61] Gregory of Tours mentions that Childeric was recognized as king by the Franks together with Aegidius after he had returned from Thuringia, where he stayed for eight years in exile. Gregory, The History of the Franks, 2.12. Remigius of Rheims implies in his letter to Clovis that Childeric was a Roman provincial ruler of Belgica Secunda when he says that Clovis was taking his father's position in the province of Belgica Secunda. Remigius, "Epistulae Austrasiacae," in Merovingici et Karolini Aevi 1, ed. Bruno Krusch and Wilhelm Levison, MGH Epp., vol. 3 (Hannover: Hahn, 1896), 113.

[62] Remigius, 112-114.

times did not include kings as we know them today. The Frankish leaders were called *duces* or *regulus* and their positions of leadership were mainly connected with military enterprises. [63]

Even if Clovis was not recognized as king when he started to rule over the Salian Franks, his style of rulership matched those of other kings who lived after him. He was an absolute monarch with a despotic leadership and loyal subjects, and his elimination of relatives who could threaten his kingdom and monarchal succession demonstrated his ambition in favor of a centralized government.[64]

War against Syagrius (486)

According to Gregory of Tours,[65] in 486, with the help of Ragnachar (465-? 508),[66] Clovis defeated Syagrius (487 d.), the last Roman official in northern Gaul, whose rule covered the area around Soissons in present-day Picardie. Syagrius was the son of the Roman general Aegidius (464 d.), the Gallo-Roman *magister militum*[67] in the reign of Emperor Majorian.[68] Aegidius is considered the last powerful Roman representative in Gaul. The kind of political influence that Syagrius had in Gaul after his father's death is not clear from historical documents.[69] According to Dill, Syagrius was more concerned with the administration of his own farm than with the political and military affairs of his domains. He considers Syagrius's lack of management of the state to be a sign of the weakness that made Clovis's victory easy.[70] Edward James questions whether Syagrius was a political force in Gaul at all, and suggests that Gregory's inclusion of Syagrius as *Rex Romanorum* was his way of "inflating Syagrius' position, since it also inflated Clovis's victory over him."[71]

Another point to be considered concerning Clovis's victory over Syagrius is that Bishop Remigius of Rheims recognized Clovis as ruler over Belgica Secunda.

---

[63] Gear sees Clovis as a chieftain of the Franks, following barbarian traditions of rulership by military success and not by inheritance (51-62, 82-84).

[64] Ormonde Maddock Dalton, The History of the Franks, vol. 1 (Oxford: Clarendon Press, 1927), 191-194.

[65] Gregory of Tours did not give a date for this event; he only described it. The date of A.D. 486 for Clovis's control over Soissons is recognized by the majority of the historians.

[66] The Frankish king at Cambrai. See Gregory, The History of the Franks, 2.18.

[67] Magister militum is a Latin phrase meaning "master of the soldiers." This term was commonly used in the later Roman Empire to refer to the senior military officer of the empire, and it was also used with a provincial name to indicate a regional position.

[68] Julius Valerius Majorianus, commonly known as Majorian, was Roman emperor in the West (457–461).

[69] See James, The Franks, 67-71.

[70] Dill, Roman Society in the Western Empire, 201.

[71] James, The Franks, 71.

According to James, this province included Reims, Tournai, and Soissons.[72] If Clovis undertook the command of Belgica Secunda when he started his rulership in 481, Soissons was already under his dominion, and Syagrius could have been considered, as James suggests, a count of Soissons. On the other hand, if Clovis undertook the command of Belgica Secunda after defeating Syagrius (? 486), Remigius's letter was sent to Clovis after this war. However, in his letter Remigius did not mention anything that indicated a military enterprise when Clovis assumed the command of Belgica Secunda; rather, he implied a natural succession of power.[73]

Since all the available historical information about Syagrius's life is found in Gregory of Tours's *History of the Franks*, historians assume that Clovis took over part of Gaul by defeating Syagrius, following Gregory's account, or that he gradually aggregated to his kingdom those regions of Gaul left without a strong political power after the deaths of Aegidius and Euric (king of the Visigoths).[74]

Clovis's Marriage (492-493)

In 492 or 493, Clovis married Clotilda, the niece of Gondebad, king of the Burgundians. Clotilda was a Catholic and, according to the tradition, very pious. For Gregory of Tours, she was the major cause of Clovis's conversion to Catholicism. He stated that after the baptism of Clovis's second son,[75] who was miraculously saved from death by God, Clotilda strongly urged Clovis to embrace the Catholic faith. Clovis's conversion, according to Gregory's account, came after a battle against the Alamanni: Clovis's troops were on the point of yielding, but when he invoked the aid of Clotilda's God and promised to become a Christian, the Alamanni fled and Clovis returned victorious.[76]

War against the alamanni (496 or 506) and clovis's baptism (496 or 508)

Gregory of Tours chronologically sets Clovis's baptism after a war against the Alamanni and before the war against the Visigoths. According to him, Clovis's

---

[72] Ibid., 65.

[73] Remigius's letter congratulates Clovis on his new position as administrator of Belgica Secunda, replacing his father, and advises him to follow the counsel of the bishops. See Remigius, 112-114.

[74] See Geary, 82-83; James, The Franks, 67-71; Wood, The Merovingian Kingdoms, 40-41.

[75] The first son died after being baptized, and Clovis believed the baptism was the cause of his death. See Gregory, The History of the Franks, 2.29.

[76] Ibid., 2.30. More details on Clovis's conversion will be given in the next section.

conversion and baptism, like Constantine's conversion, marked a turning point in Catholic history. Clovis became the Catholic champion against Arianism, and Gregory describes Clovis's conversion as a supernatural event.

Clovis's conversion and baptism can be analyzed in different ways. Historians disagree on the dates of Clovis's conversion and baptism and on his motives for choosing Catholicism.[77] Regarding the date of Clovis's baptism, there are three main theories: that Clovis's baptism followed his conversion after the war against the Alamanni in 496; that his baptism followed his conversion after the battle against the Alamanni in 506 or 508; and that his conversion and baptism took place at different times, with the former around 496 and the latter around 506 or 508.

The date of 496 for Clovis's baptism and conversion is defended primarily by Gregory of Tours. His chronology is generally accepted by the majority of general historians. However, critical analysis of Gregory's *History of the Franks* and of other primary and secondary sources from the fifth and sixth centuries has led some historians to reevaluate the dates proposed by Gregory and suggest a later date for Clovis's baptism. Among these historians are A. Van de Vyver,[78] Wilhelm Junghans,[79] Godefroid Kurth,[80] Ferdinand Lot,[81] Georges Tessier,[82] and Ian Wood.[83]

The critics challenge Gregory's chronology on points like the distinction between reality and mythology in Gregory's chronology, Gregory's particular choice of events to support his theology,[84] Bishop Avitus's letter to Clovis, the war against the Alamanni, the war against the Visigoths, and Clovis's baptism description by Bishop Nicetius of Trier (566 d.).[85]

---

[77] For further studies on Clovis's conversion, see Moorhead, "Clovis' Motives for Becoming a Catholic Christian," 329-339; Tessier, 87-104.

[78] Van de Vyver, "La Victoire (1re partie)," 895-914.

[79] Wilhelm Junghans and Gabriel Monod, Histoire Critique Des Règnes De Childerich Et De Chlodovech (Paris: F. Vieweg, 1879), 57-69.

[80] Kurth, Clovis, 314-340.

[81] Lot, 906-911.

[82] Tessier, 87-96.

[83] Wood, The Merovingian Kingdoms, 43-48; I. N. Wood, "Gregory of Tours and Clovis," in Debating the Middle Ages: Issues and Readings, ed. Barbara H. Rosenwein and Lester K. Little (Malden, MA: Blackwell Publishers, 1998), 73-91.

[84] This topic will be discussed in the next section.

[85] For the Latin text of Bishop Avitus's letters see Avitus, Alcimi Ecdicii Aviti Viennensis Episcopi Opera Quae Supersunt, ed. R. Peiper, MGH Scr. AA, vol. 6.2 (Hannover: Hahn, 1883), epistolae 46. For an English translation see Avitus, Avitus of Vienne, Letters and Selected Prose, trans. Danuta Shanzer and I. N. Wood, Translated Texts for Historians, vol. 38 (Liverpool: Liverpool University Press, 2002), 369-374. For the Latin text of Bishop Nicetius's letter see: Nicetius of Trier, "Excerpta Ex Epistola Ad Chlodosindam " in PL, ed. J. P. Migne, vol. 71 (Paris: J.-P. Migne, 1845), col. 1166-1168. For an English translation see: idem, "Bishop Nicetius of Trier

Commenting on this criticism, Tessier points out that the chronological description of Gregory of Tours is more like a romance than a real description of historical events.[86] Gregory's account sets the major events of Clovis's life in a perfect sequence in years: the fifth year of his reign (victory over Syagrius), the tenth (victory over the Thuringians), the fifteenth (victory over the Alamanni and Clovis's baptism), and the twenty-fifth (victory over the Visigoths).[87] He also mentions Clovis being baptized in the thirtieth year of his life, like Jesus[88] (which could be a great coincidence). Wood points out that Gregory's account is chronologically confused because he "did not have reliable evidence on which to base his computations," and that "the most general chronological indications in the second half of Book Two of the *Libri Historiarum*, with the possible exceptions of the quinquennial dates for the defeat of Syagrius and the Thuringian war, are invalid as historical evidence."[89]

The letter from Bishop Avitus to Clovis is used in different ways by historians to support a late date for Clovis's baptism. Van de Vyver stresses that all of Avitus's other letters were sent only after 501 and his letter-writing became stronger toward the end of his episcopal work. He points out that it would be unusual for Clovis's letter to be the only exception to this rule.[90]

Another historian who uses Bishop Avitus's letter to support a later date for Clovis's baptism is Ian Wood. Wood points out that Avitus did not "ascribe [any] role either to the queen or to the outcome of a battle"[91] for Clovis's conversion to Catholicism. Wood says that Avitus "sees Clovis's decision to become a Catholic as the personal choice of an intelligent monarch."[92] Wood identifies three main points in relation to Clovis's baptism emphasized by Avitus: "First, he comments on the king's astuteness in seeing through the arguments of the heretics, though he implies that for some while Clovis had been persuaded by them. Second, he congratulates the king on breaking with the tradition of his ancestors. Finally, after conjuring up an image of the royal baptism, he exhorts the king to further the cause of Catholi-

---

to Clotsinda, Queen of the Lombards (563-565)," in Christianity and Paganism, 350-750: The Conversion of Western Europe, ed. J. N. Hillgarth, The Middle Ages (Philadelphia: University of Pennsylvania Press, 1986), 79-81.

[86] Tessier, 87.

[87] Ibid., 80-81.

[88] Ibid., 82.

[89] Wood, "Gregory of Tours and Clovis," 77.

[90] A. Van de Vyver, "La Victoire Contre Les Alamans Et La Conversion De Clovis (1re Partie)," Revue belge de Philologie et d'Histoire 15, no. 3-4 (1936): 882-887.

[91] Wood, The Merovingian Kingdoms, 43.

[92] Ibid., 44.

cism, while praising his recent action of freeing an unnamed captive people."[93]

Wood implies that the heretics mentioned by Avitus are the Visigoth Arians, and he suggests that the unnamed captive people freed by Clovis were the Gallo-Roman Catholics.[94] He argues that after the battle against the Alamanni in 496, there were no specific people who would properly match Avitus's mention of a recent captive people freed by Clovis. He shares Van de Vyver's position on a later date for the battle and mentions Enodius's letter to Theodoric that refers to the migration of Alamanni into the territory of the Goths[95] as a natural result of "the beginning of Frankish annexation of their territory."[96]

Wood also mentions that the reference in Avitus's letter to a close link between Clovis and Anastasius would be difficult to place before 508. He says, "The degeneration of relations between Theodoric and the Emperor Anastasius, leading to open hostility in 508, coincides suggestively with Gregory's record of the conferment of some notable office on Clovis at Tours in that year."[97] According to him, Clovis received higher status before Anastasius than Theodoric, and the reference to a "consulship" of 508 is a fine interpretation of Avitus's letter.[98]

Another sixth-century document used by historians to challenge Gregory's chronology is the work of Bishop Nicetius of Trier. Tessier mentions that Nicetius describes Clovis's baptism as happening after the miraculous war that happened in Tours near the tomb of Saint Martin.[99] For him Clovis's decision was directly connected with his experience at Saint Martin's tomb. He does not mention Clovis's supernatural experience in the battle against the Alamanni. Kurth, Vyver, and others consider Nicetius's account to be the most reliable one because his letter is earlier than Gregory's *History*

[93] Ibid.

[94] Dallais suggests that the captive people freed by Clovis were his own people, the Franks, and cites the three thousand soldiers baptized with Clovis as a clear proof of this. However, Bishop Avitus refers to the freeing of the captives as a work of evangelization initiated by Clovis, freeing them from a heretical power, and the Franks were not under a heretical rulership when Clovis was baptized. See Dallais, 119.

[95] Herwig Wolfram, History of the Goths, New and completely rev. from the 2nd German ed. (Berkeley: University of California Press, 1988), 313-314.

[96] Wood, The Merovingian Kingdoms, 46.

[97] Wood, "Gregory of Tours and Clovis," 88.

[98] Ibid., 89.

[99] "Nizier, évêque de Trèves de 525 à 566, contemporain par conséquent du premier âge mérovingien, écrivait à la fin de son épiscopat à une petite-fille de Clovis, Clotsinde ou Chlodosvinde, femme d'alboin, roi arien des Lombards. Après lui avoir donné une copieuse leçon de théologie, il la presse de s'en pénétrer et d'en exposer la substance à son mari en vue de le convertir. Puis il rappelle les guérisons miraculeuses qui s'opèrent à Tours, auprès du tombeau de saint Martin." Tessier, 91.

of the Franks and he was a contemporary of Clotilda, Clovis's wife.[100]

There are two major points of controversy concerning the story of Clovis's baptism after the battle against the Alamanni: first, the existence of two battles, one around 496 and the other around 506, and second, the period between Clovis's conversion and his baptism. One advocate of a later date for the battle of Tobiac against the Alamanni is Van de Vyver, who does not see a major problem in Gregory's account of Clovis's conversion after the battle. However, he argues that Gregory did not pay attention to the testimony of Bishop Nicetius stressing the impact of St. Martin on Clovis's conversion. According to Van de Vyver, Gregory's chronological order of the battle and the baptism is right, but both events should come 10 or more years after Gregory's dates. He mentions that when Gregory's account of the battle is compared with other sources, there are three events that make 506 the only possible date for the battle: (1) the death of the king of the Alamanni, (2) their submission to Clovis, and (3) Theodoric's establishment of a protectorate over the Alamanni who did not stay on Clovis's side. Theodoric's letter to Clovis (506-507) mentions all three points. The Panegeric of Enodius to Theodoric (507) mentions points one and three. The historical work of Agathias of Constantinople (570) mentions point three. Gregory's own account of the battle (575) mentions points one and two. For Van de Vyver, then, all this evidence indicates later dates for the battle against the Alamanni (around 506) and for Clovis's baptism (around 508).[101]

Wood presents two other sources that support a later date: Cassiodorus's *Varia*, which mentions a battle between the Franks and the Alamanni in 506, and the letter of Avitus congratulating Clovis for his baptism, which could not have been sent earlier than 502 because of the relations between Franks and Burgundians before that.[102]

Another point that may indicate Clovis's baptism after the battle of Vouillé against Alaric and the Visigoths is the way that Bishop Caesarius of Arles (470?-542) refers to Clovis and his son Childebert (d. 558) in his *Vita Caesarii*. Caesarius does not identify Clovis as Catholic,[103] but he clearly mentions Childebert as Catholic.[104] His description of Childebert indicates an obvious satisfaction with Childebert's religious preference.[105] Even though, like Avitus, Caesarius was living under Arian rulership, he did not congratulate Clovis for his conversion or even mention that Clovis had

---

[100] Kurth, 277-286; A. Van de Vyver, "L'unique Victoire Contre Les Alamans Et La Conversion De Clovis En 506," Revue belge de Philologie et d'Histoire 17, no. 3-4 (1938): 793-813.

[101] Van de Vyver, "L'unique Victoire," 793-813.

[102] Wood, "Gregory of Tours and Clovis," 83, 88.

[103] Caesarius, Sancti Caesarii Episcopi Arelatensis Opera Omnia Nunc Primum in Unum Collecta, ed. Germain Morin (Maretioli: Sanctum Benedictum, 1937), 1.28.

[104] Ibid., 2.45.

[105] Ibid., 1.34.

become a Catholic. This does not mean that he did not know anything about Clovis's conversion and baptism, but it may imply that the event happened so close to Clovis's death that it was not crucial for him to mention it, or that Clovis's Catholicism did not represent a political appeal to break with the Arian rulership.

The possibility that Clovis's baptism did not immediately follow his conversion is presented by Edward James. Commenting on Ian Wood's reasons for Clovis's baptism in 508, James suggests three steps in Clovis's adoption of Catholicism:

> A date of 508 for Clovis's baptism (rather than the traditional 496), as recently argued by Ian Wood, does not mean that Clovis's conversion was similarly near the end of his reign. Gregory of Tours's account of the conversion makes clear one aspect which modern historians have not always remembered in their discussions of the conversion of kings. There may be at least three stages in the process: first of all, intellectual acceptance of Christ's message, the "conversion" proper; secondly, the decision to announce this publicly, to followers who may be hostile to the change; thirdly, the ceremony of baptism and membership of the community of Christians. The Emperor Constantine reached the first stage in 312, never seems to have grasped the nettle of the second stage, and reached the third only on his death-bed in 337. The Burgundian king Gundobad, according to Gregory of Tours, reached the first stage of conversion from Arianism to Catholicism, but did not dare to progress to the second stage for fear of his followers. Avitus himself struggled to convert Gundobad, and so was very aware of the problems. In his letter to Clovis he remarked that many could not bring themselves to convert because of the traditions of their people and respect for their ancestors' worship, and praised Clovis for having had the courage to overcome these obstacles. Clovis progressed through all three stages, even if he may have taken ten or more years to do so. Gregory of Tours, for various reasons, because of what his sources told him, or because of his desire to tell a good, effective story, describes these three stages, but collapses the scale and presents them as happening in a relatively short space of time.[106]

Another important point related to Clovis's baptism is the importance that Bishops Avitus and Gregory of Tours gave to the event. For Avitus and Gregory, the baptism was the apex of Clovis's life. Avitus's letter congratulating Clovis for his baptism reveals its importance to the church-state relationship after the barbarian invasions and presents some reasons why Clovis's baptism was a turning point, not only for the Frankish kingdom, but also for the whole western part of the empire.

Avitus pointed out that Clovis had been appointed by God as judge for the cause of Catholicism and his decision in favor of the Catholic faith was a victory for the Catholic church. He wrote that through Clovis's baptism, "Divine foresight

---

[106] James, The Franks, 123.

has found a certain judge for our age," that Clovis's choice enabled him to "judge in behalf of everyone," and that his faith was a victory for the Catholic Church.[107] Clovis had broken with the tradition of his ancestors and established a kingdom based not on earthly traditions, but on heavenly ones—Catholic traditions. [108]

For Avitus, Clovis's baptism marked the beginning of a new rule for the church in the western part of the empire. He argued that the west could rejoice because it had a Catholic king—a privilege previously reserved for the Greeks in the east— and mentioned that Clovis had been merciful to the Catholic inhabitants of Gaul that he had liberated from Arian Visigoth control. Furthermore, Avitus argued that Clovis's battles before his baptism had been won by good luck, but now his victories would be more effective because of their religious motive and blessings.[109]

For Avitus, the key point in Clovis's life was his baptism and not any of his victories. Clovis's victories were a natural result of his commitment to God and the Catholic Church, as demonstrated in his baptism. Avitus stated that Clovis had demonstrated great respect for bishops since the beginning of his reign, even though he was only obliged to do so after his baptism: "You long ago paid it [humility] to me by your service, even though only now do you owe it to me through your profession of faith."[110] Avitus then pointed out Clovis's mission as a Catholic Christian king: to defend the Catholic Church and to be active in the conversion of pagans by sending envoys and expanding his power over the surrounding pagan tribes.

> Since God, thanks to you, will make of your people His own possession, offer a part of the treasure of Faith which fills your heart to the peoples living beyond you, who, still living in natural ignorance, have not been corrupted by the seeds of perverse doctrines [that is, Arianism]. Do not fear to send them envoys and to plead with them the cause of God, who has done so much for your cause. So that the other pagan peoples, at first being subject to your empire for the sake of religion, while they still seem to have another ruler, may be distinguished rather by their race than by their prince.[111]

Gregory of Tours, like Avitus, stressed the importance of Clovis's baptism. Even though 508 is the best date for the baptism of Clovis, it is possible to understand why Gregory set an earlier date: Gregory wanted to portray everything in Clovis's life as a result of the commitment to the church sealed in his baptism. Gregory even compared

---

[107] Avitus, 369.

[108] Ibid., 370.

[109] Ibid.

[110] Ibid., 371.

[111] Avitus, "Bishop Avitus to King Clovis," in *Christianity and Paganism, 350-750: The Conversion of Western Europe*, ed. J. N. Hillgarth, The Middle Ages (Philadelphia: University of Pennsylvania Press, 1986), 78.

Clovis's baptism to that of Jesus by setting it in the thirtieth year of his life. In the same way that Jesus initiated his ministry at his baptism, Clovis started his defense of Catholicism after his baptism, and from Gregory's viewpoint, Clovis's campaign against the Visigoths could be considered a Catholic Christian crusade only if Clovis was baptized. Gregory wanted to portray Clovis as an example for all Frankish kings and include all his deeds that could be related to patronage of Catholic Christianity in this ideal of kingship. Placing Clovis's baptism at an earlier date allowed him to validate all of Clovis's actions as a pattern for later generations of Catholic kings.[112]

When we accept Clovis' baptism in 508 how shall we interpret the events prior to his baptism such as Clovis' marriage to the Catholic queen Clotilda and her pushing for his conversion to Catholicism; the influence of Bishop Remigius; his spiritual experiences in the war against the Alamanni at Tobiac in 506 (according to Cassiodorus)[113] as presented by Gregory of Tours, and in the tomb of Saint Martin as presented by Bishop Nicetius; and his religious words of motivation to the army in the battle against the Visigoths in 507. All these events would simply represent a gradual process of conversion to Catholicism over a number of years which finally culminated in Clovis's baptism and complete commitment to the Catholic faith in 508. As Wood says, "In order to disprove the 508 dating it would be necessary to find another context which fitted all the contemporary evidence more clearly."[114] Thus Clovis' growth and development in the Catholic faith seems to be similar to Constantine's experience with Catholicism. Although Constantine was favorable towards Christianity, it was not until many years later that he made his full commitment to the Catholic Church and was baptized. So it was with Clovis, king of the Franks.

WAR AGAINST THE VISIGOTHS

The war against the Visigoths is described by Gregory of Tours as one battle where Clovis defeated the Arian heretics in defense of the Catholic faith. The generally accepted date for this battle is A.D. 507, and the victory against the Visigoths was Clovis's most important military achievement.[115] The points of controversy here are whether or not the war consisted of only one battle and whether or not Clovis was fighting for religious reasons.

According to James, the war between the Franks and the Visigoths was "far from

---

[112] Gregory, The History of the Franks, 2.27-43.

[113] The date of 506 for Clovis's battle against the Alamanni can be substantiated by the writings of Cassiodorus, who mentions how many Alamanni sought refuge in Italy after they had been defeated. Cassiodorus, "Variae," 2.41.

[114] Wood, "Gregory of Tours and Clovis," 90.

[115] James, The Franks, 86.

being confined to one battle"[116] and "contemporary annals relate how the Visigoths retook Saintes from the Franks in 496 and the Franks took Bordeaux in 498."[117] James notes that after 502, they had a temporary period of peace in which Alaric probably agreed to pay tribute to Clovis, which "would explain the remark made by Avitus of Vienne that the downfall of the Visigothic kingdom had been due to the drastic debasement of the Visigothic coinage."[118] He implies that the reasons for Clovis's invasion were more economic than religious.

Wood mentions that the religious motive for the war against the Visigoths is more a construction of Gregory's to suit the theological purpose of his book than a reality. He argues that even the stories of Arian persecution against Catholic bishops are not historical fact, and Clovis's motive for the battle was not religious. Also, he mentions that the Arian king Gundobad would not have allied with Clovis in an anti-Arian crusade, and that for Theodoric and Cassiodorus the war was caused by trivial things.[119]

Wood presents strong reasons to dismiss the religious motive for Clovis's attack on Alaric II. However, wars usually have more than one trigger factor. The war against the Goths in Italy demonstrated that the population would shift between supporting the Romans and the Gothic army for convenience, but they would not shift their allegiance away from the Catholic Church.[120] Clovis, as a politician, used the religious expedient to secure support for his military enterprise against the Visigoths, and promised the bishops living under Arian rulership that church property would be preserved. If the war was not an anti-Arian crusade, Clovis still took the religious motive into account as part of his strategy to win the war, and even though the Gallo-Roman clergy did not express their support for a Catholic king, they made their view of the war clear, as in Gregory's account.[121] Even Clovis's anti-Arian speech before the war, as reported by Gregory of Tours, could have been an assurance of victory for the soldiers, in the same way that Constantine used his vision of the cross to motivate his army.[122]

---

[116] Ibid.

[117] Ibid.

[118] Ibid.

[119] Wood, "Gregory of Tours and Clovis," 84-85.

[120] See the section "The Gothic War" in chapter 3.

[121] David Stewart Bachrach, Religion and the Conduct of War, C. 300-1215, Warfare in History (Woodbridge, Suffolk, UK; Rochester, NY: Boydell Press, 2003), 22-23; Peter N. Stearns and William L. Langer, The Encyclopedia of World History: Ancient, Medieval, and Modern, Chronologically Arranged (Boston: Houghton Mifflin, 2001), 171.

[122] According to Gregory, Clovis said, "It irketh me sore that these Arians hold a part of Gaul. Let us go forth, then, and with God's aid bring the land under our own sway." Gregory, The History of the Franks, 2.27.

It is important to mention that both Romans and barbarians viewed religion as part of the military affairs of the state. Geary writes, "The religion of the Frankish king was an integral component of the identity and military success of a whole people, who drew their identity and cohesion from him. The conversion of the king necessarily meant the conversion of his followers. . . . The conversion was clearly a military affair—the adoption by the commander and his army of a new and powerful victory-giver."[123] He also mentions that Christianization made the union between the Gallo-Romans and Franks possible; both groups rejected the idea that their neighbors' religious traditions represented a threat to their kingdoms.[124]

Whether or not Clovis was fighting for religious reasons, the outcome of the battle against the Visigoths was very positive for his kingdom and for the Catholic Church. He doubled the territory of his kingdom and consolidated Catholic supremacy in Gaul, he was recognized as ally and champion of the Catholic Church, and he made an alliance with Emperor Anastasius in 508 that rendered him a "legitimate ruler of Romans as well as his own Franks."[125]

After 508, the relationship between Clovis and the Catholic Church became closer. According to the hagiographic tradition, Clovis founded many churches, but there is historical evidence for only one: the church of the Apostles, later of Sainte-Geneviève, in Paris. He and his wife were buried in that church.[126] Clovis had a good relationship with the bishops in Gaul, but one of his most important acts was the convocation of the Council of Orléans.

THE COUNCIL OF ORLÉANS

From an ecclesiastical point of view, the Council of Orléans in 511 was the first important event of Clovis's reign. It is important to stress that Clovis at this point had already established total control over the Frankish tribes, Aquitaine, and all of Gaul except for a small part under Burgundian control. Clovis's victories in Gaul upheld his religious preferences: the Catholic faith was reaffirmed and Arianism was completely eliminated in his dominions. Clovis's devotion to the Catholic faith can clearly be seen in his pilgrimage to the shrines of St. Martin and St. Hilary in

---

Even later, at the time of Chlotar and Chilperic, Frankish soldiers believed in divine intervention in battle; see Bachrach, 23.

[123] Geary, 85.

[124] Ibid., 86.

[125] James, The Franks, 88.

[126] Ralph W. Mathisen, People, Personal Expression, and Social Relations in Late Antiquity (Ann Arbor: University of Michigan Press, 2003), 196.

the south of Gaul.[127] The Frankish kingdom became a Catholic kingdom, and the Council of Orléans sealed this new national unity. This was the beginning of the close church-state relationship that characterized all of medieval French history.[128]

The Council of Orléans was attended by thirty-two bishops, mainly from Aquitaine and the south of Gaul. Bishops from the distant northeastern frontier were not present.[129] Many of the decisions made at the council were related to ecclesiological problems of the church in Aquitaine and Gaul. However, some other decisions were made that affected the whole Catholic Church; for example, it was decided that monks who married should be expelled from the ecclesiastical order because the church was to be considered the spouse of the priest.[130] Another example is the adoption for the first time of the term "litany" or "rogation," meaning both penitential procession and litany in an official document. The council also prescribed that the Frankish church emulate Bishop Mamertus of Vienne's (477 d.) observance of penitential exercises for the three days before the Feast of the Ascension.[131] The final decisions of the council were summarized in thirty-three canons and addressed to Clovis, seeking his support and validation.[132]

---

[127] Gregory, The History of the Franks, 2.27.

[128] The significance of the Council of Orléans to church-state relationships at the time of Clovis will be discussed in the section "The Council of Orléans" below.

[129] Hefele, 4:87.

[130] Ibid., 4:91.

[131] "Though not the inventor of Rogations or Litanies, Mamertus was undoubtedly the founder of the Rogation Days. Litanies of the kind were, on the evidence of Basil, in use in the East and, on that of Sidonius, in the West, but Mamertus first systematized them on the three days preceding Ascension Day. The story of their institution has been given by his contemporary Sidonius, by Avitus, Gregory of Tours, and others. Vienne, in some year before 474, had been terrified by portents and calamities. To atone for the sins of which these calamities were thought to be the penalties, Mamertus, with the joyful assent of the citizens, ordained a three days' fast, with processions and an ordered service of prayer and song, which, for greater labour, was to take place outside the city. Its successful issue ensured its permanence, and from Vienne it spread over France and the West. Already in 470 or 474 Sidonius had established these services at Clermont, and looked to them as his chief hope in the threatened invasion of the Goths." Henry Wace, William C. Piercy, and William Smith, A Dictionary of Christian Biography and Literature to the End of the Sixth Century A.D., with an Account of the Principal Sects and Heresies (London: J. Murray, 1911), 681.

[132] This is a literal translation of the letter sent by the bishops to Clovis together with the canons: "To our lord, the much glorious King Clovis, son of the Catholic Church, from all bishops which you have ordained to attend the council. Because so many cares have impelled you to honor the religion of the glorious Catholic faith, you have, in order to have access to the priestly opinion, ordered the bishops to come together to discuss necessary questions. In accordance with your will, we reply that this is what appeared to be the best solution to the consultation and to the items that you gave us. So that, if this that we determined is also approved by your judgment, this is the right. The agreement of a so-great king and master, will confirm that the authoritative sentence of so many bishops must be observed" (Domno suo catholicae ecclesiae filio Chlothouecho gloriosissimo regi omnes sacerdotes, quos ad

The Salic Law

The Salic law was the Frankish law code that, according to scholars, was written down between 507 and 511. This code differed from Roman and other barbarian codes of law in its content and to whom it was addressed. Roman laws distinguished between private and public spheres of justice, whereas the Salic code was based on individuals seeking compensation for wrongs suffered. As Drew says, "the Frankish law, like the law of the other Germanic peoples, did not distinguish between what might call civil and criminal causes. The Franks did not have a police force to bring criminals before police courts (as did the Romans); instead, what we would call criminal cases were handled as civil suits for damages."[133]

The Salic law did not defer to the church as an organization, but it included special provisions for church buildings and bishops. The compensation owed for destroying a church by fire was 200 *solidi*.[134] Bishops were ranked among those who were liable to receive the highest amount of money—1800 *solidi*.[135] Bishops were not appointed as chief judicial officers under the Salic code, but as leaders in their communities, they retained their knowledge of Roman law in applying it to the Gallo-Roman population. As Avé Lallemant says, "Several documents contain an admonition [from the king] to a bishop or count to render justice to one of their subjects, who had come to the king with the complaint that he could not receive justice at home."[136]

Another point regarding the content, as Charles de Secondat Montesquieu points out, is that "the laws of the Burgundians and Visigoths were impartial; but it was otherwise with regard to the Salic law, for it established between the Franks and Romans the most mortifying distinctions."[137] The amount of money to be paid for an offense against a Frank was at least double the amount required

---

concilium uenire iussistis. Qui tanta ad religionis catholicae cultum gloriosae fidei cura uos excitat, ut sacerdotalis mentis affectum sacerdotes de rebus necessaries tractaturos in unum college iusseritis, secundum uoluntates uestrae consultationem et titulos, quos dedistis, ea quae nobis uisum est definitione respondimus ; ita ut, si ea quae nos statuimus etiam uestro recta esse iudicio conprobantur, tanti consensus Regis ac domini maiori auctoritate seruandam tantorum firmet sententiam sacerdotum). Charles de Clercq, Concilia Galliae A. 511-A. 695, Corpus Christianorum, Series Latina, vol. 148A (Turnholti: Typographi Brepols Editores Pontificii, 1963), 4.

[133] Katherine Fischer Drew, The Laws of the Salian Franks, Middle Ages Series (Philadelphia: University of Pennsylvania Press, 1991), 33.

[134] A solidi at the time of Clovis was a silver coin weighting 4.55 grams.

[135] Ibid., 162-163.

[136] W. Marjolijn J. de Boer Avé Lallement, "Early Frankish Society as Reflected in Contemporary Sources: Sixth and Seventh Centuries" (Ph.D. diss., Rice University, 1982), 94.

[137] Charles de Secondat Montesquieu, The Spirit of Laws (London: George Bell and Sons, 1878), 185.

for the same offense against a Roman.[138]

The Salic law differed from other barbarian codes in that it was the first Germanic code that included both Romans and barbarians.[139] The Visigoths and Burgundians had set up different law codes for Romans and barbarians.[140] However, Clovis did not promulgate a specific code for Gallo-Romans in his kingdom, and scholars suggest that issues not covered in the Salic laws were judged by the national laws of each nation under Frankish control.[141]

Since religion was not considered in the Salic code of the Franks, and Clovis did not create a separate code for his Gallo-Roman subjects as other barbarian kings had done, he adopted the council's procedures as religious law and implemented them as the law of the state. This differed from the Roman judicial system, where religion was part of the body of laws of the state. Religious laws for the Franks then had state approval, but became a separate code of laws by themselves.[142]

---

[138] For example, the murderer of a Frank had to pay 200 solidi (4.55 grams silver coin) to the family of the victim, the murderer of a Roman landowner had to pay 100 solidi, and the murderer of a Roman freeman had to pay 62.5 solidi. Drew, 104-105.

[139] Theodoric issued a code known as Edictum that was a compilation of Roman laws and did not have any Germanic content. See Guy Carleton Lee, Historical Jurisprudence: An Introduction to the Systematic Study of the Development of Law (New York: Macmillan, 1900), 376.

[140] The Burgundians had two law codes: the Lex Gundobada for the Burgundian invaders, and the Lex Romana Burgundiorum, known also as Papianus, for the Romans. The Visigoths also had two codes: one known as Forum Judicum and Judicum Liber, for the barbarians, and the Liber Legum Romanorum, which was by the thirteenth century called Breviarium Alarici, for the Roman inhabitants. King Chindasuinth, in the second year of his reign (642/643), promulgated a new Visigoth code in Spain for both Romans and Visigoths, the Lex Visigothorum, eliminating social differences before the law. See Katherine Fischer Drew, The Burgundian Code: The Book of Constitutions or Law of Gundobad; Additional Enactments (Philadelphia: University of Pennsylvania Press, 1972), 1-16; Harold Dexter Hazeltine, "Roman and Canon Law in the Middle Ages," in The Cambridge Medieval History, ed. J. B. Bury et al. (New York: Macmillan, 1926), 721-723; P. J. Heather, The Visigoths from the Migration Period to the Seventh Century: An Ethnographic Perspective, Studies in Historical Archaeoethnology (Woodbridge, UK; Rochester, NY: Boydell Press; Center for Interdisciplinary Research on Social Stress, 1999), 225-258; P. D. King, Law and Society in the Visigothic Kingdom (Cambridge; New York: Cambridge University Press, 2006), 1-22; Lee, 369-385.

[141] The Breviarium Alarici was still in use during the time of the Merovingian rulers, but it was only officially adopted by the Franks as a law code for those Gallo-Roman citizens living in Septimania, Aquitania, and other parts of southern Gaul, and for Frankish church matters at the time of Charlemagne. Drew, The Laws of the Salian Franks, 28-30; Luitpold Wallach, Alcuin and Charlemagne: Studies in Carolingian History and Literature, Cornell Studies in Classical Philology (Ithaca, NY: Cornell University Press, 1959), 130-139.

[142] For more information on the Salic law, see Joseph Balon, Traité De Droit Salique; Étude D'exégèse Et De Sociologie Juridiques (Namur, Les Anc: Éts Godenne, 1965); Karl August Eckhardt, Die Gesetze Des Merowingerreiches, 481-714, Germanenrechte, Bd. 1 (Witzenhausen: Deutschrechtlicher Instituts-Verlag, 1961); Jan Hendrik Hessels and H. Kern, Lex Salica: The Ten Texts with the Glosses, and the Lex Emendata (London: J. Murray [etc.], 1880); Micheline

SUMMARY

Gregory's chronology of Clovis's reign is accepted by the majority of historians as sequentially faithful on the majority of the facts. The two major points of criticism concern Clovis's baptism and the war against the Alamanni. Historians have also criticized Gregory's writing style, considering his *History of the Franks* to be more a romance than a historical book.

The most important event of Clovis's reign at the time was his victory over the Visigoths, but the most important event of Clovis's life in the history of the Middle Ages was his conversion to Catholicism. Besides his marriage to Clotilda, there are two suggested motivations for Clovis's conversion: the battle against the Alamanni and Clovis's visit to St. Martin's tomb. Those who agree with Gregory's explanation of Clovis's conversion set the battle and Clovis's baptism around 496. Those who disagree with Gregory's explanation set the battle and Clovis's conversion in 506 and his baptism in 508.

The most important years of Clovis's reign were 507 and 508, which marked Clovis's final victory over the Visigoths, his alliance with Emperor Anastasius, and the best date for his baptism. After that, Clovis was recognized as an ally and champion of the Catholic Church; he paid homage to St. Martin in acknowledgment of divine help, he established Paris as the capital of his kingdom, and he began dealing in the affairs of the church (building churches, appointing bishops, and later convening the Council of Orléans).

FRANKISH EXPANSION AND THE CHURCH-STATE RELATIONSHIP DURING CLOVIS'S REIGN

INTRODUCTION

The Franks occupied the lowlands near the mouth of the Rhine River at the end of the fourth century and beginning of the fifth century.[143] In 481, when Clo-

---

Peyrebonne, La Véritable Histoire De La Loi Salique (Paris: M. Peyrebonne; distribution, Europe notre patrie, 1980); John Milton Potter, The Development and Significance of the Salic Law of the French (n.p.: 1937); Theodore John Rivers, Laws of the Salian and Ripuarian Franks, Ams Studies in the Middle Ages, No. 8 (New York: AMS Press, 1986); Hans-Achim Roll, Zur Geschichte Der Lex Salica-Forschung, Untersuchnungen Zur Deutschen Staats- Und Rechtsgeschichte, N. F., Bd. 17 (Aalen: Scientia Verlag, 1972); Ruth Schmidt-Wiegand, Fränkische Und Frankolateinische Bezeichnungen Für Soziale Schichten Und Gruppen in Der Lex Salica (Göttingen: Vandenhoeck & Ruprecht, 1972); Mary Agnes Somers, "The Source and Development of the Salic Law in France before A.D. 1600" (1916).

[143] For maps on the Frankish territory before and after Clovis see appendix C.

vis became chieftain of the Salian Franks, they began expanding south from their homeland into Roman-controlled Gaul. In approximately twenty-five years, Clovis defeated the last Roman army in Gaul, the Thuringians (489), the Alamanni (496 and 506), the Visigoths (507/508), and the other Germanic tribes, and unified the Frankish tribes, becoming king of all the Franks and ruler of much of western Europe. At Clovis's death, his kingdom was a mixture of different ethnicities. Small minorities of Franks were living among the Gallo-Romans, and numerous other Germanic peoples were united by the Catholic religion.

FRANKISH EXPANSION

The Frankish expansion under Clovis was an extraordinary achievement for a Germanic tribe that did not have great numbers or the most powerful army. Possible decisive factors in this vast territorial expansion include the fact that it was an expansion rather than a migration, the assimilation of local institutions and rulers, the geographical position, and religious factors.

EXPANSION, NOT MIGRATION

The Frankish expansion differed from the invasions of other German tribes because the Franks did not abandon their homeland when moving into the conquered territory, but rather added them together. They expanded, rather than migrating. After a successful military venture, they would move the capital of the realm to a new centralized position; a few Frankish landlords would move into the new territory and the majority of the warriors would return to their homelands. The Franks were constantly increasing in number, but not at a fast enough rate to populate the new territories.[144]

ASSIMILATION OF LOCAL INSTITUTIONS AND RULERS

Clovis's expansion policy allowed the established local authorities in many places to continue to exercise responsible and responsive government. His administration blended Frankish and Roman traditions. In the north, the predominantly Frankish population had been Romanized after years of service to the Roman administration. In the south, the local administration and infrastructure suffered few changes. The *civitas* with its local senate was added to the Frankish

---

[144] Francis Owen, The Germanic People: Their Origin, Expansion, and Culture (New York: Bookman Associates, 1960), 108-111.

aristocracy. The Franks were used to working with the Roman bureaucracy and absorbed it into their administrative system.[145]

However, the Franks did not assimilate the whole Roman administrative system. The Frankish government was more primitive and decentralized, with a high level of local autonomy in most places. The army was not paid by the central government. Each duke worked independently for the maintenance of its army and was connected to central government by oath. The general Roman institutions that levied heavy and unfair taxes were rejected; the Franks had a tendency to exempt their state from taxation and inflict it on others. The local aristocracy was responsible to provide assistance to the state and the Frankish lords with military protection.[146]

GEOGRAPHICAL POSITION

The geographical position of the Franks was another important factor in their process of expansion. The eastern part of the Roman Empire was occupied with the Persian and barbarian threat. The majority of the barbarian tribes moved into the empire in a southern direction. The Scandinavian tribes north of Gaul did not come down to invade Roman lands. The Turigians and the Alamanni were not strong enough to defeat the Franks. The barbarians in control of the south (Spain and Italy) were constantly being threatened by other barbarian tribes or the eastern Roman Empire. The Roman authorities left in Gaul were mostly corrupt and unable to gather an army big enough to defeat the barbarians; the only possible source of military resistance was the Catholic Church, which preserved the Roman ideals and traditions that were still valuable for the Gallo-Romans, but did not strongly oppose the Franks.[147]

---

[145] Geary, 92-95; Eleanor L. Turk, The History of Germany, The Greenwood Histories of the Modern Nations (Westport, CT: Greenwood Press, 1999), 25.

[146] The fall of the Roman Empire brought the same problems of high taxation to the Visigoths and Burgundians. Previously, the barbarians had had to pay taxes to the Roman emperor to live in his territory. With the fall of the empire, the barbarian kings continued to use the same taxation system, but now on their own behalf. However, the Franks did not assimilate the Roman taxation system like the other barbarian tribes because, since Julius's time, they had had the status of federates. For further information on barbarian settlements in Gaul, see Walter A. Goffart, Barbarians and Romans, A.D. 418-584: The Techniques of Accommodation (Princeton, NJ: Princeton University Press, 1980), 103-161.

[147] See J. F. Drinkwater and Hugh Elton, Fifth-Century Gaul: A Crisis of Identity? (Cambridge: Cambridge University Press, 2002), 165-176; Guy Halsall, "The Barbarian Invasions," in The New Cambridge Medieval History 1, C. 500-C. 700, ed. Paul Fouracre (Cambridge: Cambridge University Press, 2006), 35-65; Andrew Louth, "The Eastern Empire in the Sixth Century," in The New Cambridge Medieval History 1, C. 500-C. 700, ed. Paul Fouracre (Cambridge: Cambridge University Press, 2006), 93-117; Van Dam, 193-231.

RELIGIOUS FACTORS

The barbarian tribes who had taken over Gaul were Arian Christians or pagans. The Gallo-Roman society included a mix of religions. However, because of the strong diocesan system rooted in the cities, the Catholic Church inherited political control of the cities in times of distress after the fall of the Western Roman Empire. Catholic bishops were viewed as saviors when they took over from the inefficient and often absent Roman officers as defenders of the cities. Many fifth- and sixth-century bishops are named with the epithet *defensor civitatis,* reflecting these political works.[148] Among the city residents, there was great appreciation for and fidelity to the bishops, and consequently, to the church. Therefore, the most important point about a ruler to them was not whether he would be a good Christian, but whether he was Catholic.[149]

Those who opposed the Franks in Gaul were either weak Roman aristocrats or Arian Christian barbarians. The political and military instability of the Western Roman Empire in the fifth century led most of the aristocratic families to withdraw from political responsibilities and focus on their own financial interests. In this atmosphere of social and political disorganization, bishops from aristocratic families with more administrative than theological qualifications became more valuable to the people. As Dill states, "He [bishop] had wealth for sacred or charitable objects, to build or renovate churches, to redeem the captive among the barbarians, to relieve the miseries of the lower classes who were suffering from the disorder and insecurity caused by the invasions. He had also the authority derived from rank, and the social tact which made him able to defend his flock against the violence of the German chiefs, or the not less dreaded oppression of the Roman officials."[150]

Even though they were Arian, the Visigoths and Burgundians were not generally hostile to their Catholic subjects, and they did not normally persecute or destroy Catholic churches. The historical accounts of Catholic persecution in Gaul by Arian governments are connected more to political problems than religious problems.[151] Nevertheless,

---

[148] Wood, The Merovingian Kingdoms, 75.

[149] Heuclin, 9.

[150] Dill, Roman Society in the Western Empire, 216.

[151] One of Gregory of Tours's reasons for Clovis becoming a Catholic champion against Arianism is the persecution of Catholic bishops in Gaul. However, the events he presented as proof of this persecution are not supported by historical evidence. This does not mean that Catholics and Arians were living in peace and enjoying each other, but as Wood writes, "Alaric II's reign suggests that he was concerned to establish good relations with the Catholic Gallo-Romans in the years immediately before 'Vouillé'. He was responsible for the compilation of a Roman law-book, the Breviary. He also supported a Catholic Church Council presided over by Caesarius of Arles at Agde in 506, and he approved the holding of another council in the following year, although it did not meet because of the king's defeat and death at the hands of Clovis." Wood, The Merovingian Kingdoms, 47. See also Moorhead, "Clovis' Motives for Becoming a Catholic Christian," 329-339.

some Catholics who feared Arian expansion worked against their Arian masters and welcomed the Franks, who had a good relationship with the Catholic Church.[152]

St. Remigius's letter welcoming Clovis in his ascendance to the throne implies a good relationship between Clovis's son Childeric and the bishops in Belgica Secunda. Remigius reminded Clovis of the importance of "continuing the traditions of his ancestors" and told him that he "should respect your bishops and always have recourse to their counsel, for if there is good interchange between you and them your province can be more secure."[153] Another example of Clovis leaning toward the Catholic Church is his edict issued just before the war against the Visigoths in 507. Clovis sent a letter addressed to the bishops in the Visigoth dominions telling them that he had issued an edict stating that all church properties would be protected and not destroyed.[154]

Clovis not only sought to have a good relationship with the Catholics, but also used Catholic bishops as part of the administration system of his domains. The Catholic Church had the skilled personnel that he needed for administrative positions. Most of the clergy were part of the aristocracy and well educated, and they already had the respect of the population of the *civitas*.[155] John William Burgess, commenting on the role of the church in Clovis's kingdom and his good relationship with the clergy, points out that the church became an important factor in the balance of power in the Frankish kingdom, since it was

> well organized under its Bishops, and possessing, according to the Roman public law, the power of intercession with the Government in behalf of the individual and of the people, and the power of controlling and administering education and charity, and the law of domestic relations. The authority of the Frankish King over his Gallo-Roman subjects depended almost entirely upon the influence of the Bishops and lower Clergy over the people. He must, therefore, in his Government not only leave them in possession of the powers recognized to them by the public law of the Roman Empire, but he must increase those powers from time to time, in order to maintain their friendship and co-operation.[156]

George William Kitchin also writes, "The bishops became the advisers, and, in

---

[152] Paul Van Dyke, The Story of France from Julius Caesar to Napoleon III (New York: C. Scribner's Sons, 1929), 44-45.

[153] William M. Daly, "Clovis: How Barbaric, How Pagan?," Speculum 69, no. 3 (1994): 632.

[154] Wood, The Merovingian Kingdoms, 47.

[155] Laurent Theis, "Au Commencement Était La Gaule Romaine," Notre Histoire Sommaire, April 1996, 9.

[156] John William Burgess, The Reconciliation of Government with Liberty (New York: C. Scribner's Sons, 1915), 87.

some sense, the educators of the chieftains . . . as they [chieftains] brought into Gaul their old dislike of town-life, they left the bishops with sole authority in the cities: and the clergy consequently continued to be the special representatives of the old Roman municipal life."[157] Even later on, the church played a very important role in pacifying non-Christian lands that were added to Frankish territory.[158]

The church-state relationship in Clovis's kingdom was very important for Frankish expansion because the umbrella of the Catholic faith unified the various groups of subjects. The Frankish expansion was parallel to that of Catholicism in Gaul and other parts of Europe, which culminated in the formation of the Holy Roman Empire centuries later.

THE COUNCIL OF ORLÉANS

After Emperor Theodosius's proclamation of Catholicism as the official religion of the Roman Empire in 392, the Catholic Church had influence in the political sphere but was not strong enough to eradicate Arianism or prevent the Roman emperors from interfering in church affairs. The fall of the Roman Empire and the rise of the independent barbarian kingdoms brought a new kind of relationship between church and state. The Arian rulers generally granted the Catholic bishops autonomy to deal with ecclesiastical affairs; this meant church and state were legislating almost totally independently of one another.[159] Nevertheless, the leadership exerted by the bishops of Gaul to defend the *civitas* against barbarian invasion led society to recognize the preeminence of spiritual power over temporal power.[160] Such bishops as Remigius and Avitus became not only spiritual leaders, but also counselors of the political leaders.[161] Clovis's administrative ability is demonstrated in his utilization of these powerful spiritual leaders, drawing them to his side.[162]

In the war against Alaric, Clovis's edict promising to spare church property from destruction and pillage demonstrated his strategic use of religious preference for political advantage.[163] Shortly after his victory over the Visigoths, his gifts to the shrines of St. Martin and donations to build churches like the church

---

[157] G. W. Kitchin, A History of France, Clarendon Press Series (Oxford: Clarendon Press, 1892), 73.

[158] Ibid.

[159] For more information, see the above section "The Church in the West and Barbarian Invasion."

[160] See the above section "The Catholic Diocesan System."

[161] The content of Remigius's and Avitus's letters to both Frankish and Burgundian kings indicates that they worked for these kings not only as religious leaders, but also as political advisors. See Avitus, "Opera Quae Supersunt," 1-14, 29-31, 35-102; Remigius, 112-114.

[162] Turk, 25.

[163] Gregory, The History of the Franks, 2.27.

of Paris increased the confidence of the bishops and Gallo-Roman Catholics in Clovis's leadership of the Catholic faith.[164] The need for an immediate solution to local church problems that the bishops presented led Clovis to summon a council at Orléans in 511. The final decisions of the council were validated by Clovis's political power. Thus, some historians such as Jean Heuclin call the Council of Orléans a concordat.[165]

Constantine and other Roman emperors had been part of church councils before Orléans, but the council summoned by Clovis was different because of how the bishops and the king worked out the problems to be solved. The king summoned the council and provided a list of topics to be addressed. The bishops discussed the topics without state supervision, provided solutions, and submitted the canons to the king, not for his opinion or any further suggestions, but only for his validation and political implementation of their decision.[166]

The topics addressed by the council went beyond religious affairs to judicial and political subjects. Heuclin discusses it as follows:

> La premièe partie des canons répondait à des interrogations politiques. Les problèmes du droit d'asile et des mariages incestueux, abordés dans le Code théodosien, avaient pris une acuité nouvelle de par la présence des Francs. La loi romaine avait délimité l'espace du droit d'asile. Elle en avait exclu les débiteurs publics et les juifs et avait infligé des peines sévères aux violateurs de ce droit. Le concile s'attacha à protéger de la mort et de la mutilation les homicides, adultères, ravisseurs des jeunes filles et esclaves fugitifs, catégories particulièrement exposées au droit de vengeance privée (la *faide*) des lois barbares. Le concile menaça d'excommunication et de la colère divine les poursuivants. Les évêques bénéficiaient ici d'une reconnaissance légale de leur intercession, en obtenant la commutation des peines capitales en compensation pécunière (*wergeld*), dont les tarifs étaient fixés par la Loi salique.[167]

The Council of Orléans confirmed the political power attributed to the bishops in Clovis's reign. There was now a new concept of clergy: A bishop could now be appointed by the king and play the role not only of a religious leader, but also of a political leader. The bishops then had the authority to control violence and civil affairs in their bishoprics.[168] The council confirmed the new relationship between church

---

[164] Ibid.

[165] Heuclin, 41.

[166] See a translation of the letter sent to Clovis by the bishops after the Council of Orléans in fn. 126 in this chapter. Clercq, 4.

[167] Heuclin, 43. See John C. Murray, "Leo XIII: Separation of Church and State," Theological Studies 14 (June 1953), 193.

[168] Canon 1. Hefele, 4:88.

and state present in Clovis's kingdom and those of all other Merovingian kings.

Kitchin comments that in this new relationship between church and state in the Frankish kingdom, the church gained most of all. He says, "Before the emperors she [the church] had been submissive, dependent; towards the Franks, she assumed the air of a benefactor, of a superior: she had 'made their fortune'; she guided their policy, blessed their arms, partially tempered their fierceness, standing between them and the conquered inhabitants of Gaul: she lived under and administered the Roman law, not the rude Custom-law of the Franks."[169] It was the council that sealed this concordat between church and state. As Heuclin says, "Ce fut le concile des compromissions."[170]

SUMMARY

The Frankish expansion was facilitated by several different factors. The Franks expanded their territories rather than migrating to new ones; they were relatively unthreatened by other barbarian tribes due to their geographic location and their greater military power; and they assimilated part of the Roman administrative structure left in Gaul and adopted the religion of the Gallo-Roman population—Catholicism.

The conversion of Clovis to Catholicism was one of the most important factors in the Frankish expansion and led to the development of a new type of church-state relationship. The bishops became political leaders in their communities and political advisors to the king, while the king acquired political influence in such ecclesiastical affairs as the appointment of bishops and had to implement the rules proposed by the bishops. Bishops and kings worked together for the benefit of church and state.

THE IMPACT OF CLOVIS'S CONVERSION DESCRIBED BY HISTORIANS AND THEOLOGIANS

INTRODUCTION

The most significant event in the beginning of the history of the Frankish people is Clovis's conversion. The Franks became a Catholic nation, and gradually all the other Germanic tribes in Europe adopted Catholicism. The "episcopal lordship" model of Frankish Gaul was the basis for the establishment of the Holy Roman

---

[169] Kitchin, 75.

[170] Heuclin, 43.

Empire. Clovis became the eldest son and the Franks became the eldest daughter of the Catholic Church, and they were strong supporters of papal supremacy.[171]

The scholars discussing the impact of Clovis's conversion in the historical and theological milieus can be divided into three major groups: one group that says the Franks were champions of the Roman church, another group that used him to justify a movement for Frankish Catholic independence from the Roman church; and a third group, critics of early secondary sources, that suggested a political rather than a religious reason for Clovis's acceptance of Catholicism.

Clovis, the Champion of Catholicism

The first historian to describe Clovis as a champion of Catholicism was Gregory of Tours, in his *History of the Franks*. For him, Clovis was God's hand punishing the heretics and promoting the Catholic faith. During the Middle Ages, chroniclers and theologians continued to portray him this way. Even after historical criticism challenging Gregory's account, Clovis is still seen as a Catholic champion by the majority of historians.

For Gregory of Tours, Clovis's wars after his baptism had a religious motive. His description of Clovis's political and military enterprises is more a theological treatise than a historical work. He uses Clovis's reign as a reference point in support of his theological assumptions. Heinzelmann summarizes Gregory's theological description of Clovis's life in the following way:

> First, the bishop announces the birth of Clovis with the same words the evangelist Luke had used for that of the Saviour in order next to allude to the good inclinations of the still-pagan king and to his later baptism. Cleansed of his previous sins at the time of baptism and becoming in that way part of the church of Christ, Clovis is finally ready for what appears to be his true historic calling: with the assistance of several prestigious saints, principally Saint Martin and Saint Hilary, he strikes the heretic kings, Gundobad and, especially, Alaric the Visigoth. Having fulfilled his messianic role, he is fully rewarded by God, who gives him victory over all his enemies.[172]

---

[171] Elizabeth Missing Sewell, Popular History of France from the Earliest Period to the Death of Louis XIV (London: Longmans, Green, 1876), 13. Even today, the Catholic church recognizes France as the eldest daughter of the church due to the conversion of Clovis and the Franks. "Having embraced Christianity at the initiative of its King, Clovis, it was rewarded by this most honourable testimony to its faith and piety, the title of eldest daughter of the Church." Pope Leo XIII, "Nobilissima Gallorum Gens," Encyclical of Pope Leo XIII on the Religious Question in France. http://www.vatican.edu/holy_father/leo_xiii/encyclicals/documents/hf_l-xiii_enc_08021884_nobilissima-gallorum-gens_en.html (accessed 18 March 2009).

[172] Martin Heinzelmann, "Heresy in Books I and II of Gregory of Tours' Historiae," in After Rome's Fall: Narrators and Sources of Early Medieval History: Essays Presented to Walter Goffart, ed. Alexander C. Murray (Toronto: University of Toronto Press, 1998), 69.

According to Heinzelmann, Gregory's *History of the Franks* parallels Augustine's description of Christ and the church as the kingdom of God. He says that "the chief purpose of Gregory of Tours was to demonstrate the historical presence of Christ and, through this reality, a 'society of the saints,' taken in the literal sense."[173] He stresses that mainly the bishops, but also the king, had an important role in the formation of this ideal society. Heinzelmann points out three roles played by the bishops. First was "the representation of the universal church and its continuity."[174] Through the apostolic succession represented by the bishop's office, the universality and orthodoxy of the church was preserved. Second was the relationship between bishops and king. Heinzelmann points out that Gregory mentions Clovis as being assisted by such bishops as Saint Remigius and Saint Avitus, and stresses that the "royal government was highly dependent on episcopal participation."[175] Third, and most important for him, was the "role of the prelates in their city, that is, to put it simply, the governance of Christian society."[176]

Kathleen Anne Mitchell also states that Gregory's *History* is more theologically than historically oriented. Mitchell says that, to Gregory, keeping the law of God was the only way to have a successful society, and the political leaders were responsible for enforcing this. "These are the bishops and the kings, and God's law demands that they obeyed. A subordinate, therefore, has no right of rebellion against them. . . . The practice of good rule can be best achieved when bishops and kings work together, bishops guiding and kings implementing."[177]

The fact that Gregory is the major source for information on Clovis's reign means that the majority of historians see Clovis's conversion as the beginning of a closer relationship between church and state, as well as the alliance between the Catholic Church and the Franks.[178] Clovis is seen as a great unifier. As Victur Dutry says, "Clovis was the first to unite all the elements from which the new social order was to be formed, - namely, the barbarians whom he established in power; the Roman civilization to which he rendered homage by receiving the insignia of Patrician and of Consul from the Emperor Anastasius; and finally, the Catholic Church, with which he formed that fruitful alliance which was continued by his successors."[179]

---

[173] Ibid., 80.

[174] Ibid., 71.

[175] Ibid., 72.

[176] Ibid.

[177] Mitchell, 76-77.

[178] Among the historians who see Clovis as a Catholic champion are Bertier de Sauvigny and Pinkney; Dallais; Dalton; Victor Duruy and George Burton Adams, The History of the Middle Ages (New York: H. Holt, 1904); Guizot and Guizot de Witt; Haine; and Verseuil.

[179] Duruy and Adams, 32.

Movement toward Independence

In the sixteenth century Frankish historians and theologians began openly rejecting papal supremacy, although they did not reject Catholicism. The great debate at this time in France was over clerical and royal jurisdiction, and they often referred to events from early Frankish history such as the Council of Orléans to support the thesis that the Frankish church had always been independent from Rome, that the ecclesiastical power in France had been subordinated to secular jurisdiction. The alliance was not between the king and Rome, but between the kings in the Frankish Catholic Church.

Both sides used Clovis's reign to support their positions. The main argument related to Clovis's reign was whether or not the relationship between Rome and France had begun in his time. The royalists argued that the Frankish kings had taken the duty of protecting the church from the Roman emperors, while the papists argued that the Frankish kings were acting in defense of the interests of the church. The question was not whether Clovis had become a champion of Catholicism, but rather, for whom was the Catholic king acting. This discussion brought to light a lot of primary and secondary sources, such as those used by Jean Du Tillet in his *Chronicle of the Kings of the France.*[180]

Historical Criticism

The historians who criticize the religious motivation for Clovis's conversion do not deny his adoption of the Catholic faith and its future impact on the history of the Franks and European countries. In most cases, they compare Clovis with Constantine and see Clovis's conversion as a way to get the support of the Gallo-Roman Catholics.[181] Their major criticism is of Gregory's account, which they argue is more a careful choice of events portrayed in a miraculous way to support his theological presuppositions.

---

[180] For further studies, see J. H. M. Salmon, "Clovis and Constantine: The Uses of History in Sixteenth-Century Gallicanism," Journal of Ecclesiastical History 41, no. 4 (1990): 584-605; Jean Du Tillet, La Chronique Des Roys De France, Puis Pharamond Iusques Au Roy Henry, Second Du Nom, Selon la Computation Des Ans, Iusques in L'an Mil Cinq Cens Quarante & Neuf (Paris: Paris Galiot du Pré, 1550); idem, Recueil Des Roys De France Plus Une Chronique Abregée (Paris: I. Du Puys, 1580); Jean Du Tillet and Henri Auguste Omont, Portraits Des Rois De France Du Recueil De Jean Du Tillet (Paris: Imprimerie Berthaud Frères, 1908); Mack P. Holt, The French Wars of Religion, 1562-1629, New Approaches to European History (Cambridge; New York: Cambridge University Press, 2005); Victor Martin, Les Origines Du Gallicanisme (Paris: Bloud & Gay, 1939).

[181] Some of the historians who propose statements like this are Matthieu-Maxime Gorce, Clovis, 456-511 (Paris: Payot, 1935); James, The Franks; Kurth; Lot; Périn and Feffer; Tessier; Van de Vyver, "L'évolution"; Wood, The Merovingian Kingdoms.

Ian Wood did one of the latest analyses of the historicity of Gregory's chronology. He points out that basically everything in Gregory's chronology of Clovis's life is invalid, with the exception of the dates for the defeat of Syagrius and the Thuringian war.[182] Wood says that Gregory's major source was oral history, which is the hardest to validate for the modern historian, and that his other sources must be carefully examined to unveil the historical method underlying Gregory's account. He argues that any historian approaching Gregory's account of Clovis should be careful in separating the real Clovis from Gregory's Clovis, but at the same time he recognizes that "it would be unreasonable to expect a 'scientific' approach to history in the sixth century; allowance must be made for the moralizing aspects of Catholic historiography. Once that is done, Gregory's achievement in drawing together material of very different kinds—sometimes admittedly with comic results—stands out as a formidable one, even if his interpretation of Clovis lacks credibility."[183]

CONCLUSION

From A.D. 481 to 511, in the years of Clovis's reign, the adoption of Catholicism by the Franks brought key changes in the relationship between the Catholic Church and the state in Gaul. In this period, the Catholic Church experienced a major shift in its power on secular issues and in its relationship with the state. The years before Clovis's reign marked the fall of the western Roman Empire, the incursion of barbarian tribes, the revival of paganism, and the spread of Arianism supported by barbarian kings. The Catholic influence in the political sphere that had started with Constantine and peaked with Theodosius's proclamation of Catholicism as the official religion of the state in 392 was shaken.

The fall of the Roman Empire and the rise of independent barbarian kingdoms led to a new relationship between church and state. The Arian rulers generally granted the Catholic bishops autonomy to deal with ecclesiastical affairs; church and state were legislating independently of one another. This lack of recognition as the official religion of the state was more positive than negative for Catholicism. The leadership exerted by the bishops of Gaul in defense of the *civitas* against barbarian invasion increased the bishops' political influence and led to the recognition of the preeminence of spiritual power over temporal power. Such bishops as Remigius and Avitus became not only spiritual leaders, but also counselors of political authorities.

Clovis, considered the first king of the Franks, expanded his territorial power

---

[182] Wood, "Gregory of Tours and Clovis," 77.
[183] Ibid., 91.

by assimilating Roman territories and defeating other barbarians. By 508, he was the lord of all Gaul and Aquitaine, except for the region under Burgundian control. The most significant events during his reign were his victory over the Alamanni in 506, his victory over the Visigoths in 507-508, his appointment to the consulship by Emperor Anastasius in 508, his homage to the shrine of Saint Martin of Tours in recognition of God's help in the battle of Vouillé in 508, his baptism in 508, and his involvement in? the Council of Orléans in 511.

Among these events, Clovis's baptism in 508 is the most significant, since it consummated a process of conversion, where the Frankish kingdom became a Catholic kingdom and a concordat between the Catholic Church and the Franks was completed. After 508, the political and military power of the Franks was enlisted to defend the Catholic faith in the western part of the Roman Empire. Clovis was the first barbarian king to convert to Catholicism, and he established a new system of Christian society under the authority of the Catholic bishops—a union of the Frankish king with the ecclesiastical authorities of the Catholic Church. As Wood says, "What was important was the fact that after 508 the Catholic Church defined the Christian community which constituted the *regnum Francorum*."[184]

Clovis's conversion to Catholicism and his territorial expansion that eliminated Arianism from Gaul solidified Catholic supremacy. He not only adopted the Catholic faith, but also drew powerful Catholic leaders to his side. After 508, Clovis's administrative model of the church-state relationship set the tone for the new European political system of independent kingdoms united by the bonds of the Catholic Church: a partnership of throne and altar. Bishops and kings began working together, with the bishop's role being to guide and the king's to implement.[185]

---

[184] Wood, The Merovingian Kingdoms, 72.

[185] Mitchell, 76-77.

CHAPTER V

ANALYSIS OF ANCIENT AND CONTEMPORARY AND CONTEMPORARY VIEWS ON CHURCH-STATE RELATIOSHIPS FROM POPE GREGORY THE GREAT TO CHARLAMAGNE

INTRODUCTION

After Clovis's expansion of power in Gaul and founding of the Frankish kingdom, Charlemagne (768–814) was the next great reformer of the Frankish monarchy; he is considered by some to be the founder of the Holy Roman Empire.[1]

Charlemagne, as Einhard portrays him, was a great monarch who expanded his territory to control almost all of the old western part of the Roman Empire and promoted the set of economic, administrative, religious, cultural, and educational reforms known as the Carolingian Renaissance.[2] He was a faithful Catholic, a defender of the church and papacy, and devoted to fulfilling his mission as appointed by God to save the subjects of his empire. He was a great military leader and led successful military campaigns during most of his reign; he freed the papacy from the Lombard threat, and in 800 was crowned emperor by the pope.

---

[1] There is a debate over the beginning of the Holy Roman Empire. Some historians of the 19th century and some historians today have considered the coronation of Charlemagne in 800 to be the beginning of the Holy Roman Empire. Modern historians date the foundation of the Holy Roman Empire to the coronation of Otto I by Pope John XII in 962. For more information, see Morris Bishop, The Middle Ages (Boston; London: Houghton Mifflin; Hi Marketing, 2001), 47; W. Michael Blumenthal, The Invisible Wall: Germans and Jews: A Personal Exploration (Washington, DC: Counterpoint, 1998), 131; James Bryce, The Holy Roman Empire (Oxford: T. & G. Shrimpton, 1864), 36-64; Earle Edwin Cairns, Christianity through the Centuries: A History of the Christian Church (Grand Rapids: Zondervan Publication, 1996), 189; Krijnie N. Ciggaar, Western Travellers to Constantinople: The West and Byzantium, 962-1204: Cultural and Political Relations, The Medieval Mediterranean, vol. 10 (Leiden: Brill, 1996), 201; Albert Henry Newman, A Manual of Church History (Philadelphia: American Baptist Publication Society, 1900), 439-441; Frederic Austin Ogg, A Source Book of Mediaeval History: Documents Illustrative of European Life and Institutions from the German Invasion to the Renaissance (New York, Cincinnati: American Book, 1907), 130-131.

[2] For maps on the Frankish territory at the time of Charlemagne se appendix C.

Analysis of the historical records pertaining to Charlemagne, his relationship with the pope and the Catholic Church, and his coronation as Roman emperor by the pope raises some questions relating to historical developments before and after his coronation and their implications for church-state relationships prior and during his time, and in the Middle Ages. What was the relationship between popes, Eastern emperors, and Frankish kings prior to Charlemagne? What were the roles of the king and the bishops in his kingdom? What was the relationship between Charlemagne, the bishops, and the papacy? Did Charlemagne exert political supremacy over the Papal States?

This chapter will analyze church-state relationships at the time of Charlemagne, focusing on his religious policies, his relationship with the papacy, his coronation, and the question of ecclesiastical and secular authority. Directly related to these issues are the development of the political supremacy of the papacy and the relationship between the Carolingians and the papacy.

The chapter will begin by discussing historical events during the Merovingian dynasty of the Frankish kingdom, and then move on to the first two kings in the Carolingian dynasty and their relationship with the papacy, Charlemagne's reign and relationship with the papacy, the historical development of the political supremacy of the papacy, Charlemagne's religious reforms, and his coronation and its implications for church-state relationships in his kingdom. Finally, a summary will be given and conclusions will be drawn.

The Merovingian Kingdom and Its Decline after Clovis

The Merovingians, a dynasty of Frankish kings who were descendants of the Salian Franks, had in Clovis their first great king and the founder of the Frankish monarchy. After Clovis's death in 511, following the Frankish Merovingian tradition, the kingdom was divided among his descendants and split into independent kingdoms, later known as Austrasia, Neustria, and Burgundy. The borders of these kingdoms often shifted during the Merovingian dynasty, and they were unified under a single monarch during the reigns of Clotaire the Old (558-61), Clotaire the Young (613-23), and Dagobert I (629-39).[3] The Merovingian dynasty had strong and weak kings and gradually lost its political influence after Dagobert I, when the mayors of the palace[4] became active

---

[3] For a list of Franlish kings and mayors of the palace see appendix A. for maps on the Frankish territory after Clovis see appendix C.

[4] In the Frankish kingdom, originally the officers were divided as mayors and domestics of the palace. At the end of the sixth century one of the officers of the palace reached the highest rank before the king, receiving

rulers. The last Merovingian king was Childeric III, who was deposed in 751 by Pepin the Short, the first king of the Carolingian dynasty.[5]

The political structure of the Merovingian kingdom was centralized in the court. At the end of the fifth and the beginning of the sixth century, Gaul under the Frankish government had moved from the city-based state of the Romans to a rural-based state.[6] The political structure of the empire had been broken down by the barbarian invasions of the fifth century, and the newly established barbarian kingdoms maintained order and peace in their territories through the leadership of a king and a body of men who served him faithfully as his representatives in their districts or counties.[7]

After Clovis, his sons kept his policy of distributing land and wealth to ensure loyalty to the king.[8] This policy created a rural nobility of counts, dukes, and lords connected to the land under their control. This rural nobility appointed by the king to keep order, collect taxes, promote justice, and assist in the king's military actions formed the royal court and became the political power of the Merovingian kingdom.[9]

Along with this rural nobility, the clergy was another political force in Gaul. Bishops were responsible for all the clergy in their dioceses, the administration of church properties, and the care of the poor, widows, slaves, and captives. During the Merovingian period, the Catholic church in Gaul received copious donations: aristocrats who became bishops left their property to the church, and kings and other members of the nobility even disinherited their heirs, leaving their properties to the church. Also, the church received exemption from some taxes and could even levy tithes with state sanction in some places. This

---

the title of mayor-domus. At first the king appointed the mayor-domus and later on the nobles elected him. Gradually the mayors-domus centralized the government of the kingdom in their hands and the title mayor of the palace was restricted to the mayor-domus. The Pippinids made the function hereditary. For more information see: W. H. Jervis, The Student's France, a History of France from the Earliest Times to the Establishment of the Second Empire in 1852 (New York: Harper and Brothers, 1867), 56-57; George Spence, An Inquiry into the Origin of the Laws and Political Institutions of Modern Europe, Particularly of Those of England (Clark, NJ: Lawbook Exchange, 2006), 273-274.

[5] For more information, see Geary, 117-220; James, The Origins of France: From Clovis to the Capetians, 500-1000, 123-156; Wood, The Merovingian Kingdoms, 55-70, 88-101, 120-158, 221-292.

[6] Brown, 12.

[7] Chris Wickham, Framing the Early Middle Ages: Europe and the Mediterranean: 400-800 (Oxford: Oxford University Press, 2007), 103-104.

[8] During Clovis and his sons' expansion of power, most of the territories conquered were added to the patrimonomy of the Merovingian monarchs. Wood, The Merovingian Kingdoms, 64.

[9] Paul Fouracre and Richard A. Gerberding, Late Merovingian France: History and Hagiography, 640-720, Manchester Medieval Sources Series (Manchester, NY: Manchester University Press, 1996), 2.

converted bishops into great landowners, and prosperous monasteries were founded in Gaul.[10] As Fouracre says, "If for no other reason, then certainly because of its landed wealth, the seventh-century Frankish Church had become a very important part of the political system."[11]

Bishops also acted in areas outside the interest of the state, such as judicial work—wills and testaments, marriage and legitimacy—and carried out civil administration in many areas of the public life of the *civitas*.[12] Pfister says, "The bishop thus took the place of the former municipal magistrates, whose office had died out; he received the town to govern *(ad gubernandum)*; by the end of the Merovingian period certain cities are already episcopal cities. The bishop maintains the cause of his parishioners before the officials of the State, and even before the king himself; he obtains for them alleviation of imposts and all kinds of favours.[13] James mentions that bishops acquired local prestige, power, and influence in their cities due to their work as judges and other administrative tasks.[14] Fouracre also argues that this judicial authority exerted by a bishop "put him in competition with the count, the Frankish king's local representative."[15]

The growing political power of the episcopate did not mean its spiritual power was growing. The first Council of Orléans (511) had bestowed upon the king the right to confirm or appoint bishops; thus, many bishops at that time were aristocrats who were appointed for political, not spiritual, reasons. "The barbarian rulers were accustomed to appoint as bishops their relatives and military followers, without reference to their literary, moral, or spiritual qualifications. Bishops so appointed spent their time in revelry, hunting, warfare, the management of their estates, etc."[16] The result was decadence in the church and in society; manners and morals deteriorated, and education and society faded out.[17]

---

[10] The levy of tithe became mandatory by the state only at the time of Charlemagne. See Christian Pfister, "Gaul under the Merovingian Franks," in The Cambridge Medieval History, ed. J. B. Bury et al. (New York: Macmillan, 1926), 143-145.

[11] Fouracre and Gerberding, Late Merovingian France: History and Hagiography, 640-720, 4.

[12] John Bossy, Disputes and Settlements: Law and Human Relations in the West, Past and Present Publications (Cambridge: Cambridge University Press, 2003), 45-46; Jeremiah Francis O'Sullivan and John Francis Burns, Medieval Europe (New York: F.S. Crofts, 1943), 178; F. Prinz, "Die Bischöfliche Stadtherrschaft Im Frankenreich Vom 5. Bis Zum 7. Jahrhundert," Historische Zeitschrift 217 (1973): 1-35.

[13] Pfister, 144.

[14] James, The Franks, 184.

[15] Fouracre and Gerberding, Late Merovingian France: History and Hagiography, 640-720, 4.

[16] Newman, 406.

[17] Wood argues that the religious decadence of the Frankish church was not as generalized as St. Boniface portrayed it in his fight for reform. Wood, The Merovingian Kingdoms, 250-252.

The Frankish church had a history of close connection with the Roman See. During the Merovingian period, secularization of the episcopate made the episcopal office a more political than religious position, brought profound decadence to the church, and gradually diminished the influence of the papacy in France.[18] The religious reform promoted by St. Boniface and Chrodegang, bishop of Metz, under the firm hands of the Carolingians brought back the Frankish church under the influence of the papacy.[19] Boniface was consecrated at Rome, pledging "himself to work as a bishop under papal direction." He promised "to hold no intercourse with bishops who disobeyed the canons, to work against them and to denounce them to the Pope."[20] The pope gave Boniface a collection of canons to guide his work, and he also received a letter of commendation from Charles Martel to fulfill his work of rebuilding the Frankish church. "Henceforth, Boniface could depend even more than before upon papal direction, help, and sympathy: we find him, like St Augustine of Canterbury, sending difficulties to Rome for decision."[21]

The balance of power between king, nobility, and clergy changed in the Frankish kingdom between the sixth and eighth centuries. The first Merovingian kings were able to keep their power as rulers, but by the end of the seventh century, their political and military power died out, and the provincial aristocracy usurped the governmental power of the Merovingian dynasty. Even the bishops who had given legitimacy to Clovis's Frankish monarchy now lined up with the political interests of the nobility.[22] Kings from the Merovingian dynasty continued to exist, but the mayors of the palace ruled the state.[23] The provinces of the Frankish kingdom became more independent, the power of local authorities—notably bishops—increased, and they started to act as autonomous units.[24]

---

[18] Bossy, 45.

[19] Barbara H. Rosenwein, Negotiating Space: Power, Restraint, and Privileges of Immunity in Early Medieval Europe (Ithaca, NY: Cornell University Press, 1999), 99-114. For more information on Chrodegang, see M. A. Claussen, The Reform of the Frankish Church: Chrodegang of Metz and the Regula Canonicorum in the Eighth Century, Cambridge Studies in Medieval Life and Thought (New York: Cambridge University Press, 2004).

[20] J. P. Whitney, "Conversion of the Teutons," in The Cambridge Medieval History, ed. J. B. Bury et al. (New York: Macmillan, 1926), 537.

[21] Ibid. For more information on the life of St. Boniface, see David Cook, St. Boniface: 675-754; The First European (Exeter: Bartlett Printing, 2004); Joanne Therrien, St. Boniface, Manitoba Country Scapes Series (Winnipeg: Vidacom, 2008); James Mann Williamson, The Life and Times of St. Boniface (Ventnor: W. J. Knight, 1904); Willibald, The Life of Saint Boniface, trans. George W. Robinson (Cambridge: Harvard University Press, 1916).

[22] Norman F. Cantor, The Civilization of the Middle Ages (New York: HarperPerennial, 1994), 115-116.

[23] James Mackinnon, A History of Modern Liberty (London; New York: Longmans, Green, and Co., 1906), 6.

[24] Wickham, Framing the Early Middle Ages Europe and the Mediterranean: 400-800, 104.

Even though the mayor of the palace ruled the state, the royal family in the figure of the king "remained indispensable for the legitimation of even such powerful
mayor domo as Charles Martel and Ebroin."[25] The courts in Burgundy, Neustria, and
Austrasia continued to be the centers of political power, but "they were the places
where magnates needed to go if they wanted to settle their disputes peacefully. . . .
Indeed, the courts were full of aristocrats and bishops seeking honours and preferment, even at the low points for strictly royal authority."[26] Wood argues that even
during the government of the Pippinids (Pepin the Old and his sons), "as long as the
body of witnesses was made up largely of independent members of the aristocracy,
the Pippinids did not have complete control of government," and that "the judicial
function of the Merovingian kings remained a crucial aspect of their office."[27] For
Pepin the Short, then, being anointed as king by the pope was imperative to legitimize
his rulership and the change of dynasty, and symbolized the approval of God.[28]

CAROLINGIAN DYNASTY

The Carolingian dynasty, named after its major king, Charlemagne, was the dynasty of the descendants of the aristocratic family of Pepin the Elder, who were the
mayors of the palace for the Merovingian kings of the Franks from 584 to 751. After
Pepin the Middle (c. 635-714) and his illegitimate son Charles Martel (686-741), the
Carolingians had effective rule over the Frankish kingdom, even though they were
still under the Merovingian monarchs. Pepin the Short's deposing of Merovingian
king Childeric III in 751 and his coronation as Frankish king by a bishop of the Roman church as ordered by Pope Zacharias is considered to be the beginning of the
Carolingian dynasty. Pepin the Short was the first Frankish king to legitimize his reign
by coronation and consecration through the Roman Catholic Church.

CHARLES MARTEL

---

[25] Cantor, 116.

[26] Wickham, Framing the Early Middle Ages Europe and the Mediterranean: 400-800, 105.

[27] Wood, The Merovingian Kingdoms, 262.

[28] There are two versions of the coronation of Pepin the Short. According to the Annales Regni Francorum,
Pepin the Short was crowned king of the Franks by Saint Boniface. "Annales Regni Francorum," 149. According
to the continuator of Fredegar, Pope Stephen II came to Pepin requesting his support against the Lombards, and
since he agreed to defend the church's interests, he was anointed king of the Franks by the pope. Maybe in his
visit to Pepin the Short, Pope Stephen anointed him as king. Fredegar, c. 28. Ronald Cohen and Judith D. Toland
followed Fredegar's account and since the main idea of this paragraph is taken from them, it was stated that the
king was anointed by the pope. Ronald Cohen and Judith D. Toland, State Formation and Political Legitimacy
(New Brunswick, NJ: Transaction Books, 1988), 28.

The weak Merovingian dynasty at the end of the seventh century fragmented the political unity of the Frankish kingdom. Most of the time, the mayors of the palace were powerless to face the local aristocratic families, who had control of the land, the monasteries, and often the local dioceses with dynastic bishoprics. Under the leadership of Charles Martel, the reunification of Gaul started to take place.

After the death of Pepin the Middle, there was no legitimate son to claim his position as mayor of the palace of Austrasia. Plectrude, his wife, imprisoned Charles Martel and tried to govern in the names of her grandchildren. However, Charles escaped and started a campaign to establish himself as mayor of the palace of Austrasia in his father's place. At the same time, he directed his attention to the Neustrians and Frisians. Ratbod, the leader of the Frisians, defeated him in 716. In the same year and again in 717, Charles retaliated and defeated the Frisians and their Neustrian allies, who fought under the leadership of Ragamfred, mayor of the palace of the Neustrians, and the Merovingian king Chilperic II (715-721). His next move was to legitimize his conquests by making himself mayor of the palace and proclaiming Clotaire IV (717-719) king of Austrasia. Chilperic II and Ragamfred joined forces with Eudo, duke of Aquitaine, but Charles defeated them in 719. After Clotaire IV was dead, Charles made Childeric II king of the Franks, but under his authority. [29]

After 719, having solidified his position in Austrasia, Charles attacked the other regions still hostile to his rulership. He fought against the Frisians and finally subdued the Neustrians in 724. Then, he directed his attention to reasserting Frankish authority over the other Germanic tribes and the south of Gaul, and marched against Aquitaine, Burgundy, Saxony, Bavaria, Provence, and Septimania. Charles Martel's victories over the Muslims from 732 to 737 were another significant military achievement, especially his victory at the Battle of Tours in 732. [30]

---

[29] Liber Historiae Francorum, ed. Bernard S. Bachrach (Lawrence, KS: Coronado Press, 1973), 59-53; Fredegar, c. 27.

[30] Some historians today tend to distance themselves from Gibbon's belief that the battle of Tours prevented Europe from becoming Muslim. They argue that Gibbon greatly overrated the battle, that the Arabs did not intend to conquer Gaul, only to pillage it, and that even if the Franks had lost the battle, they could have recovered their independence as the Visigoths did in Spain. Alessandro Barbero, Charlemagne: Father of a Continent (Berkeley: University of California Press, 2004), 9-11; Ernest Mercier, "La Bataille De Poitiers Et Les Vraies Causes Du Recul De L'invasion Arabe," Revue Historique 7 (1878): 1-13; Leon Levillain and Charles Samaran, "Sur Le Lieu Et La Date De La Bataille Dite De Poitiers De 732," Bibliotheque de l'Ecole de Chartres 99 (1938): 243-267. For another group of modern historians the battle of Tours is a macrohistorical event that decided that Europe would be Christian and not Muslim. See Edward Gibbon and J. B. Bury, The End of the Roman Empire in the West: The Barbarian Conquests and the Transition to the Middle Ages: A.D. 439-565, The Library of Religion and Culture (New York: Harper, 1958), 6:16-19; Guizot and Guizot de Witt, 1:154; William E. Watson,

Although Charles Martel ruled France, he never took the title of king. After Childeric II's death, Charles Martel made Theodoric IV (721-737) king of the Franks, but after Theodoric IV's death he did not bother appointing a new king. By the time of his death, he was ruling over all three of the Frankish kingdoms; his two legitimate sons, Pepin the Short and Carloman, succeeded him as rulers of France.[31]

According to some historians, Charles Martel caused the church to sink into profound decadence through his ecclesiastical endowments. Pfister argues that he conferred bishoprics and abbeys on uneducated men. He says, "These bishops and abbots never wore clerical vestments, but always sword and baldric. They dissipated the property of the Church and sought to bequeath their offices to their bastards. For eighty years no council was called. Every vestige of education and civilization was in danger of being swamped."[32]

Newman, however, does not see any difference between Charles Martel's treatment of the church and that of other Frankish kings and mayors of the palace before him. He says, "Charles Martel dealt with ecclesiastical endowments as with any other portion of the royal domain. He gave to his liege Milo, the archbishoprics of Rheims and Trier; to his nephew Hugh, the archbishoprics of Rouen, Paris, and Bayeux, with the abbeys of Fontenelle and Jumieges."[33] Wood also mentions that Charles Martel did what other rulers had done before him. The major difference for him is that Martel defeated more enemies in battle, which at that time naturally led to a change of leadership in the dioceses.[34] Charles Martel was a Catholic and promoted Catholicism in his reign. Although he did not agree to help the pope against the Lombards, it was under his rulership that the Frisians were converted to Catholic Christianity, through his support for the missionary efforts of Saint Boniface, papal legate, and others like him in the hope of consolidating his military victories.[35]

PEPIN THE SHORT

After Charles Martel's death in 741, his two legitimate sons, Pepin the Short and Carloman, divided the kingdom between them. As had happened with their father,

---

"The Battle of Tours-Poitiers Revisited," Providence: Studies in Western Civilization 2, no. 1 (1993), http://www.deremilitari.org/resources/articles/watson2.htm (accessed April 13, 2009); Wood, The Merovingian Kingdoms, 281-284.

[31] Wood, The Merovingian Kingdoms, 272, 286-287.

[32] Pfister, 146.

[33] Milo was the Bishop of Rheims (717-744) and Trier (717-744). Newman, 407.

[34] Wood, The Merovingian Kingdoms, 287.

[35] Dana Carleton Munro and Raymond James Sontag, The Middle Ages, 395-1500 (New York; London: Century Corporation, 1928), 76-77.

some aristocrats refused to acknowledge their authority as rulers. The throne had been vacant since the death of Theodoric IV in 737, but to avoid more resistance from the nobility, Pepin the Short and Carloman crowned Childeric III of the Merovingian dynasty as king of the Franks in 743. Meanwhile, their illegitimate brother Grifo treacherously sought to secure the throne for himself. Even though Pepin defeated Grifo more than once, he still kept him alive and gave him twelve counties in the kingdom of Neustria.[36]

In 747, Pepin became sole ruler of the Frankish empire as mayor of the palace after his brother Carloman retired to monastic life.[37] He then successfully campaigned against Bavaria, Saxony, and Alamania. He also promoted religious reformation in the liturgy of the Frankish church following the guidelines of the Church of Rome,[38] and sent representatives from the clergy to Pope Zacharias asking his approval for Chilperic III's deposition and Pepin's elevation as king of the Franks. With the approval of the pope, Pepin the Short was consecrated king of the Franks by Saint Boniface, and Pepin promised to protect the church against the Lombards.[39]

Pepin fulfilled his promise, campaigning against the Lombards and rendering homage and obedience to the church.[40] He also promoted reforms for the financial benefit of the Catholic Church and even attacked Waifer, Duke of Aquitaine, because he held the income of the church back for himself.[41] Before his death, Pepin divided the kingdom between his two sons, Charles and Carloman.[42]

CHARLEMAGNE

In 768, Charlemagne and his brother Carloman succeeded their father Pepin the Short as kings of the Franks.[43] With the death of Carloman in 771, Charlemagne became sole ruler of the Frankish kingdom. Even before Carlo-

---

[36] Fredegar, c. 28.

[37] Annales Regni Francorum, ed. Bruno Krusch and Wilhelm Levison, MGH Scr. SRG, vol. 6 (Hannover: Hahn, 1895), 746; Fredegar, c. 28.

[38] Fredegar, c. 28.

[39] "Annales Regni Francorum," 149. According to the continuator of Fredegar, Pope Stephen II came to Pepin the Short requesting his support against the Lombards, and since he agreed to defend the church's interests, he was anointed king of the Franks by the pope. Fredegar, c. 28.

[40] "Annales Regni Francorum," 755, 756.

[41] Fredegar, c. 29.

[42] Ibid., c. 30.

[43] In the Annales Regni Francorum there are indications that Pepin the Short did not divide the kingdom between Charlemagne and Carloman. However, the continuator of Fredegar mentions that Pepin made the division. See "Annales Regni Francorum," 769; Fredegar, c. 53.

man's death, Charlemagne had to suppress revolts in Aquitaine and Gascony to remove those who threatened his power.[44]

After Carloman's death, Charlemagne expanded his territory, adding Saxony (772-804), Lombardy (773-775), Bavaria (787-788), Spanish March (778-801), and the Slavic kingdom of the Avars (791-802) to his kingdom. His longest military enterprise resulted in the conversion of the Saxons to Catholic Christianity.[45]

Among his wars, the campaign against Lombardy is significant because he intervened in defense of the papacy. The Lombards were a constant threat to the city of Rome and the power of the papacy. In 773 Desiderius (756-774), king of the Lombards, invaded the papal states in northern Italy and laid siege to Rome. Pope Hadrian I (772-795) asked for help from Charlemagne, who invaded Italy and defeated the Lombards in 774. In 800, Charlemagne came again to aid Pope Leo III, who had been mistreated by the Romans. The pope cleared himself of the charges brought against him—he had been accused of adultery and perjury—swearing his innocence, and on Christmas Day, he crowned Charlemagne as Roman emperor.[46]

Charlemagne promoted political, educational, religious, economic, military, monetary, and cultural reforms. His patronage of learning, combined with effective military, administrative, and legislative actions, promoted intellectual and cultural achievements that left their mark on Europe for hundreds of years after him; this was named the Carolingian Renaissance.[47]

Even though there was a significant renaissance of culture during Charlemagne's reign, the motivation for this learning was associated with worship of the true God.[48] Religion was not only part of the reforms he promoted—it was the center of all his other reforms. As Rosamond McKitterick says, "His patronage was designed to promote his royal power as a Christian king and to consolidate the Christian faith by disseminating the key texts on which that faith was based.[49]

---

[44] Einhard, Life of Charlemagne, trans. Samuel Epes Turner (New York; Cincinnati: American Book Co., 1880), 3.

[45] Rosamond McKitterick, The Frankish Kingdoms under the Carolingians, 751-987 (London; New York: Longman, 1983), 47-72.

[46] Ibid.

[47] Rosamond McKitterick, "The Carolingian Renaissance of Culture and Learning," in Charlemagne: Empire and Society, ed. Joanna Story (Manchester; New York: Manchester University Press, 2005), 151-166.

[48] In a letter sent to all bishops of his kingdom c. 800, Charlemagne linked learning with the Christian faith, exhorting the bishops "not to neglect for the study of letters" in order for them "more correctly to penetrate the mysteries of divine scripture." Charlemagne, "De Litteris Colendis," in Charlemagne: Translated Sources, trans. P.D. King (Lambrigg, Kendal, Cumbria: P.D. King, 1987), 232-233.

[49] McKitterick, "The Carolingian Renaissance of Culture and Learning," 165.

Since religion was at the center of Charlemagne's administrative structure, this section will first analyze his religious reforms, then the development of the temporal authority of the papacy up to Charlemagne, and finally authority and the church-state relationship at the time of Charlemagne.

RELIGIOUS REFORM

Charlemagne promoted religious reform in the church of France. At the beginning of his reign, there was an undercurrent of disorder in the church, and apocalyptic visions urging reform can be found throughout the literature of that time. For example, according to the reckoning of Alcuin of York and the studies of Eusebius and Jerome, the seventh millennium would begin when Charlemagne was crowned in the year 800. This expectation led men to prepare themselves for the end of the world and bolstered Charlemagne's program of church reform.[50]

Charlemagne's religious reforms were not the fruit of his own imagination. He trusted in the clergy, the Roman church, canon law, and well-established traditions of the church, such as the Benedictine monastic rules. Charlemagne was assisted in his administration by educated clergymen such as Alcuin of York (c. 735-804), Theodulf, bishop of Orléans (c. 750-821), Paul the Deacon (c. 719-799), Paulinus of Aquileia (c. 730-802), Angilbert, abbot of Centulum (d. 814), and Waldo of Reichenau (c. 740-814).[51] These men not only helped Charlemagne with his religious reforms, but also worked in the administrative structure of the empire and promoted the revival of study and learning throughout the kingdom that scholars today call the Carolingian Renaissance.[52]

Charlemagne's relationship with the church of Rome went beyond the political sphere in seeking legitimacy. Rome was the place where the apostles Peter and Paul were martyred. Charlemagne's reforms involved the proper worship to receive God's salvation, and prayer was an integral part of it. Prayer would not only bring salvation to the penitent, but would also channel God's power into the military enterprises of the king and protection of the kingdom. In a letter to Pope Leo III lamenting the death of Pope Hadrian, Charlemagne expressed the importance of the pope's prayer as the best channel of God's power, comparing him to Moses, who ensured the victory for God's people while holding up his hands.[53]

---

[50] Mayke de Jong, "Charlemagne's Church," in Charlemagne: Empire and Society, ed. Joanna Story (Manchester; New York: Manchester University Press, 2005), 105.

[51] Patricia Ranft, Women in Western Intellectual Culture, 600-1500 (New York: Palgrave Macmillan, 2002), 12.

[52] Lawrence Cunningham and John Reich, Culture and Values: A Survey of the Humanities (Belmont, CA: Thomson/Wadsworth, 2006), 348.

[53] Alcuin, "Alcuini Sive Albini Epistolae," in EKA, ed. Bruno Krusch and Wilhelm Levison, MGH Epp., vol. 4 (Berlin: Weidmans, 1895), no. 93.

The papal chair was also the place where the true doctrine was defined. Since the time of Clovis, the canonical law had been the religious law of the state, as the Salic law was for civil cases.[54] During the Merovingian period, even though aristocrats and the king participated in Frankish synods along with bishops, church decisions were considered to be part of canon law. However, in the time of Pepin the Short and Charlemagne, Rome and not the Frankish synods were consulted for guidance on religious matters. Such popes as Zacharias and Hadrian provided the Frankish monarchs with authoritative collections of the canon law.[55]

Another aspect that influenced the religious reforms promoted by Charlemagne at the beginning of the ninth century was the Old Testament (OT) system of laws and government. "The levying of Tithes, the observance of Sunday, royal anointing, sexuality and marriage, the oblation of Children, the purity of priests, fair weights and measures—in all these spheres the 'Old Law' (*Vetus Lex*) was a source of inspiration and regulation."[56] The reading of the OT was not literal, but allegorical. "Israel" did not refer to the Jewish nation, but the Christian Franks—as the preface of the Salic Law states, a people founded by God who, because of their devotion to church martyrs, replaced the Romans who had mutilated the martyrs, meriting God's favor.[57]

Worship was at the core of Charlemagne's religious reforms. Like the Romans, he saw proper worship as the way to earn the favor of God. However, theology did not play a central role as it had in the time of Constantine and Justinian. Charlemagne's major concern was with the liturgy. Intercessory prayers were essential for the prosperity of the kingdom, and the lives of those who prayed had to be pure for the prayer to be effective. Also, by this time, "mass had become a sacrificial gift to God, to be offered in order to secure the salvation of the soul, the victory of armies, the stability of the realm—and to ward off illness, infertility, crop failure and a whole host of other disasters."[58]

The emphasis on prayer increased the importance of the monastic communities. The patronage of monasteries had become an important function of the Frankish nobility. In the Merovingian period, many monasteries were established

---

[54] See the section "The Salic Law" in chapter 4 above.

[55] "Admonitio Generalis," in Charlemagne: Translated Sources (Lambrigg, Kendal, Cumbria: P. D. King, 1987), 209-220.

[56] de Jong, 112.

[57] The first article of the preface of the Salic Law says, "The whole Frankish people, established by the power of God, are strong in arms, weighty in council, firm in the compact of peace, pure in body, distinguished in form, brave, swift, and austere. Recently converted to the Catholic faith, they are free from heresy, rejecting barbarian rites with the help of God, keeping the faith; and according to their customs they seek the key to wisdom and desire justice." Katherine Fischer Drew, The Laws of the Salian Franks, Middle Ages Series (Philadelphia: University of Pennsylvania Press, 1991), 171.

[58] de Jong, 119.

with large donations of money and land; the abbots became powerful and influential figures in the kingdom, which led to disputes among the aristocracy.[59] By the time of the Pippinids, the king had more direct control over the monasteries. Monasteries were purged of all impurity, became places for educating the youth, and were used by Charlemagne as a "crucial instrument for implementing many of his political, cultural, and religious goals."[60] As Michael Ronald Lines summarizes, scholars recognize that monasteries were important to the Carolingians because they "generated wealth, performed multiple social functions, acted as a complement to military colonization and cultural domination, and played a material part in politics and economics at the local level."[61]

Charlemagne's goal with his religious reforms was to achieve a union of worship. He admonished the bishops to pay attention to whether their local priests were celebrating mass, performing baptisms, and properly teaching doctrinal beliefs. Especially in the mass, he believed that the psalms, the preaching, the Lord's Prayer, and singing should synchronize with the harmony of the heavenly angels.[62] Union in worship would bring salvation to the people and economic and military prosperity and unity to the empire.

THE TEMPORAL AUTHORITY OF THE PAPACY UP TO CHARLEMAGNE

After Constantine's incorporation of Christianity as the legal religion of the empire, the bishop of Rome sought ecclesiastical supremacy, which was recognized and enforced by Justinian.[63] During the reign of the Arian barbarians Odoacer and Theodoric in Italy (476-526), the papacy enjoyed religious freedom, but worked for the reunification of the empire under the government of a Christian emperor. Justinian's reconquest of the West freed the church from the Arian rulers while restraining papal ecclesiastical and political autonomy. The papacy was the only remaining political institution in Rome that had survived the Gothic wars, and Justinian recognized the political authority of the pope in Rome through his *Pragmatic Sanction*; Pope Vigilius and his successors recognized the importance of political supremacy and fought for it without breaking with the eastern emperor and the idea of a Christendom.[64]

---

[59] John J. Butt, Daily Life in the Age of Charlemagne (Westport, CT: Greenwood Press, 2002), 123.

[60] M. M. Hildebrandt, The External School in Carolingian Society, Education and Society in the Middle Ages and Renaissance, vol. 1 (Leiden; New York: E.J. Brill, 1992), 54.

[61] Michael Ronald Lines, "Charlemagne's Monastic Policy and the Regula Benedicti: Frankish Capitularies Front 742 to 813" (University of Toronto, 2000), 10-11.

[62] "Admonitio Generalis," no. 22.

[63] See chapter 3 above.

[64] See chapter 3 above.

The Lombard conquest of Italy threatened the political survival of the Roman See and also reduced the political power of Constantinople over the city of Rome and the papacy. The eastern emperor and his representative in Ravenna could not always help defend Rome from the Lombards, and the pope was left alone to conduct the defense of the city and form an independent political state.[65]

By the time of Pope Gregory the Great (590-604), "the Church had become de facto the key power in Italy."[66] Noble even argues that the Catholic Church in Byzantine Italy was "older, richer, and potentially more significant than the whole secular ruling apparatus."[67] The Catholic Church under the leadership of the pope earned the allegiance of the people not only because of its care for the poor, but also because it took charge of economic and military affairs in the defense of the Roman people.[68]

Gregory the Great, born to a wealthy patrician family in Rome and trained in the monastic life, served as prefect of the city, deacon, and *apocrisiarius*—papal legate at Constantinople—of Pope Pelagius II before being ordained as pope. In his pontificate, Gregory the Great promoted liturgical and administrative reforms in the church, a missionary outreach sending Augustine to England, and the defense of the Duchy of Rome from Lombard attacks.[69]

Besides the liturgical reform attributed to Gregory the Great,[70] he is considered the last of the Latin Fathers and helped to solidify other theological doctrines. Hans Küng states, "Gregory was also without doubt responsible for the theological sanctioning not only of a massive veneration of saints and relics but also for the ideas of purgatory and of masses for souls. He was excessively interested in sacrifices, penitential ordinances, categories of sins, and punishments for sins, and he put excessive emphasis on fear of the eternal judge and hoped for reward for good works."[71]

During his reign, Gregory the Great extended the political power of the papacy in the face of the Lombard threat and the emperor's legislation. The exarch of Ravenna was

---

[65] John Moorhead, "Ostrogothic Italy and the Lombard Invasion," in The New Cambridge Medieval History 1: C. 500 - C. 700, ed. Paul Fouracre (Cambridge: Cambridge University Press, 2006), 155-160.

[66] Thomas F. X. Noble, The Republic of St. Peter: The Birth of the Papal State, 680-825, The Middle Ages (Philadelphia: University of Pennsylvania Press, 1984), 9.

[67] Ibid.

[68] Ibid., 12.

[69] R. H. C. Davis and R. I. Moore, A History of Medieval Europe (Harlow, England; New York: Pearson Longman, 2006), 86-88.

[70] For more information on Gregory's liturgical reform, see Michael S. Driscoll, "The Conversion of the Nations," in The Oxford History of Christian Worship, ed. Geoffrey Wainwright and Karen B. Westerfield Tucker (New York: Oxford University Press, 2006), 185-188.

[71] Hans Küng and John Bowden, The Catholic Church: A Short History, Modern Library Chronicles Book, vol. 5 (New York: Modern Library, 2003), 65.

responsible for the defense of Italian territory under the control of the eastern empire, and an imminent attack from the Ariulf (d. 602), Duke of Spoleto, led Gregory to seek the exarch's support. Since his request was not attended, Gregory organized military operations against the duke and negotiated peace. Against King Agilulf, Gregory even had to pay the troops and again negotiate peace.[72] He also protested and negotiated with Emperor Maurice (582-602), who changed his law regarding *curiales* and ecclesiastical offices.[73] Gregory strongly objected to Emperor Maurice's support for granting the title of Oecumenical Patriarch to the bishop of Constantinople John the Faster (582-595). The crisis was resolved only in 607 when Emperor Phocas murdered the emperor and his family and reaffirmed to Pope Boniface III the primacy of Rome.[74]

Even though he was loyal to the emperor in Constantinople, Pope Gregory the Great acted as temporal ruler of Rome, leading and commissioning civil, military, and ecclesiastical offices, making peace independently of the empire, and using monastic missionaries to establish the faith and convert nations, in a prototype of the medieval papacy.[75]

In the seventh century, from the death of Pope Gregory until the peace with the Lombards in 680/681, the papacy faced problems with the exarch of Ravenna, the emperor, and the Monothelite controversy,[76] which culminated in the imprisonment and death of Pope Martin I (649-653). This widened the gap between Rome and Constantinople and fostered the loyalty of the Romans to the papacy.[77] The policies

---

[72] Richards, 173-174.

[73] Emperor Maurice decreed that those enrolled in public offices could not join ecclesiastical orders and soldiers could do so only after retirement from the army. Gregory I, "Epistolae," in Gregorii I Papae Registrum Epistolarum, ed. Bruno Krusch and Wilhelm Levison, MGH, Epp., vols. 1-2 (Berlin: Weidmans, 1891), 1:3.61, 2:8.10.

[74] LP, 64.

[75] Richards, 174.

[76] Monothelitism is the belief that Christ had two natures but only one will. The controversy began in the time of Emperor Heraclius (610–641) and was promulgated by Patriarch Sergius I of Constantinople (patriarch 610–638) as a means to reunify the Monophysites with the Church. Since Pope Honorius I (pope 625–638) did not take a stand against it, he was condemned at the Third Council of Constantinople (680-681) when Monothelitism was declared to be a heresy. See Klaus Schatz, Papal Primacy: From Its Origins to the Present (Collegeville, MN: Liturgical Press, 1996), 54-55.

[77] For the peace between the east and the Lombards, see Erich Ludwig Eduard Caspar, Geschichte Des Papsttums Von Den Anfängen Bis Zur Höhe Der Weltherrschaft (Tübingen: J.C.B. Mohr, 1933), 724; Giorgio Falco, The Holy Roman Republic; a Historic Profile of the Middle Ages (London: G. Allen & Unwin, 1964), 110; Guy Halsall, "The Barbarian Invasions," in The New Cambridge Medieval History 1: C. 500 - C. 700, ed. Paul Fouracre (Cambridge: Cambridge University Press, 2006), 294; Andreas N. Stratos, Byzantium in the Seventh Century (Amsterdam: Adolf M. Hakkert, 1968), 49. For the history of the Byzantine Empire and the papacy and the Monothelite controversy, see Joseph Cullen Ayer, A Source Book for Ancient Church History (New York: C. Scribner's Sons, 1922), 660-671; William Holden Hutton, The Church and the Barbarians: Being an Outline of

of Emperors Constantine the Bearded (641-688) and Constantine IV (688-685) and those of Popes Martin I (649-655) and Agatho (678-681) reveal their understanding of their roles in religious matters. For the emperors, religion was a matter of the state and the emperor should lead for the welfare of the empire. For the popes, the emperor had a leading role in defending and implementing the Catholic faith, but the pope established the definition of Catholic orthodoxy, and they would not fear to defy the emperor when the Roman definition of Catholic orthodoxy was challenged.

By the end of the seventh century, the new military and administrative structure of the Byzantine Empire in *themes*[78] strengthened local leaders' power politically and militarily. In Rome, the papacy increased its political influence and bound the aristocracy and the army to its leadership. Emperor Justinian II (685-695 and again from 705-711) ordered the imprisonment of Pope Sergio I (687-701), but the army and people of Rome stopped Zacharias, the emperor's representative, from taking the pope prisoner. Then Zacharias's life was spared by the intervention of the pope.[79] As Richards says, "Gradually, as their composition and their outlook changed, the army came to identify the pope as the figurehead of Italian aspirations. It was, after all, the popes, such as Gregory the Great and Honorius I, who frequently acted as their paymasters. They were strongly committed to the orthodox faith, which the pope defended. Their officers received land grants from the papacy and settled down to become a new aristocracy."[80]

The relationship between Emperor Leo III (717-741) and Pope Gregory II (715-731) demonstrates the loyalty of the army to the papacy. Leo III's losses in the war against the Arabs led him to increase taxation in Italy. Pope Gregory II refused to pay the taxes, and the emperor ordered his imprisonment, but the Roman army did not allow the pope to be taken as a prisoner to Constantinople. Also, in the iconoclast controversy, the pope refused to enforce the emperor's decree and the Italian army sided with the pope.[81]

Gregory's II political and military position was difficult. The Lombard king Liutprand (712-744) had expanded his power in Italy, and even though he had

---

the History of the Church from A.D. 461 to A.D. 1003 (Charleston, SC: Bibliolife, 2008), 82-89; Andrew Louth, "The Byzantine Empire in the Seventh Century," in The New Cambridge Medieval History 1: C. 500-C. 700, ed. Paul Fouracre (Cambridge: Cambridge University Press, 2006), 291-316; Richards, 181-200.

[78] Themes were the administrative divisions of the Byzantine Empire that replaced the provincial system implemented by Diocletian, where a specific geographical area was designated to an army and a plot of land to the soldiers for farming; see John F. Haldon, Warfare, State, and Society in the Byzantine World, 565-1204, Warfare and History (London; New York: Routledge, 2003), 67-138; Warren T. Treadgold, Byzantium and Its Army, 284-1081 (Stanford, CA: Stanford University Press, 1995), 98-108.

[79] Le Liber Pontificalis, ed. L. Duchesne, 3 vols. (Paris: E. de Boccard, 1955), 1:372-374.

[80] Richards, 205.

[81] LLP, 1:403-404.

acted benevolently toward Rome, Gregory II foresaw Liutprand's plan to have all of Italy under his control. On the other hand, Emperor Leo III was enforcing an iconoclastic religious policy that Gregory II refused to adopt, but he needed the emperor's protection in case of a Lombard attack. Gregory made alliances with the dukes of Spoleto and Benevento, which caused Liutprand dissatisfaction; King Liutprand then attacked and subdued Spoleto and Benevento, coming close to the gates of Rome. In 729, Gregory II and Liutprand came to terms that left the Lombard king at peace with Rome for almost ten years[82]

Gregory II was able to place himself between the two political and military forces around him: the eastern emperor and the Lombard king. He knew that to fall under the authority of "a powerful and strong-handed Italian king would have been fatal to the secular power of the papacy."[83] His political diplomacy kept Liutprand far from the doors of Rome and made him, as Noble points out, more an ally of Leo III than a subject.[84] Gregory II opposed the iconoclastic religious policy of the emperor, but put the papal army at the disposal of the exarch of Ravenna, Eutychius (c. 727-752), to help him overcome Tiberius Petasius, an imperial pretender. Gregory's dealings with the emperor and the Lombard king show his "control of the civil and ecclesiastical life of the city and of its duchy, even if that control was not yet absolute. From 719 on, and in certain respects for several years already, it is meaningless to speak any longer of imperial Rome. Some new but still inchoate papal Rome now existed."[85]

Pope Gregory III (731-741) followed his predecessor's policies against iconoclasm. He summoned a Roman synod (November 731) and condemned iconoclasm as heresy.[86] He sent papal legates to Constantinople, condemning Leo III's religious policy, but the emperor was able to avoid these unwelcome guests, holding them in Sicily. The emperor also took measures to retaliate against the pope and transferred the properties of the Holy See in the south of Italy, Sicily, and Illyricum to the patriarchate of Constantinople.[87] According to Noble, Leo's decisions isolated central Italy from the rest of the eastern empire and "the Duchy of Rome was now de facto an autonomous region under the pope." He says, "The creation of a papal Republic may be dated to the years between 729 and 733."[88]

---

[82] Ibid., 1:405-409.

[83] Charles Oman, The Dark Ages, 476-918, Periods of European History (London: Rivingtons, 1908), 283.

[84] Noble, 36.

[85] Ibid., 38.

[86] LLP, 1:416.

[87] L. Duchesne and Arnold Harris Mathew, The Beginnings of the Temporal Sovereignty of the Popes, A.D. 754-1073 (London: K. Paul, Trench, Trübner Company, 1907), 6-7.

[88] Noble, 40.

Even though Gregory III openly opposed the emperor, he desired unity of the empire in Italy. He intervened to restore Ravenna to the exarch Eutychius when the Duchy of Vicenza attacked it and paid Transamund, duke of Spoleto, for the restitution of Castrum Gallesium to the empire.[89]

The increased papal power in Rome and the lack of military support from Constantinople enfeebled the exarch of Ravenna before the Lombards. Gregory III's defense of Ravenna from Lombard attack was possibly a way of checking King Liutprand. Like Gregory II, he also sought allegiance with the Duchy of Spoleto to release the pressure of Transamund Duke of Spoleto from Rome. Liutprand's response was to ensure his autonomy over the Duchies of Spoleto and Benavento by attacking them. Transamund sought refuge in Rome, and when the Romans refused to release him to Liutprand, the Lombard king captured four cities from the Duchy of Rome. In vain, Pope Gregory III sent envoys to negotiate the return of the cities. The Romans then agreed to help Transamund restore his position as duke of Spoleto, and he promised to return the four cities to the papacy, but did not fulfill his promise.[90]

Liutprand then directed his armies against Spoleto and Rome, which sought Frankish help. Gregory III sent envoys to Charles Martel asking for his support against the Lombards. However, Martel did not help the pope, since he and Liutprand had been allies in the war against the Saracens. The Romans and Transamund had one victory against the Lombard king (739).[91] Zacharias (741-752), who succeeded Gregory III, came to terms with Liutprand, who restored his autonomy over Spoleto and returned the four cities to the papacy (741).[92]

Pope Zacharias exerted great diplomatic influence over Liutprand and Ratchis (744-749), his successor as king of the Lombards. He was able to save Ravenna twice from the hands of these kings.[93] However, when Aistulf (749-756) took the throne of the Lombards, Zacharias was not able to persuade him, and he conquered Ravenna and even threatened Rome.[94]

By the time of Pope Stephen II (752-757), Aistulf was menacing Rome and the eastern emperor did not come to assist the pope.[95] Stephen II turned to the Frankish ruler Pepin the Short, who in 751 had received official approval from Pope Zacharias to depose the Merovingian king, Childeric III, and ascend to the

---

[89] LLP, 1:420-421; Paul, "Pauli Historia Langobardorum," in SRL, ed. Alfredus Boretius, MGH Scr. AA, vol. 1 (Hannover: Hahn, 1878), 6.54.

[90] Paul, 6.56.

[91] Fredegar, c. 22; LLP, 1:420.

[92] LLP, 1:427.

[93] Ibid., 1:428-429.

[94] Ibid., 1:441.

[95] Ibid., 1:442.

throne as king of the Franks. After Pope Stephen II personally visited Pepin in France, Pepin came down with his army, defeated Aistulf, and took possession of the exarchate of Ravenna, giving it to the pope.[96]

The pope gave the title *Patricius Romanorum* to Pepin and his sons, which created a "legal entitlement for Pepin's having assumed the obligation of defending the Republic."[97] The Frankish kings, who had been faithful Catholics since the time of Clovis, were now brought into close union with the papacy. The papacy found in the Frankish king a protector who had a great veneration for Saint Peter and his vicar, the pope, and did not challenge its supremacy. Even though the pope already had acted as leader of the republic of Rome for many years, his temporal dominion was recognized by the donation of Pepin.[98] This marked the final break between Rome and the eastern empire.

Pepin was loyal to the Catholic faith and to Saint Peter. His campaign against the Lombards did not eliminate their power, but it was enough to eliminate the immediate pressure on the papacy and to restore order in Italy. The narrator of the life of Saint Stephen II in the *Liber Pontificalis* records a Pepin who was strongly committed to the papacy and Saint Peter, and mentions that Pepin refused to alienate those territories claimed by the eastern emperor's representative from the Roman Jurisdiction because of his faithfulness to God and love for Saint Peter. He adds that Pepin declared that nothing would persuade him to take away what had been offered to Saint Peter and to the pontiff of the apostolic see.[99]

Also, according to Philip Schaff, Pope Stephen II tested the faithfulness of Pepin to the church and its saints, by promising eternal life and large properties in heaven if the king would obey his command to rescue the Holy See in the names of Peter and the holy Mother of God.[100] Schaff also comments, "To such a height of blasphemous as-

---

[96] Ibid., 1:444-454.

[97] Noble, 87.

[98] Scholars discuss the Donation of Pepin related to the Quierzy document. The Quierzy document was produced as a result of the agreement between the pope and Pepin, and determined the territories that should be given to the papacy if Pepin was victorious over Aistulf. In 774, this same document is mentioned by the writer of the life of Pope Hadrian, affirming that Charlemagne confirmed to Rome all his father had promised in Quierzy. Scholars also discuss the content of the document as well as the cities mentioned in it. See Erich Ludwig Eduard Caspar, Pippin Und Die Römische Kirche: Kritische Untersuchungen Zum Fränkisch-Päpstlichen Bunde Im VIII: Jahrhundert (Berlin: Springer, 1914), 148-150; Paul Kehr, "Die Sogenannte Karolingische Schenkung Von 754," Historische Zeitschrift 70, no. (1893): 385-441; Noble, 83-94; Louis Saltet, "La Lecture D'un Text Et La Critique Contemporaine: La Prétendue Promesse De Quierzy Dans Le 'Liber Pontificalis,'" Bulletin de Litterature Ecclésiastique 41, no. (1940): 176-207; Louis Saltet, "La Lecture D'un Text Et La Critique Contemporaine: La Prétendue Promesse De Quierzy Dans Le 'Liber Pontificalis,'" Bulletin de Litterature Ecclésiastique 42, no. (1941): 61-85.

[99] LLP, 1:452-454.

[100] Philip Schaff and David S. Schaff, History of the Christian Church (New York: C. Scribner's Sons, 1882), 4:232-234.

sumption had the papacy risen already as to identify itself with the kingdom of Christ and to claim to be the dispenser of temporal prosperity and eternal salvation."[101]

The years that followed Pepin's intervention during the reign of Stephen were relatively peaceful. In 756, with the death of Lombard king Aistulf, Ratchis assumed again the throne, but was convinced by Pope Stephen to resign in favor of Desiderius (756-774). Desiderius had promised to hand over the cities taken from the republic in the time of Liutprand, but he did not. Pope Paul I (757-767), Stephen's brother, who succeeded him in the Roman See, urged Pepin to intervene in Italy to force Desiderius to fulfill his promises of 756, but in vain. Desiderius extended his authority over Spoleto and Benavento, but did not challenge the Roman Duchy.[102]

After Pope Paul's death, the nomination of a new pope caused confusion in Rome. Toto, the duke of Nepi, and a body of Tuscans invaded Rome and forced the appointment of his brother Constantine II as pope. With Lombard help, the papal chancellor Christophorus and his brother Sergius deposed Constantine II and set Philip on the throne, but on the same day the clergy chose Stephen III and forced Philip to return to his monastery. The fight among the Romans led Desiderius to challenge the Roman Duchy. Desiderius went to Rome and made a treaty of peace with Pope Stephen. Christophorus and Sergius were killed, and Paul Afiarta became a representative of the king in Rome.[103]

With the election of Hadrian I as pope, Desiderius lost ground in Rome. Hadrian required Desiderius to restore the cities to the Roman Duchy according to the pact of 756, and Desiderius's response was to invade the pope's territory. Hadrian appealed to Charlemagne, who invaded Italy, defeated Desiderius, and made himself king of the Lombards.[104] One of Hadrian's letters to Charlemagne is significant because the pope not only asked him to support the Roman See, but also mentioned the temporal rights that the papacy had over the Duchy of Rome and other territories in Italy since the time of Pope Silvester, who had received them from Constantine. In this letter some historians such as Johann Lorenz von Mosheim see a reference to the forged document known as the Donation of Constantine.[105] Mosheim argues that

---

[101] Philip Schaff and Samuel Macauley Jackson, Theological Propaedeutic: A General Introduction to the Study of Theology, Exegetical, Historical, Systematic, and Practical, Including Encyclopaedia, Methodology, and Bibliography: A Manual for Students (New York: Charles Scribner's Sons, 1892), 298.

[102] "Codex Carolinus," in EKA, ed. W. Gundlach, MGH Epp., vol. 4 (Berlin: Weidmans, 1892), no. 10-39; LLP, 1:454-456.

[103] LLP, 1:468-480.

[104] "Annales Regni Francorum," 773-774; LLP, 1:480-493.

[105] The Donation of Constantine is a document written probably at the end of the eighth century advocating papal authority and temporal power. In this document Constantine donated to Pope Silvester the whole territory of the western empire, North Africa, and other parts of Asia. The document also mentions

in this letter Adrian exhorts Charles before his elevation to the empire, to order the restitution of all the grants and donations that had formerly been made to St. Peter, and to the church of *Rome*. In this demand also he distinguishes, in the plainest manner, the donation of Constantine from those of the other princes and emperors, and, what is particularly remarkable, from the *exarchate* which was the gift of Pepin, and even from the additions that Charles had already made to his father's grant; from whence we may justly conclude that by the *donation of Constantine*, Adrian meant the city of *Rome* and its annexed territory.[106]

---

that the bishop of Rome was the head over all other sees and earthly ruler over those territories granted to him. According to the document, Constantine was miraculously cured of leprosy by Silvester, who instructed him in the faith and baptized him. In 1440 the Catholic priest Lorenzo Valla proved the document to be a forgery. Contemporary scholarship debates whether or not the document was used by the papacy to legitimate its temporal authority. For more information see: John N. Deely, Four Ages of Understanding: The First Postmodern Survey of Philosophy from Ancient Times to the Turn of the Twenty-First Century, Toronto Studies in Semiotics (Toronto; Buffalo: University of Toronto Press, 2001), 193-201; Alfred Hiatt, The Making of Medieval Forgeries: False Documents in Fifteenth-Century England, British Library Studies in Medieval Culture (London: British Library and University of Toronto Press, 2004), 136-155; Henry Charles Lea, Studies in Church History: The Rise of the Temporal Power; Benefit of Clergy; Excommunication (Philadelphia; London: H.C. Lea; S. Low, Son, & Marston, 1869), 153-167; Joseph Wheless, Forgery in Christianity: A Documented Record of the Foundations of the Christian Religion (New York: A. A. Knopf, 1930), 251-269. For the text of the Donation of Constantine and Valla's work demonstrating it was a forgery, see Lorenzo Valla and Christopher Bush Coleman, The Treatise of Lorenzo Valla on the Donation of Constantine, Text and Translation into English (New Haven: Yale University Press, 1922).

[106] Johann Lorenz Mosheim, An Ecclesiastical History, Ancient and Modern, from the Birth of Christ to the Beginning of the Eighteenth Century, vol. 2 (London: R. Baines, 1819), 238. Mosheim also argues that Hadrian "speaks first of this grant in the following terms: 'Deprecamur vestram Excellentiam . . . pro Deiamore et ipsius clavigeri regni coelorum . . . ut secundum promissionem quam polliciti estis eidem Dei apostolo proanimae vestra mercede et stabilitate regni vestri, omnia nostris temporibus adimplere jubeatis . . . et sicut temporibus beati Silvestri Romani pontificis, a sanctae recordationis piissimo Constantino M. Imperatore, per ejus largitatem (here Constantine's donation is evidently mentioned) sancta Dei catholica et apostolica Romana ecclesia elevata atque exaltata est, et potestatem in his Hesperiae partibus largiri dignatus est ita et in his vestris felicissimis temporibus atque nostris sancta Dei ecclesia germinet... et amplius atque amplius exaltata permaneat . . . quia ecce novus Christianissimus Dei gratia Constantinus imperator (here we see Charles, who at that time was only a king, styled emperor by the pontiff, and compared with Constantine) his temporibus surrexit, per quem omnia Dues sanctae suae ecclesiae . . . largiri dignatus est.' So much for that part of the letter that relates to Constantine's grant: as to the other donations which the pontiff evidently distinguishes from it, observe what follows: 'Sed et cuncta alia quae per diversos Imperatores, Patricios, etiam et alios Deum timentes, pro eorum animae mercede et venia delictorum, in partibus Tusciae, Spoleto, seu Benevento, atque Corsica, simul et Pavinensi patrimonio, beato Petro apostolo concessa sunt, et per nefandam gentem Longobardorum per annorum spatia abstracta et ablata sunt vestris temporibus, restituantur.' (The pontiff intimates further, that all these grants were carefully preserved in the office of the Lateran, and that he sends them to Charles by his legates.) 'Unde et plures donationes in sacro nostro sacrinio Lateranensi recon-

Charlemagne's attitude towards the papal request was different from that of his father Pepin the Short. Charlemagne eliminated the Lombard kingdom, organizing it under his supervision, and enlarged the papacy's territories, fulfilling the promise made by his father.[107] A few years later, acting again in favor of the pope, Charlemagne went to Rome and was crowned emperor of the Romans by Pope Leo III.

The papacy's relations with Charlemagne were closer than with his father, and the papacy benefited greatly from it. Charlemagne's coronation impacted the future of Europe and of the Frankish church. As J. F. Hurst says, "The emperor was no sooner crowned than he threw off his Northern costume, and put on the tunic, the chlamys, and the sandals of the Roman. When he came to leave Rome, and Leo III exchanged kisses with him, and he was lost to sight behind the hills of the Champagne, Europe entered on a new career."[108]

CHURCH-STATE RELATIONSHIPS

Among the difficult subjects related to the church-state relationship in the time of Charlemagne, scholars and historians consider his coronation as Roman emperor one of the most complex. The authority and role of the papacy in the coronation, Charlemagne's understanding of it, his reaction to it, and the results of it in his administrative and religious reforms are integral parts of the debate.[109]

The question of authority in the Carolingian period and the distribution of power in the political structure of Europe in 800 sheds light on the roles and status of popes and kings. In addition, the story of Charlemagne has been rewritten to suit the pur-

---

ditas habemus, tamen et pro satisfactione Christianissimi regni vestri, per jam fatos viros ad demonstrandum eas vobis direximus, et pro hoc petimus eximiam praecellentiam vestram, ut in integro ipsa patrimonia beato Petro et nobis restituere jubeatis.' By this it appears that Constantine's grant was now in being among the archives of the Lateran, and was sent to Charlemagne with the other donations of kings and princes, whose examples were made use of to excite his liberality to the church" (238-239).

[107] LLP, 1:498. According to Noble, the promisse of Pepin the Short was the promise of Quierzy. Noble, 83-86. For maps on Italy and the papal states after Charlemagne see appendix D.

[108] J. F. Hurst, Short History of the Christian Church (New York: Harper, 1893), 110.

[109] See François Louis Ganshof, The Carolingians and the Frankish Monarchy; Studies in Carolingian History (Ithaca, NY: Cornell University Press, 1971), 41-54; Vivian Hubert Howard Green, A New History of Christianity (New York: Sutton Publication, 2000), 60-61; Karl Heldmann, Das Kaisertum Karls Des Grossen: Theorien Und Wirklichkeit, Quellen Und Studien Zur Verfassungsgeschichte Des Deutschen Reiches Im Mittelalter Und Neuzeit, 6, 2 (Weimar: Böhlaus, 1928); Noble, 291-299; Martin D. Stringer, A Sociological History of Christian Worship (Cambridge; New York: Cambridge University Press, 2005), 107-113; Walter Ullmann, The Growth of the Papal Government in the Middle Ages: A Study of the Ideological Relation of Clerical to Lay Power (London: Methuen, 1955), 87-118.

poses of political leaders and the papacy, affirming him as a defender of the church and papacy or a despotic controller of the church, a holy man who promoted justice and education and spread the knowledge of salvation to other lands or a tyrannical lord who murdered Saxons and others who rejected his Christ and lordship.[110]

Ganshof points out three different interpretations of the imperial coronation of Charlemagne. The first group of scholars maintains that "Charlemagne was led to the imperial coronation through the following circumstances: He was master of almost all Western Christendom and even of Rome. He was the defender of faith and Church. He had conquered for Christ huge territories. He had preserved the purity of the dogma and protected the successor of St Peter."[111] The coronation would be a natural result of Charlemagne's actions. The second group argues that the coronation was initiated by the pope and not Charlemagne's counselors. The third group argues that the idea for the coronation came at least partially from Charlemagne, influenced by his advisors, mainly Alcuin. Ganshof himself leans toward this third position.[112]

These three theories address the question of authority in different ways: In the first position, Charlemagne was crowned emperor as a natural result of his own actions as a good administrator and military leader; in the second, the papacy was the sole source of authority for Charlemagne to be declared emperor; and in the third, he sought church legitimacy for his own imperial authority achieved by military actions.

In the historical accounts of Charlemagne's life, all three theories can be true depending on the perspective from which each is seen: the narrators of the history from a papal perspective, the Catholic clergy and advisors of Charlemagne, and the actions taken by Charlemagne and the popes after the event.

The Carolingian rulers before Charlemagne had trouble asserting their authority after they took the throne. The kingdom was divided into dukedoms, and political power was fragmented. The local leader—normally a count—was responsible for the defense of his territory. Each new central political leader had to affirm his authority, either by building up alliances with dukes, princes, and feudal lords or by suppress-

---

[110] Joanna Story, Charlemagne: Empire and Society (Manchester; New York: Manchester University Press, 2005), 2.

[111] Ganshof, 43.

[112] For works on these three positions, see Ganshof, 41-49; Louis Halphen, Charlemagne and the Carolingian Empire, Europe in the Middle Ages, vol. 3 (Amsterdam; New York: North-Holland, 1977); Hans Hirsch, "Der Mittelalterliche Kaisergedanke in Den Liturgischen Gebeten," Mitteilungen des Österreichischen Instituts für Geschichtsforschung 44 (1930): 1-20; Arthur Jean Kleinclausz, Charlemagne (Paris: Hachette, 1934); M. Lintzel, "Das Abendländische Kaisertum Im Neunten Und Zehnten Jahrhundert. Der Römische Und Der Fränkisch-Deutsche Kaisergedanke Von Karl Dem Großen Bis Auf Otto Den Großen," Welt als Geschichte 4 (1938): 423-447; Elisabeth Pfeil, Die Fränkische Und Deutsche Romidee Des Frühen Mittelalters, Forschungen Zur Mittelalterlichen U. Neueren Geschichte, Bd. 3 (Munich: Verlag der Münchner Drucke, 1929); E. E. Stengel, "Kaisertitel Und Suveranitatsidee," Geschichte des Mittelalters 3 (1939): 1-23.

ing them through military actions. In this context, the king's authority was derived from his ability to get the support and legitimacy of other local powers.[113]

This understanding of authority that was more connected to the ruler's personal capacity for gaining legitimacy differed from the Roman concept, where the "authority of the state had something of the abstract and impersonal; obedience was due rather to the office than to the person."[114] In addition, the administrative organization of the Frankish empire was different from that of the Roman Empire. The Roman Empire was centered around the cities, the ideology of the *pax romana*, and a hierarchical network of officials who preserved Roman political and religious traditions and implemented imperial legislation.[115]

For the Carolingians, the political authority of the king was drawn from Christian ideology. Authority in Germanic tradition was connected to each tribal deity and carried out by the tribal leader (*dux*). The conversion to Christianity eliminated the ties to local deities and brought many tribes under the universal authority of the Christian God, represented on earth by the leadership of the church—the bishops—and of the state—the king.[116] Therefore, the Carolingian empire was a group of regional leaders united by the Catholic faith under the leadership of a king who "had both the military task of maintaining a coalition of tribal armies which would defend the empire against enemies from without and the spiritual task of maintaining the Christian faith of the empire against a reversion to paganism."[117]

In this context, Charlemagne's coronation as emperor by the pope in 800, independent of his personal feelings about it, gave him more legitimacy as the ruler of the different nations under his dominion. He was not only the king or chieftain of a tribe, but the supreme leader of all Europe under God, set up to promote justice and defend His church.

It is hard to say whether Charlemagne's relationship with the pope and religious reform was politically or religiously motivated, because it was hard to separate the two in Charlemagne's time. Yet his father's commitment to the Catholic faith and Saint Peter and Charlemagne's own statements on matters of faith imply a great belief in the defense of faith, which included the Papal States and reforms in the Frankish church, as part of his mission as ruler and even his personal salvation. As Janet L. Nelson comments, "As far as Charlemagne was concerned, his obligations to protect

---

[113] See the sections on "Charles Martel" and "Pepin the Short," above.

[114] Jean Brissaud, A History of French Public Law, Law Classic (Washington, DC: Beard Books, 2001), 68.

[115] Harold J. Berman, Law and Revolution: The Formation of the Western Legal Tradition (Cambridge, MA: Harvard University Press, 1983), 66.

[116] Ibid.

[117] Ibid., 89.

Peter's Church were indeed scrupulously fulfilled, on a higher plane than the merely geographical. In Charlemagne's mind, that fulfillment was inseparable from continuing manifestations of divine blessings secured by Peter's intercession."[118]

Noble argues that Charlemagne did not consider the imperial office to be bestowed by the pope, but by God. He comments, "Charlemagne did not bequeath his imperial title until after the Byzantine emperor had recognized its legitimacy. Charlemagne's years of negotiations with the Byzantines suggest that he did not believe that the legitimacy of his imperial office depended upon the pope and the Romans; at least not upon them exclusively."[119]

However, even if he did think the imperial office was of divine origin, the pope, as the head of the church on earth, could have the legitimacy to bestow it. Charlemagne's program of imperial government promulgated in 802, even before he had been recognized as emperor by the eastern empire, demonstrates his awareness of the importance of the coronation by the pope.[120] In this capitulary,[121] Charlemagne is addressed for the first time as emperor,[122] and articles 2 to 9 require all subjects of the empire over the age of 12 to take a new oath of fidelity to the emperor, even those who had sworn fidelity to him as king. As François Louis Ganshof says, "This distinction underlies the difference between the two dignities, showing how much the imperial dignity was superior to the royal, from which it differed fundamentally."[123]

---

[118] Janet L. Nelson, "Charlemagne the Man," in Charlemagne: Empire and Society, ed. Joanna Story (Manchester; New York: Manchester University Press, 2005), 31.

[119] Noble, 297-298.

[120] G. Waitz disputes that this text can be classified as a capitulare missorum. Ganshof argues that it is more appropriate to identify it as a "programmatic capitulary." See Charlemagne, "Capitulare Missorum Generale," in Cap., ed. Alfredus Boretius, MGH Leges, vol. 1 (Hannover: Hahn, 1883), no. 33; Ganshof, 56; Gerhard Wolfgang Seeliger, Die Kapitularien Der Karolinger (Munich: Lindauer, 1893), 69.

[121] The capitularies made up a certain code of law, gathered from various synods, that was intended for the government of the church by the kings of France, especially Charlemagne, under the advice of an assembly of bishops. Not all the articles in the capitularies had religious content: civil laws and other orders addressing different matters between the king and his subjects were also part of what was organized as the body of capitularies. Guizot argues that the collection of capitularies as organized today cannot be considered part of the main body of Frankish legislation. He classifies the capitularies in eight categories: moral, political, penal, civil, religious, canonical, domestic, and occasional. M. Guizot, The History of Civilization, from the Fall of the Roman Empire to the French Revolution, trans. William Hazlitt, 3 vols. (New York: Appleton, 1846), 2:219-221.

[122] Capitularies from 19 to 28 addressed Charlemagne as rex francorum and capitularies from 28 to 32 added the title patricius romanorum. From capitulary 33 on, he is addressed as christianissimus domnus imperator Karolus. See Charlemagne, "Karoli Magni Capitularia," in Cap., ed. Alfredus Boretius, MGH Leges, vol. 1 (Hannover: Hahn, 1883), no. 19-33.

[123] Ganshof, 58.

The coronation also drove Charlemagne's proposed reforms. He was not only reforming religion, but using religious authority and influence to foster his political administration. His patronage of monasteries was not only part of his religious reforms, but also played a part in extending his political power over the Frankish empire. He extended his authority to local communities by integrating monasteries into his "royal lordship with privileges, grants of immunity from lordly control and the confirmation of property rights."[124] Hummer comments that these ties between the Carolingian kings and the monasteries "co-opted not merely an ecclesiastical elite, but also the clusters of families tied to the monks by kinship, friendship and property . . . reinforce local order," and enabled them "to project their authority into localities with as little disruption of local sensibilities as possible."[125]

The other point related to authority in the relations between the Carolingians and the popes is the issue of rulership. Scholars following Albert Hauck portray Charlemagne and his father as lords of Rome even before his coronation in 800.[126] Noble properly refutes Hauck and his followers, pointing out that their "sources are cryptic, enigmatic, scanty, and in truth, susceptible of multiple interpretations," and that their conclusion "is richer in assumptions and speculations than it is in concrete, sustained demonstrations."[127]

After describing the weakness of Hauck's arguments, Noble concludes that any lordship of Pepin and Charlemagne over the Roman republic ruled by the papacy before 800 cannot be proved, and that even after Charlemagne's coronation, his only action at Rome was the condemnation of the accusers of Pope Leo III (who was not considered innocent by Charlemagne; he cleared himself by oath of innocence). Furthermore, he states that there was no mention of the papacy or the republic of Italy in Charlemagne's program of imperial government that began in 802.[128]

Even though Charlemagne did not interfere in the political and ecclesiastical affairs of the Duchy of Rome, he followed the traditional custom of the Frankish rulers by legislating religious matters for the Frankish church. Since Clovis, the Franks had had only one body of civil law for their subjects—the Salic laws. Capitularies were issued by kings to regulate everything not covered in this code, and other issues were regulated according to the laws of the peoples under Frankish

---

[124] Hans J. Hummer, Politics and Power in Early Medieval Europe: Alsace and the Frankish Realm, 600-1000, Cambridge Studies in Medieval Life and Thought (Cambridge, UK; New York: Cambridge University Press, 2005), 24.

[125] Ibid.

[126] Albert Hauck, Kirchengeschichte Deutschlands, vol. 2 (Leipzig: Hinrichs, 1935), 87-93. Noble gives an extensive list of scholars who follow this position. See Noble, 277.

[127] Noble, 277.

[128] Ibid., 277-299.

control. Church legislation was also enforced by the state as a separate body of laws, and most of the capitularies had religious content. Charlemagne legislated through capitularies, and even though he followed the canons provided by the Roman See, he promulgated many ecclesiastical laws in his capitularies.[129]

Kings after Clovis considered ecclesiastical affairs to be matters of state, and Charlemagne, as Ganshof points out, considered that "within his realm, God had entrusted the Church to his keeping, that he might watch over its destinies in the midst of so many besetting dangers."[130]

For the church, the main impact of the alliance between Charlemagne and the papacy was his military conquest in Italy that eliminated the Lombard threat to the pope's temporal power. Since Vigilius, the papacy had been increasing its political independence from the eastern empire, but after the Lombard invasion of north Italy, the papacy faced a greater threat to its temporal power over the Duchy of Rome than the eastern empire posed. The rise of the Carolingian dynasty and their alliance with the papacy provided the military help that the papacy needed without challenging its sovereignty in Italy.

The popes knew that the eastern emperors would never fully recognize their temporal supremacy. As Tierney says, "The only real hope of establishing beyond doubt the legitimacy of the papal claim lay in the institution of a new Roman emperor in the West on whom the popes could rely as a friend and protector. It was probably this factor more than any other which led to the dramatic climax of the Frankish-papal alliance: the coronation of Pepin's son Charlemagne as emperor of the Romans in St. Peter's church at Rome on Christmas Day, A.D. 800."[131]

Charlemagne's elimination of the Lombard kingdom advanced the cause of the papacy and stabilized the political situation in Italy. As William Prall says,

> By it [Lombard elimination] the great and holy see of Rome became emancipated from all allegiance to the emperors of the East and entered on the splendid role it afterward played so fearlessly—the role of arbiter of kings and supreme ruler over the peoples of the western world. And by it, it received immediately the territory that had belonged to the exarchate of northern Italy, which gradually grew into the States of the Church, and which, making the pope a temporal, as well as a spiritual monarch, enabled him the easier to enter into the political life of Europe.[132]

---

[129] Ibid.; Matthew Innes, "Charlemagne's Government," in Charlemagne: Empire and Society, ed. Joanna Story (Manchester; New York: Manchester University Press, 2005), 76-79.

[130] Ganshof, 205.

[131] Brian Tierney, The Crisis of Church and State, 1050-1300: With Selected Documents (Toronto; Buffalo: University of Toronto Press in Association with the Medieval Academy of America, 1988), 17.

[132] William Prall, The State and the Church (New York: T. Whittaker, 1900), 159.

The impact of Charlemagne's coronation was seen more after his death than before. It helped to establish the medieval hierarchical theory that all authority came from God through the Catholic Church. Brian Tierne states, "By one brilliant gesture Pope Leo established the precedent, adhered to throughout the Middle Ages, that papal coronation was essential to the making of an emperor, and thereby implanted the germ of the later idea that the empire itself was a gift to be bestowed by the papacy."[133]

Charlemagne's relationship with the bishop of Rome and his coronation laid the foundation for the formation of the Holy Roman Empire. According to Einhard, Charlemagne's official biographer, his favorite work was Augustine's *The City of God*.[134] According to John Neville Figgis, what captured Charlemagne's attention in *The City of God* was Augustine's vision of the heavenly city and the role of the ruler in this city. Figgis points out that for Augustine, a good emperor would promote the true worship of God, not only for earthly benefits, but also for eternal salvation. Charlemagne's vision was to form a "Christian Empire, the City of God on earth."[135]

The implications of this understanding are that the emperor and the bishops would adopt hierarchical roles to achieve eternal salvation in a Christian empire. Augustine stressed that the church was the source of justice and churchmen should be the ones responsible for promoting the knowledge of universal salvation in society.[136] Augustine did not assign a political role to the church in his book; as Vernon Bourke argues, the city of God for Augustine was not a political institution, but the regeneration of the inner heart of a human being.[137] The stress that Charlemagne put on reforming the clergy demonstrates the importance he assigned to the clergy, as the ones who bestowed salvation, and to the Catholic Church, as the source of it. Bishops in his administration undertook more secular duties than they had under any Frankish king before him—not to neglect the word of God, but to fulfill the needs of the people.[138] This policy of empowering bishops with secular duties strengthened the claim of ecclesiastical superiority over secular authorities; years later, with the decline of royal power, Hincmar

---

[133] Tierney, 18.

[134] Einhard, 24.

[135] John Neville Figgis, The Political Aspects of St. Augustine's 'City of God' (Gloucester, MA: Peter Smith, 1963), 84.

[136] Augustine, The Political Writings of St. Augustine, ed. Henry Paolucci and Dino Bigongiari (Washington, DC: Regnery Publication, 1996), 245-246, 271, 287-288.

[137] Vernon J. Bourke, Wisdom from St. Augustine (Houston, TX: Center for Thomistic Studies, University of St. Thomas, 1984), 162.

[138] R. W. Southern, Western Society and the Church in the Middle Ages, The Penguin History of the Church, vol. 2 (Harmondsworth: Penguin, 1990), 173-174.

would state "the episcopal dignity is greater than the royal, for bishops consecrate kings, but kings do not consecrate bishops."[139]

SUMMARY AND CONCLUSION

The Merovingian kings after Clovis continued to have a close relationship with the Catholic Church. The Frankish church received great donations from the nobility and became very wealthy, making the office of bishop a powerful and desirable position. Bishops were appointed by the king and became a political force in the Frankish kingdom; this political use of the office of bishop led to spiritual and moral decadence in Frankish society. The Merovingian dynasty then lost political power and the country was administered by the mayor of the palace.

By the end of the seventh century, the mayor of the palace of the Austrasian house, Charles Martel, unified the Frankish kingdom under his leadership, but still in the name of the Merovingian dynasty. In the time of his son Pepin the Short, the Merovingian king Childeric III was deposed and Pepin was crowned king of the Franks.

The pope granted legitimacy to Pepin's coronation as king; Pepin and the pope made an alliance in which the king would support the papacy with military force against the Lombards and the pope would give legitimacy to the Carolingian dynasty. Charlemagne continued his father's alliance with the popes and helped free the Roman See from the Lombard threat to its political supremacy in the Roman Duchy.

Since the time of Vigilius, the Roman See had been seeking political independence in Italy. The invasion of the Lombards in Italy threatened the supremacy of the papacy in Italy, but it also helped the papacy fight for independence from the East. The papacy could have claimed total control of the Italian territory and freed itself from eastern interference, but it needed military help to keep the Lombards away. With the alliance between the papacy and the Franks, the church was able to claim political supremacy over the papal state without fear of the Lombards or the Byzantines.

The relationship between the Church of Rome and the Frankish state during the Carolingians raised some relevant points:

1. The administration of the Frankish church was initially handled by local synods headed by clergymen, nobles, and sometimes the king. After Saint Boniface, the Church was organized following the Roman church system (754).

---

[139] Hendrik Spruyt, The Sovereign State and Its Competitors: An Analysis of Systems Change, Princeton Studies in International History and Politics (Princeton, NJ: Princeton University Press, 1994), 47.

2. The title of patrician given by the pope to Pepin the Short indicates that the papacy had assumed responsibility for appointing political leaders and replaced the eastern Roman Empire as the source of political power in the West.

3. The Church of Rome had political power, but lacked military strength.

4. The Roman See recognized itself as politically independent from the eastern Roman Empire and from other Germanic kingdoms. Its relationship with these kingdoms was based on its need for military power to defend its religious efforts throughout the empire and its political prerogatives.

5. According to Pope Hadrian, the papal claim of temporal power and legitimacy to crown rulers is connected to the donation of Constantine to Pope Silvester.

6. The Carolingian kings were despotic rulers who promoted religious reforms according to their political interest and religious convictions, regulating the affairs of the church and state together. However, they were Catholic Christians, and as such they had great concern for religious matters: They considered the papacy to be the see of Saint Peter and the head of the Catholic Church, promoted religious reforms according to the Roman See, recognized the papacy as a temporal state and ally, and accepted its political authority in conferring legitimacy on kings and rulers.

7. The Frankish kings and the papacy were allies and leaders of independent kingdoms, but the Franks would give protection to the Holy See, the chair of Saint Peter.

8. The Frankish kingdom was a heterogenic group of Germanic peoples and the Catholic faith became the strongest force binding them together.

9. The coronation of Charlemagne strengthened his power and sealed the political independence of the Roman republic under the leadership of the papacy and the authority of the chair of Saint Peter.

10. It revived the idea of Europe as a unified Catholic Christian empire, now under two monarchs—the spiritual and the temporal, the pope and the king.

Charlemagne's religious policy prepared the way for the medieval church to exert political authority over the state. He had bishops as close advisors, and the clergy promoted his political, educational, religious, and cultural reforms. The Frankish church was molded according to the orientation of the Church of Rome, and the clergy were empowered with civil authority, paving the way for the formation of the Holy Roman Empire.

CHAPTER VI

Analysis and comparison of the models of church-state relationships during the rulerships of Constantine, Clovis, Justinian, and Charlemagne

Introduction

From Constantine to Charlemagne, Catholic Christianity moved from a small religious group in the empire to the most powerful religious force in Europe; it replaced paganism as the official religion of the empire and became a state religion. After the barbarian invasions, Catholic Christianity won the battle against Arianism and, in time, all the barbarian kingdoms converted to Catholicism.

This change of religious forces in the Roman Empire affected both the empire and the Catholic Church. New policies on church-state relationships were established, and such rulers as Constantine, Clovis, Justinian, and Charlemagne were important characters in this process.

This chapter analyzes and compares the models of church-state relationships discussed in the prior chapters. All these models share common points, but also have their own peculiarities. Only the most critical historical, descriptive, and analytical information from the previous chapters will be repeated, with general references to the sections from which it was drawn. Credits to external works previously mentioned will be provided only for information and phrases that express the whole idea of the author.

The chapter is divided into two sections. The first section discusses the similarities and differences in the religious policies adopted by Constantine, Justinian, Clovis, and Charlemagne, and provide some information on the reaction of the church to these policies. The second section discusses the historical development of church-state relationships, focusing on the results for the state and church from the application of these religious policies. Finally, a conclusion is drawn.

SIMILARITIES AND DIFFERENCES

EMPERORS AND CATHOLICISM

All of the four emperors studied promoted Catholic Christianity and suppressed heresies and non-Christian religions. All four saw Catholic Christianity as a source of unity in the empire and sought the favor of God by favoring Catholicism. The major difference between them in their general relations with Catholicism was that Clovis and Charlemagne were less involved in defining doctrine than were Constantine and Justinian. Furthermore, Constantine and Clovis had "miraculous conversions" to Catholicism, while Justinian and Charlemagne were born under Catholic rulers.

Constantine's religious policy retained the main tenets of the Roman pagan religion: he sought divine favor, not by following the traditional pagan Roman religious policy, but by sponsoring Catholic Christianity. Constantine adopted a more pluralistic approach to religion in the beginning of his reign and then gradually narrowed it down to the patronage of only Catholic Christianity. His battles were not a crusade against the enemies of the Catholic Church, but he attributed his victories to the Christian God. The result was his dedication to Catholic Christianity and suppression of paganism and non-Catholic Christians. Constantine favored Catholicism, but it was not yet the state religion. After Constantine, Catholic Christianity not only became the official religion of the state, but also gradually became part of the state. As Burckhardt comments, after Constantine, the church had turned into the state and the state into the church.[1]

For Justinian, Catholicism was the religion of the empire, and the task of preserving the faith and defending it against heresies and non-Christians rested on the shoulders of the emperor. He was motivated by political ambitions, but presented his wars as having a religious motivation—the elimination of the heretics. During Justinian's time, paganism was dealt its final deadly blow and non-Christians were persecuted and had their civil rights taken away.

Clovis, like Constantine and Justinian, sought God's favor through Catholic Christianity. According to Gregory of Tours, Clovis favored Catholic Christianity by fighting against Arianism and building churches, and like the emperors, he attributed his victories to the Christian God.[2] His conversion to Catholicism made it the official religion of the Franks. However, unlike Constantine and Justinian, Clovis did not interfere in church doctrine. He

---

[1] Burckhardt, 308.
[2] Gregory, The History of the Franks, 2.18-27.

summoned councils and enforced their canons as prepared by the bishops. In his time, the church-state relationship was more like a contract between two independent institutions united in an exchange of benefits.

Charlemagne also related the prosperity of the state to God's favor. Like Clovis, he did not emphasize theological debate. He sought uniformity of worship following the guidance of the Roman See. Like Constantine, Justinian, and Clovis, Charlemagne fought in defense of the Catholic cause, and like Gregory of Tour's view of Clovis, he sent his army to protect the Catholic Church. Like Justinian, Charlemagne forced pagans (the Saxons) to convert to Catholicism. His church-state relationship followed the model of Clovis, an alliance between the Franks and the church. However, Charlemagne's relations included the papacy and not only the bishops of France.

Constantine's and Clovis's conversions were similar in several ways. They were both related to miraculous intervention of the Christian God in battle; they both introduced Catholicism as an official state religion in their dominions; they both began important phases for the Catholic Church in the Roman and Frankish empires; and they both were presented by Catholic writers as examples for future rulers. However, Constantine and Clovis differed in the timing of their baptisms. While Constantine did not baptize until close to his death, Clovis did it at the apex of his reign. This difference marks the historical significance of Clovis's baptism for the church. While Constantine did not make Catholicism the official religion of the empire, since his full commitment to the church came only on his deathbed, Clovis's baptism in 508 represented a union between the Catholic Church and the Franks—a new model of church-state relationships that found its full expression in the Concordat of 511 of the Council of Orleans that would become the pattern for the new European states under barbarian rulers.

Emperor's Appointment

All four emperors shared the understanding that they were appointed by God to promote the welfare of the state and the church, but Justinian and Charlemagne had a deeper perception of their responsibility before God for the resolution of internal church matters than did Constantine and Clovis.

Constantine had a vision that he was appointed by God to promote the well-being, not only of the state, but also of the Catholic Christian faith. He intervened in church schisms to avoid bringing the anger of God down on himself and the empire and to promote the welfare of the nation. As Jones comments, Constantine believed that "schism would provoke God's anger against the empire and particularly against himself, to whose care the empire had been committed."[3]

---

[3] Jones, "Church and State from Constantine to Theodosius," 270.

Constantine exerted the same comprehensive judicial authority, as had the previous pagan Roman emperors. He was Augustus, the divine ruler, emperor, the supreme commander of the army, consulate, and juridical system, which empowered him as the final, inviolable, and omnipotent authority in the empire.[4] In addition to that, he was the *pontifex maximus*, the supreme religious leader of the empire.

After Gratian, Roman emperors did not use the title *pontifex maximus*, but Justinian, Clovis, and Charlemagne also acted as religious leaders in their domains. They shared Constantine's vision of state intervention in church issues to avoid provoking the anger of God, and of being appointed by God to preserve the state and the church. Justinian had a deeper understanding of the role of the emperor as God's representative on earth than did Constantine. He expressed the idea that the empire was "God's agent for bringing divine order to an otherwise chaotic world"[5] and that "God has sent us [the emperor and the empire] from heaven so that it [the empire] might remedy difficulties through its perfection, and adapt the laws to the varieties of nature."[6] Charlemagne related his work to his appointment by God, understanding that the salvation of the country was his responsibility before God.

THEOLOGY AND RELIGIOUS TOLERANCE

Constantine and Justinian became more involved in the theological debate. Clovis and Charlemagne focused more on the worship aspect of religion. Even though Constantine dealt with theological matters, he was more pluralist in religious matters. Justinian, Clovis, and Charlemagne adopted a policy of religious intolerance.

Even though Constantine dealt with theological matters, some of his statements indicate that he believed the cultic or worship aspects of religion were more important than the theological aspects. Ecclesiological or theological differences could exist, since they did not threaten the unity and welfare of the state. Dissidents and troublemakers could cause civil disorder and bring divine disfavor upon the empire. Constantine compared the bishops' theological debates to trivial matters, not because he did not understand them, but because he considered unity of worship to be more important than theological matters.[7] In a sense, Constantine was more nearly pluralistic in religious matters: He favored Catholic Christianity but did not bother to intervene in religious issues if the unity of the state was not threatened.

Justinian had a different perspective on religious matters than did Constantine.

---

[4] Saxer, 13-14.
[5] Olster, 166.
[6] Novel, 73.
[7] Drake, Constantine and the Bishops, 96; Eusebius, VC, 1:2.71.

For Justinian, theology and the proper definition of faith were the most important parts of the true religion. Like Constantine, he tried to reach a compromise between opposing groups—the Chalcedonians and Monophysites—but he would not compromise the main tenets of the Nicaean-Chalcedonian faith. He worked hard to eradicate theological differences, although he did not completely succeed. His problems with Pope Vigilius reflect his emphasis on theology. He believed that the Roman See was the guardian of Catholic orthodoxy and that the pope's support for Justinian theology would bring the whole West to his side. Justinian was not pluralistic, and during his reign there was no place for religious tolerance.

Clovis and Charlemagne differed from Justinian and Constantine in their approach to theology. Clovis delegated the theological debate to the bishops and supported their decisions. Charlemagne, even though he revived the study of religious matters, lined up more with Clovis, concentrating more on the cultic aspect of religion than on theology. Like Justinian, Clovis and Charlemagne were not pluralistic on religious matters, and in their kingdoms there was no room for religious freedom.

Relationship with Bishops

All four emperors used bishops in the administration of the empire. Constantine used bishops as a source of political legitimacy to the imperial throne instead of the senate.[8] Clovis and Charlemagne used bishops in their expansion of power. Constantine and Clovis did not have a special relationship with the bishop of Rome. Charlemagne and Justinian had a distinctive relationship with the bishop of Rome, who occupied the chair of Saint Peter and the pope was the head of the church.

Constantine's policy on religion gave him a new constituency. According to Drake, he sought legitimacy for his reign from the bishops, as previous emperors had from the senate. The senate had lost contact with the population, and bishops, because of their work to help the poor and fulfill the spiritual needs of the people, were representatives for a large part of the population.[9] Constantine started a policy of giving the church the right to legitimize state authorities; he employed bishops in administrative positions due to their "long experience in organizing opinion and administering resources."[10]

Clovis and Charlemagne also used bishops in their expansion of power. They were important figures in Clovis's conquest and administration of Gaul and in Charlemagne's religious reform.

---

[8] See the section "Constantine, the Bishops, and the Church" in chapter 3 above.

[9] Drake, 103-108.

[10] Fredriksen, 37.

Constantine's appointment of bishops to imperial offices bestowed a distinctive power and prestige on the bishops, raised the clergy "above society," and made the position of bishop more a political than a spiritual one.[11] This particularly affected the Roman church, which acquired political ascendancy in Rome over the senate and magistrates. By the time of Leo I, bishop of Rome, the papacy was already developing diplomatic relations with the barbarians and defending the city from their attacks. By the time of Justinian, two popes were sent as political representatives to intercede in favor of the Ostrogoths.

In the time of Clovis, bishops were acting as defenders of their cities against barbarian attacks and assuming most of the political responsibilities of the cities. Before going to war against the Visigoths, Clovis recognized the bishops' political role in the cities by sending letters to them, assuring them that church properties would not be destroyed. By the time of Charlemagne, bishops were a powerful force in the political and ecclesiastical life of the empire. He used them to promote his administrative, educational, cultural, and religious reforms.

Constantine did not hold the bishop of Rome in higher regard than other bishops. In the Donatist controversy, he asked Melchiades, bishop of Rome, and other bishops from Gaul to solve the issue together. When the result was not satisfactory, he followed the procedures that became the norm for the rest of his reign: negotiation through letters, holding church councils, and enforcement of council decisions. The fact that he sent Bishop Hosius of Cordoba as the church representative to solve the Arian controversy[12] demonstrated that his choice of Melchiades to solve the Donatist issue was not related to the primacy of the Roman See over other sees. After the Donatist controversy, there is no mention of any special relations between Constantine and the bishops of Rome.[13] However, Constantine's introduction of the bishops to the political life of the empire led to a gradual integration between church and state. Bishops were integrated as a new social class of the empire. To belong to this class became a desire of the aristocracy, which later began to dominate it.

From Constantine to Justinian, a bishop's influence depended on the individual man and not the see where he was exerting his office. Ambrose had more influence over the emperor Theodosius than did Julian, bishop of Rome. The Cappadocian fathers had more influence over Emperor Valens

---

[11] Burckhardt, 309.

[12] Eusebius, VC, 2.63.

[13] The only reference to special relations between Constantine and a Roman bishop is found in the Donation of Constantine, a document that, according to scholars, was prepared no earlier than the eighth century. See the section, "The Temporal Authority of the Papacy up to Charlemagne" in chapter 5 above.

than other bishops. In the Acacian schism, the bishops of Constantinople were more influential than the bishops of Rome.[14]

Clovis, like Constantine, had a closer connection with the bishops of his domains than with the bishop of Rome. Clovis's relationship with the bishops in Gaul was an agreement that also resembled Charlemagne's later relationship with the papacy.

Justinian differed from Constantine and Clovis in his relationship with the bishop of Rome. He attributed special dignity to the bishop of Rome. He gave primacy to the bishop of Rome over other sees and sought his approval for his religious policy. For Justinian, to win the support of the bishop of Rome was to win the support of the whole West.[15]

Charlemagne, like Justinian, differentiated the bishop of Rome from other bishops. However, he related to the bishop of Rome as an ally, not as a subordinate. He appointed religious leaders in France, but did not interfere in the administration of the papal republic.

Legislation

Constantine and Justinian are similar in their legislative work related to church matters. For them, there was one body of state laws for secular and religious issues. Justinian's legislation continued that of Constantine and other emperors, deepening the relationship between church and state. Clovis and Charlemagne were similar in their legislative work related to church matters. They had a civil code—the Salic Law—and religious legislation was outside of it.

Constantine incorporated the Catholic Church under the umbrella of the state. Theodosius made the Catholic Church the official religion of the state. Justinian made the state Catholic.

Constantine legislated in favor of Catholicism. Emperors after Constantine, as expressed in the Theodosian code, gave a distinctive position to Catholic Christianity, reserving a whole section of the Roman law book for regulating religious affairs. Justinian made Catholic beliefs the foundation of Roman legislation. He not only enforced canon law, but made it fundamental to other legislation.

Constantine tried to solve church issues by first giving the church an opportunity to solve its own problems. If that did not work, he summoned councils for the church to reach a consensus on the matter and actively participated in the councils to ensure unity. Afterwards, he enforced the decisions of the councils over the Christian world. Finally, he suppressed opponents of the councils' decisions through military action.

---

[14] See the section "Bishops' Responses to Imperial Intervention in Church Affairs" in chapter 4 above.

[15] See the section "Justinian's Ecclesiastical Policies" in chapter 4 above.

The emperors after Constantine followed his policies, except Zeno and Anastasius, who formulated a theological treatise and imposed it as a formula of concord. Justinian blended the two approaches. He issued an imperial decree on theological matters and tried to gain the support of the clergy, mainly the pope, for his formula. When he encountered, he summoned a council and worked to have his wishes included into the canons of the council.

Clovis did not involve himself in theological discussions. He summoned a council, but did not participate in it, and enforced the decisions as law in his territory. However, other Frankish kings after Clovis interfered in church affairs as Constantine and Justinian had. Charlemagne, in particular, adopted two different approaches to church-state relationships. He promoted religious reform in France, issuing laws to regulate many aspects of the ecclesiastical, liturgical, and theological life of the church. At the same time, he acted as an ally of the papacy and did not interfere in the religious or administrative government of the Roman Republic headed by the pope. Charlemagne helped defend the papacy against its enemies and sought guidance from the pope regarding Christian theology and ways to reform the Catholic Church in France.

HISTORICAL DEVELOPMENT

CONSTANTINE

Constantine's religious policy continued that of the old Roman emperors except that it introduced Catholic Christianity as one of the official religions of the empire. Throughout his reign, he advocated the main tenets of Roman religion: Proper worship was essential to achieve the favor of the gods, religion was an affair of the state, and the well-being of the state was more important than that of the individual. Also, he emphasized the cultic aspect of religion over the theological aspect.

Eusebius describes Constantine's patronage of Catholic Christianity as the result of a miracle conversion—his vision of the labarum that ensured him victory over his enemies and became the symbol of his army.[16]

Constantine envisioned Christianity as a better way than paganism to promote the unity of the empire, and used the administrative abilities of the bishops in his reorganization of the empire. The responsibilities of Bishops in their dioceses and their close contact with the people made them well suited to replace the senate as the source of legitimacy for Constantine's government.[17] He empowered the church

---

[16] Eusebius, VC, 1.28-31.
[17] Drake, Constantine and the Bishops, 54-56.

with donations, made the episcopacy a court of appeal, and suppressed heresy and non-Christian religions. Constantine introduced the church into the political life of the empire and favored Catholic Christianity over other religions, but Catholicism did not become the sole state religion during his reign.[18]

Constantine's procedures to deal with church affairs were first to allow the church leadership to solve its own problems through diplomatic means, second to summon a church council and work through the council to achieve unity, and finally to enforce the council's decisions by law and military action if needed.

Catholic bishops did not oppose Constantine's patronage of Christianity, but they sought the emperor's support for their own understanding of Catholic orthodoxy. Bishops such as Eusebius presented Constantine not only as appointed by God to promote peace and justice in the secular world, but as the representative of the godhead on earth.[19]

At the time of Constantine, Catholic bishops accepted the emperor as a court of appeal for church matters. They even accepted the intervention of the state in church matters for the promotion of Christian moral values.[20] This included using the political and military power of the state to suppress anyone who threatened the sound doctrine of the Catholic Church.

The recognition of the emperor as a judge appointed by God to promote peace and justice led to struggles between bishops for the political support of the emperor throughout the Donatist and Arian controversies. However, after the Arian controversy, state intervention against bishops' understandings of Catholic orthodoxy made the church leaders realize the necessity of autonomy in ecclesiastical matters. This leadership role was more effectively developed through the Roman See in the person of its bishop.

From Constantine's Sons to Justinian

After Constantine, the state and the church began to develop different understandings of the roles of ecclesiastical and political leaders. The differences were not related to the separation of church and state, but rather the proper way to settle ecclesiastical and theological issues. The church leadership even increased its political activities in the administration of the empire.

On the side of the state, the emperors continued the religious policy of Constantine. They legislated in favor of Catholic Christianity and suppressed heresy and

---

[18] Saxer, 13.

[19] See Eusebius, VC, 1:2.20, 4.29; idem, OC, 1:3; Eusebius and Ferrar, 141, 349-351, 393.

[20] For more information on Christians' views of church and state relationships before Constantine, see the section "The Christian Church and the State before Constantine" in chapter 2 above.

non-Christian religions. By the time of Theodosius, Catholic Christianity became the official religion of the empire. Emperors' patronage of Christianity enriched the church and made the bishopric an important political position.

It remained one of the emperor's prerogatives to legislate on religious matters, and emperors summoned councils and regulated the religious life of the empire. They went further than Constantine, legislating in theological matters without the convocation of a council. Religion continued to be a force for unity, and proper worship was considered essential to attain God's favor for the prosperity of the empire.

The church's pursuit of independence in theological and ecclesiastical decisions followed distinct routes in the East and West. In the East, the presence of the emperor in Constantinople meant he had more control over church affairs. Bishops could not act independently and emperors imposed their wishes on the clergy, even deposing bishops who refused to abide by their rules.

In the West, the gradual disintegration of the Roman administration because of the barbarian invasions and the absence of the emperor from Rome gave the Roman See more ecclesiastical and political power. Also, the major theological controversies happened in the East and not the West, which meant the eastern church was not united as a political force under the leadership of the bishop of Constantinople or another see.

After the final disintegration of the Roman Empire in the West, when the government was in the hands of Arian barbarians, the Roman See was politically independent and had a stronger claim to ecclesiastical supremacy. Even before the fall of Rome, the bishops of Rome had developed a theory of ecclesiastical supremacy based on the apostolic succession and the Roman See as the chair of Saint Peter, the founder of the Catholic Christian church. The eastern emperor Justinian finally recognized the ecclesiastical supremacy of the bishop of Rome in 533.

The Arian barbarian government in Rome hindered full recognition of the supremacy of the bishop of Rome, but after the end of the siege of Rome by the Ostrogoths in 538, the papacy was fully free from this non-Catholic Christian government and could exert its ecclesiastical supremacy. Even though Totila took control of Rome three times during 546 to 552, the papacy did not come under barbarian government because Pope Vigilius was at Constantinople during this time.[21]

CHURCH-STATE UNDER BARBARIAN GOVERNMENT

The barbarian invasions introduced a new perspective on church-state relationships to the West. Most of the barbarian rulers preserved the administrative structure of the Roman Empire, especially in Italy: The Heruls under the lead-

---

[21] For more information see "Justinian's Ecclesiastical Policies" in chapter 3 above.

ership of Odoacer and then the Goths under Theodoric sought legitimacy for their rule from the senate. The senate thus reacquired some of its prestige and importance as a political force in Italy.

The clergy also continued to gain influence in the political life of the new barbarian kingdoms. In Italy, the Goths did not enforce their Arian beliefs on their Catholic subjects: Catholics had freedom of worship. Only in North Africa under the Vandals was there persecution against Catholics. The Goths did not interfere in the government of the church, and in this period, the papacy solidified its ecclesiastical supremacy over the western sees. The eastern emperor's lack of influence in the West led the papacy to challenge him on religious matters. The popes recognized the legitimacy of the emperor's authority on secular matters, but argued that emperors should accept the church's guidance on religious matters, as Catholics who received the salvation of their souls from the church.[22]

At this time, popes not only defended their ecclesiastical supremacy of jurisdiction, but also elaborated on the specific roles of emperors and clergy in the church-state relationship. Pope Gelasius I explored this topic through the theory of the two swords. In a letter to Emperor Anastasius, he conveyed a dualist structure of power as spiritual and temporal, the former headed by the pope and the latter by the emperor. As a member of the church, he wrote, the emperor should humbly subordinate himself to the authority of the church in ecclesiastical and theological matters, as the clergy did to the emperor in civil matters. Both powers received their authority from God, and while any faithful member of the church submitted to all priests, more obedience should be shown to the pope, as the head of the see appointed by God to be over all others.[23]

Even under barbarian government, the clergy and aristocrats maintained open communication with the East. Senators in Rome still had properties in the eastern part of the empire, and many of them considered themselves part of the empire. The ties that had bound senators to emperors in the past were now transferred to the papacy. Aristocratic life revolved around the church, its interests, and its leader, the pope. Even the literary works produced at this time were intended to further Catholic Christianity.[24]

The period of barbarian rule in Italy increased the political power of the senate and fostered the independence of the church from the eastern emperors. However, it did not erase the desire of aristocrats and clergy to be under the leadership of a Catholic Christian emperor. Although Catholics had more freedom under the Goths than under Roman emperors, Arianism was a heresy and the clergy wanted it eliminated.

---

[22] See the section "Bishops' Responses to Imperial Intervention in Church Affairs," in chapter 3 above.

[23] Gelasius, "Epistolae et Decreta," 42.

[24] See the section "The Church in the West and the Barbarian Invasion" in chapter 3 above.

Catholic bishops' desire for the elimination of Arianism became very notorious in Gaul with the conversion of Clovis. Bishops such as Gregory of Tours described Clovis's war against the Visigoths as a Christian crusade against Arians. Bishop Avitus even declared that God had raised Clovis to be the judge of His people, saying, "Divine foresight has found a certain judge for our age. In making a choice for yourself, you judge on behalf of everyone. Your faith is our victory."[25] It is important to mention that Clovis's victory over Arian Visigoths in Gaul did not eliminate Arianism from the western part of the Roman Empire. The Visigoths converted to Catholicism only at the end of the sixth century, and Arianism prevailed among the Lombards close to the end of the seventh century.

Clovis's conversion to Catholicism also brought about key changes in the relationship between the Catholic Church and the state in Gaul. Catholic influence in the political sphere, which had peaked with Theodosius's proclamation of Catholicism as the official religion of the state in 392, had been shaken by Arian rule, but there would be another major shift in favor of Catholicism.

Bishops in Gaul who had acquired temporal power due to their defense of the cities from barbarian invasion also became counselors of political authorities.[26] In his territorial expansion, Clovis incorporated these powerful Catholic leaders into his administration. His victories against the Visigoths in 507-508 and his baptism in 508[27] solidified the formation of a new society in Gaul, united the Frankish king with the ecclesiastical authorities of the Catholic Church, and established a Christian community under the authority of the Catholic bishops. As Wood says, "What was important was the fact that after 508 the Catholic Church defined the Christian community which constituted the *regnum Francorum*."[28]

Clovis's model of church-state relationships was the union of two powers for the benefit of the Frankish kingdom: the civil and military power, represented by the king, and the moral and religious power, represented by the clergy. In this model, bishops and kings began working together for strengthening of the kingdom, with the bishop's role being to guide and the king's to implement.[29] It contrasts with other barbarian models of church-state relationships, like the one implemented in Italy by Odoacer and Theodoric that granted religious freedom to Catholics, Jews, and others. For the first time, a barbarian king defended Catholicism and religious

---

[25] Avitus, Avitus of Vienne, Letters and Selected Prose, 369.

[26] See, for example, the bishops Remigius and Avitus. For more information, see the section "Clovis's Kingdom" in chapter 4 above.

[27] See the section "War against the Alamanni and Clovis's Baptism (496 or 508)" in chapter 4 above.

[28] Wood, The Merovingian Kingdoms, 72.

[29] Mitchell, 76-77.

tolerance was withdrawn. Gradually, with the help of the state, the Catholic Church eradicated all forms of paganism from Gaul.

After Clovis's baptism in 508, the Frankish kingdom consolidated its union with the Catholic Church, and the spreading of Catholicism became the spreading of Roman tradition. Catholicism became the bridge between barbarians and Romans and represented the continuity of the Roman Empire, carrying on the old Roman traditions under the leadership of barbarian rulers. Clovis's administrative model of the church-state relationship set the tone for the new European political system of independent kingdoms united by the bonds of the Catholic Church. His baptism in 508, as a consummation of this alliance between church and state, throne and altar, can be considered the point of transition from the old Roman Empire to the new empire under Germanic kings that would later be called the Holy Roman Empire.

JUSTINIAN

Justin and his nephew Justinian started the shift of religious policy toward reunion with the Roman See. Their first move was to heal the thirty-year Acacian schism: They abided by Pope Hormidas's demands and the reconciliation was made. In the final analysis, this victory might belong more to the papacy than the emperor, but Justinian still understood religion to be an integral part of the state and the emperor's responsibility.[30]

Justinian was an autocratic ruler. He envisioned the reunification of the empire and saw that the Catholic Christian church had an important part to play in it. His religious legislation went beyond that of any other emperor before him. Constantine had put the Catholic Church under the umbrella of the state, and Theodosius made Catholic Christianity the official religion of the empire, but Justinian made the state Catholic. He started his code with a definition of faith and explained the link between law and religion, affirming in his *Institutions* that "learning in the law entails knowledge of God and man."[31] Moorhead says, "While the legal code issued by Theodosius II in 438 concluded with a statement of belief, the code of Justinian opened with one."[32]

Justinian surpassed previous emperors' persecution of heretics and non-Christians. He was running a Catholic state and his legislation denied civil rights to non-Christians. His policies did not feature the same religious tolerance as those of the Arian barbarian rulers, and Catholic bishops would praise him for his defense

---

[30] See the section "Justinian's Policies on Church-State Relationships" in chapter 3 above.

[31] Justinian, Birks, and McLeod, 37.

[32] Moorhead, Justinian, 119.

of the faith.[33] In his time, paganism was dealt its final blow, Jews and Samaritans lost their civil rights, and even small non-Catholic Christian communities were forced to convert to Catholicism or be punished according to the law. At first, Justinian did not persecute the Arians, but after 538, when he considered himself lord of Italy,[34] according to John Malalas and Procopius, he resumed his policy of religious intolerance, destroying Arian churches and forbidding them to hold worship meetings.[35]

Justinian's reconquest of the West, according to Procopius, happened due to God's commandment. Procopius says that after Justinian was dissuaded from attacking North Africa by John the Cappadocian, the praetorian prefect, a bishop came to the emperor and told him that God had visited him in a dream and said that Justinian should not be afraid of protecting the Christians and going against the tyrants. The bishop affirmed that God Himself would join Justinian in the war and give him the victory. Procopius states that this was enough for Justinian to make the preparations for the war and send Belisarius to Africa.[36]

Justinian legislated in favor of Catholic Christianity. Besides reenacting previous emperors' laws supporting Catholicism, such as the laws on Sunday observance,[37] Justinian issued new laws confirming the Trinitarian creed,[38] according legal force to the canons of church councils,[39] protecting monastic estates,[40] and reinforcing the power of the clergy to help with political leadership in their cities, defending the poor, orphans, children, foreigners, and women. Yet he exempted them from all civil and criminal jurisdictions, stating that the church would judge only spiritual cases.[41]

The church responded to Justinian's legislation with strong support. After 538, when Justinian recognized Italy as part of the empire again, his law code was enforced and Pope Vigilius openly campaigned in favor of imperial control over Italy and the

---

[33] See, for example, Pope Vigilius's letters of 540 and 553 praising Justinian's faithfulness to, defense of, and imposition of the canons of the ecumenical councils. Vigilius, "Constitutum De Tribus Capitulis," 230; Vigilius, "Epistola IV," in Sacrorum Conciliorum, Nova Et Amplissima Collectio, 9:35.

[34] The first mention of Justinian as lord of Italy is found in Novel 69, addressed to the people of Constantinople on June 1, 538.

[35] Iohannes Malalas, The Chronicle of John Malalas, trans. Elizabeth Jeffreys et al., Byzantina Australiensia (Melbourne: Australian Association for Byzantine Studies, 1986), 143; Procopius, The Secret History of Procopius, 62.

[36] Procopius, History of the Wars Books III-IV, trans. H.B. Dewing, vol. 2 (Cambridge, MA: Harvard University Press, 1990), 3.10.7-22.

[37] Justinian reissued the Sunday laws of emperors Constantine (321) and Leo I (469). CJ 3.12.3, 10.

[38] CJ 1.1.5-7.

[39] Novel 131.

[40] Novels 5, 67, 79.

[41] Stein and Palanque, Bas-Empire, 395-402.

reestablishment of the Catholic Christian empire without Arian rule.[42] As Hunter said, "Greater than a shifting territorial supremacy were the influence and the authority of the Church in supporting and fostering the Justinian legislation. For the Popes and the pontifical courts ranked the Roman civil law only a little lower than the canon law, and consistently upheld its authority; their influence penetrating far beyond the borders of the States of the Church, wherever an ecclesiastic found his way."[43]

Justinian had great respect for the pope. Even though he legislated on religious matters before asking the pope's approval, he considered the pope to be "the head of all the holy churches," and included it as law in his code.[44] However, he had an understanding that emperors did not create laws, but only preserved through centuries these eternal precepts handed out by God. Justinian wrote, "God has sent us [the emperor and the empire] from heaven so that it [the empire] might remedy difficulties through its perfection, and adapt the laws to the varieties of nature."[45] For him, emperors just received this "power from God in order to establish laws."[46]

Justinian legislated both secular and religious laws, not in order to challenge the papal leadership; but because he believed he had an obligation from God to preserve order and defend the faith. The church was the final authority in defining faith, but the emperor enforced the creed throughout the kingdom. Olster, commenting on Justinian's letter to Pope John, summarizes this point: "Justinian did not entirely resign all authority to the church; underlying even this most respectful address was the imperial prerogative to enforce order and law that left open the door to imperial intervention in the church."[47]

By the time of Justinian, the papacy's view on church-state relationships was different from that of the emperor. Under barbarian rule, the papacy had enjoyed ecclesiastical and theological freedom and had developed an understanding of church and state as independent institutions working together for mutual benefit. Thus, Pope John's letter to Justinian described distinctive roles and areas of authority for the pope and the emperor. Olster comments,

> The Pope at all times maintained a distinction between the authority that he possessed, and the power that the emperor possessed. The Pope contrasted the authority through which he approved Justinian's confession of faith, to the imperial power that preserved the unity of the church and the imperial harmony. He

---

[42] See the section "Justinian and Popes Silverius, Vigilius, and Pelagius I" in chapter 3 above.

[43] Hunter, Gaius, and Cross, 98.

[44] CJ 1.1.8.

[45] Novel 73.

[46] Novel 72.

[47] Olster, 174.

contrasted "that edict you have proposed to the faithful populace out of love for the faith, with the desire to suppress the heretics," to that confirmation of its orthodoxy that could only be given by the Pope, "which, because it accords with the apostolic doctrine, we confirm by our authority." He further reserved the right to define heresy and judge heretics solely to the Papacy.[48]

Pope Vigilius had the same ideal of church-state relationships expressed by Pope Gelasius in the theory of the two swords and by Pope John's letter to Justinian described above. However, Vigilius did not expect Justinian to intervene in church matters and impose his will as he did in the Three Chapters controversy. The western bishops were against the imperial will and Vigilius was pressed by the emperor to support his theological proposition. As a result, Vigilius made a political maneuver that did not satisfy either the bishops or the emperor. His political moves preserved his life, but his reputation with the bishops in Italy and North Africa was tarnished. Vigilius was the first pope not to be canonized as a saint.[49]

Vigilius's political moves had a positive side for the papacy. His diplomatic actions in the face of Justinian's intervention and intransigence on matters of faith led the church to reevaluate its relations with the empire. His pontificate after 538, as Amory comments, "was a 'fundamental caesura' in church history—inseparably the caesura of Justinian's momentous reign. This time of synthesis marked the beginning of the consolidation of the notion that the pope led a distinctively western and Latin Christian community."[50]

East and West were going in different directions in their religious understanding, and while the emperor had a prominent role in the religious life of the eastern empire, the West was united under the leadership of the papacy. The Gothic war had weakened Italy economically and politically. The senate, which had supported the Gothic rulers, lost prestige before Belisarius, and with the end of the siege of Rome and the political reorganization of Italy, the Goths and the senate in Rome basically disappeared as political powers in Italy after 538.[51] The only solid institution left in Italy with coalition power was the Catholic Church, headed by the bishop of Rome. As Lançon argues, "The long Gothic war, which devastated Italy for nearly thirty [535-553] years in the mid-sixth century, delivered some hard blows to the Senate, leading to its inevitable decline. . . . The vast

---

[48] Ibid., 175.

[49] Sotinel, "Autorité Pontificale," 441.

[50] Amory, 233.

[51] After Constantine had moved the Capital of the empire to Constantinople—the new Rome—a new senate was created in Constantinople and worked as a separate body from the senate of Rome. For more information see chapter 2 above.

senatorial order of the fourth and fifth centuries had become a small assembly dominated by the figure of the pope."[52]

After 538, the papacy became the strongest political force representing the interests of Italian citizens. Now the door was open for the political supremacy and temporal power of the papacy to increase, which culminated with the formation of the Republic of Saint Peter, as Noble calls it, in the first half of the eighth century.[53] Vigilius's pontificate after 538, then, marks the consummation of the legal recognition of papal primacy on ecclesiastical matters and the beginning of the notion of papal political independence and leadership in the West away from the Constantinian, Eusebian, and Justinian views of the priestly function of the king.[54]

Justinian's reign marks the final marriage between secular and religious and the making of a Catholic state, but from the church's side, this relationship might be more precisely expressed as a relationship of fornication, where church and state united only in an exchange of interest, exploiting one another and changing allegiance according to the occasion. The Catholic Church would stay connected with the eastern empire while the empire was able to defend Catholic interests, but it gladly sided with Germanic kings when that suited its political goals.

CHARLEMAGNE

The years that followed Justinian's reign demonstrated an increasing separation between the papacy and the eastern empire. The pope did not advocate independence from the empire until the time of the Carolingians, but he acted as a political power in Rome, and gradually transferred the allegiance of the Roman duchy from the empire to himself.

The union between the papacy and the Carolingians differed from Constantine's and Justinian's models of church-state relationships, since it was an alliance between the papacy and the king. The king would give military protection to the papacy and the popes would give legitimacy to the king's rule. The Roman See would have an army to fight against its enemies, whether they were pagans, heretics, or Catholics, and would extend the blessings of Saint Peter and grant salvation to the defenders of the papacy.

While the Roman emperors had emphasized the definition of faith by summoning the major church councils, the Frankish notion of the sacramental power

---

[52] Lançon, 52-53.

[53] Noble, xxiii.

[54] For the Constantinian and Eusebian views on the priestly function of the king, see chapter 3 above. For Justinian's view, see the section "The Corpus Juris Civilis" in chapter 4 above.

of the mass led the Carolingian rulers to stress proper worship according to Roman canons. The chair of Saint Peter became the source of salvation, and the defense of the Vicar of Christ on earth, the pope, would grant great rewards in heaven. As de Jong says, "The mass had become a sacrificial gift to God, to be offered in order to secure the salvation of the soul, the victory of armies, the stability of the realm—and to ward off illness, infertility, crop failure and a whole host of other disasters."[55]

Popes Stephen II, Hadrian, and Stephen III would largely follow these premises in their dealings with the Carolingian kings. As Schaff says, "To such a height of blasphemous assumption had the papacy risen already as to identify itself with the kingdom of Christ and to claim to be the dispenser of temporal prosperity and eternal salvation."[56]

Summary and Conclusion

This chapter analyzed and compared the models of church-state relationships during the reigns of Constantine, Justinian, Clovis, and Charlemagne. The main points of this analysis and comparison are as follows:

1. All four rulers were autocratic and found it within their rights to interfere in church affairs.

2. All shared the belief that Catholic Christianity was a means of bringing about unity in the empire.

3. All believed that the interference of the state in religious matters was essential to achieve the favor of God, and the prosperity of the empire was related to the proper veneration of God.

4. All four rulers were patrons of Catholic Christianity and suppressed heresies and non-Christian religions.

5. All four legislated in favor of Catholicism and used bishops in their administrations.

6. Constantine's religious policy was a policy of continuity; he kept all the main tenets of the Roman pagan religion.

7. Constantine introduced the Catholic Church into the political life of the empire, but Catholicism was not yet the state religion.

8. Theodosius made Christianity the official religion of the empire.

---

[55] Jong, 119.

[56] Schaff and Jackson, Theological Propaedeutic, 298.

9. Justinian completed the merging of church and state.

10. Justinian dealt the final blow to paganism.

11. Even though Constantine was an absolutist monarch, he had a more pluralistic vision of religious matters than did the later rulers.

12. Clovis, Justinian, and Charlemagne adopted policies of religious intolerance in their territories.

13. Justinian, Clovis, and Charlemagne presented their wars as crusades against heresy and paganism.

14. Catholic authors presented Clovis's victory over the Visigoths as a victory of Catholicism over Arianism, but Arian barbarian states continued to exist in the western part of the Roman Empire for hundreds of years after Clovis.

15. Constantine legislated in favor of Catholic Christianity.

16. Justinian made Catholic beliefs the center of Roman legislation.

17. Constantine's policies for solving religious problems included diplomatic action, church councils, and imperial enforcement of council decisions.

18. Justinian's policies for solving religious problems included imperial legislation, diplomatic work to gain bishops' support, church councils, and imperial enforcement of council decisions.

19. Clovis's policies for solving religious problems included summoning councils, decision-making by the bishops, and enforcement by the king.

20. Charlemagne's policies for solving religious problems included imperial legislation, guided by church synods and Roman canons, and followed by imperial enforcement.

Analysis and comparison of the church-state models of Constantine, Justinian, Clovis, and Charlemagne suggests that Justinian's model was more similar to Constantine's, and Charlemagne's model was more similar to Clovis's. Constantine started the union between church and state, making Catholic Christianity part of the state. Justinian consummated the union between church and state, making the state part of the church. Clovis introduced Catholic Christianity to the Franks (as the first barbarian king), making an alliance with the bishops. Charlemagne solidified Catholicism in Europe, making an alliance with the papacy. Constantine and Justinian interfered in the church's theological decisions, while Clovis and Charlemagne followed Rome and the Frankish bishops in theological matters. Constantine and Justinian considered the church to be subordinate to the state, while Clovis and Charlemagne worked as allies of the church. Constantine and Justinian saw the church as an integral part of the state, while Clovis and Charlemagne dealt with the church more as an independent institution.

The analysis of these models also suggests two phases and systems in the history of church-state relationships in this period. In the first period, Catholicism was introduced to the life of the empire, and gradually, over almost 200 years, the church replaced paganism and the senate as guardian of the empire and Roman traditions; Constantine and Justinian were the central characters in this process. In the second period, Catholicism became the basis for the formation of a new Roman Empire—the Holy Roman Empire—with the church and its leader, the pope, as sources of coalition and legitimacy; Clovis and Charlemagne were the central characters in this process. In this second period, A.D. 508 and 538 are singled out as the key dates when the models of relationships between church and state and between rulers and clergy changed.

CHAPTER VII

Conclusion

The goal of this study was to analyze and compare the development of the church-state relationship from Constantine to Charlemagne. Constantine's conversion to Catholic Christianity was a turning point in the history of the Roman Empire. In a few centuries, Catholic Christianity expanded enough to replace the Roman pagan religion, and even became the continuator of Roman traditions. By the time of Charlemagne, Catholicism was more than a religious force in Europe; it was a political power and source of legitimacy for rulers.

In this study, we have seen that the changes brought by Constantine's patronage of Catholic Christianity impacted the Christian church and the Roman state differently. Constantine's patronage affected the social, political, and religious spheres of the state. On the religious side, Catholic Christianity gradually replaced paganism as the official religion of the empire. This shift in religious patronage affected the social life of the empire, since the clergy became a new rank in the social strata of the empire, causing aristocratic families to fight for church offices. This especially impacted the senate, which had been the former guardian of Roman traditions. The conversion of the aristocracy to Catholic Christianity connected senators to Catholic values, and the Catholic Church became the new guardian of Roman traditions. Also, emperors used the Catholic Church as a source of political legitimacy instead of the senate.

The theological understanding, social life, and political influence of the church were all affected. Before Constantine, Christians recognized the state as established by God to promote justice in earthly things; their focus was on spiritual development rather than politics, and their allegiance was directed only to God. The favoring of Catholic Christianity by the emperor led some of the clergy to associate human rulership with God's providence. Heavenly aspects of the kingdom of God were thought to be incorporated into earthly imperial affairs. The emperors not only became a court of appeal in ecclesiastical matters, but also took charge of settling theological differences by summoning councils and influencing their final decisions. For the first time, the state participated in the definition of faith, the appointment of bishops, the suppression of heresies, and the embellishment of church properties. Also, some aspects of pagan religion were incorporated into

Catholic Christianity. The clergy became a privileged class in society, exempt from taxes and responsible for philanthropic work, and the bishopric became a court of appeal. Even though some bishops rose against some of Constantine's decisions on church matters, the trend among bishops was to get the emperor's support for their theological understandings or against rival sees. Constantine's patronage of Catholic Christianity enriched the church, extended the influence of bishops to secular matters, and expanded the power of the church in the empire.

Even though Constantine was the first emperor to sponsor Catholic Christianity instead of any pagan religion, his religious policies were similar to those of previous emperors. In Roman society, religion was an integral part of the state, and the state regulated religious practices because its success was related to the favor of the gods and proper worship. Throughout Constantine's reign, he manifested the view that earning the favor of God through proper worship was essential to the welfare of the state; however, he envisioned Catholicism as better suited for unifying the empire than paganism, and he chose the bishops as a source of political legitimacy instead of the senate.

In this study, I suggest that the most important events at the time of Constantine related to the church-state relationship are the Edict of Milan, the Council of Nicaea, and the Donatist and Arian controversies. In the Edict of Milan, Constantine incorporated Christianity into the state and favored it over paganism. Throughout his reign, Constantine managed Christian theological controversies that threatened his plans to unify the empire through Catholicism, establishing a religious policy that encompassed (1) diplomatic work, allowing the church to solve its own problems, (2) summoning of church councils, and (3) imposition of council decisions. At the end of Constantine's reign, Catholic Christianity did not become the state church, but it replaced paganism as the source of the empire's prosperity.

I have argued that after Constantine, the merging of Catholic Christianity with the Roman state was consummated through Justinian's legislation. Emperors before Justinian had already legislated in favor of Catholic Christianity and suppressing non-Christian religions and heresies. By the time of Emperor Theodosius, Catholic Christianity was declared the official religion of the Roman Empire, and emperors after him issued many laws suppressing paganism. However, it was Justinian who completely integrated Catholic Christianity into the state.

Justinian did not differ from Constantine and other emperors in his understanding of the importance of religion to the prosperity of the empire. However, he went beyond other emperors' views by not only making Catholicism the official religion of the state, but also making the state Catholic. Religion was at the center of his legislation. For him, there was no division between secular and sacred. All the civil and criminal aspects of his legislation were religious because he believed men did not create laws; they were derived from God. Emperors were only God's representatives on earth to adapt the laws of nature and to preserve order.

Justinian's high regard for the role of religion in the welfare of the empire was perhaps why he gave preference to the bishop of Rome over those of other sees, since Justinian considered the Roman See to be the chair of Saint Peter and the guardian of the apostolic faith. He did not wait for the pope to define and defend Catholic Christianity, but he considered papal authority essential to the true definition of faith. For him, the pope was the head of the Catholic Church and had ecclesiastical supremacy over other sees.

Besides his religious legislation, the reconquest of the West and the Three Chapters controversy were the most significant events during Justinian's reign. Justinian had a political motivation for reconquering the West, even though his dedication to Catholicism might suggest that for him the war was a religious crusade against heresy. However, the results of the war were more important to the church than the elimination of heretics.

This study also provided evidence that Justinian's war against the Goths in Italy did not strengthen the emperor's position in the West, but that the great winners of the war were the church and the bishop of Rome. The Goths had intended to legitimize their rule in Italy by reviving the senate's political power, but the war decimated the senatorial aristocracy and impoverished Italy. The long war against the Goths, with cities being taken by opponent armies more than once, led the population to side with local institutions, and the only powerful institution left in Italy was the Catholic Church. Even though Italy would still be part of the eastern empire for centuries, the church under the leadership of the papacy would represent the interests of Italy more than the eastern emperor.

It has been argued that the strengthening of the Catholic Church as an independent institution during barbarian rule, even though it worked in unity with the state, affected the relationship between Justinian and the bishop of Rome in the Three Chapters controversy. Justinian's attitude toward religion was first to legislate and then to get the support of the clergy for his formulas of faith. Sometimes he would weigh the political consequences of his acts and give in to religious leaders, but he would come back again with a religious formula with similar content. After 538, considering himself to be in control of the whole empire, Justinian acted boldly in religious matters. Since he was not able to reach a consensus of the clergy or get the open support of the pope for the condemnation of the Three Chapters, he decided to summon a council, which worked only to confirm his position and give him grounds to enforce it. In the end, Justinian did not achieve his goal of unity, and the bishops were still divided in the matter.

This study suggests that the outcome of Justinian's wars, his religious policies throughout his reign, and his relationship with the papacy was the solidification of the ecclesiastical supremacy of the Roman See, the final integration between church and state—but at the same time, these events mark a meaningful break in the pattern of the history of the relationship between church and state. As

Amory comments, "Vigilius's pontificate was a 'fundamental caesura' in church history—inseparably the caesura of Justinian's momentous reign. This time of synthesis marked the beginning of the consolidation of the notion that the pope led a distinctively western and Latin Christian community."[1] What could have been a great marriage became more a relationship of fornication, where the church and the state were united but would try to supplant each other and take the best from each circumstance. The church would use the state to defend its interests and the state would use the church to ensure that God favored the empire.

Justinian's style of state control over church affairs, the lack of strong political leadership in Italy after the reconquest of the West, the distance between the eastern and western parts of the empire, and the constant threat of the invasions of the Arian Lombards to the political stability of the Duchy of Rome led the papacy to seek a new ally to help fight its battles. This ally the Catholic Church found in the Franks.

After Clovis's conversion to Catholicism, the Franks became faithful Catholics. Clovis was the first barbarian king to become Catholic, and the Catholic clergy saw his conversion as a great opportunity to counterattack the barbarian Arians who had invaded the empire. Clovis's conversion to Catholicism and his baptism in 508 are important because they led to a new type of relationship between church and state.

As presented in this study, the Catholic Church was well established in Gaul before the dominion of the Franks. Bishops had actively participated in the defense of cities against barbarians. Their duties had expanded from spiritual to political in their domains. During Clovis's rapid expansion of power in Gaul, he incorporated the bishops as a political force in his administration. In addition to using bishops as administrators, Clovis converted to Catholic Christianity, sealed his alliance with Catholicism through his baptism in 508, and joined forces with the church in defense of Christian values. In his relationship with the church, he kept civil and religious matters separate. He promulgated a body of laws—the Salic Law—that regulated only secular areas of society; he summoned councils, but did not intervene in their decisions, and he enforced the canons of the councils as religious laws of the state. Clovis's relationship with the church was a alliance in which the two institutions—the state and the church—worked together for the benefit of the state. It paved the way for the future establishment of the European states.

The Franks maintained their allegiance to the Catholic faith, and by the time of Pepin the Short, they sought legitimacy from the church to establish a new monarchic dynasty. Pepin the Short, the mayor of the palace, but in reality the ruler, got permission from Pope Zacharias to be crowned king. In return, he stopped the Lombard threat to the Roman Duchy.

---

[1] Amory, 233.

In the time of Charlemagne, Pope Hadrian again requested the services of the Franks against the Lombards. Charlemagne not only eliminated the Lombard threat, but also recognized the temporal authority of the papacy over its territories. Charlemagne saw the papacy as an ally and did not intervene in the government of the Papal States, even though he acted as supreme ruler in both secular and sacred matters in France. Even when Charlemagne came to rescue Pope Leo III, who had been accused of perjury and adultery and deposed from his see by the Roman population, he did not act as ruler of Rome except by condemning the accusers of the pope. The pope then crowned Charlemagne as Roman emperor, and after that, Charlemagne promoted great religious reform in France.

It has been demonstrated in this study that even before Charlemagne eliminated the Lombards in Italy, the papacy had temporal power in Rome. However, the struggle between the papacy and the eastern Roman Empire and the alliance between the Roman See and the Frankish kings culminated with the final separation of East and West. The papacy became the temporal leader of the Duchy of Rome and started a new relationship with European monarchs that led to the formation of the Holy Roman Empire and the fight for political control between church and state.

The analysis and comparison of the church-state relationships from Constantine to Charlemagne presented in this study suggests that the model of church-state relationships adopted by Constantine was similar to the one adopted by Justinian, and that Clovis and Charlemagne also had similar models of church-state relationships. This study also proposes that Constantine and Clovis were the starting points of the systems that were enlarged by Justinian and Charlemagne.

This study proposes that A.D. 508 is the most significant year for the church-state relationship in Clovis's reign, since it marked the culmination of the union between the Franks and the Catholic Church. In this year, Clovis eliminated the Arian threat in Gaul, paid homage to Saint Martin, and confirmed his allegiance to the Catholic Church through his baptism. The alliance between Clovis and the Catholic Church in Gaul that was created in 508 with Clovis's baptism represented a union between throne and altar, a model of church-state relationship where the king and the bishops would work together in distinct roles—bishops as guiders and kings as executors—for the benefit of the state. Clovis's baptism in 508 can be considered the point of transition between the old Roman Empire and the new empire under Germanic kings that would later be called the Holy Roman Empire.

This study suggests A.D. 538 as the most significant year for the establishment of political power of the papacy, since it was the year of Justinian's recognition of Italy as part of the empire, which made implementation and enforcement of Justinian's code in the West possible. His code recognized the ecclesiastical supremacy of the pope, made the canons of church councils into state laws, and the Catholic definition of faith became the foundation of Roman law. Also, after 538 the papacy became the strongest political power in Rome, since the Gothic war had impoverished Italy, decimated the senate and its political power, reduced the Goths' political and military power, and strengthened the allegiance of Italians to the only local institution that survived the war—the Catholic Church.

Further, this study also suggests that after 538, Vigilius's pontificate represents a change of pattern in the relationship between emperors and popes. The popes, being recognized as heads of the church, stopped fighting for ecclesiastical supremacy and began to fight for political supremacy. They were not trying to separate the church from the state, but to establish its political influence in the West and the proper roles of emperors and clergy. As Amory says, it was a change of paradigm (caesura) in the relations between emperors and popes. The "music" was the same—a union between church and state for the promotion of the empire and the Catholic faith—but the theme had changed: The papacy was now taking a leading role in the Latin Christian community in the West. [2] According to my study,[3] after 538, Vigilius's activities and of other popes after him increased the temporal power and political supremacy of the papacy, which culminated in the formation of the Republic of Saint Peter with the pope as its king.

Focusing on the changes and developments that occurred in the Roman Empire and in the Catholic Christian church, whereas Constantine's and Charlemagne's reigns can be considered turning points in the history of Christianity, the alliance between Clovis and the Catholic Church that culminated with his defeat of the Arian Visigoths (507-508) and his baptism in 508, as well as the reign of Pope Vigilius in Rome after 538 and his troubled relationship with Justinian, can be considered the tipping points that introduced the new European model of church-state relations and the papacy's fight for political supremacy.

Several areas of study still need attention concerning the relationships between church and state from Constantine to Charlemagne. Understanding the relationship between the papacy and the elimination of Arian barbarians in Italy and other parts of the empire is crucial to understanding the influence of the bishop of Rome in the development of the political power of the papacy. Also, by examining papal influence in the Frankish regions before the Peppinids helps us to understand the influence of the popes outside Rome and Constantinople during this period. Most of the works on the papacy after Justinian focus on the eastern empire and not on the events that took place in the West in relation to the papacy.

---

[2] Amory, 233.

 BIBLIOGRAPHY

PRIMARY SOURCES

Acta Conciliorum et Epistolae Decretales, ac Constitutiones Summorum Pontificum. ed. Jean Hardouin, Philippe Labbe and Gabriel Cossart. Parisiis: Ex Typographia Regia, 1714.

"Acta Martyrum Saturnini, Felicis, Dativi, Ampelii et Aliorum." In *PL*, ed. J. P. Migne, 8. [Paris]: Excecudebatur et venit apud J.-P. Migne, 1844.

"Admonitio Generalis." In *Charlemagne: Translated Sources*, 209-220. Lambrigg, Kendal, Cumbria: P.D. King, 1987.

Alcuin. "Alcuini Sive Albini Epistolae." In *MGH Epp. Epistolae Karolini Aevi II*, ed. Bruno Krusch and Wilhelm Levison, 4, 1-481. Berlin: Weidmans, 1895.

Ammianus, Marcellinus, and Charles Duke Yonge. *The Roman History of Ammianus Marcellinus: During the Reigns of the Emperors Constantius, Julian, Jovianus, Valentinian, and Valens.* London; New York: G. Bell, 1894.

Anastasius bibliothecarius. "Historia de Vitis Romanorum Pontificum." In *PL*, ed. J. P. Migne, 128, 9-1403. Paris: Excecudebatur et venit apud J.-P. Migne, 1880.

"Annales Regni Francorum." In *MGH SRG*, ed. Bruno Krusch and Wilhelm Levison, 6. Hannover: Hahn, 1895.

Athanasius. "Apologia Contra Arianos." In *NPNF2*, ed. Philip Schaff and Henry Wace, 4. Grand Rapids, MI: Eerdmans, 1983.

Athens, Aristides of. "The Apology of Aristides the Philosopher ": Early Christians Writings, 125.

Augustine. "Epistolae." In *PL*, ed. J. P. Migne, 33. Paris: Excecudebatur et venit apud J.-P. Migne, 1845.

_____. *The City of God*. New York: Modern Library, 1950.

_____. *Letters*. Vol. 18. Fathers of the Church. New York: Fathers of the Church, 1951.

_____. *The Teacher. The Free Choice of the Will. Grace and Free Will.* Vol. 59. Washington, DC: Catholic University of America Press, 1968.

Augustine, Edmund Hill, John E. Rotelle, and Augustinian Heritage Institute. *The Works of Saint Augustine: A Translation for the 21st Century*. Brooklyn, NY: New City Press, 1990.

_____. *The Works of Saint Augustine: A Translation for the 21st Century*. Brooklyn, NY: New City Press, 1991.

_____. *The Works of Saint Augustine: A Translation for the 21st Century*. New Rochelle: New City Press, 1992.

_____. *The Works of Saint Augustine: A Translation for the 21st Century*. New Rochelle: New City Press, 1993.

_____. *The Works of Saint Augustine: A Translation for the 21st Century*. Hyde Park: New City Press, 1994.

_____. *The Works of Saint Augustine: A Translation for the 21st Century*. New Rochelle: New City Press, 1995.

Augustine, Henry Paolucci, and Dino Bigongiari. *The Political Writings of St. Augustine*. Washington, DC: Regnery Publication, 1996.

Avitus. " Alcimi Ecdicii Aviti Viennensis Episcopi Opera Quae Supersunt." In *MGH AA*, ed. R. Peiper, 6, 2. Hannover: Hahn, 1883.

_____. *Avitus of Vienne, Letters and Selected Prose*. Vol. 38. Translated Texts for Historians. Liverpool: Liverpool University Press, 2002.

Bachrach, Bernard S. *Liber Historiae Francorum*. Lawrence, KA: Coronado Press, 1973.

Basil. "Epistolae." In *NPNF2*, ed. Philip Schaff and Henry Wace, 8. Grand Rapids, MI: Eerdmans, 1983.

Caesarius. *Sancti Caesarii Episcopi Arelatensis Opera Omnia Nunc Primum in Unum Collecta*. Maretioli, 1937.

Cassiodorus. *Variae*. Vol. 12. MGH AA, ed. T. Mommsen. Berlin: Weidmannos, 1894.

Celestine I. "Vita Operaque." In *PL*, ed. J. P. Migne, 50. Paris: Excecudebatur et venit apud J.-P. Migne, 1845.

Charlemagne. "Capitulare Missorum Generale." In *MGH Cap.*, ed. Alfredus Boretius, 1, 91-99. Hannover: Hahn, 1883.

_____. "Karoli Magni Capitularia." In *MGH Cap.*, ed. Alfredus Boretius, 1. Hannover: Hahn, 1883.

_____. "De Litteris Colendis." In *Charlemagne: Translated Sources*, 232-233. Lambrigg, Kendal, Cumbria: P.D. King, 1987.

Chronica Minora Saec. IV, V, VI, VII. MGH AA, ed. Theodor Mommsen and Johannes Lucas. Berolini: Weidmannos, 1892.

Claudianus, Claudius, and Maurice Platnauer. *Claudian.* The Loeb Classical Library. London; New York: W. Heinemann; G.P. Putnam's Sons, 1922.

Clement. *The Epistles of St. Clement of Rome and St. Ignatius of Antioch.* Westminster, MD: The Newman bookshop, 1946.

"Codex Carolinus." In *MGH Epp. Epistolae Karolini Aevi I*, ed. W. Gundlach, 3, 470-687. Berlin: Weidmans, 1892.

Coleman-Norton, Paul Robinson. *Roman State & Christian Church: A Collection of Legal Documents to A.D. 535.* London: S.P.C.K., 1966.

Council of, Constantinople, J. Straub, and Eduard Schwartz. *Concilium Universale Constantinopolitanum Sub Iustiniano Habitum.* Vol. 2. Aco. Berolini: W. de Gruyter, 1914.

_____. *Gesta Concilii.* Vol. 1. Aco. Berolini: W. de Gruyter, 1914.

_____. *Sententia Dogmatica.* Vol. 1. Aco. Berolini: W. de Gruyter, 1914.

Davis, Raymond. *The Book of Pontiffs (Liber Pontificalis): The Ancient Biographies of the First Ninety Roman Bishops to Ad 715*, Rev. ed. Translated Texts for Historians. Liverpool: Liverpool University Press, 2000.

Dioscorus to Hormidas. "Collectio Veronensis, 167." In *CSEL*, ed. Karl Ziwsa, 35, 2:618-621. Vindobonae: F. Tempsky, 1893.

Einhard. *Life of Charlemagne.* New York; Cincinnati: American Book Co., 1880.

Eusebius. "The Church History of Eusebius." In *NPNF2*, ed. Philip Schaff and Henry Wace, 1. Grand Rapids, MI: Eerdmans, 1983.

_____. "The Life of the Blessed Emperor Constantine." In *NPNF2*, ed. Philip Schaff and Henry Wace, 1. Grand Rapids, MI: Eerdmans, 1983.

_____. "The Oration of Eusebius Pamphilus, in Praise of the Emperor Constantine. Pronounced on the Thirtieth Anniversary of His Reign." In *NPNF2*, ed. Philip Schaff and Henry Wace, 1. Grand Rapids, MI: Eerdmans, 1983.

Eusebius, and W. J. Ferrar. *The Proof of the Gospel Being the Demonstratio Evangelica of Eusebius of Caesarea.* London: Society for Promoting Christian Knowledge, 1920.

Eutropius. *Eutropii Historiae Romanae Breviarium: Cum Versione Anglica, in Qua Verbum de Verbo Exprimitur: Notis Quoque & Indice: Or Eutropius's Compendious History of Rome; Together with an English Translation, as Literal as Possible, Notes and an Index.* London: J. F. and C. Rivington ... and T. Evans, 1793.

Eutychius, J. Straub, and Eduard Schwartz. *Euthycii Epistula ad Vigilium*. Aco. Berolini: W. de Gruyter, 1914.

Evagrius, and Michael Whitby. *The Ecclesiastical History of Evagrius Scholasticus*. Translated Texts for Historians, V. 33. Liverpool: Liverpool University Press, 2000.

Facundus. "Adversus Mocianum " In *PL*, ed. J. P. Migne, 67, 853-868. Paris: Excecudebatur et venit apud J.-P. Migne, 1862.

_____. "Pro Defensione Trium Capitulorum Concilii Chalcedoniensis Libri Xii " In *PL*, ed. J. P. Migne, 67, 527-852. Paris: Excecudebatur et venit apud J.-P. Migne, 1862.

_____. *Facundi Episcopi Ecclesiae Hermianensis Opera Omnia*. Vol. 90a. 519 vols. Turnholti: Brepols, 1974.

Felix III. "Epistolae." In *PL*, ed. J. P. Migne, 58. Paris: Excecudebatur et venit apud J.-P. Migne, 1862.

Festus, Sextus Pompeius, Marcus Verrius Flaccus, Paul, Emil Thewrewk, and W. M. Lindsay. *Sexti Pompei Festi de Verborum Significatu Quae Supersunt Cum Pauli Epitome*. Bibliotheca Scriptorum Graecorum et Romanorum Teubneriana. Lipsiae: B.G. Teubneri, 1913.

Firmilian. "Firmilian, Bishop of Cæsarea in Cappadocia, to Cyprian, against the Letter of Stephen." In *ANF*, ed. Alexander Roberts, James Donaldson and A. Cleveland Coxe, 5. Grand Rapids, MI: Eerdmanns, 1989.

Fredegar. *The Fourth Book of the Chronicle of Fredegar with Its Continuations*. Medieval Classics: Nelson, 1960.

Gelasius. "Epistolae et Decreta." In *PL*, ed. J. P. Migne, 59. Paris: Excecudebatur et venit apud J.-P. Migne, 1862.

_____. "Decretalis de Recipiendis et Non Recipiendis Libris. Epistolae 42." In *Epistolae Romanorum Pontificum Genuinae et Quae ad Eos Scriptae Sunt: Tomus 1. A S. Hilaro Usque ad Pelagium II*, ed. Andreas Thiel, 454-471. Hildesheim; New York: Olms, 1974.

Gregory. *The History of the Franks*. Vol. 2. Oxford: Clarendon Press, 1927.

_____. *Glory of the Martyrs*. Liverpool: University Press, 1988.

Gregory I. "Epistolae." In *MGH Epp. Gregorii I Papae Registrum Epistolarum*, ed. Bruno Krusch and Wilhelm Levison, 1 - 2. Berlin: Weidmans, 1891.

Hilarus. "Epistolae." In *PL*, ed. J. P. Migne, 58. Paris: Excecudebatur et venit apud J.-P. Migne, 1862.

Hilary of Poitiers. *Collectanea Antiariana Parisina* Vol. 65. CSEL, ed. Alfred Leonhard Feder. Vienna: F. Tempsky, 1916.

Hippolytus. "Antichrist." In *ANF*, ed. Alexander Roberts, James Donaldson and A. Cleveland Coxe,

5. Grand Rapids, MI: Eerdmanns, 1989.

_____. *Kommentar Zu Daniel*. Vol. 7, 2d ed. Griechischen Christlichen Schriftsteller Der Ersten Jahrhunderte, ed. G. Nathanael Bonwetsch and Marcel Richard. Berlin: Akademie Verlag, 2000.

Hormidas. "Exemplum Libelli." In *CSEL*, ed. Karl Ziwsa, 35, 2:521. Vindobonae: F. Tempsky, 1893.

Innocent I. "Epistolae et Decreta." In *PL*, ed. J. P. Migne, 20. Paris: Excecudebatur et venit apud J.-P. Migne, 1845.

Innocent of Maroneia. In *Acta Conciliorum Oecumenicorum*, ed. Rudolf Schieffer, Eduardus Schwartz, Johannes Straub, Gesellschaft Wissenschaftliche and Gesellschaft Strassburger Wissenschaftliche, 169-184. Berlin: de Gruyter, 1914.

Iohannes, Malalas, Elizabeth Jeffreys, Michael Jeffreys, Roger Scott, and Brian Croke. *The Chronicle of John Malalas*. Byzantina Australiensia. Melbourne: Australian Association for Byzantine Studies, 1986.

Jerome. *The Letters of St. Jerome*. New York: Newman Press, 1963.

Justinian. "Adversus Nonnullos, Impium Theodorum Atque Iniqua Ejus Dogmata." In *PL*, ed. J. P. Migne, 69, 273-328. Paris: Excecudebatur et venit apud J.-P. Migne, 1845.

_____. "Confessio Rectæ Fidie Adversus Tria Capitula " In *Pg*, ed. J. P. Migne, 86, 994-1095. [Paris]: Excecudebatur et venit apud J.-P. Migne, 1857.

Justinian, Peter Birks, and Grant McLeod. *Justinian's Institutes*. Ithaca, NY: Cornell Unversity Press, 1987.

Krueger, Paul, Theodor Mommsen, Rudolf Schoell, and Wilhelm Kroll. *Corpus Iuris Civilis*. Berlin: Weidmannos, 1895.

Lactantius. "Of the Manner in Which the Persecutors Died." In *ANF*, ed. Alexander Roberts, James Donaldson and A. Cleveland Coxe, 7. Grand Rapids, MI: Eerdmanns, 1989.

_____. "Divine Institutes." ed. Kevin Knight, 7: New Advent, 2007.

Le Liber Pontificalis. 3 vols., ed. L. Duchesne. Paris: E. de Boccard, 1955.

Leo. "Epistolae." In *PL*, ed. J. P. Migne, 54. Paris: Excecudebatur et venit apud J.-P. Migne, 1845.

_____. "Sermones in Praecupuis Totius Anni Festivitatibus ad Romanam Plebem Habiti." In *PL*, ed. J. P. Migne, 54. Paris: Excecudebatur et venit apud J.-P. Migne, 1845.

Leo XIII. *Encyclical Satis Cognitum of Leo Xiii*. 1896. Accessed August 05 2008. Web page. Available from http://www.vatican.va/holy_father/leo_xiii/encyclicals/documents/hf_l-xiii_enc_29061896_satis-cognitum_en.html.

Liberatus Carthaginensis Diaconus. "Breviarium Causae Nestorianorum et Eutychianorum." In *PL*, ed. J. P. Migne, 68, 969-1050. Paris: Excecudebatur et venit apud J.-P. Migne, 1848.

Livy. *Livy, with an English Translation by B. O. Foster*. 13 vols. The Loeb Classical Library. Latin Authors. Cambridge, MA: Harvard University Press, 1939.

Marcellinus. *The Chronicle of Marcellinus: A Translation and Commentary : (with a Reproduction of Mommsen's Edition of the Text)*. Byzantina Australiensia, 7. Sydney: Australian Association for Byzantine Studies, 1995.

Martyr, Justin. "The First Apology." In *ANF*, ed. Alexander Roberts, James Donaldson and A. Cleveland Coxe, 1. Grand Rapids, MI: Eerdmanns, 1989.

————. "The Second Apology." In *ANF*, ed. Alexander Roberts, James Donaldson and A. Cleveland Coxe, 1. Grand Rapids, MI: Eerdmanns, 1989.

Maunder, Chris, and Henry Scowcroft Bettenson. *Documents of the Christian Church*, 3rd / ed. Oxford: Oxford University Press, 1999.

Nicetius. "Excerpta Ex Epistola ad Chlodosindam " In *PL*, ed. J. P. Migne, 71, col. 1166-1168. Paris: Excecudebatur et venit apud J.-P. Migne, 1845.

Optatus. *S. Optati Milevitani Libri VII*. Vol. 26. CSEL, ed. Karl Ziwsa. Vindobonae: F. Tempsky, 1893.

Origen. "Homily 1 in Psalm 36." In *Pg*, ed. J. P. Migne, 12, 161 v. in 168. [Paris]: Excecudebatur et venit apud J.-P. Migne, 1857.

Orosius, Paulus. *The Seven Books of History against the Pagans; the Apology of Paulus Orosius*. Records of Civilization, Sources and Studies, No. Xxvi. New York: Columbia University Press, 1936.

"Passio Donati." In *PL*, ed. J. P. Migne, 8. [Paris]: Excecudebatur et venit apud J.-P. Migne, 1844.

Paul. "Pauli Historia Langobardorum." In *MGH SRL*, ed. Alfredus Boretius, 1, 13-192. Hannover: Hahn, 1878.

Pelagius I, and Robert Devreesse. *Pelagii Diaconi Ecclesiae Romanae in Defensione Trium Capitulorum: Texte Latin Du Manuscrit Aurelianensis 72 (70)*. Studi E Testi Pubblicati Per Cura Degli Scittori Della Biblioteca Vaticana E Degli Archivisti Dell'archivio Vaticano, 57. Città del Vaticano: Biblioteca Apostolica Vaticana, 1932.

Pharr, Clyde. *The Theodosian Code and Novels, and the Sirmondian Constitutions*. [Princeton]: Princeton University Press, 1952.

Pitra, J. B. *Juris Ecclesiastici Graecorum Historia et Monumenta*. Romae: typis collegii urbani, 1868.

Pontius. "The Life and Passion of Cyprian." In *ANF*, ed. Alexander Roberts, James Donaldson and

A. Cleveland Coxe, 5. Grand Rapids, MI: Eerdmanns, 1989.

Procopius. *Books III-IV*. Vol. 2. History of the Wars / Procopius. Cambridge, MA: Harvard University Press, 1990.

Procopius, and Henry Bronson Dewing. *Procopius*. Vol. 3. New York: The Macmillan, 1914.

Procopius, of Caesarea. *The Secret History of Procopius*. New York: Covici Friede, 1934.

Ranft, Patricia. *Women in Western Intellectual Culture, 600-1500*. New York: Palgrave Macmillan, 2002.

Remigius. "Epistulae Austrasiacae." In *MGH Epp. 3, Merovingici et Karolini Aevi 1*, ed. Bruno Krusch and Wilhelm Levison, 112-114. Hannover: Hahn, 1896.

Sacrorum Conciliorum, Nova et Amplissima Collectio. 54 vols., ed. Philippe Labbe and Giovan Domenico Mansi. Graz: Akademische Druck- u. Verlagsanstalt, 1960.

Scott, Samuel Parsons. *The Civil Law, Including the Twelve Tables the Institutes of Gaius, the Rules of Ulpian, the Opinions of Paulus, the Enactments of Justinian, and the Constitutions of Leo*. Cincinnati: Central Trust Company, 1973.

Sidonius Apollinaris. *Carmen 5*. Vol. 8. MGH AA, ed. C. Luetjihann. Berlin: Weidmannos, 1887.

Sidonius, Apollinaris, and Ormonde Maddock Dalton. *The Letters of Sidonius: Translated with Introduction and Notes*. Oxford: Clarendon Press, 1915.

Simplicius. "Epistolae." In *PL*, ed. J. P. Migne, 58. Paris: Excecudebatur et venit apud J.-P. Migne, 1845.

Siricius. "Epistulae et Decreta." In *PL*, ed. J. P. Migne, 13. Paris: Excecudebatur et venit apud J.-P. Migne, 1845.

_____. "Incipit Consilium Thelense Super Tractoriam Sancti Sirici Episcopi Urbus Romae Per Africam." In *Concilia Africae, A. 345-A. 525*, ed. Charles Munier, xxxviii, 429. Turnholti: Brepols, 1974.

Socrates. "Historia Ecclesiastica." In *NPNF2*, ed. Philip Schaff and Henry Wace, 2. Grand Rapids, MI: Eerdmans, 1983.

Sozomen. "Historia Ecclesiastica." In *NPNF2*, ed. Philip Schaff and Henry Wace, 2. Grand Rapids, MI: Eerdmans, 1983.

Tacitus, Cornelius. *The Annals*. London: W. Heinemann, 1931.

Tertulian. "The Apology." In *ANF*, ed. Alexander Roberts, James Donaldson and A. Cleveland Coxe, 3. Grand Rapids, MI: Eerdmanns, 1989.

_____. "To Scapula." In *ANF*, ed. Alexander Roberts, James Donaldson and A. Cleveland Coxe, 3. Grand Rapids, MI: Eerdmanns, 1989.

Theodoret. "Historia Ecclesiastica." In *NPNF2*, ed. Philip Schaff and Henry Wace, 3. Grand Rapids, MI: Eerdmans, 1983.

Theophanes, and Cyril A. Mango. *The Chronicle of Theophanes Confessor : Byzantine and near Eastern History: ad 284 - 813*. Oxford: Clarendon Press, 1997.

Victor, and John Moorhead. *Victor of Vita: History of the Vandal Persecution*. Vol. 10. Translated Texts for Historians. Liverpool: Liverpool University Press, 1992.

Victor vitensis. "Historia Pesecutionis Africanae Provinciae, Temporibus Geiserici et Hunirici Regum Wandalorum." In *PL*, ed. J. P. Migne, 58, 179-276. Paris: Excecudebatur et venit apud J.-P. Migne, 1845.

Vigilius. "Constitutum de Tribus Capitulis." In *CSEL*, ed. Karl Ziwsa, 35, 230-234. Vindobonae: F. Tempsky, 1893.

_____. "Epistola IV." In *Sacrorum Conciliorum, Nova et Amplissima Collectio*, ed. Giovan Domenico Mansi, 34-38. Graz: Akademische Druck- u. Verlagsanstalt, 1960.

Vigilius pope, J. Straub, and Eduard Schwartz. *Epistula ad Rusticum et Sebastianum*. Vol. 2. Aco. Berolini: W. de Gruyter, 1914.

_____. *Ex Tribus Capitulos*. Vol. 2. Aco. Berolini: W. de Gruyter, 1914.

_____. *Vigilii Epistula I ad Eutychium*. Vol. 1. Aco. Berolini: W. de Gruyter, 1914.

_____. *Vigilii Epistula II ad Eutychium*. Vol. 1. Aco. Berolini: W. de Gruyter, 1914.

_____. *Vigilii Iuramenti Testificatio*. Vol. 1. Aco. Berolini: W. de Gruyter, 1914.

Wallace-Hadrill, J. M. *The Fourth Book of the Chronicle of Fredegar, with Its Continuations*. Westport, CN: Greenwood Press, 1981.

Zosimus. *New History* Vol. 2. Byzantina Australiensia. Canberra: Australian Association for Byzantine Studies, 1982.

Zosimus, and Ludwig Mendelssohn. *Zosimi Comitis et Exadvocati Fisci Historia Nova*. Lipsiae: B. G. Teubneri, 1887.

Zozimus. "Epistolae II: ad Epistolae Africanus." In *PL*, ed. J. P. Migne, 20. Paris: Excecudebatur et venit apud J.-P. Migne, 1845.

Secondary Sources

Alföldy, Géza. *The Social History of Rome*. Baltimore, MD: Johns Hopkins University Press, 1988.

Allen, Pauline. "Justin I and Justinian." In *The Cambridge Ancient History. Empire and Successors, ad 425-600 Vol. 14, Late Antiquity*, 820-828. Cambridge: Cambridge University Press, 2000.

Altheìm, Franz. *History of Roman Religion*. New York: E. P. Dutton, 1937.

Altizer, Thomas J. J. *History as Apocalypse*. Suny Series in Religion. Albany: State University of New York Press, 1985.

Amory, Patrick. *People and Identity in Ostrogothic Italy, 489-554*. Cambridge Studies in Medieval Life and Thought. New York: Cambridge University Press, 2003.

Anastos, Milton V. "Justinian's Despotic Control over the Church as Illustrated by His Edicts on the Theopaschite Formula and His Letter to Pope John II in 553." In *Melanges Georges Ostrogorsky*, 2, 1-11. Belgrade: Institut d'Etudes Byzantines, 1963.

_____. "The Edict of Milan (313): A Defence of Its Traditional Authorship and Designation." In *Conversion, Catechumenate, and Baptism in the Early Church*, ed. Everett Ferguson, 11, xv, 435. New York: Garland, 1993.

Armstrong, Gregory T. "Church and State Relations: The Changes Wrought by Constantine." *The Journal of Bible and Religion* 32, no. 1 (1964): 1-7.

_____. "Politics and the Early Christian." *Journal of Church and State* 10 (1968): 448-450.

Avé Lallement, W. Marjolijn J. de Boer. "Early Frankish Society as Reflected in Contemporary Sources: Sixth and Seventh Centuries." Rice University, 1982.

Ayer, Joseph Cullen. *A Source Book for Ancient Church History*. New York: C. Scribner's Sons, 1922.

Azkoul, Michael. "Sacerdotium et Imperium: The Constantinian Renovatio According to the Greek Fathers." *Theological Studies* 32 (1971): 431-464.

Bachrach, David Stewart. *Religion and the Conduct of War, C. 300-1215*. Warfare in History. Woodbridge, Suffolk, UK; Rochester, NY: Boydell Press, 2003.

Bailey, Cyril. *Phases in the Religion of Ancient Rome*. Westport, CO: Greenwood Press, 1972.

Bainton, Roland. "The Christian and the War." *The christian century* 61 (1944): 560.

Baker, G. P. *Constantine the Great and the Christian Revolution*. New York: Cooper Square Press, 2001.

Balon, Joseph. *Traité de Droit Salique; Étude D'exégèse et de Sociologie Juridiques*. Namur, Les Anc:

Éts Godenne, 1965.

Barbero, Alessandro. *Charlemagne: Father of a Continent*. Berkeley: University of California Press, 2004.

Barker, Ernest. "Italy and the West, 410-476." In *The Cambridge Medieval History*, ed. J. B. Bury, J. R. Tanner, C. W. Previté-Orton and Z. N. Brooke, 5, 392-432. New York: MacMillan, 1926.

_____. *From Alexander to Constantine; Passages and Documents Illustrating the History of Social and Political Ideas, 336 B.C.-A.D. 337*. Oxford: Clarendon Press, 1956.

Barnard, Leslie W. "Church-State Relations, ad 313-337." *Journal of Church and State* 24 (1982): 337-355.

Barnes, Timothy David. "Beginnings of Donatism." *Journal of Theological Studies*, no. 26 (1975): 13-22.

_____. *Constantine and Eusebius*. Cambridge, MA: Harvard University Press, 1981.

_____. "The Constantinian Settlement." In *Eusebius, Christianity, and Judaism*, ed. Harold W. Attridge and Gohei Hata, 42, 635-657. New York: E.J. Brill, 1992.

_____. *Athanasius and Constantius: Theology and Politics in the Constantinian Empire*. Cambridge, MA: Harvard University Press, 1993.

Baronio, Cesare, Giovan Domenico Mansi, Odorico Rinaldi, Giacomo Laderchi, Augustin Theiner, and Antoine Pagi. *Annales Ecclesiastici, Denuo Excusi et ad Nostra Usque Tempora Perducti Ab Augustino Theiner*. Barri-Ducis: L. Guerin, 1864.

Barzun, Jacques. *The French Race: Theories of Its Origins and Their Social and Political Implications Prior to the Revolution*. Port Washington, NY: Kennikat Press, 1966.

Batiffol, Pierre. *La Paix Constantinienne et le Catholicisme*, 2nd ed. Paris: Librairie Victor Lecoffre, 1914.

Bauman, Michael, and David W. Hall. *God and Caesar*. Camp Hill, PA: Christian Publications, 1994.

Baynes, Norman Hepburn. *Constantine the Great and the Christian Church*. London: H. Milford, 1930.

_____. "Idolatry and the Early Church." In *Byzantine Studies and Other Essays*. London: University of London Athlone Press, 1955.

_____. *Byzantine Studies and Other Essays*. [London]: University of London Athlone Press, 1960.

Beard, Mary, and John A. North. *Pagan Priests: Religion and Power in the Ancient World*. Ithaca,

N.Y.: Cornell University Press, 1990.

Beard, Mary, John A. North, and S. R. F. Price. *Religions of Rome*. Vol. 1. Cambridge: Cambridge University Press, 1998.

Beck, Henry G. J. *The Pastoral Care of Souls in South-East France During the Sixth Century*. Rome: Aedes Universitatis Gregorianae, 1950.

Becker, Jürgen. *Paul: Apostle to the Gentiles*. Louisville, KY: Westminster/John Knox Press, 1993.

Beet, William Ernest. *The Rise of the Papacy: A.D. 385-461*, 1st ed. London: C. H. Kelly, 1910.

Berkhof, Hendrik. *Die Theologie Des Eusebius Von Caesarea*. Amsterdam: Uitgeversmaatschappij Holland, 1939.

_____. *Kirche Und Kaiser.Eine Untersuchung Der Entstehung Der Byzantinischen Und Der Theokratischen Staatsauffassung Im Vierten Jahrhundert.: Aus Dem Holländischen Übers. Von Gottfried W. Locher*. Zollikon-Zürich,, 1947.

Berman, Harold J. *Law and Revolution: The Formation of the Western Legal Tradition*. Cambridge, MA: Harvard University Press, 1983.

Bertier de Sauvigny, Guillaume de, and David H. Pinkney. *History of France*, Rev. and enl. ed. Arlington Heights, Ill.: Forum Press, 1983.

Bettenson, Henry Scowcroft, and Chris Maunder. *Documents of the Christian Church*, 3rd / ed. Oxford: Oxford University Press, 1999.

Bishop, Morris. *The Middle Ages*. Boston, Mass.; London: Houghton Mifflin ; Hi Marketing, 2001.

Blumenthal, W. Michael. *The Invisible Wall: Germans and Jews: A Personal Exploration*. Washington, DC: Counterpoint, 1998.

Boles, David B., and Harold W. Boles. *Withers-Davis Ancestry: With the Families of Abraham, Babb, Bachiler, Chandler, Collet, David, Davies, Hollingsworth, Hussey, Jefferis, Lewis, Martin, May, Nash, Nowell, Perkins, Powell, Ree, Roberts, Sloper, Tarrant, Wise, Wood, and Woolaston*. Decorah, Iowa: printed for Anundsen Pub. Co., 1998.

Bondi, Roberta C. *Three Monophysite Christologies: Severus of Antioch, Philoxenus of Mabbug and Jacob of Sarug*. Oxford Theological Monographs. London: Oxford University Press, 1976.

Boojamra, John L. "Constantine and the Council of Arles: The Foundations of Church and State in the Christian East." *Greek Orthodox Theological Review* 43, no. 1-4 (1998): 129-141.

Book, World. *The World Book Encyclopedia*. Chicago: World Book, 1997.

Bossy, John. *Disputes and Settlements: Law and Human Relations in the West*. Past and Present Publications. Cambridge: Cambridge University Press, 2003.

Boularand, Ephrem. *L'hérésie D'arius et La "Foi" de Nicée*. 2 vols. Paris: Letouzey & Ané, 1972.

Bourke, Vernon J. *Wisdom from St. Augustine*. Houston, TX: Center for Thomistic Studies, University of St. Thomas, 1984.

Bower, Archibald, and Samuel H. Cox. *The History of the Popes: From the Foundation of the See of Rome to A.D. 1758*. 3 vols. Philadelphia: Griffith & Simon, 1844.

Boyd, William Kenneth. *The Ecclesiastical Edicts of the Theodosian Code*. New York: Columbia University Press, 1905.

Brent, Allen. *The Imperial Cult and the Development of Church Order: Concepts and Images of Authority in Paganism and Early Christianity before the Age of Cyprian*. Supplements to Vigiliae Christianae ; V. 45. Boston: Brill, 1999.

Brissaud, Jean. *A History of French Public Law*. A Law Classic. Washington, D.C.: Beard Books, 2001.

Brown, Peter Robert Lamont. *The World of Late Antiquity, ad 150-750*. New York: Harcourt Brace Jovanovich, 1971.

_____. "Christianization and Religious Conflict." In *The Cambridge Ancient History: The Late Empire, A.D. 337-425*, ed. Averil Cameron and Peter Garnsey, 13, 632-664. Cambridge: Cambridge University Press, 1998.

_____. *The Rise of Western Christendom: Triumph and Diversity, A.D. 200-1000*. The Making of Europe. Malden, MA: Blackwell Publishers, 2003.

Bryce, James Bryce. *The Holy Roman Empire*. London: MacMillan, 1919.

Bryce, James Vc. *The Holy Roman Empire by James Bryce*. Oxford: T. & G. Shrimpton, 1864.

Burckhardt, Jacob. *The Age of Constantine the Great*. Garden City, NY: Doubleday, 1949.

Burgess, John William. *The Reconciliation of Government with Liberty*. New York: C. Scribner's Sons, 1915.

Burgess, R. W. "The Date of the Deposition of Eustathius of Antioch." *Journal of Theological Studies* 51, no. 1 (2000): 150-160.

_____, to Bryan Ward-Perkins, Spring-Summer, 2007. Canadian Journal of History/Annales Canadiennes d'Histoire

Buri, Fritz. *Clemens Alexandrinus Und Der Paulinische Freiheitsbegriff*. Zürich: M. Niehans, 1939.

Burn-Murdoch, Hector. *The Development of the Papacy*. London: Faber and Faber, 1954.

Burn, A. E. *The Council of Nicaea: A Memorial for Its Sixteenth Centenary*. London: Society for

Promoting Christian Knowledge, 1925.

Bury, J. B. *History of the Later Roman Empire: From the Death of Theodosius I to the Death of Justinian*. New York: Dover, 1958.

Butler, Alban, David Hugh Farmer, and Paul Burns. *Butler's Lives of the Saints*. Tunbridge Wells, Kent; Collegeville, MN: Burns & Oates; Liturgical Press, 1995.

Butt, John J. *Daily Life in the Age of Charlemagne*. Westport, CN: Greenwood Press, 2002.

Cadoux, Cecil John. *The Early Church and the World: A History of the Christian Attitude to Pagan Society and the State Down to the Time of Constantinus*. Edinburgh: T. & T. Clark, 1955.

_____. *Christian Pacifism Re-Examined*. New York: Garland Publishing, 1972.

_____. *The Early Christian Attitude to War: A Contribution to the History of Christian Ethics*. New York: Seabury Press, 1982.

Cairns, Earle Edwin. *Christianity through the Centuries: A History of the Christian Church*. Grand Rapids: Zondervan Publication, 1996.

Calderone, Salvatore. *Constantino E Il Cattolicesimo*. Firenze: F. Le Monnier, 1962.

Cameron, Averil. "Religious Police: The Three Chapters and the Fifth Oecumenical Council." In *The Cambridge Ancient History. Empire and Successors, ad 425-600 Vol. 14, Late Antiquity*, 79-82. Cambridge: Cambridge University Press, 2000.

Cameron, Avril. *The Later Roman Empire*. Cambridge, MA: Harvard University Press, 1993.

Campenhausen, Hans Freiherr von. *Ambrosius Von Mailand Als Kirchenpolitiker*. Berlin, Leipzig: W. de Gruyter, 1929.

Cantor, Norman F. *The Civilization of the Middle Ages*. New York: HarperPerennial, 1994.

Capizzi, Carmelo. *Giustiniano I Tra Politica E Religione*. Accademia Angelica Costantiniana Di Lettere Arti E Scienze. Saggi, Studi, Testi ; 1. Soveria Mannelli: Rubbettino, 1994.

_____. "La Politica Religiosa Ed Ecclesiastica Di Giustiniano." In *Christian East. Rome: Pontificio Ist Orientale*, 55-84, 1996.

Caspar, E. "Das Papsttum Unter Fränkischer Herrschaft." *Zeitschrift für Kirchengeschichte* 54, no. 3. Folge 5 (1935): 132-266.

Caspar, Erich Ludwig Eduard. *Pippin Und Die Römische Kirche: Kritische Untersuchungen Zum Fränkisch-Päpstlichen Bunde Im VIII. Jahrhundert*. Berlin: Springer, 1914.

_____. *Geschichte Des Papsttums Von Den Anfängen Bis Zur Höhe Der Weltherrschaft*. Tübingen: J.C.B. Mohr, 1930.

_____. *Geschichte Des Papsttums Von Den Anfängen Bis Zur Höhe Der Weltherrschaft*. Tübingen: J.C.B. Mohr, 1933.

Cerfaux, Lucien, and Julien Tondriau. *Le Culte Des Souverains: Un Concurrent Du Christianisme Dans La Civilisation Gréco-Romaine*. Tournai: Desclée, 1957.

Chadwick, Henry. "The Fall of Eustathius at Antioch." *Journal of Theological Studies* 49 (1948): 27-35.

_____. "Faith and Order at the Council of Nicea: A Note on the Background of the Sixth Canon." *Harvard Theological Review* 53, no. 3 (1960): 171-195.

_____. *The Early Church*, Rev. ed. Penguin History of the Church. London, New York: Penguin Books, 1993.

Châlons, Vincent-Claude. *The History of France: From the Establishment of That Monarchy under Pharamond, to the Death of Lewis Xiii*. Dublin: printed by George Faulkner, 1752.

Chapman, John. "Donatists." In *The Catholic Encyclopedia; an International Work of Reference on the Constitution, Doctrine, Discipline, and History of the Catholic Church*, ed. Charles George Herbermann, Edward Aloysius Pace, Condé Bénoist Pallen, Thomas J. Shahan, John J. Wynne and Knights of Columbus. Catholic Truth Committee., V, 121-129. New York: Encyclopedia Press Incorporation, 1913.

Ciggaar, Krijnie N. *Western Travellers to Constantinople: The West and Byzantium, 962-1204: Cultural and Political Relations*. The Medieval Mediterranean, 10. Leiden: Brill, 1996.

Clark, Gillian. *Christianity and Roman Society*. Key Themes in Ancient History. Cambridge: Cambridge University Press, 2004.

Claussen, M. A. *The Reform of the Frankish Church: Chrodegang of Metz and the Regula Canonicorum in the Eighth Century*. Cambridge Studies in Medieval Life and Thought. New York: Cambridge University Press, 2004.

Clercq, Charles de. *La Legislation Religieuse Franque de Clovis a Charlemagne: Étude Sur Les Actes de Conciles et Les Capitulaires, Les Statuts Diocesains et Les Règles Monastiques*. Louvain: Bureau du Recueil Bibliothèque de l'Université, 1936.

_____. *Concilia Galliae A. 511-A. 695*. Vol. 148A. Corpus Christianorum. Series Latina. Turnholti: Typographi Brepols Editores Pontificii, 1963.

Cohen, Ronald, and Judith D. Toland. *State Formation and Political Legitimacy*. New Brunswick, U.S.A.: Transaction Books, 1988.

Coleman, Christopher Bush. *Constantine the Great and Christianity*. New York: Columbia University Press, 1914.

Collins, J. J. "The Sibylline Oracles." In *The Old Testament Pseudepigrapha*, 1st ed., ed. James H.

Charlesworth, 1, 317-472. Garden City, NY: Doubleday, 1983.

Cook, David, and Bonifacius. *St. Boniface: 675 - 754; the First European.* Exeter: Bartlett Printing, 2004.

Costigan, Richard F. "State Appointment of Bishops." *Journal of Church and State* 8, no. 1 (1966): 82-96.

Courcelle, Pierre Paul. *Recherches Sur Saint Ambroise; "Vies" Anciennes, Culture, Iconographie.* Paris: Études augustiniennes, 1973.

Cranz, Ferdinand Edward. "Kingdom and Polity in Eusebius of Caesarea." *Harvard Theological Review* 45 (1952): 47-66.

Crowe, Eyre Evans. *The History of France.* New York: Harper & Brothers, 1869.

Cullmann, Oscar. "The State in the New Testament." In *Church and State in the Middle Ages,* ed. Bennett D. Hill, 6-15. New York: Wiley, 1970.

Cunningham, Agnes. *The Early Church and the State.* Philadelphia: Fortress Press, 1982.

Cunningham, Lawrence, and John Reich. *Culture and Values: A Survey of the Humanities.* Belmont, CA: Thomson/Wadsworth, 2006.

Cutts, Edward Lewes. *Constantine the Great: The Union of the State and the Church.* Home Library. London: Society for Promoting Christian Knowledge, 1881.

Dagron, Gilbert. *Emperor and Priest: The Imperial Office in Byzantium.* Cambridge, U.K.; New York: Cambridge University Press, 2003.

Dallais, F. *Clovis, Ou, le Combat de Gloire.* La Roche Rigault: PSR éditions, 1996.

Dalton, Ormonde Maddock. *The History of the Franks.* Vol. 1. Oxford: Clarendon Press, 1927.

Daly, William M. "Clovis: How Barbaric, How Pagan?" *Speculum* 69, no. 3 (1994): 619-664.

Davies, Wendy, Guy Halsall, Andrew Reynolds, and Alex Langlands. *People and Space in the Middle Ages, 300-1300.* Vol. 15. Studies in the Early Middle Ages Turnhout: Brepols, 2006.

Davis, R. H. C., and R. I. Moore. *A History of Medieval Europe.* Harlow, England; New York: Pearson Longman, 2006.

de Clercq, Victor C. "Ossius of Cordova; a Contribution to the History of the Constantinian Period." Ph.D. diss. diss., Catholic University of America Press, 1954.

de Jong, Mayke "Charlemagne's Church." In *Charlemagne: Empire and Society,* ed. Joanna Story, 103-135. Manchester; New York: Manchester University Press, 2005.

Deely, John N. *Four Ages of Understanding: The First Postmodern Survey of Philosophy from Ancient Times to the Turn of the Twenty-First Century*. Toronto Studies in Semiotics. Toronto; Buffalo: University of Toronto Press, 2001.

Del Mar, Alexander. *The Worship of Augustus Caesar, Derived from a Study of Coins, Monuments, Calendars, Aeras, and Astronomical and Astrological Cycles, the Whole Establishing a New Chronology and Survey of History and Religion*. New York: Cambridge, 1900.

Delogu, Paolo. "Lomabard and Carolingian Ytaly." In *The New Cambridge Medieval History 2, C. 700-C. 900*, ed. Rosamond McKitterick, 290-319. Cambridge: Cambridge University Press, 1995.

Denny, Edward. *Papalism. A Treatise on the Claims of the Papacy as Set Forth in the Encyclical Satis Cognitum*. London: Rivingtons, 1912.

Dill, Samuel. *Roman Society in the Last Century of the Western Empire*, 2d rev. ed. New York: Macmillan Company, 1899.

_____. *Roman Society in Gaul in the Merovingian Age*. London: MacMillan, 1926.

_____. *Roman Society in the Last Century of the Western Empire*, 2d rev. ed. New York: Meridian Books, 1962.

Drake, H. A. "Athanasius' First Exile." *Greek, Roman and Byzantine Studies* 27 (1986): 193-204.

_____. "Constantine and Consensus." *Church History* 64 (1995): 1-15.

_____. *Constantine and the Bishops: The Politics of Intolerance*. Ancient Society and History. Baltimore, MD: Johns Hopkins University Press, 2000.

_____. *Constantine and the Bishops: The Politics of Intolerance*. Ancient Society and History. Baltimore, MD: Johns Hopkins University Press, 2002.

Drew, Katherine Fischer. *The Barbarian Invasions; Catalyst of a New Order*. New York: Holt Rinehart and Winston, 1970.

_____. *The Burgundian Code: The Book of Constitutional or Law of Gundobad; Additional Enactments*. Philadelphia: University of Pennsylvania Press, 1972.

_____. *The Laws of the Salian Franks*. Middle Ages Series. Philadelphia: University of Pennsylvania Press, 1991.

Drinkwater, J. F., and Hugh Elton. *Fifth-Century Gaul: A Crisis of Identity?* Cambridge: Cambridge University Press, 2002.

Driscoll, Michael S. "The Conversion of the Nations." In *The Oxford History of Christian Worship*, ed. Geoffrey Wainwright and Karen B. Westerfield Tucker, 175-215. New York: Oxford University Press, 2006.

Du Tillet, Jean. *La Chronique Des Roys de France, Puis Pharamond Iusques Au Roy Henry, Second Du Nom, Selon La Computation Des Ans, Iusques in L'an Mil Cinq Cens Quarante & Neuf.* Paris: Paris Galiot du Pré, 1550.

_____. *Recueil Des Roys de France Plus Une Chronique Abregée.* Paris: I. Du Puys, 1580.

Du Tillet, Jean, and Henri Auguste Omont. *Portraits Des Rois de France Du Recueil de Jean Du Tillet.* Paris: Imprimerie Berthaud Frères, 1908.

Duchesne, L. *Early History of the Christian Church, from Its Foundation to the End of the Fifth Century.* Vol. 2. London: J. Murray, 1911.

Duchesne, L., and Arnold Harris Mathew. *The Beginnings of the Temporal Sovereignty of the Popes, A.D. 754-1073.* London: K. Paul, Trench, Trübner Company, 1907.

Duchesne, M. l'abbé. "Vigile et Pélage, Étude Sur L'histoire de L'église Romaine Au Milieu Du VI Siècle." *revue des questions historiques* 19, no. 36 (1884): 369-438.

Dudden, F. Homes. *The Life and Times of St. Ambrose, by F. Homes Dudden.* 2 vols. Oxford: The Clarendon Press, 1935.

Duggan, Charles. "Decretals." In *New Catholic Encyclopedia*, ed. Editorial Staff of the Catholic University of America, 4, 707-713. New York: McGraw-Hill, 1967.

Dumézil, Georges. *Archaic Roman Religion, with an Appendix on the Religion of the Etruscans.* 2 vols. Chicago: University of Chicago Press, 1970.

Duruy, Victor, and George Burton Adams. *The History of the Middle Ages.* New York: H. Holt, 1904.

Duval, Yves-Marie. *Ambroise de Milan: Xvie Centenaire de Son Élection Épiscopale.* Paris: Études augustiniennes, 1974.

Dvornik, Francis. "Emperors, Popes, and General Councils." In *Dumbarton Oaks Papers*, 1-23. Washington, DC: Dumbarton Oaks Center for Byzantine Studies Trustees for Harvard University, 1951.

_____. "Early Christian and Byzantine Political Philosophy: Origins and Background." In *Dumbarton Oaks Papers.* Washington, DC: Dumbarton Oaks Center for Byzantine Studies Trustees for Harvard University, 1966.

Eckhardt, Karl August. *Die Gesetze Des Merowingerreiches, 481-714.* Germanenrechte, Bd. 1. Witzenhausen: Deutschrechtlicher Instituts-Verlag, 1961.

Edwards, Mark J. "The Arian Heresy and the Oration to the Saints." *Vigiliae christianae* 49, no. 4 (1995): 379-387.

Elliott, Thomas G. "Constantine's Early Religious Development." *Journal of Religious History* 15

(1989): 283-291.

_____. "Constantine's Preparation for the Council of Nicaea." *Journal of Religious History* 17, no. 2 (1992): 127-137.

_____. "Constantine and 'the Arian Reaction after Nicaea." *Journal of Ecclesiastical History* 43 (1992): 169-194.

Eno, Robert B. *The Rise of the Papacy*. Wilmington, DE: M. Glazier, 1990.

Ensslin, Wilhelm. "Gottkaiser Und Kaiser Von Gottes Gnaden: Staat Und Kirche V Konstantin D Grossen Bis Theodosius D Grossen: Cäsaropapismus." In *Byzantinische Herrscherbild*, 54-85. Darmstadt: Wissenschaftliche Buchgesellschaft, 1975.

Falco, Giorgio. *The Holy Roman Republic; a Historic Profile of the Middle Ages*. London: G. Allen & Unwin, 1964.

Ferguson, Everett. *Church and State in the Early Church*. Vol. 7. Studies in Early Christianity. New York: Garland, 1993.

Ferguson, John. *The Religions of the Roman Empire*. Ithaca, N.Y.: Cornell University Press, 1970.

Ferreiro, Alberto. "Braga and Tours: Some Observations on Gregory's de Virtutibus Sancti Martini." *Journal of Early Christian Studies* no. 3 (1995): 195-210.

Figgis, John Neville. *The Political Aspects of St. Augustine's 'City of God'.*. Gloucester, MA: Peter Smith, 1963.

Forstman, Jack. "Nicene Mind in Historical Perspective and Its Significance for Christian Unity." *Encounter* 38 (1977): 213-226.

Fouracre, Paul. *The New Cambridge Medieval History 1, C. 500-C. 700*. Cambridge: Cambridge University Press, 2006.

Fouracre, Paul, and Richard A. Gerberding. *Late Merovingian France: History and Hagiography, 640-720*. Manchester Medieval Sources Series. Manchester, NY: Manchester University Press, 1996.

Fowden, Garth. "Bishops and Temples in the Eastern Roman Empire ad 320-435." *Journal of Theological Studies* 29, no. 1 (1978): 53-78.

Fredriksen, Paula. "Lambs into Lions." *The New Republic* (2001): 35-39.

Frend, W. H. C. *The Donatist Church: A Movement of Protest in Roman North Africa*. Oxford: Clarendon Press, 1952.

_____. *The Rise of the Monophysite Movement; Chapters in the History of the Church in the Fifth and Sixth Centuries*. Cambridge, [Eng.]: University Press, 1972.

Frend, W. H. C., and K. Clancy. "When Did the Donatist Schism Begin?" *Journal of Theological Studies*, no. 28 (1977): 104-109.

Friesen, Steven J. *Twice Neokoros: Ephesus, Asia, and the Cult of the Flavian Imperial Family*. Religions in the Graeco-Roman World ; V. 116. Leiden ; New York: E.J. Brill, 1993.

Fuhrmann, Horst. "Justinians Edictum de Recta Fide (551) Bei Pseudoisidor." In *Melanges G Fransen*, 1, 217-223. Rome: Libreria Ateneo Salesiano, 1976.

Gaddis, Michael. *There Is No Crime for Those Who Have Christ: Religious Violence in the Christian Roman Empire*. The Transformation of the Classical Heritage. Berkeley: University of California Press, 2005.

Ganshof, François Louis. *The Carolingians and the Frankish Monarchy; Studies in Carolingian History*. Ithaca, NY: Cornell University Press, 1971.

Garnsey, Peter, and Richard P. Saller. *The Roman Empire: Economy, Society, and Culture*. Berkeley: University of California Press, 1987.

Geanakoplos, Deno John. "Church and State in the Byzantine Empire: A Reconsideration of the Problem of Caesaropapism." *Church History* 34, no. 4 (1965): 381-403.

_____. "Church Building And "Caesaropapism" ad 312-565." *Greek, Roman and Byzantine Studies* 7 (1966): 167-186.

Geary, Patrick J. *Before France and Germany: The Creation and Transformation of the Merovingian World*. New York: Oxford University Press, 1988.

Gebru, Mebratu Kiros. "Miaphysite Christology a Study of the Ethiopian Tewahedo Christological Tradition on the Nature of Christ." Library and Archives Canada / Bibliothèque et Archives Canada, 2006.

Gennep, Arnold van. *The Rites of Passage*. [Chicago]: University of Chicago Press, 1960.

Gibbon, Edward, and J. B. Bury. *The End of the Roman Empire in the West: The Barbarian Conquests and the Transition to the Middle Ages: A.D. 439-565*. The Library of Religion and Culture. New York: Harper, 1958.

Gibbon, Edward, and William Youngman. *The History of the Decline and Fall of the Roman Empire*. London: William Ball, 1839.

Ginn, Craig Warryn Clifford "Prestige of the Bishop in Eusebius' "Ecclesiastical History"." University of Lethbridge, 1999.

Goffart, Walter A. *Barbarians and Romans, A.D. 418-584: The Techniques of Accommodation*. Princeton, NJ: Princeton University Press, 1980.

_____. *The Narrators of Barbarian History (A.D. 550-800): Jordanes, Gregory of Tours, Bede, and Paul the Deacon*. Princeton, NJ: Princeton University Press, 1988.

González Fernández, Rafael. "Legislación Y Personalidad de Justiniano: Su Matrimonio Con Teodora." In *Arte, Sociedad, Economía Y Religión Durante El Bajo Imperio Y La Antigüedad Tardía* 169-175. Murcia, Spain: Universidad de Murcia, 1991.

Goodenough, Erwin Ramsdell. *The Church in the Roman Empire*. New York: H. Holt and Company, 1931.

Gorce, Matthieu-Maxime. *Clovis, 456-511*. Paris: Payot, 1935.

Gottlieb, Gunther. *Ambrosius Von Mailand Und Kaiser Gratian*. Göttingen: Vandenhoeck und Ruprecht, 1973.

Gradel, Ittai. *Emperor Worship and Roman Religion*. Oxford Classical Monographs. Oxford: Oxford University Press, 2004.

Grant, Edward. *God and Reason in the Middle Ages*. Cambridge UK; New York: Cambridge University Press, 2001.

Grant, Frederick C. *The Early Days of Christianity*. New York: Abingdon Press, 1922.

Grant, Robert McQueen. "Religion and Politics at the Council at Nicaea." *Journal of Religion* 55, no. 1 (1975): 1-12.

Gray, Patrick T. R. "The Legacy of Chalcedon: Christological Problems and Their Significance." In *The Cambridge Companion to the Age of Justinian*, ed. Michael Maas, 215-238. Cambridge; New York: Cambridge University Press, 2005.

Green, Vivian Hubert Howard. *A New History of Christianity*. New York: Sutton Publication, 2000.

Greenslade, S. L. *Church and State from Constantine to Theodosius*. London: SCM Press, 1954.

Gregg, Robert C., and Dennis E. Groh. "Centrality of Soteriology in Early Arianism." *Anglican Theological Review* 59, no. 3 (1977): 260-278.

Grillmeier, Alois, and Theresia Hainthaler. *Christ in Christian Tradition*. 2 vols. London; Louisville, KY: Mowbray; Westminster John Knox, 1995.

Guizot, and William Hazlitt. *The History of Civilization, from the Fall of the Roman Empire to the French Revolution*. New York: Appleton, 1864.

Guizot, Witt, and Robert Black. *The History of France from the Earliest Times to 1848*. New York: J. B. Alden, 1885.

Gummerus, Jaakko. *Die Homousianische Partei: Bis Zum Tode Des Konstantius: Ein Beitrag Zur Geschichte Des Arianischen Streites in Den Jahren 356-361*. Leipzig: A. Deichert'sche, 1900.

Guterman, Simeon L. *Religious Toleration and Persecution in Ancient Rome*. London: Aiglon Press, 1951.

Gwatkin, Henry Melvill. *The Arian Controversy*. London: Longmans Green, 1908.

Haine, W. Scott. *The History of France*. The Greenwood Histories of the Modern Nations,. Westport, Conn.: Greenwood Press, 2000.

Haldon, John F. *Warfare, State, and Society in the Byzantine World, 565-1204*. Warfare and History. London; New York: Routledge, 2003.

Halliday, William Reginald. *Lectures on the History of Roman Religion from Numa to Augustus*. Liverpool: The University press of Liverpool, 1923.

Halphen, Louis. *Charlemagne and the Carolingian Empire*. Europe in the Middle Ages, V. 3. Amsterdam; New York: North-Holland, 1977.

Halsall, Guy. *Settlement and Social Organization: The Merovingian Region of Metz*. Cambridge; New York: Cambridge University Press, 1995.

————. *Warfare and Society in the Barbarian West, 450-900*. Warfare and History. London; New York: Routledge, 2003.

————. "The Barbarian Invasions." In *The New Cambridge Medieval History 1, C. 500-C. 700*, ed. Paul Fouracre, 35-55. Cambridge: Cambridge University Press, 2006.

————. *Barbarian Migrations and the Roman West, 376-568*. Cambridge Medieval Textbooks. Cambridge: Cambridge University Press, 2007.

Hansen, Günther Christian. "Eine Fingierte Ansprache Konstantins Auf Dem Konzil Von Nikaia." *Zeitschrift für antikes Christentum* 2, no. 2 (1998): 173-198.

Hanson, Richard P. C. "The Doctrine of the Trinity Achieved in 381." *Scottish Journal of Theology* 36, no. 1 (1983): 41-57.

————. "The Fate of Eustathius of Antioch." *Zeitschrift für Kirchengeschichte* 95, no. 2 (1984): 171-179.

————. *The Search for the Christian Doctrine of God: The Arian Controversy, 318-381*. Grand Rapids: Baker Academic, 2005.

Hardy, Ernest George. *Christianity and the Roman Government: A Study in Imperial Administration*. London: G. Allen & Unwin, 1925.

Harnack, Adolf von. *Outlines of the History of Dogma*. New York, London and Toronto: Funk and Wagnalls, 1893.

————. *Militia Christi: The Christian Religion and the Military in the First Three Centuries*.

Philadelphia: Fortress Press, 1981.

Hauck, Albert. *Kirchengeschichte Deutschlands*. Vol. 2. Leipzig: Hinrichs, 1935.

Hazeltine, Harold Dexter. "Roman and Canon Law in the Middle Ages." In *The Cambridge Medieval History*, ed. J. B. Bury, J. R. Tanner, C. W. Previté-Orton and Z. N. Brooke, 5, 697-763. New York: MacMillan, 1926.

Heather, P. J. *The Visigoths from the Migration Period to the Seventh Century: An Ethnographic Perspective*. Studies in Historical Archaeoethnology. Woodbridge, UK; Rochester, NY: Boydell Press; Center for Interdisciplinary Research on Social Stress, 1999.

_____. *The Fall of the Roman Empire: A New History of Rome and the Barbarians*. Oxford; New York: Oxford University Press, 2007.

Hefele, Karl Joseph von. *A History of the Councils of the Church: From the Original Documents*. 5 vols. Edinburgh: T. & T. Clark, 1883.

_____. *Histoire Des Conciles D'aprèS Les Documents Originaux*. Paris: Letouzey, 1907.

Heinzelmann, Martin. *Bischofsherrschaft in Gallien: Zur Kontinuität Römischer Führungsschichten Vom 4. Bis Zum 7. Jahrhundert: Soziale, Prosopographische Und Bildungsgeschichtliche Aspekte*. München: Artemis, 1976.

_____. "Heresy in Books I and II of Gregory of Tours' Historiae." In *After Rome's Fall: Narrators and Sources of Early Medieval History: Essays Presented to Walter Goffart*, ed. Alexander C. Murray, 67-82. Toronto: University of Toronto Press, 1998.

Heldmann, Karl. *Das Kaisertum Karls Des Grossen: Theorien Und Wirklichkeit*. Quellen Und Studien Zur Verfassungsgeschichte Des Deutschen Reiches Im Mittelalter Und Neuzeit, 6, 2. Weimar: Böhlaus, 1928.

Henderson, Ernest F. *Select Historical Documents of the Middle Ages*. London: G. Bell, 1916.

Héring, Jean. *A Good and a Bad Government, According to the New Testament*. American Lecture Series ; Publication No. 221. Springfield, Ill.,: C.C. Thomas, 1954.

Hershberger, Guy F. *War, Peace, and Nonresistance*, 3d rev. ed. Scottdale, PA: Herald Press, 1969.

Hessels, Jan Hendrik, and H. Kern. *Lex Salica: The Ten Texts with the Glosses, and the Lex Emendata*. London: J. Murray [etc.], 1880.

Heuclin, Jean. "Un Premier Concordat En 511." *Notre Histoire Sommaire*, April 1996, 41-43.

Hiatt, Alfred, and Library British. *The Making of Medieval Forgeries: False Documents in Fifteenth-Century England*. British Library Studies in Medieval Culture. London: British Library and University of Toronto Press, 2004.

Hildebrandt, M. M. *The External School in Carolingian Society*. Vol. 1. Education and Society in the Middle Ages and Renaissance. Leiden; New York: E.J. Brill, 1992.

Hill, Bennett D. *Church and State in the Middle Ages*. New York: Wiley, 1970.

Hirsch, Hans. "Der Mittelalterliche Kaisergedanke in Den Liturgischen Gebeten." *Mitteilungen des Öesterreichischen Instituts für Geschichtsforschung* 44 (1930): 1-20.

Hoare, F. R. *The Western Fathers; Being the Lives of Ss. Martin of Tours, Ambrose, Augustine of Hippo, Honoratus of Arles, and Germanus Auxerre*. New York: Sheed and Ward, 1954.

Hodgkin, Thomas. *Italy and Her Invaders: 535-553*. Vol. 4, 2. ed. Oxford: Clarendon Press, 1896.

Hoey, Allan S. "Official Policy Towards Oriental Cults in the Roman Army." *Transactions and Proceedings of the American Philological Association* 70 (1939): 456-481.

Hollerich, Michael J. "Religion and Politics in the Writings of Eusebius: Reassessing the First "Court Theologian"." *Church History* 56, no. 3 (1990): 309-325.

Holsapple, Lloyd Burdwin. *Constantine the Great*. New York: Sheed & Ward, 1942.

Holt, Mack P. *The French Wars of Religion, 1562-1629*. New Approaches to European History. Cambridge; New York: Cambridge University Press, 2005.

Howarth, Patrick. *Attila, King of the Huns: Man and Myth*. New York: Barnes & Noble Books, 1995.

Hughes, David. *The British Chronicles*. Westminster, MD: Heritage Books, 2007.

Hughes, Philip. *A History of the Church*. 3 vols., Rev. , 1948. ed. London: Sheed & Ward, 1960.

Hummer, Hans J. *Politics and Power in Early Medieval Europe: Alsace and the Frankish Realm, 600-1000*. Cambridge Studies in Medieval Life and Thought. Cambridge, UK; New York: Cambridge University Press, 2005.

Hunt, Lynn Avery. *The Making of the West: Peoples and Cultures, a Concise History*. Boston: Bedford/St. Martin's, 2007.

Hunter, William Alexander, Gaius, and J. Ashton Cross. *A Systematic and Historical Exposition of Roman Law in the Order of a Code*. London: Sweet & Maxwell, Limited; [etc., etc.], 1897.

Hurst, J. F. *Short History of the Christian Church*. New York: Harper, 1893.

Hutton, William Holden. *The Church and the Barbarians; Being an Outline of the History of the Church from A.D. 461 to A.D. 1003*. Charleston, SC: Bibliolife, 2008.

Innes, A. Taylor. *Church and State: A Historical Handbook*, 2d ed. Edinburgh: T. & T. Clark.

Innes, Matthew. "Charlemagne's Government." In *Charlemagne: Empire and Society*, ed. Joanna

Story, 71-89. Manchester; New York: Manchester University Press, 2005.

Jalland, Trevor. *The Life and Times of St. Leo the Great*. London: Society for promoting Christian knowledge, 1941.

————. *The Church and the Papacy; an Historical Study, Being Eight Lectures Delivered before the University of Oxford, in the Year 1942, on the Foundation of the Rev. John Bampton, Canon of Salisbury*. London

New York: Society for Promoting Christian Knowledge

Morehouse-Gorham, 1949.

James, Edward. *The Origins of France: From Clovis to the Capetians, 500-1000*. New York: St. Martin's Press, 1982.

————. "Beati Pacifici: Bishops and the Law in Sixth-Century Gaul." In *Disputes and Settlements: Law and Human Relations in the West*, ed. John Bossy, 25-46. Cambridge: Cambridge University Press, 1983.

————. *The Franks*. The Peoples of Europe. Oxford, UK: Basil Blackwell Ltd, 1988.

Jasper, Detlev, and Horst Fuhrmann. *Papal Letters in the Early Middle Ages*. History of Medieval Canon Law. Washington, DC: Catholic University of America Press, 2001.

Jervis, W. H. *The Student's France, a History of France from the Earliest Times to the Establishment of the Second Empire in 1852*. New York: Harper & Brothers, 1867.

Johanny, Raymond. *L'eucharistie, Centre de L'histoire Du Salut, Chez Saint Ambroise de Milan*. Paris: Beauchesne et ses fils, 1968.

Johnson, Edward A. "Constantine the Great: Imperial Benefactor of the Early Christian Church." *Journal of the Evangelical Theological Society* 22, no. 2 (1979): 161-169.

Jones, A. H. M. *Constantine and the Conversion of Europe*. New York: Macmillan, 1949.

————. "Church and State from Constantine to Theodosius." *Journal of Theological Studies* 5, no. 2 (1954): 269-271.

————. "Notes in the Genuineness of the Constantinian Documents in Eusebius's Life of Constantine." *Journal of Ecclesiastical History* 5, no. 2 (1954): 196-200.

————. *The Later Roman Empire, 284-602: A Social Economic and Administrative Survey*. 2 vols. Baltimore, MD: Johns Hopkins University Press, 1986.

Jones, Arnold Hugh Martin, John Robert Martindale, and J. Morris. *The Prosopography of the Later Roman Empire A. D. 395-527*. Vol. 2. Cambridge: Cambridge UP, 1980.

Junghans, Wilhelm, and Gabriel Monod. *Histoire Critique Des Règnes de Childerich et de Chlod-ovech*. Paris: F. Vieweg, 1879.

Kee, Alistair. *Constantine Versus Christ: The Triumph of Ideology*. London: SCM Press Ltd, 1982.

Kehr, Paul. "Die Sogenannte Karolingische Schenkung Von 754." *Historische Zeitschrift* 70 (1893): 385-441.

Kellett, Frederick William. *Pope Gregory the Great and His Relations with Gaul*. Cambridge: University Press, 1889.

Kelly, J. N. D. *Early Christian Creeds*, 3d ed. New York: D. McKay, 1972.

Keresztes, Paul. "The Peace of Gallienus: 260-303 ad." *Wiener Studien* 1975, 174-185.

_____. *Imperial Rome and the Christians*. Lanham: University Press of America, 1989.

Kik, Jacob Marcellus. *Church and State in the New Testament*. Philadelphia: Presbyterian and Reformed Publishing Corporation, 1962.

_____. *Church and State: The Story of Two Kingdoms*. New York: Nelson, 1963.

King, P. D. *Law and Society in the Visigothic Kingdom*. Cambridge; New York: Cambridge University Press, 2006.

Kitchin, G. W. *A History of France*. Clarendon Press Series. Oxford: Clarendon Press, 1892.

Kleinclausz, Arthur Jean. *Charlemagne*. Paris: Hachette, 1934.

Kousoulas, D. George. *The Life and Times of Constantine the Great: The First Christian Emperor*. Bethesda, MD: Provost Books, 2003.

Krautheimer, Richard. *Early Christian and Byzantine Architecture*, 3d ed. Harmondsworth: Penguin Books, 1979.

_____. *Rome, Profile of a City, 312-1308*. Princeton, NJ: Princeton University Press, 1980.

Kriegbaum, B. "Ein Neuer Löisungsverschlag Fur Ein Altes Problem: Die Sogennanten Preces Der Donatisten (Optatus 1.22)." In *Studia Patristica, Papers Presented to the 10th International Conference on Patristic Studies Held in Oxford, 1987*, ed. Elizabeth A. Livingstone, 22, 277-282. Leuven: Peeters Press, 1989.

Krusch, Bruno. *Scriptores Rerum Merovingicarum*. Hannover: Hahn, 1888.

Küng, Hans, and John Bowden. *The Catholic Church: A Short History*. Vol. 5. Modern Library Chronicles Book. New York: Modern Library, 2003.

Kunkel, Wolfgang. *An Introduction to Roman Legal and Constitutional History*. Oxford: Clarendon

Press, 1966.

Kurth, Godefroid. *Histoire Poétique Des Mérovingiens*. Paris: A. Picard, 1893.

_____. *Clovis*. Vol. 1, 2nd rev. corr. ed. Paris: V. Retauz, 1901.

_____. *Études Franques*. Vol. 2. Paris: H. Champion, 1919.

_____. *Clovis: Le Fondateur*. Paris: Tallandier, 2000.

Lacam, Guy. *Ricimer: Un Barbare Au Service de Rome*. Paris: Atelier National Reproduction des Theses, Universite Lille III, 1986.

Lançon, Bertrand. *Rome in Late Antiquity: ad 313-604*. New York: Routledge, 2001.

Latouche, Robert. *Caesar to Charlemagne: The Beginnings of France*. London; New York: Phoenix House; Barnes & Noble, 1968.

Le Nain de Tillemont, Louis-Sébastien. *MéMoires Pour Servir à L'histoire EccléSiastique Des Six Premiers SièCles, Justifiez Par Les Citations Des Auteurs Originaux: Avec Une Chronologie, Où L'on Fait Un AbréGé de L'histoire EccléSiastique; & Avec Des Notes Pour ÉClaircir Les Difficultez Des Faits & de La Chronologie*. Vol. 16. Paris: Charles Robustel, 1701.

Lea, Henry Charles. *Studies in Church History. The Rise of the Temporal Power. Benefit of Clergy. Excommunication*. Philadelphia; London: H.C. Lea; S. Low, Son, & Marston, 1869.

Lecler, Joseph. *The Two Sovereignties: A Study of the Relationship between Church and State*. London: Burns Oates and Washbourne, 1952.

Lee, Guy Carleton. *Historical Jurisprudence: An Introduction to the Systematic Study of the Development of Law*. New York: MacMillan, 1900.

Lenox-Conyngham, Andrew. "The Church in St Ambrose of Milan." *International Journal for the Study of the Christian Church* 5, no. 3 (2005): 211-225.

Levillain, L. "Le Couronnement Impérial de Charlemagne." *Revue d'histoire de l'Eglise de France* 18, no. 78 (janvier-mars 1932): 5-9.

Lewis, Catrin M. "Gallic Identity and the Gallic Civitas from Caesar to Gregory of Tours." In *Ethnicity and Culture in Late Antiquity*, 69-81. London Duckworth and the Classical Press of Wales, 2000.

Lietzmann, Hans. *Symbolstudien I-Xiv*, Sonderausg. ed. Darmstadt: Wissenschaftliche Buchgesellschaft, 1966.

Lines, Michael Ronald. "Charlemagne's Monastic Policy and the Regula Benedicti: Frankish Capitularies Front 742 to 813." University of Toronto, 2000.

Lintzel, M. "Das Abendländische Kaisertum Im Neunten Und Zehnten Jahrhundert. Der Rö-mische Und Der Fränkisch-Deutsche Kaisergedanke Von Karl Dem Großen Bis Auf Otto Den Großen." *Welt als Geschichte* 4 (1938): 423-447.

Logan, Alistair H. B. "Marcellus of Ancyra and the Councils of ad 325: Antioch, Ancyra, and Nicaea." *Journal of Theological Studies* 43 (1992): 428-446.

Long, George. "Foederatae Civitates " In *A Dictionary of Greek and Roman Antiquities*, 2nd ed., improved and enlarged ed., ed. William Smith, 542-543. London: John Murray, 1875.

Loofs, Friedrich, and Kurt Aland. *Leitfaden Zum Studium Der Dogmengeschichte*, 6., durchgesehene Aufl. ed. Tübingen: M. Niemeyer, 1959.

Lorenz, Rudolf. "Die Eustathius Von Antiochien Zugeschriebene Schrift Gegen Photin." *Zeitschrift für die neutestamentliche Wissenschaft und die Kunde der älteren Kirche* 71, no. 1-2 (1980): 109-128.

Loseby, S. T. "Gregory's Cities: Urban Functions in Sixth-Century Gaul." In *Franks and Alamanni in the Merovingian Period: An Ethnographic Perspective*, ed. I. N. Wood. Woodbridge; Rochester, NY: Boydell Press, 1998.

Lot, Ferdinand. *Naissance de La France*. Paris: Fayard, 1970.

Loughlin, James F. "The Sixth Nicene Canon and the Papacy." *American Catholic Quarterly Review* 5 (1880): 220-239.

Louth, Andrew. "The Byzantine Empire in the Seventh Century." In *The New Cambridge Medieval History 1, C. 500-C. 700*, ed. Paul Fouracre, 291-316. Cambridge: Cambridge University Press, 2006.

———. "The Eastern Empire in the Sixth Century." In *The New Cambridge Medieval History 1, C. 500-C. 700*, ed. Paul Fouracre, 93-117. Cambridge: Cambridge University Press, 2006.

Macdonald, Jeffrey Lee. "The Christological Works of Justinian." Ph.D. diss. diss., The Catholic University of America, 1995.

Mackinnon, James. *A History of Modern Liberty*. London; New York: Longmans, Green, and Co., 1906.

Madec, Goulven. *Saint Ambroise et La Philosophie*. Paris: Études augustiniennes, 1974.

Mangnall, Richmal. *Historical and Miscellaneous Questions*. New York: D. Appleton, 1866.

Marsh, Frank Burr. *The Reign of Tiberius*. New York: Barnes & Noble, 1959.

Martin, Victor. *Les Origines Du Gallicanisme*. Paris: Bloud & Gay, 1939.

Mathisen, Ralph W. "Barbarian Bishops and the Churches 'in Barbaricis Gentibus' During Late

Antiquity." *Speculum* 72, no. 3 (1997): 664-697.

————. *People, Personal Expression, and Social Relations in Late Antiquity*. Ann Arbor: University of Michigan Press, 2003.

Mattingly, H. B. "The Origen of the Name "Christians"." *Journal of theological studies* 9 (1958): 26-37.

Mayer, Wendy, and Pauline Allen. *John Chrysostom*. London: Routledge, 2000.

McGinn, Bernard. *Antichrist: Two Thousand Years of the Human Fascination with Evil*. New York: Harper SanFrancisco, 1994.

McGuckin, John A. "The "Theopaschite Confession" (Text and Historical Context): A Study in the Cyrilline Re-Interpretation of Chalcedon." *Journal of Ecclesiastical History* 35, no. 2 (1984): 239-255.

————. "The Legacy of the 13th Apostle: Origins of the East Christian Conceptions of Church and State Relation." *St Vladimir's Theological Quarterly* 47, no. 3-4 (2003): 251-288.

————. "The Legacy of the 13th Apostle: Origins of the East Christian Conceptions of Church and State Relation Other Titles: Legacy of the Thirteenth Apostle." *St Vladimir's Theological Quarterly* 47, no. 3-4 (2003): 251-288.

McKenzie, Jonh L. "The Power and the Wisdom." In *Church and State in the Middle Ages*, ed. Bennett D. Hill, 6-15. New York: Wiley, 1970.

McKitterick, Rosamond. *The Frankish Kingdoms under the Carolingians, 751-987*. London; New York: Longman, 1983.

————. *The New Cambridge Medieval History 2, C. 700-C. 900*. Cambridge: Cambridge University Press, 1995.

————. "The Carolingian Renaissance of Culture and Learning." In *Charlemagne: Empire and Society*, ed. Joanna Story, 151-166. Manchester; New York: Manchester University Press, 2005.

McLynn, Neil B. *Ambrose of Milan: Church and Court in a Christian Capital*. Berkeley: University of California Press, 1994.

Mercier, Ernest. "La Bataille de Poitiers et Les Vraies Causes Du Recul de L'invasion Arabe." *Revue Historique* 7 (1878): 1-13.

Merdinger, J. E. *Rome and the African Church in the Time of Augustine*. New Haven: Yale University Press, 1997.

Mesot, Jean. *Die Heidenbekehrung Bei Ambrosius Von Mailand*. Schöneck-Beckenried, Schweiz: Neuen Zeitschrift für Missionswissenschaft, 1958.

Meyendorff, John. "Justinian, the Empire and the Church." In *Dumbarton Oaks Papers*, 22, 43-60. Washington: Dumbarton Oaks Center for Byzantine Studies Trustees for Harvard University, 1968.

_____. *Imperial Unity and Christian Divisions: The Church, 450-680 A.D.* Crestwood, N.Y.: St. Vladimir's Seminary Press, 1989.

Millar, Fergus. *The Emperor in the Roman World: (31 Bc-ad 337)*, 2nd ed. London: Duckworth, 1992.

Mitchell, Kathleen. *History and Christian Society in Sixth-Century Gaul: An Historiographical Analysis of Gregory of Tours' Decem Libri Historiarum.* Ann Arbor, MI: UMI, 1983.

Monceaux, Paul. *Histoire Littéraire de L'afrique Chrétienne Depuis Les Origines Jusquä L'invasion Arabe.* 7 vols. Bruxells: Culture et civilization, 1966.

Montesquieu, Charles de Secondat. *The Spirit of Laws.* London: George Bell and Sons, 1878.

Moorhead, John. "Clovis' Motives for Becoming a Catholic Christian." *Journal of Religious History* 13, no. 1-4 (1984-1985): 329-339.

_____. *Theoderic in Italy.* Oxford; New York: Clarendon Press; Oxford University Press, 1992.

_____. *Justinian.* The Medieval World. London; New York: Longman, 1994.

_____. "Ostrogothic Italy and the Lombard Invasion." In *The New Cambridge Medieval History 1, C. 500-C. 700*, ed. Paul Fouracre, 140-161. Cambridge: Cambridge University Press, 2006.

Moreira, Isabel. *Dreams, Visions, and Spiritual Authority in Merovingian Gaul.* Ithaca: Cornell University Press, 2000.

Morino, Claudio. *Church and State in the Teaching of St. Ambrose.* Washington, DC: Catholic University of America Press, 1969.

Mosheim, Johann Lorenz. *An Ecclesiastical History, Antient and Modern, from the Birth of Christ to the Beginning of the Eighteenth Century.* Vol. 1. West Jordan, UT: s.n., 1980.

Muhlberger, Steven. *The Fifth-Century Chroniclers: Prosper, Hydatius, and the Gallic Chronicler of 452.* Arca, Classical and Medieval Texts, Papers, and Monographs, 27. Leeds: F. Cairns, 1990.

Munro, Dana Carleton, and Raymond James Sontag. *The Middle Ages, 395-1500.* New York; London: The Century Corporation, 1928.

Murphy, Francis Xavier. *Politics and the Early Christian.* New York: Desclée, 1967.

Murray, Alexander C., and Walter A. Goffart. *After Rome's Fall: Narrators and Sources of Early Medieval History: Essays Presented to Walter Goffart.* Toronto: University of Toronto Press, 1998.

Murray, John C. "Leo Xiii: Separation of Church and State." *Theological Studies* 14 (June 1953): 145-214.

Murvar, Vatro. "Max Weber's Concept of Hierocracy: A Study in the Typology of Church-State Relationships." *Sociological Analysis* 28, no. 2 (1967): 69-84.

Nadeau, Jean-Benoît, and Julie Barlow. *The Story of French*. New York: St. Martin's Press, 2006.

Nelson, Janet L. "Charlemagne the Man." In *Charlemagne: Empire and Society*, ed. Joanna Story, 22-37. Manchester; New York: Manchester University Press, 2005.

Newman, Albert Henry. *A Manual of Church History*. Philadelphia: American Baptist Publication Society, 1900.

Nicholas, Barry. *An Introduction to Roman Law*. Clarendon Law Series. Oxford: Clarendon Press, 1962.

Nirenberg, David. "Truth and Consequences." *New Republic* 235, no. 24 (2006): 34-37.

Noble, Thomas F. X. *The Republic of St. Peter: The Birth of the Papal State, 680-825*. The Middle Ages. Philadelphia: University of Pennsylvania Press, 1984.

Noll, Mark A. *Turning Points: Decisive Moments in the History of Christianity*. Grand Rapids, MI: Baker Books, 1997.

Norderval, Øyvind. "The Emperor Constantine and Arius: Unity in the Church and Unity in the Empire." *Studia theologica* 42, no. 2 (1988): 113-150.

Novak, Ralph Martin. *Christianity and the Roman Empire: Background Texts*. Harrisburg, PA: Trinity Press International, 2001.

Nthamburi, Zablon. "The Donatist Controversy as a Paradigm for Church and State." *Africa Theological Journal* 17, no. 3 (1988): 196-206.

O'Sullivan, Jeremiah Francis, and John Francis Burns. *Medieval Europe*. New York: F.S. Crofts, 1943.

Odom, Robert Leo. *Sunday in Roman Paganism: A History of the Planetary Week and Its 'Day of the Sun' in the Heathenism of the Roman World During the Early Centuries of the Christian Era*. Brushton, NY: TEACH Services, 2003.

Ogg, Frederic Austin. *A Source Book of Mediaeval History: Documents Illustrative of European Life and Institutions from the German Invasion to the Renaissance*. New York; Cincinnati: American Book, 1907.

Olster, David M. "Justinian, Imperial Rhetoric, and the Church." *Byzantinoslavica* 50 (1989): 165-176.

Oman, Charles. *The Dark Ages, 476-918*. Periods of European History. London: Rivingtons, 1908.

Optatus. *S. Optati Milevitani Libri VII*. Vol. 26. Corpus Scriptorum Ecclesiasticorum Latinorum, ed. Karl Ziwsa. Vindobonae: F. Tempsky, 1893.

Orlin, Eric M. *Temples, Religion, and Politics in the Roman Republic*. Boston: Brill Academic, 2002.

Ors, Alvaro d. "La Actitud Legislativa Del Emperador Justiniano." *Orientalia Christiana Periodica* 13, no. 1-2 (1947): 119-142.

Ortolan, J. L. E. *The History of Roman Law from the Text of Ortolan's Histoire de La Legislation Romaine et Generalisation Du Droit (Edition of 1870)*. London: Butterworths, 1871.

Owen, Francis. *The Germanic People: Their Origin, Expansion, and Culture*. New York: Bookman Associates, 1960.

Palmer, Robert E. A. *Roman Religion and Roman Empire: Five Essays*. Philadelphia: University of Pennsylvania Press, 1974.

"Papacy." In *Encyclopædia Britannica*, 2008.

Paredi, Angelo. *Saint Ambrose, His Life and Times*. Notre Dame: University of NotreDame Press, 1964.

Pelikan, Jaroslav Jan. *The Emergence of the Catholic Tradition (100-600)*. Vol. 1. 5 vols. Christian Tradition, ed. Jaroslav Jan Pelikan. Chicago: University of Chicago Press, 1971.

————. *The Emergence of the Catholic Tradition (100-600)*. The Christian Tradition; a History of the Development of Doctrine, ed. Jaroslav Jan Pelikan. Chicago: University of Chicago Press, 1971.

Penner, Archie. *The Christian, the State, and the New Testament*. Scottdale, PA: Herald Press, 1959.

Périn, Patrick, and Laure-Charlotte Feffer. *Les Francs: A L'origine de La France*. Vol. 2. Paris: A. Colin, 1987.

————. *Les Francs: A La Conquête de La Gaule*. Vol. 1. Paris: A. Colin, 1987.

Peterson, Erik, and Giuseppe Ruggieri. *Il Monoteismo Come Problema Politico*. Vol. 147. Giornale Di Teologia. Brescia: Queriniana, 1983.

Peyrebonne, Micheline. *La Véritable Histoire de La Loi Salique*. Paris: M. Peyrebonne ; distribution, Europe notre patrie, 1980.

Pfeil, Elisabeth. *Die Fränkische Und Deutsche Romidee Des Frühen Mittelalters*. Forschungen Zur Mittelalterlichen U. Neueren Geschichte, Bd. 3. München: Verlag der Münchner Drucke, 1929.

Pfister, Christian. "Gaul under the Merovingian Franks " In *The Cambridge Medieval History*, ed. J.

B. Bury, J. R. Tanner, C. W. Previté-Orton and Z. N. Brooke, 5, 133-159. New York: MacMillan, 1926.

Pietras, Henryk. "Le Ragioni Della Convocazione Del Concilio Niceno da Parte Di Constantino Il Grande: Un'investigazione Storico-Teologica." *Gregorianum* 82, no. 1 (2001): 5-35.

Pietri, Charles. "La Politique de Constance II: Un Premier "Césaropapisme" Ou L'imitatio Constantini." In *Église et L'empire Au Ive Siècle*, 113-172. Geneva Fondation Hardt, 1989.

Pilgrim, Walter E. *Uneasy Neighbors: Church and State in the New Testament*. Overtures to Biblical Theology. Minneapolis, MN: Fortress Press, 1999.

Poggi, Vincenzo. "La Controverse Des Trois Chapitres." *Istina* 43, no. 1 (1998): 99-110.

Pohl, Walter. *Die Völkerwanderung: Eroberung Und Integration*. Stuttgart: Kohlhammer, 2002.

Pohl, Walter, and Max Diesenberger. *Integration Und Herrschaft: Ethnische Identitäten Und Soziale Organisation Im Frühmittelalter*. Denkschriften / Österreichische Akademie Der Wissenschaften, Philosophisch-Historische Klasse. Vienna: Verlag der Österreichischen Akademie der Wissenschaften, 2002.

Popa, Mihail S. "New Testament Principles Governing the Relationship between the Christian and Civil Authorities and Their Elaboration in the Writings of Ellen G. White with Their Reflection in the Adventist Church in Romania." Project report diss., Andrews, University, 1980.

Pope Leo XIII. "Nobilissima Gallorum Gens." In *ENCYCLICAL OF POPE LEO XIII ON THE RELIGIOUS QUESTION IN FRANCE*.

Potter, John Milton. *The Development and Significance of the Salic Law of the French*. n.p., 1937.

Prall, William. *The State and the Church*. New York: T. Whittaker, 1900.

Price, S. R. F. *Rituals and Power: The Roman Imperial Cult in Asia Minor*. New York: Cambridge University Press, 1984.

Prinz, F. "Die Bischöfliche Stadtherrschaft Im Frankenreich Vom 5. Bis Zum 7. Jahrhundert." *Historische Zeitschrift* 217 (1973): 1-35.

Rahner, Hugo. *Church and State in Early Christianity*. San Francisco: Ignatius Press, 1992.

Ramsay, William Mitchell. *The Church in the Roman Empire before A.D. 170*, [5th] ed. Grand Rapids: Baker Book House, 1954.

Ramsey, Boniface. *Ambrose*. London, New York: Routledge, 1997.

Rawson, Elizabeth. *Roman Culture and Society: Collected Papers*. Oxford: Oxford University Press, 1991.

Ray, Stephen K. *Upon This Rock: St. Peter and the Primacy of Rome in Scripture and the Early Church*. Modern Apologetics Library. San Francisco: Ignatius Press, 1999.

Richards, Jeffrey. *The Popes and the Papacy in the Early Middle Ages, 476-752*. Boston: Routledge & Kegan Paul, 1979.

Ring, Thomas Gerhard. *Auctoritas Bei Tertullian, Cyprian Und Ambrosius*. Würzburg: Augustinus-Verlag, 1975.

Rivers, Theodore John. *Laws of the Salian and Ripuarian Franks*. Ams Studies in the Middle Ages, No. 8. New York: AMS Press, 1986.

Roll, Hans-Achim. *Zur Geschichte Der Lex Salica-Forschung*. Untersuchungen Zur Deutschen Staats- Und Rechtsgeschichte, N. F., Bd. 17. Aalen: Scientia Verlag, 1972.

Romanides, John S. *Franks, Romans, Feudalism, and Doctrine: An Interplay between Theology and Society*. Brookline, MA: Holy Cross Orthodox Press, 1981.

Rose, H. J. *Ancient Roman Religion*. London: Hutchinson's University Library, 1948.

Rosenwein, Barbara H. *Negotiating Space: Power, Restraint, and Privileges of Immunity in Early Medieval Europe*. Ithaca, NY: Cornell University Press, 1999.

Rossi, Giovanni Battista de. *Inscriptiones Christianae Urbis Romae Septimo Saeculo Antiquiores*. Romae: Ex Officina Libraria Pontificia, 1857.

Rostovtzeff, Michael Ivanovitch. *The Social and Economic History of the Roman Empire*. Oxford: Clarendon Press.

Rouche, Michel. *Clovis*. [Paris]: Fayard, 1996.

_____. "L'occident Sous La Menace Ariene." *Notre Histoire Sommaire*, April 1996, 14-17.

Ruhbach, Gerhard. "Euseb Von Caesarea." In *Alte Kirche*, 1, 224-235. Stuttgart: Verlag W Kohl-hammer, 1984.

Salmon, J. H. M. "Clovis and Constantine. The Uses of History in Sixteenth-Century Gallicanism." *Journal of Ecclesiastical History* 41, no. 4 (1990): 584-605.

Saltet, Louis. "La Lecture D'un Text et La Critique Contemporaine. La Prétendue Promesse de Quierzy Dans le 'Liber Pontificalis.'" *Bulletin de Litterature Ecclésiastique* 41 (1940): 176-207.

_____. "La Lecture D'un Text et La Critique Contemporaine. La Prétendue Promesse de Qui-erzy Dans le 'Liber Pontificalis.'" *Bulletin de Litterature Ecclésiastique* 42 (1941): 61-85.

Salzman, Michele Renee. *The Making of a Christian Aristocracy: Social and Religious Change in the Western Roman Empire*. Cambridge, MA: Harvard University Press, 2002.

Samaran, Leon Levillain and Charles. "Sur le Lieu et La Date de La Bataille Dite de Poitiers de 732." *Bibliotheque de l'Ecole de Chartres* 99 (1938): 243-267.

Sansterre, Jean Marie. "Eusèbe de Césarée et La Naissance de La Théorie "Césaropapiste"." *Byzantion* 62, no. 1 (1972): 131-195.

Santosuosso, Antonio. *Storming the Heavens: Soldiers, Emperors, and Civilians in the Roman Empire*. Boulder, Colo.: Westview Press, 2004.

Saxer, Victor. "L'église et L'empire Chrétien Au Ive Siècle: La Difficile Séparation Des Compétences Devant Les Problèmes Doctrinaux et Ecclésiologiques." *Revue des sciences religieuses* 77, no. 1 (2003): 11-30.

Schaff, Philip, and Samuel Macauley Jackson. *Theological Propaedeutic: A General Introduction to the Study of Theology, Exegetical, Historical, Systematic, and Practical, Including Encyclopaedia, Methodology, and Bibliography: A Manual for Students*. New York: Charles Scribner's Sons, 1892.

Schaff, Philip, and David S. Schaff. *History of the Christian Church*. New York: C. Scribner's sons, 1882.

Schaff, Philip, and Henry Wace. *A Select Library of Nicene and Post-Nicene Fathers of the Christian Church*. 14 vols. Grand Rapids: Eerdmans, 1983.

Schaidinger, Heinz. "Historial Confirmation of the Year 538 as the Beginning of the 1260 Day Prophecy." Austria: Bogenhofen Seminary, 2009.

Schardius, Simon, Hieronymus Thomas, Seiler, and Friedrich Karger. *Schardius Redivivus, Sive, Rerum Germanicarum Scriptores Varii*. Giessae Germany: Ex officina Seileriana, 1673.

Schatz, Klaus. *Papal Primacy: From Its Origins to the Present*. Collegeville, MN: Liturgical Press, 1996.

Scheid, John, and Janet Lloyd. *An Introduction to Roman Religion*. Bloomington: Indiana University Press, 2003.

Scheidweiler, Felix. "Ein Glaubensbekenntnis Des Eustathius Von Antiochien." *Zeitschrift für die neutestamentliche Wissenschaft und die Kunde der älteren Kirche* 44, no. 3-4 (1953): 237-249.

Schmemann, Alexander. "Byzantine Theocracy and the Orthodox Church." *St Vladimir's Seminary Quarterly* 1, no. 2 (1953): 5-22.

Schmidt-Wiegand, Ruth. *Fränkische Und Frankolateinische Bezeichnungen Für Soziale Schichten Und Gruppen in Der Lex Salica*. Göttingen: Vandenhoeck & Ruprecht, 1972.

Schmidt, Joël. *Lutèce: Paris, Des Origines À Clovis: 9000 Av. J.-C.--512 Ap. J.-C.* Paris: Librairie Académique Perrin, 1986.

Schowalter, Daniel N. *The Emperor and the Gods: Images from the Time of Trajan*. Vol. 27. Harvard Dissertations in Religion. Minneapolis: Fortress Press, 1991.

Schwartz, Eduard. *Gesammelte Schriften*. Vol. 3. 5 vols. Berlin: W. de Gruyter, 1956.

————. *Kaiser Constantin Und Die Christliche Kirche: Fünf Vorträge*, 3rd ed. Stuttgart: B. G. Teubner, 1969.

Scott, Kenneth. *The Imperial Cult under the Flavians*. New York: Arno Press, 1975.

Seeck, Otto. *Regesten Der Kaiser Und Päpste Für Die Jahre 311 Bis 476 N. Chr. Vorarbeit Zu Einer Prosopographie Der Christlichen Kaiserzeit*. Stuttgart: J.B. Metzler, 1919.

————. *Geschichte Des Untergangs Der Antiken Welt*. Darmstadt: Wissenschaftliche Buchgesellschaft, 1966.

Seeck, Otto, and Manlio Sargenti. *Die Zeitfolge Der Gesetze Constantins*. Materiali Per Una Palingenesi Delle Costituzioni Tardo-Imperiali, Vol. 2. Milano: Giuffrè, 1983.

Seeliger, Gerhard Wolfgang. *Die Kapitularien Der Karolinger*. München: Lindauer, 1893.

Sergeant, Lewis D. *The Franks from Their Origin as a Confederacy to the Establishment of the Kingdom of France and the German Empire*. London, New York: T. Fisher Unwin; G. P. Putnam's sons, 1898.

Setton, Kenneth Meyer. *Christian Attitude Towards the Emperor in the Fourth Century, Especially as Shown in Addresses to the Emperor*. New York, London: Columbia University Press; P.S. King & Son, 1941.

Sewell, Elizabeth Missing. *Popular History of France from the Earliest Period to the Death of Louis Xiv*. London: Longmans, Green, 1876.

Sherman, Charles Phineas. *Roman Law in the Modern World*. Boston, U.S.A.: Boston Book Co., 1917.

Sigebertus, Gemblacensis. *Sigeberti Gemblacensis Monachi Opera Omnia, Accedit Chronicon Polonorum, Auctore Anonymo, Intermiscentur Beti Odonis Cameracensis ... [et Al.] ; Scripta Vel Scriptorum Fragmenta Quae Supersunt*. Vol. 160. Patrologiae Cursus Completus. Series Secunda Latina, ed. J. P. Migne. Paris: Excecudebatur et venit apud J.-P. Migne, 1857.

Sigüenza, José de, and Mariana Monteiro. *The Life of Saint Jerome, the Great Doctor of the Church, in Six Books*. London: Sands, 1907.

Silk, Mark. "Numa of Pompilius and the Idea of Civil Relion in the West." *Journal of the American Academy of Religion* 72, no. 4 (2004): 863-896.

Skarsaune, Oskar. "A Neglected Detail in the Creed of Nicaea (325)." *Vigiliae christianae* 41, no. 1 (1987): 34-54.

Smith, John Holland. *Constantine the Great*. New York: Scribner, 1971.

Somers, Mary Agnes. "The Source and Development of the Salic Law in France before A.D. 1600." 1916.

Sordi, Marta. *The Christians and the Roman Empire*. Norman: University of Oklahoma Press, 1986.

Sotinel, Claire. "Autorité Pontificale et Pouvoir Impérial Sous le Règne de Justinien: le Pape Vigile." *Mélanges de l'école française de Rome. Antiquité* 104, no. 1 (1992): 439-463.

sotinel, claire. "Emperors and Popes in the Sixth Century." In *The Cambridge Companion to the Age of Justinian*, ed. Michael Maas, 267-290. Cambridge; New York: Cambridge University Press, 2005.

Southern, R. W. *Western Society and the Church in the Middle Ages*. Vol. 2. The Penguin History of the Church. Harmonsworth: Penguin, 1990.

Spanneut, Michel. "Position Théologique D'eustathe D'antioche." *Journal of Theological Studies* 5 (1954): 220-224.

Spence, George. *An Inquiry into the Origin of the Laws and Political Institutions of Modern Europe, Particularly of Those of England*. Clark, NJ: Lawbook Exchange, 2006.

Spruyt, Hendrik. *The Sovereign State and Its Competitors: An Analysis of Systems Change*. Princeton Studies in International History and Politics. Princeton, NJ: Princeton University Press, 1994.

Stearns, Peter N., and William L. Langer. *The Encyclopedia of World History: Ancient, Medieval, and Modern, Chronologically Arranged*. Boston: Houghton Mifflin, 2001.

Stein, Ernest, to Erich Ludwig Eduard Caspar, 1935. Catholic University of America Press. The Catholic Historical Review.

Stein, Ernest, and Jean-Rémy Palanque. *Histoire Du Bas-Empire*. Amsterdam: A. M. Hakkert, 1968.

Stengel, E.E. "Kaisertitel Und Suveranitatsidee." *Geschichte des Mittelalters* 3 (1939): 1-23.

Stevens, Courtenay Edward. *Sidonius Apollinaris and His Age*. Oxford: Clarendon Press, 1933.

Storch, Rudolph H. "Eusebian Constantine." *Church History* 40, no. 2 (1971): 145-155.

Story, Joanna. *Charlemagne: Empire and Society*. Manchester; New York: Manchester University Press, 2005.

Stratos, Andreas N. *Byzantium in the Seventh Century*. Amsterdam: Adolf M. Hakkert, 1968.

Stringer, Martin D. *A Sociological History of Christian Worship*. Cambridge; New York: Cambridge University Press, 2005.

Tacitus, Cornelius. *The Annals and the Histories*. Vol. 15. Chicago: Encyclopædia Britannica, 1952.

Telfer, W. "When Did the Arian Controversy Begin?" *The Journal of Theological Studies* 47 (1946): 129-142.

Tessier, Georges. *Le Baptême de Clovis: 25 Décembre 496 (?)*. Trente Journées Qui Ont Fait La France. [Paris]: Gallimard, 1996.

Theis, Laurent. "Au Commencement Était La Gaule Romaine." *Notre Histoire Sommaire*, April 1996, 4-9.

Therrien, Joanne. *St. Boniface*. Manitoba Country Scapes Series. Winnipeg: Vidacom, 2008.

Thompson, E. A. "The Conversion of the Spanish Suevi to Catholicism." In *Visigothic Spain: New Approaches*, ed. Edward James, 80-81. Oxford; New York: Clarendon Press ; Oxford University Press, 1980.

_____. "Barbarian Collaborators and Christians." In *Romans and Barbarians: The Decline of the Western Empire*, 230-250. Madison: University of Wisconsin Press, 1982.

_____. "Spain and Britain." In *Romans and Barbarians: The Decline of the Western Empire*, 208-229. Madison: University of Wisconsin Press, 1982.

Thompson, Glen L. "Trouble in the Kingdom: Church and State in the Fourth Century." In *Essay Life*, 1999.

Thornton, Robinson. *St. Ambrose: His Life, Times, and Teaching*. London: Society for promoting Christian knowledge, 1898.

Tierney, Brian. *The Crisis of Church and State, 1050-1300: With Selected Documents*. Toronto; Buffalo: Published by University of Toronto Press in association with the Medieval Academy of America, 1988.

Tilley, Maureen A. *Donatist Martyr Stories: The Church in Conflict in Roman North Africa*. Vol. 24. Translated Texts for Historians. Liverpool: Liverpool University Press, 1996.

_____. *The Bible in Christian North Africa: The Donatist World*. Minneapolis: Fortress Press, 1997.

Todd, Malcolm. "The Germanic People and Germanic Society." In *The Cambridge Ancient History*, ed. I. E. S. Edwards, 12, 440-460. Cambridge; New York: Cambridge University Press, 1970.

Tomka, Miklós, and Giuseppe Ruggieri. *The Church in Fragments: Towards What Kind of Unity?* London

Maryknoll, NY: SCM Pres ;

Orbis Books, 1997.

Tompkins, Charles. "Their Word to Our Day: Constantine, Secular Christian (C ad 280-337)." *Expository Times* 80 (1969): 178-181.

Torrance, Iain R., Severus, and Sergius. *Christology after Chalcedon: Severus of Antioch and Sergius the Monophysite.* Norwich: Canterbury Press, 1988.

Treadgold, Warren T. *Byzantium and Its Army, 284-1081.* Stanford, Calif.: Stanford University Press, 1995.

Trigg, Joseph W. "Eustathius of Antioch's Attack on Origen: What Is at Issue in an Ancient Controversy?" *Journal of Religion* 75, no. 2 (1995): 219-238.

Troeltsch, Ernst, and Olive Wyon. *The Social Teaching of the Christian Churches,* 1st Harper torchbook ed. New York: Harper, 1960.

Trombley, Frank R. *Hellenic Religion and Christianization, C. 370-529.* Boston: Brill Academic Publishers, 2001.

Turcan, Robert. *The Cults of the Roman Empire.* Oxford: Blackwell, 1996.

Turk, Eleanor L. *The History of Germany.* The Greenwood Histories of the Modern Nations. Westport, CN: Greenwood Press, 1999.

Ullmann, Walter. *The Growth of the Papal Government in the Middle Ages: A Study of the Ideological Relation of Clerical to Lay Power.* London: Methuen, 1955.

————. *Gelasius I. (492-496): Das Papsttum an Der Wende Der Spätantike Zum Mittelalter.* Stuttgart: Hiersemann, 1981.

Ulrich, Jörg. "Nicaea and the West." *Vigiliae christianae* 51, no. 1 (March 1997): 10-24.

Valla, Lorenzo, and Christopher Bush Coleman. *The Treatise of Lorenzo Valla on the Donation of Constantine, Text and Translation into English.* New Haven: Yale university press, 1922.

Van Dam, Raymond. "Merovingian Gaul and the Frankish Conquest." In *The New Cambridge Medieval History 1, C. 500-C. 700,* ed. Paul Fouracre, 193-231. Cambridge: Cambridge University Press, 2006.

Van de Vyver, A. "La Victoire Contre Les Alamans et La Conversion de Clovis (1re Partie)." *Revue belge de Philologie et d'Histoire* 15, no. 3-4 (1936): 895-914.

————. "La Victoire Contre Les Alamans et La Conversion de Clovis (Suite)." *Revue belge de Philologie et d'Histoire* 16, no. 1-2 (1937): 35-94.

————. "L'unique Victoire Contre Les Alamans et La Conversion de Clovis En 506." *Revue belge de Philologie et d'Histoire* 17, no. 3-4 (1938): 793-813.

Van Dyke, Paul. *The Story of France from Julius Caesar to Napoleon III.* New York: C. Scribner's

Sons, 1929.

Vermès, Géza. *Scrolls, Scriptures, and Early Christianity.* Vol. 56. Library of Second Temple Studies. London; New York: T & T Clark International, 2005.

Verseuil, Jean. *Clovis, Ou, La Naissance Des Rois.* L'histoire En Tête. Série Les Grandes Familles. Paris: Criterion, 1992.

Wace, Henry, William C. Piercy, and William Smith. *A Dictionary of Christian Biography and Literature to the End of the Sixth Century A.D., with an Account of the Principal Sects and Heresies.* London: J. Murray, 1911.

Wallace-Hadrill, J. M. *The Long-Haired Kings, and Other Studies in Frankish History.* London: Methuen, 1962.

_____. *The Frankish Church.* Oxford: Clarendon Press, 1983.

_____. *The Barbarian West, 400-1000,* Rev. ed. Oxford; Cambridge, MA: B. Blackwell, 1996.

Wallace-Hadrill, J. M., and John McManners. *France: Government and Society.* London: Methuen, 1957.

Wallace-Hadrill, J. M., Patrick Wormald, Donald A. Bullough, and Roger Collins. *Ideal and Reality in Frankish and Anglo-Saxon Society: Studies Presented to J.M. Wallace-Hadrill.* Oxford: B. Blackwell, 1983.

Wallach, Luitpold. *Alcuin and Charlemagne: Studies in Carolingian History and Literature.* Cornell Studies in Classical Philology. Ithaca, NY: Cornell University Press, 1959.

Wand, J. W. C. *The Latin Doctors.* London: Faith Press, 1948.

Ward-Perkins, Bryan. *The Fall of Rome: And the End of Civilization.* Oxford; New York: Oxford University Press, 2005.

Wardman, Alan. *Religion and Statecraft among the Romans.* Baltimore, MD: Johns Hopkins University Press, 1982.

Warmind, Morten Lund. "The Cult of the Roman Emperor before and after Christianity." In *The Problem of Ritual: Based on Papers Read at the Symposium on Religious Rites Held at Åbo, Finland, on the 13th-16th of August, 1991,* ed. Tore Ahlbäck, 211-220. Åbo, Finland: Donner Institute for Research in Religious and Cultural History, 1993.

Warmington, B. H. "The Sources of Some Constantinian Documents in Eusebius' Ecclesiastical History and Life of Constantine." In *Studia Patristica,* 1, 93-98. Kalamazoo: Cistercian Publications, 1985.

Watson, Alan. *The State, Law, and Religion: Pagan Rome.* Athens, GA: University of Georgia Press, 1992.

Watson, William E. "The Battle of Tours-Poitiers Revisited." In *Providence: Studies in Western Civilization*, 2, 1993.

Weinstock, Stefan. *Divus Julius*. Oxford: Clarendon Press, 1971.

Weiss, Rolf. *Chlodwigs Taufe: Reims 508. Versuch Einer Neuen Chronologie Für Die Regierungszeit Des Ersten Christlichen Frankenkönigs Unter Berücksichtigung Der Politischen Und Kirchlich-Dogmatischen Probleme Seiner Zeit.* Bern, Frankfurt/M: Herbert Lang, 1971.

Westcott, Brooke Foss, and Arthur Westcott. *The Two Empires, the Church and the World*. London: Macmillan, 1909.

Wheless, Joseph. *Forgery in Christianity; a Documented Record of the Foundations of the Christian Religion*. New York: A. A. Knopf, 1930.

Whitney, J. P. "Conversion of the Teutons " In *The Cambridge Medieval History*, ed. J. B. Bury, J. R. Tanner, C. W. Previté-Orton and Z. N. Brooke, 5, 415-542. New York: MacMillan, 1926.

Wickham, Chris. "The Other Transition: From the Ancient World to Feudalism." *Past and Present*, no. 103 (1984): 3-36.

_____. *Early Medieval Italy: Central Power and Local Society, 400-1000*. Ann Arbor: University of Michigan Press, 1989.

_____. *Framing the Early Middle Ages Europe and the Mediterranean; 400-800*. Oxford: Oxford University Press, 2007.

Widukind, Henry, Conrad Vecerius, Hermann Graf von Neuenar, Einhard, Pius, and Liudprandus. *Rervm Ab Henrico et Ottone I Impp. Gestarum Libri III, Unà Cum Alijs Quibusdam Raris & Antehac Non Lectis Diuersorum Autorm Historijs, Ab Anno Alutis D. Ccc. Usq. ad Praesentem Aetatem.* Basileae: Apvd Io. Hervagivm, 1532.

Wilken, Robert L. "In Defense of Constantine." *First Things*, no. 112 (2001): 36-40.

Williams, Daniel H. "Constantine, Nicaea and the 'Fall' of the Church " In *Christian Origins: Theology, Rhetoric, and Community*, ed. Lewis Ayres and Gareth Jones, 117-136. London and New York: Routledge, 1998.

Williams, Stephen. *Diocletian and the Roman Recovery*. New York: Methuen, 1985.

Williamson, James Mann. *The Life and Times of St. Boniface*. Ventnor: W.J. Knight, 1904.

Willibald, and George W. Robinson. *The Life of Saint Boniface*. Cambridge: Harvard University Press, 1916.

Willis, Geoffrey Grimshaw. *Saint Augustine and the Donatist Controversy*. London: S. P. C. K., 1950.

Wissowa, Georg. *Religion Und Kultus Der Römer.* Munich: C.H. Beck, 1912.

Wojtowytsch, Myron. *Papsttum Und Konzile Von Den Anfängen Bis Zu Leo I. (440-461): Studien Zur Entstehung Der Überordnung Des Papstes Über Konzile.* Stuttgart: A. Hiersemann, 1981.

Wolff, Hans Julius. *Roman Law: An Historical Introduction.* Norman: University of Oklahoma Press, 1951.

Wolfram, Herwig. *History of the Goths,* New and completely rev. from the 2nd German ed. Berkeley: University of California Press, 1988.

Wood, I. N. *The Merovingian Kingdoms, 450-751.* London and New York: Longman, 1994.

_____. "Gregory of Tours and Clovis." In *Debating the Middle Ages: Issues and Readings,* ed. Barbara H. Rosenwein and Lester K. Little, 73-91. Malden, MA: Blackwell Publishers, 1998.

Wood, James Edward. *Church and State in Scripture, History, and Constitutional Law.* Waco, TX: Baylor University Press, 1958.

Wood, Philip John. "Foundation Myths in Late Antique Syria and Mesopotamia: The Emergence of Miaphysite Political Thought. 400-600 A.D." Thesis diss., University of Oxford, 2007.

Woods, David. "Three Notes on Aspects of the Arian Controversy C 354-367 Ce." *Journal of Theological Studies* 44 (1993): 604-619.

Yoder, John Howard. *Discipleship as Political Responsibility.* Scottdale, PA: Herald Press, 2003.

 APPENDIX

CHRONOLOGICAL LIST OF BISHPS OF ROME, ROMAN EMPER-
ORS, AND FRANKISH KINGS FROM A.D. 280-816

Table 1. Chronological List of Bishops of Rome, Roman Emperors, and Frankish Kings from A.D. 280-816

Year	Bishop of Rome	Roman Emperor - West	Roman Emperor - East	Frankish kings
280				
290	St. Marcellinus (296-304)	Co-emperor Maximian (286 - 305; 307 - 310)	Diocletian (284 - 305)	
300		Constantius I Chlorus (305-306)	Galerius (305 - 311)	
		Severus (306-307)		
		Maxentius (306 - 312)		
	St. Marcellus I (308-309)	Constantine I, the Great (306 - 337)	Licinius (308 - 324)	
310	St. Eusebius (309 or 310)		Maximinus Daia (308 - 313)	
	St. Miltiades (311-314)		Valerius Valens (316-317)	
	St. Sylvester I (314-335)		Sextus Marcius Martinianus (324)	
320				
330	St. Marcus (336)			
	St. Julius I (337-352)	Constantine II (337 - 340)	Constantius II (337 - 361)	
		Constans (337 - 350)		

Table 1—Continued.

340		
350	Vetranio (350)	Liberius (352-366) Opposed by Felix II, antipope (355-365)
	Nepotianus (350)	
	Magnentius (350 - 353)	
360	Julian (361 - 363)	
	Jovian (363 - 364)	
	Valentinian I (364 - 375) (co-emperor Procopius 364 - 365)	
	Valens (364 - 378)	St. Damasus I (366-383) Opposed by Ursicinus, antipope (366-367)
370	Gratian (367 - 383)	
	Valentinian II (375-392)	
380	Theodosius I (379 - 395)	
	Magnus Maximus (383 - 388)	St. Siricius (384-399)
390	Eugenius (392 - 394)	
	Honorius (393-423)	
	Arcadius (395 - 408)	

Table 1—Continued.

Year			
	St. Anastasius I (399-401)		
400	St. Innocent I (401-417)	Priscus Attalus (409 - 410 and 414 - 415)	Theodosius II (408 - 450)
		Constantine III (409 - 411)	
410		Jovinus, (411 - 412)	
	St. Zosimus (417-418)		
	St. Boniface I (418-422) Opposed by Eulalius, antipope (418-419)		
420		Constantius III (421)	
	St. Celestine I (422-432)	Joannes (423-425)	
		Valentinian III (425-455)	
430	St. Sixtus III (432-440)		
440	St. Leo I (the Great) (440-461)		
450		Maximus (455)	Marcian (450 - 457)
		Avitus (455-456)	

Table 1—Continued.

Year	Bishop of Rome	Roman Emperor - West	Roman Emperor - East	Frankish kings
		Recimir (456-472)	Leo I (457 – 474)	
460	St. Hilarius (461-468)	Majorian (457-461)		
		Libius Severus (461-465)		
470	St. Simplicius (468-483)	Anthemius (467-472)		
		Olybrius (472)		
		Glycerius (473-474)	Zeno (474 – 475)	
		Julius Nepos (474-475/480)	Basiliscus (475 – 476)	
		Romulus Augustulus (475-476)	Zeno (restored) (476 – 491)	
480	St. Felix III (II) (483-492)		Anastasius I, (491 – 518)	Clovis I, (481–511 – Paris)
490	St. Gelasius I (492-496)			
	Anastasius II (496-498)			
500	St. Symmachus (498-514) Opposed by Laurentius, antipope (498-501)			

Table 1—Continued.

Year	Bishop of Rome	Roman Emperor - West	Roman Emperor - East	Frankish kings
510				Chlothar I, (511–561 - Soissons)
520	St. Hormisdas (514-523)		Justin I the Great, (518 - 527)	Childebert I, (511–558 - Paris; 524–558 - Orléans)
	St. John I (523-526)			Chlodomer, (511–524 - Orléans)
	St. Felix IV (III) (526-530)			Theuderic I, (511–533 - Reims)
530	Boniface II (530-532) Opposed by Dioscorus, antipope (530)		Justinian I the Great, (527 - 565)	Munderic, (533, rival king in the Auvergne - Reims)
	John II (533-535)			Theudebert I, (533–548 - Reims)
	St. Agapetus I (535-536) Also called Agapitus I			
	St. Silverius (536-537)			
540	Vigilius (537-555)			Theudebald, (548–555 - Reims)
550				

Table 1—Continued.

Year	Bishop of Rome	Roman Emperor - West	Roman Emperor - East	Frankish kings
	Pelagius I (556-561)			Chlothar I, (555–561 - Reims; 558–561 - Paris; 558–561 - Orléans)
560	John III (561-574)			Charibert I, (561–567 - Paris)
				Guntram, (561–592 - Orléans)
				Sigebert I, (561–575 - Reims)
570			Justin II, (565 - 578)	Chilperic I, (561–584 - Soissons;
			Tiberius II Constantine, (574 - 582)	662-675 - Austrasia; 673-675 - Burgundy/Neustria)
	Benedict I (575-579)			Childebert II, (575–595 - Reims; 592–596 - Burgundy)
580	Pelagius II (579-590)		Maurice I Tiberius, (582 - 602)	

Table 1—Continued.

286   APPENDIX

Year	Bishop of Rome	Roman Emperor - West	Roman Emperor - East	Frankish kings
580				Gundoald, (584–585, rival king in Aquitaine - Orléans)
590	St. Gregory I (the Great) (590-604)			Chlothar II, (584–629 - Neustria; 613–629 - Burgundy; 613-623 -Austrasia)
600	Sabinian (604-606)		Phocas the Tyrant, (602 - 610)	Theudebert II, (596–612 - Austrasia)
	Boniface III (607)			Theuderic II,(596–613 -Burgundy; 612–613 - Austrasia)
610	St. Boniface IV (608-615)		Heraclius, (610 - 641)	Sigebert II, (613 - Austrasia/Burgundy)
	St. Deusdedit (Adeodatus I) (615-18)			
	Boniface V (619-625)			

Table 1 —Continued.

Year	Bishop of Rome	Roman Emperor - West	Roman Emperor - East	Frankish kings
620	Honorius I (625-638)			Dagobert I, (623–632 - Austrasia; 629-639 - Neustria/Burgundy)
				Pippin I of Landen (Austrasia: 623–629 and 639–640) - MP*
				Charibert II, (629–632 - Aquitaine)
				Chilperic, (629-632 - Aquitaine)
				Sigebert III, (632–656 - Austrasia)
630				Clovis II, (639–657 - Neustria/Burgundy; 656-657 - Austrasia)
640	Severinus (640)		Constantine III Heraclius, (641)	
	John IV (640-642)		Heraclonas Constantine, (641)	
	Theodore I (642-649)		Constans II Heraclius Pogonatus (the Bearded), (641 - 668)	

Table 1—Continued.

Year	Bishop of Rome	Roman Emperor - West	Roman Emperor - East	Frankish kings
				Grimoald I (Austrasia: 643–656; died 662)
650	St. Martin I (649-655)			Grimoald II (643-656 Austrasia) MP*
	St. Eugene I (655-657)			
	St. Vitalian (657-672)			Childebert the Adopted, (656–662 - Austrasia)
660				Chlothar III, (657–673 - Neustria/ Burgundy
			Mezezius (668 to 669)	661–662 - Austrasia)
670	Adeodatus (II) (672-676)		Constantine IV, (668 - 685)	Childeric II, 662–675 - Austrasia; 673–675 - Neustria/Burgundy
				Theuderic III (673, 675-690/1 - Neustria/Burgundy; 687-690/1 - Austrasia)
				Clovis III, (675–676 - Austrasia; 690/1-4)

Table 1 —Continued.

Year	Bishop of Rome	Roman Emperor - West	Roman Emperor - East	Frankish kings
	Donus (676-678)			Dagobert II, (676-679 - Austrasia)
	St. Agatho (678-681)			Pippin II of Herstal (Austrasia: 680-714, Neustria and Burgundy: 687-695) - MP*
680	St. Leo II (682-683)			
	St. Benedict II (684-685)			
	John V (685-686)		Justinian II Rhinotmetus (the Slit-nosed), (685 - 695)	
	Conon (686-687)			
	St. Sergius I (687-701) Opposed by Theodore and Paschal, antipopes (687)			Clovis IV, (691-695)
690				Childebert III, (694-711)
			Leontius II, (ruled 695 - 698)	Drogo (Burgundy: 695-708) - MP*
700	John VI (701-705)		Tiberius III Apsimar (698 - 705)	Grimoald II (Neustria: 695-714, Burgundy: 708-714) - MP*

Table 1—Continued.

Year	Bishop of Rome	Roman Emperor - West	Roman Emperor - East	Frankish kings
	John VII (705-707)		Justinian II, Rhinotmetus (705 - 711)	
	Sisinnius (708)			
	Constantine (708-715)			
710				
			Philippicus Bardanes, (711 - 713)	Dagobert III, (711–715/6)
			Anastasius II, (713 - 715)	Theudoald (Austrasia, Neustria, and Burgundy: 714–716) - MP*
	St. Gregory II (715-731)		Theodosius III, (ruled 715 - 717)	Chilperic II, 715/6-21
				Charles Martel (Austrasia: 715–741, Neustria and Burgundy: 718–741) - MP*
				Pippin II (Austrasia 714) MP*
			Leo III the Isaurian, (717 - 741)	Chlothar IV, 717–720, rival king in Austrasia
720				
				Theuderic IV, (721–737)
730	St. Gregory III (731-741)			
				interregnum (737–743)
740				

Table 1—Continued.

Year	Bishop of Rome	Roman Emperor - West	Roman Emperor - East	Frankish kings
	St. Zachary (741-752)		Constantine V Copronymus (the Dung-named), (741-775)	Pepin III the Short (Neustria and Burgundy: 741-751, Austrasia: 747-751) - MP*
750			Artabasdus (rival emperor, 741 -743)	Childeric III, (743-751)
	Stephen II (752) Because he died before being consecrated, many authoritative lists omit him			Carloman (Austrasia: 741-747; died 754 or 755) - MP*
	Stephen III (752-757)			Pepin the Short, (751-768)
	St. Paul I (757-767)			
760	Stephen IV (767-772) Opposed by Constantine II (767) and Philip (768), antipopes (767)			Carloman I, (768-771 Burgundy, Alemannia, southern Austrasia)

Table 1—Continued.

Year	Bishop of Rome	Roman Emperor - West	Roman Emperor - East	Frankish kings
770				Charles I, called Charlemagne, (768–814, King of the Lombards 774, Emperor 800)
	Adrian I (772-795)			
780			Leo IV the Khazar, (775 - 780)	
			Constantine VI the Blinded, (776 - 797)	
790	St. Leo III (795-816)			
800			Irene the Athenian, (797 - 802)	
810			Nicephorus I the General Logothete, (802 - 811)	
			Stauracius, (ruled 811)	
			Michael I Rhangabe, (811 - 813)	
			Leo V the Armenian, (813 - 820)	

* MP – Mayor of the Palace